Praise for
Living in the Divine Flow:
Monthly Spiritual Gifts and Blessings

(In alphabetical order)

A MESSAGE OF HOPE, COMFORT AND WISDOM

How do we hold on to faith when facing illness, death of loved ones, Israeli war, the rise in Anti- Semitism? In these challenging times of uncertainty, *Living in the Divine Flow* offers us a message of hope, comfort, wisdom as well as the tools to ground ourselves in our Divine connection. *Kabbalah Month by Month* was my favorite book for many years. It helped me in my personal life and in my work as a Chaplain. I kept it by my bed stand and read it daily for years. There was no other book I read so consistently except possibly the Jewish prayer book and Bible. *Living in the Divine Flow* is an update of this book and is even better, deeper and more powerful.
—**Sarah Blum**, Chaplain, former student of Melinda Ribner

THIS BOOK BRINGS HARMONY INTO OUR LIVES

There are many wonderful Jewish books written in Hebrew offering inspiring teachings about the energies of the different months of the Jewish year. What makes this book unique and therefore a must read is that it skillfully guides the reader in English to experience this wisdom in the most personal and practical of ways. With the gift of a variety of tools, exercises, stories and teachings the reader becomes empowered to integrate the spiritual messages of the months into their personal lives, irrespective of whatever tensions may be within or surround them. In our world of increased polarization this book helps bring harmony into our lives. As such it is truly a gift that we as individuals and the world needs.
—**Rabbi Sam Intrator**, Kavannah Life Singles, Former Rabbi of the Carlebach Synagogue in Manhattan

TIME IS AN EXQUISITE DIVINE FLOW

Seasoned with personal stories, phrased in easily digestible English, grounded in impeccable sources, flowing with love and wonder, Melinda's wisdom wakes us up from the monotonous slumber induced by the fallacy that time is a generic bland blackboard upon which our lives are written. A wake up call is in order especially now, post October 7, when we are all in a state of shock and we need the healing of movement and growth. Filled with a joyous vibrancy that can be traced back to her Rebbe, Reb Shlomo zy"a , *Living in the Divine Flow* helps us all to use our time here for what it truly is; an exquisite Divine Flow that always reaches us, and teaches us in new ways.

—**Rabbi Dr. Leibish Hundert**, Rosh Yeshivat Simchat Shlomo, Jerusalem, Israel

AN ACHOR OF SUPPORT FOR TODAY

The way we have been accustomed to experiencing the flow of our lives has taken a major shift, a shift none of us could have foreseen. It's as if time has stood still since October 7th, while realizing that time can never truly stand still. How does one bridge this gap in our consciousness/experience? With the gift of *Living in the Divine Flow,* our dear friend and teacher, Melinda Miriam Shulamit Ribner, has provided for us an incredible anchor. It is an anchor of support to all those seeking meaning in the gift called TODAY. Rooted deeply in the mystical orchard of our tradition, she has brought to life the ability to rise up to the occasion of feeling aligned with the spirit that each day brings, by meeting our souls like never before, through the Divine loving flow that is presented though our calendar.

—**Rabbi Shlomo Katz**, Rav of Kehilat Shirat David, Efrat, Israel

UNPACKS COMPLEX IDEAS IN AN EASY TO UNDERSTAND WAY

This book surprised me in the best way possible. Instead of being another dry and technical exploration of Kabbalah, it offers a clear and accessible guide to this rich spiritual tradition. The author's expertise and gifts as a teacher shines through as she unpacks complex ideas in a way that is easy to understand and apply.

What truly sets this book apart is its focus on practical application. The author skillfully weaves conceptual teachings with guided meditations and exercises, empowering readers to integrate their learnings into their daily lives. The author also shares with her audience vignettes from her own life that facilitate engagement and learning. This approach makes the book valuable for anyone seeking spiritual growth and self-discovery.

Whether you're already familiar with Kabbalah or just starting your exploration, this book offers a unique and enriching journey. It masterfully blends the wisdom of Kabbalah with the broader spiritual wisdom of Judaism, making it a valuable resource for anyone on a path of personal growth.
—**Rabbi Dr. Pinchas Klein**, Psy. Scholar-in Residence Congregation Ansche Emunah (Delray Beach FL)

AN INSPIRING GUIDE TO TAP INTO THE JEWISH CALENDAR

To All Sincere Spiritual Seekers: Shalom. In Jewish thought, each changing day, hour and moment presents us with new challenges to face, affording opportunities for personal rectification and growth. Melinda Ribner is a spiritual teacher who is highly sensitive to these changes in time, and she seeks to teach others how to plug in to this consciousness. Her book, *Living in the Divine Flow: Monthly Spiritual Gifts and Blessings* is an inspiring guide that will aid the reader in tapping into the wellsprings of Israel's calendar of the Divinely-sanctified seasons. Melinda presents sublime concepts of Jewish mystical thought and makes them relatable and accessible to all. She is a truly caring individual and her writing exudes positive energy. May the fruit of Melinda's unique creativity bring blessings to her readers and help them develop a deeper relationship with the Creator and a deeper understanding and appreciation of themselves.
—**Rabbi Chaim Richman**, Director, Jerusalem Lights: Torah for Everyone

WRITTEN WITH CLARITY AND TREMENDOUS DEPTH

Melinda Ribner's *Living in the Divine Flow* is inspiring and informative written with clarity, insight and tremendous depth. This book comes at a perfect time as understanding Rosh Chodesh and working with the spiritual theme of each month as a healing practice is blossoming. This is not a book that sits on a shelf, it is useful and enriching go-to resource to use every month.

—**Kohenet Miki Raver,** author of *Listen to Her Voice: Women of the Hebrew Bible*

GET THE MOST OUT OF EVERY HEBREW MONTH

Melinda Ribner is a very inspired writer. Her writing brings people closer to finding their higher purpose and guiding them on a rich inner spiritual journey, sourced in Jewish tradition. I love her work and have used *Kabbalah Month by Month* in teaching classes in meditation and movement with rave reviews.

What I read of *Living in the Divine Flow* is really beautifully written, incredibly deep and truly a road map to getting the most out of each month. The personal examples in this new addition are very insightful and uplifting!! I will definitely use this new book in my classes as I have used her previous books in past years. Her many books and classes have inspired people all over the world. May her work continue to inspire and bring much blessing.

—**Tirzah Singer**, Jerusalem Rosh Chodesh teacher and musical composer.

HELPS US ACCESS TREASURES WITHIN OUR OWN SOUL

Mindy Ribner, an expert psychotherapist and meditation teacher for many years, has combined this work with her deep knowledge of Kabbalah in this newest book. *Living in the Divine Flow*. Based on ancient Kabbalistic wisdom regarding the growth opportunity within each Hebrew month, Mindy helps her readers access the treasures that we can find within our own soul. Rabbi Shlomo Carlebach OBM, Mindy's mentor, reminded us that the world needs teachers who believe in others. Mindy is one of those enlightened guides. Thank you Mindy for sharing yourself so intimately in this holy precious book.

—**Emuna Witt HaLevi**, editor of Kol Chèvre, an annual celebration of Reb Shlomo's wisdom, for 30 years

LIVING
IN THE
DIVINE
FLOW

LIVING
IN THE
DIVINE
FLOW

MONTHLY SPIRITUAL GIFTS
AND BLESSINGS

Melinda Ribner

Copyright © 2024 Melinda Ribner

Permission is granted to share excerpts of this book along with approbation to author, book title, and website, if appropriate.

Email: mindyribner@gmail.com
Website: www.melindaribner.com
Sign up for monthly newsletter: www.melindaribner.com
Subscribe to Melinda Ribner YouTube channel for guided meditation, interviews and talks.
www.youtube.com/@MelindaRibner

ISBN hardcover 979-8-9906964-0-2
ISBN paperback 979-8-9906964-1-9
ISBN ebook 979-8-9906964-2-6

Book design and layout by Eight Eyes
eighteyes.com

Profits from this book are donated to Israeli charities to feed, heal, and protect the holy people living in Israel.

Discounted and free book copies available for distribution to college students, Israelis experiencing trauma due to October 7th and others who are suffering with depression and need to be uplifted. Please contact via email above.

Contents

Author Statement		xiii
Introduction		xvii
1	Tishrei SEPTEMBER–OCTOBER Opening to Newness	1
2	Cheshvan OCTOBER–NOVEMBER Inner Work of Personal Transformation	53
3	Kislev NOVEMBER–DECEMBER Kindling Dreams and Faith	81
4	Tevet DECEMBER–JANUARY Purification and Liberation from Negative Emotions	111
5	Shevat JANUARY–FEBRUARY Inner Renewal	141
6	Adar FEBRUARY–MARCH The Joy of Oneness	171

Check your browser or Jewish calendar
for the Hebrew month.

7	**Nissan** MARCH–APRIL Moving Towards Freedom	207
8	**Iyar** APRIL–MAY Healing on All Levels of Being	241
9	**Sivan** MAY–JUNE The Art of Receiving	271
10	**Tammuz** JUNE–JULY Seeing Life as It Is	305
11	**Av** JULY–AUGUST The Wholeness of Brokenness	335
12	**Elul** AUGUST–SEPTEMBER Return to Inner Stillness	373
	Conclusion	401
	About the Author	404
	Acknowledgments	405

Calendar of the Year

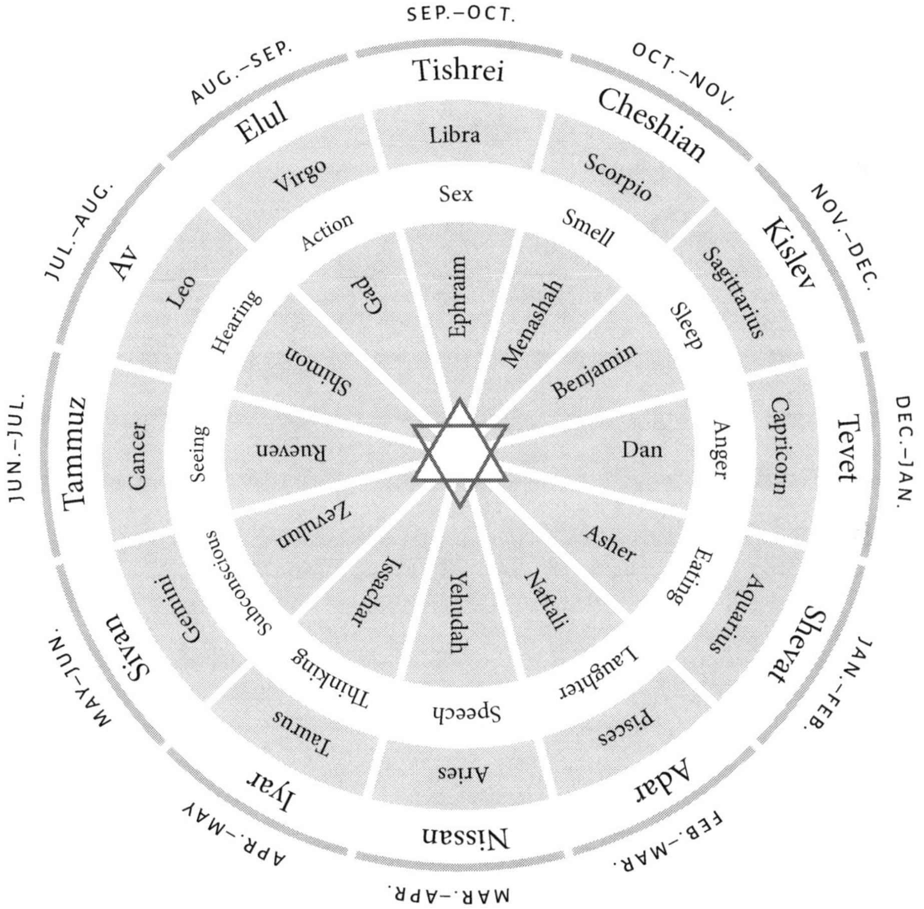

Author Statement

We live in challenging times. It is likely that life will become even more intense in the coming years before everything gets better. The challenges we face are designed to purify, strengthen and help us move out of our heads to live more fully in our hearts and souls. It is my prayer that this book helps you access the inner peace and love that is integral to who you are on a soul level. Every Hebrew month offers a sincere and unique invitation to go beyond limiting concepts of yourself and God so you can live your life more authentically. It is my hope that the wisdom in this book helps you flow gracefully with whatever is happening in your life and in the world.

If you want this book to positively impact your life, please do not just read this book, but take time to study and internalize the wisdom and practice the meditations in this book. Like a good friend, this book is here to help remind you of what you already know and empower you to live in greater accordance with your higher and inner knowing. Keep this book by your bed or at your desk and read a little bit whenever you can or feel called to do so. Consider this book like a large food buffet. You can eat whatever you want whenever you want for as long as you want. For each yearly cycle in which you study this book, you will receive even greater treats.

As important as the teachings, stories, and recommendations in this book are, the practice of the meditations may be even more important. Because meditation affords us direct access to the wisdom of our own souls, it may be the very best support for us to live our lives in a more empowered way. Prayer from the prayer book done with the heart is also a form of meditation. Meditation helps us to find this place of inner stillness where we can experience God deep within ourselves—not as a projection—but more as who and what God truly is.

Living with a greater awareness of who God is and who we are on a soul level renews us each day. Because God created this world to love and be known, according to Jewish teachings, when we love without expectation, we know God in a deeper way. Our life mission here is to love ourselves, love others and love God in our unique ways. Love is the eternal flame of God burning within our very being, a flame that can never be extinguished, no matter what happens in life. It behooves us to know and embody this love directly for ourselves.

It is no accident that we are each alive at this time. Each of us has something important to contribute and share in this world at a time such as this. Otherwise, we would not now be physically embodied at this time. You, my dear reader, are a blessing in this world, whether you experience that or not. Your life matters.

We live in extraordinary times of spiritual opportunity and blessing. Will we spiritually grow and become better people, more loving and resilient? Worry or complaining will not be helpful or serve us at this time. Let us not view the adversity of our time or what we may experience in our personal lives as a punishment but rather as our opportunity to grow as people. It may be helpful to remember that we often experience our greatest growth through adversity. There will be awesome spiritual gifts and blessings through the challenges we face as a people and as individuals today that would not have been available to us otherwise.

The profound universal teachings in this book are readily available to open-hearted people of all faiths. Jews, Christians, Buddhists, Hindus, people of other traditions, and secularists will all benefit from the universality of the holy teachings presented here. This book will serve as a daily and monthly resource of blessing for all its readers.

I want to take this opportunity to simplify and summarize for all the readers of this book the following ten points highlighted throughout this book. May these ten statements both comfort and empower you. This list just came to be rather unexpectedly without any thought on my part.

1. You do not have to be perfect for God to use you for a greater purpose nor for you to fulfill your soul purpose for being alive at this time.

2. You are essentially and sufficiently good enough to live your life with integrity and faith.
3. Your life has intrinsic value and purpose that has been gifted to you by the Creator. You are deeply loved. Anything suggesting otherwise is not true.
4. Do not waste time focusing on what is wrong with your life and the world. Life is too precious.
5. Be grateful for the privilege of being a human being and be joyful for the gifts and opportunities given to you each day.
6. Be aware that God your Creator believes in you more than you believe in yourself.
7. Life is unfolding according to Divine Will, whether we like it or not. Take comfort. There is a Divine plan for the highest good for each of us and for the world as a whole.
8. We do not always understand the why's of life when life is unfolding before us. We do not have the whole picture. Only later we may look back to see the Divine perfection in what has happened.
9. Divine blessings are flowing through you at all times, regardless of what is happening in the world and even in your life. Do your best to receive and share these blessings.
10. You are never alone.

Living in the Divine Flow is here to support you to embody your most awesome soul potential. No one, and nothing, can prohibit you from realizing this most important spiritual gift, yet it is something that you must choose actively for yourself. This indeed is the greatest opportunity of our human existence.

I end this brief introductory note with the following blessing. *May you experience love and blessing on every page of this book.* For it is there. Amen to all your prayers and blessings. I love you.

—Melinda, Mindy, Miriam (Triple M)

Introduction

Living in the Divine Flow: Monthly Spiritual Gifts and Blessings is a rebirth, an updated and expanded version of my most popular and beloved book, Kabbalah Month by Month, published in 2002. In addition to the basic information contained in the previous book, this edition offers new stories and deeper teachings to reach a larger audience. Much has happened since 2002 when Kabbalah Month by Month was first published, yet the holy wisdom in this book remains relevant, universal, and eternal.

In a similar format as the previous book, Living in the Divine Flow reveals the Jewish calendar as a road map for personal transformation. Though this knowledge remains obscure, it has influenced many current forms of healing. In many ways, the Jewish calendar is the original twelve step program. Though I have added a modern psycho-spiritual component to these teachings, I have not altered the basic fundamental components as prescribed in ancient Kabbalah texts like *Sefer Yetzirah* and expounded upon in Chassidic commentaries. As you study and work with the material in this book, keep in mind that Kabbalah is a heavenly transmission. It is not rational nor the product of the human mind.

Living in the Divine Flow offers stories, guidelines, meditations, and strategies to promote personal growth each month. The information in this work provides a framework for flowing gracefully through one's life. Knowing when the auspicious and inauspicious times for starting new projects, making business partnerships, or celebrating weddings is helpful. Although I am familiar with this knowledge and have allowed it to guide me personally and my work with clients for more than thirty years, I continue to be amazed at how relevant this material is each month. The challenges facing the individual and the world seem to mirror the spiritual opportunities available each month.

To the uninitiated, the material in this book may seem mystical or even superstitious. But that does not mean that it is not true. Many things exist that are beyond our powers of conception or reasoning. Just as there are various seasons and fluctuations in our weather there are also fluctuations in the spiritual energies available. Those who are attuned to these energies are very aware of such changes and know how to use this knowledge for their personal growth and success. Rather than promoting fatalism, this knowledge actually increases our capacity to make meaningful and effective choices for our highest good. It is my sincere intention that you be empowered by reading, studying, applying, and internalizing the wisdom in this book.

This book is a spiritual guide to support you, my dear reader, on the holy path towards receiving the gifts and blessings needed to fulfill your soul purpose and embody your highest soul potential month by month. It does not matter what your background is, what you have done and what you have not done, what your nationality is, what your religious affiliation is. The knowledge in this book is universal and beneficial to everyone.

Judaism has always taught that there is only One God who is the Creator of all creation. The word Israel means in Hebrew *Yeshar El*—straight to God. Every person has the privilege to go directly to God. According to Judaism, even non-Jews can be prophets and be filled with the Holy Spirit. This book will help you to increase access to your intrinsic Divine connection.

Some people have trouble with the word God because their image of God is of a white bearded elderly man on a throne taught to them in their childhood. Other names are less anthropomorphic and may be preferable to some. God has many names so feel free to use the names meaningful to you. The Source of Life, Universal Consciousness, True Reality, Limitless Light, Cosmic Intelligence, Infinite Love and Light, and HaShem are a few commonly used non-anthropomorphic names of God. Judaism has many Hebrew names for God as well. It is important to remember that whatever we may call God, whatever concepts we may have about God, God is ultimately beyond conceptualization and definition. God is even beyond what we call infinity for infinity is still a concept.

I generally use the simple word God in this book, yet I could appropriately use any of these more illustrious names without altering the content of the book. *Please do not allow your personal limiting concept of God to interfere with the direct experience of consciousness expansion available to you now.* A great rabbi was reported to have said to an atheist, "The God you do not believe in, I do not believe in either." The direct experience of God is so much more empowering and real than the limiting beliefs we may have about God. The experience of God as the True Reality is liberating.

In the secular calendar, a new month begins in the middle of the moon's cycle. In the Jewish calendar, a new month begins with the new moon. The Hebrew word for month is *chodesh*, which also means newness. Each of the twelve months brings in new energies and offers unique opportunities to realize one's personal potential and overcome the limitations hindering the true expression of one's essence. It is no coincidence that there are twelve months, twelve astrological signs, twelve tribes in Israel, and twelve permutations of the Tetragrammaton, the letters of the Divine Name, YHVH.

There are also twelve Kabbalistic prescriptions for healing, one for each month. For example, the Hebrew month of Tevet—December-January—is an optimal time to work on transforming anger. The month of Kislev—November-December—is healing through sleep and paying attention to one's dreams. The month of Shevat—January-February—is the time to conceive of new projects. At the beginning of each chapter and throughout the book, I share intimate stories from my personal life as well as that of a few clients to demonstrate the healing energies of each month. Of course, the names of clients have been changed, but the stories are all true.

The energy forecasted for each month reflects the various components associated with the month. According to Kabbalah, each month has a Hebrew letter, a Hebrew tribe, an astrological sign, a holiday or holidays, and a unique permutation of the Tetragrammaton associated with it. Each monthly chapter in the book reviews Torah (Biblical) portions traditionally read during that month. Each Torah portion has a hidden message relevant to the events occurring in one's life and in the world. It is for this reason that the Torah is called a Tree of Life and why the Alter Rebbe, Rabbi Shneur Zalman, the founder of the Lubavitcher Chassidic sect, said that the Jew lives with the times: he was referring to the Torah portions of the week. The Torah is considered the blueprint of creation, but one needs to know the secret codes to decipher this hidden wisdom. You will learn some of the secret codes in this book.

The holidays of each month encapsulate the energy and spiritual opportunity of the month. With one exception, every Jewish month has a holiday within it. The empty month, October-November, is reserved for a future holiday that will take place during messianic times. Many Jewish holidays are not widely known.

According to Kabbalah, a Jewish holiday is not just a celebration of a particular historical event, rather, it is a spiritual transmission of cyclical energies occurring at the time of the holiday that are actually sourced in the particular permutation of the Divine Name for that month. As you study this material your knowledge and appreciation of the holidays will be heightened whether you observe the holiday in any way or not at all. You will better understand why the holidays occur when they do. For example, it will become clear that Passover could only occur in the month of Nissan, March-April, or Chanukah could only take place in the darkest time in the calendar like December-January.

Like astrology, which reveals trends for each month according to the movement of planets, Kabbalah derives its knowledge of the energies and trends of the month from the various permutations of the letters of the Divine Name. The mysteries of the Divine Name and its permutations cannot be fully explained here. For now, suffice it to say that it is the position, sound, and shape of the letter in the permutation that makes the difference in the energy for each month. This will become clearer to you in the sections devoted to highlighting the Divine permutation for each month.

Much like a computer program, each permutation regulates and directs the flow of energy for that month. Each month corresponds to a particular permutation that is a unique conductor or grid for the flow of Divine Light for that month. Understanding each permutation is illuminating and complex. Everything that occurs in the month and everything that has occurred historically in that month is a revelation of spiritual light vibrating at different frequencies as it flows through the various spiritual worlds through the sounding of the permutation of the Divine Name.

Kabbalah proclaimed thousands of years ago that all physical matter is concentrated energy pulsating at different sound vibrations. A fundamental text of Kabbalah, the teachings of Rabbi Yitzchak Luria, *Etz Chaim, Tree of Life*, is so profound that it reads like a physics text. Much of the wisdom within Kabbalah explaining the how and why of creation has been recently confirmed in modern day physics. Nikola Tesla, the famous inventor, summed it up succinctly when he said, "If you wish to understand the universe, think of energy, frequency, and vibration."

We each live in the midst of a personal and collective vibratory field. This knowledge is hinted at in the book of Genesis. The Bible simply tells us that creation occurred through Divine speech. *God spoke … and it was so …* Though this is only a metaphor, for God does not speak as we do, it is a very important and meaningful metaphor with increasing relevance today.

According to the Bible, everything in creation was created through Divine speech. God spoke and creation happened. Yet in the Torah story of creation of the human being, God breathed as well as spoke. Rabbi Simon Jacobson, a former teacher of mine, explained that speech is used as a metaphor to describe creation because what is spoken exists, yet it does not have an independent existence. If the Bible had used the metaphor of thought, and God only thought the world, the world would not appear to have a separate existence. What we think remains internal. If the Bible had said that God made the world, the world would be separate from God. Whatever we make, once it is made, it is separate from us.

Speech is the perfect metaphor because speech depends on the speaker to be speaking. If the speaker ceases to speak, there is no speech. By using the metaphor of speech, the Bible tells us that God is constantly creating everything anew and that everything in existence is in essence a Divine communication. As such, we and our world may have a sense of a separate existence but we do not exist independently of God.

There is a Divine plan and soul purpose for creation as a whole and for every person living in this physical world. What happens in our lives may sometimes feel random, like a series of accidents, we may even feel like victims, but that is not the truth. Though God may be hidden and concealed for many, God is active, alive, and present within us and within every event that takes place.

Many of us spend considerable time and much effort each day to fortify our sense of ego identity rather than be guided by our own soul to align with Divine Will. We often accomplish so much because of the desires of our ego. We want to be recognized, we want to be loved, we want material success, and we want to feel safe. Ultimately, these pursuits will never fulfill us if they are not connected to our soul purpose for being in the world. The deeper truth is that when we define ourselves by our worldly accomplishments, we are actually invalidating ourselves on a soul level. Strengthening our ego identity, no matter how successful we may become, is no replacement for soul embodiment and Divine connection.

> Strengthening our ego identity, no matter how successful we may become, is no replacement for soul embodiment and Divine connection.

Our Jewish sages as well as saints from other traditions have told us repeatedly that there is no true reality in the world other than that of God. *Ain Od Mil vado*—There is nothing else! The Alter Rebbe in his classical book, *Shaare Hayichud,* which means Gate of Unity, provided the following illustration to explain this simple and yet most profound idea. Compare the light of the sun to the sun itself. The light may spread a great distance, but what is it in relation to the sun? The light is a part of the sun and has no existence by itself.

Similarly, we may think and we may feel that we are independent of God, but in the deepest truth we are not. We did not give birth to ourselves but rather we were each created by the same One Being frequently and simply called God in common vernacular. Furthermore, we are sustained and supported by this very Being every moment of our lives whether we recognize that or we do not. It therefore behooves us to enter and deepen our relationship with our Creator and Sustainer.

This book is here to inspire you to access, empower, and embody more of the wonder of who you really are on the deepest level of being so as to fulfill your soul purpose. This holy beautiful soul within you is the most authentic essence of who you are—who you really were before you entered into this physical world, who you really are while embodied in this world of time and space, and who you will continue to be when you eventually leave your physical body. The soul is the only part of us we will take with us when we leave the physical world. Fulfilling our soul purpose is the primary reason why we are each physically embodied for a limited period of time we are granted on this planet. Remember, we did not come here to be comfortable but to experience and radiate Divine Light and love in the unique way only possible in our human existence.

The original *Kabbalah Month by Month* was written primarily right before and in the immediate aftermath of the events of September 11, 2001. That day remains an intense wake up call to the United States and the world! Never before did the United States experience a terrorist attack of that magnitude in its homeland. Living in Manhattan at that time made the whole experience very close for me. In the immediate days that followed, the bridges and tunnels were closed. There was no way to leave Manhattan and nowhere to turn except to God, friends, and family. It was as if a veil had been lifted, and I could see so clearly how connected we all are to each other and how artificial and unnecessary were the walls we construct to separate us from one another. I cried for people murdered as if they were close friends.

This book, *Living in the Divine Flow*, has been primarily written during the COVID shutdown in 2020-2022, the onset of the war between Ukraine and Russia, and finalized in the immediate aftermath of the October 7th, 2023 attack on Israel. The COVID pandemic encouraged us to tap into our inner resources and prioritize our health and well being. Now with the threat of nuclear war emerging in this Ukraine and Russia war, rising crime rate, rising anti- semitism. increasing inflation, war in the Middle East, Iran emerging as a chief sponsor of terrorism and its potential to soon have a nuclear weapon, people in the world once again are increasingly aware of our common vulnerability and interdependence.

As challenging as these times are, in our heart of hearts, many of us know that our souls have been waiting for an extraordinary time such as this. Though this time is one of challenge and hardship for many, it has been predicted to also be a time of wondrous, positive, global transformation. We will emerge from this time more aligned with our inner selves and with God. This will be a time for each of us to shine in our own unique ways. The teachings in this book will help people undergo this upcoming global initiation and transformation with greater ease, consciousness, and patience.

When external events become increasingly intense, *Living in the Divine Flow* will help the reader find tools to move from fear and powerlessness to faith, peacefulness, and empowerment. In our unique ways, in large and small ways, we will each be privileged to contribute to spreading peace and love in the world.

When I first began to write this book, I had been sitting in my house in Florida virtually in quarantine for more than six months. Being older and having diabetes made me acutely aware of my vulnerability. My plans to return to Israel in April 2020 were thwarted by the virus and then followed with several personal health challenges. In the midst of my quarantine, I decided to rewrite and update my most popular book. Even though *Kabbalah Month by Month* had been out of print for more than ten years, a month rarely goes by to this day when I do not receive a heartfelt request for a copy of this book.

As I worked on this book update, I came to appreciate why *Kabbalah Month by Month* was the most beloved of all my books. The material in this book is succinct, practical, and relevant to what is happening in a person's life each month. This book may be likened to a delicious fast-food spiritual buffet. A reader can pick this book up at any time during the course of a month and quickly find pertinent and practical guidance to enhance their experience of life immediately. Spiritual nourishment is easily found in less than five or ten minutes. Whenever a person needs inspiration, consolation and encouragement, this book is there as a good friend to support the reader in accessible ways, every year, every month, and every day.

After the reading the Introduction and the General Guidelines and Goals section for each monthly chapter, I encourage everyone to keep a journal, diary, or record for each month. Some of you may want to list your personal spiritual, emotional, and physical goals for each month along with strategies and activities that you see possible for yourself. In the course of the month, record your actual experiences and experiences to the recommended exercises each month. At the end of the month, take time to highlight the impact of major events taking place during the month, and what soul qualities you were able to access and express more fully in your life.

This book is to be read throughout the month each year as much as you feel called to do so. Reading the material several times, practicing the meditations, completing the guidelines and practical recommendations each month will help you grow in the ways that you want to grow. Sharing the spiritual work within this book with a friend or two would be very supportive and assist you and your friends to be more focused and disciplined in your commitment to your spiritual growth.

As each month has its unique energy and its own holidays, it is best to study and meditate upon the chapter of the current month. Don't be rigid about this. Allow yourself to be guided to read any section of the book at any time. You may need to feel a little more joy in your life, no matter what the month, so you might want to read the chapter on Adar, the month of joy and laughter. If you want to feel more adventurous, read about Kislev, rekindling dreams. If you feel emotionally stuck review the month of Tevet, the month devoted to the transformation of anger.

Though holidays occur at specific times, we need to tap into the energy and grace of all of the holidays on a daily basis to be fully human. Every day we need a little taste of Rosh Hashanah to open to the newness available each moment of our lives. We need a little Yom Kippur to feel forgiveness for ourselves and others. We need a little Chanukah to be empowered to take risks and go for what we really want. And we need a little Passover to receive Divine grace to take us beyond our limitations. Let your higher wisdom guide you.

Keep this book by your bed or on your desk so it is easily accessible when you feel the urge to consult it. The monthly charting of the map of time in this book will support your personal growth in the most gentle, continuous, and practical way. You will need a Jewish or astrological calendar available at Jewish bookstores or just search on Google, or another browser, to know the current month.

Those who study the material in this book, keep it close to their hearts, practice the meditations, and seek to live from its teachings will access more of their soul purpose and be transformed in the ways that they really want. The more a person works with the energy of each month, the deeper their experience will be and the greater receptivity for the spiritual energy of the following month. Each month builds upon the preceding ones.

Finally, I extend my love and blessings to you, my dear reader, for a wonderful year of blessings. I write from the heart so I hope that my words will touch your heart. As you study this book, I pray that you have many glimpses of how holy this wisdom is, how holy God is, and how holy you are.

Please check out my website: melindaribner.com

You are invited to contact me personally, subscribe to my monthly newsletter, subscribe to my Melinda Ribner YouTube channel, participate in free meditation classes, and avail yourself of the many additional services I offer.

1

Tishrei

SEPTEMBER – OCTOBER

ENERGY
Opening to Newness

AREA OF HEALING
Sex

ASTROLOGICAL SIGN
Libra

HEBREW LETTER
Lamed ל

HEBREW TRIBE
Ephraim

DIVINE NAME PERMUTATION
VHYH

HOLIDAYS
Rosh Hashanah
Yom Kippur
Sukkot
Shemini Atzeret and Simchat Torah

A Personal Story

According to the Jewish calendar, Tishrei, the first month of the year, is the headquarters for asking and receiving blessings for ourselves, our loved ones, and the world for the upcoming year. In this introductory story to this month, I share a secret from my personal life to increase the likelihood that prayers this month will be answered. You may possibly even experience miracles as I did.

In mid 1994, before I wrote any books, I felt myself confronting a life threatening illness. My life revolved primarily around attending to my uncomfortable bodily sensations and exploring various healing options. No doctor initially offered me any explanation as to the root cause of my affliction or what I could do to return to a more normal life. Months had gone by when I struggled to walk even a few city blocks due to weakness. I lost fifteen or twenty pounds of weight quickly as it was very difficult to hold down food.

One day, a friend called to assure me that a particularly brilliant doctor in New York would be able to diagnosis my situation and even cure me. I had been living in Boston but returned to New York to see this doctor as soon as possible.

After describing my symptoms to the doctor, he immediately diagnosed my problem and prescribed very strong medication without informing me of possible side effects. He assured me that he had the correct diagnosis. No further tests were necessary. So delighted, I inwardly skipped to the pharmacy to fulfill the prescription as soon as I could.

Late that night, I experienced a health crisis. The symptoms of nausea and pain returned in spades. Frightened and distraught, I called this doctor for support and guidance, only to discover that his emergency telephone number was out of order.

What shall I do? Shall I go to the emergency room? It was after midnight. My last experience in a New York City emergency room made me too frightened to ever go there again. At that time, I shared a cubicle with a man who must have been dangerous, his mouth was taped, his hands handcuffed, and his feet chained. He sat book-cased between two strong big policemen with real guns in their holsters. We waited together in silence to see a physician for more than an hour in a very small room. No, I was not going to the hospital in the middle of the night by myself. I would prefer to die in my own home alone than revisit that trauma.

Now, with what little energy I could muster, I remembered to pray to God for relief of my discomfort and for my life. Isn't that what I always taught? There was nothing else I felt I could do. Basically I pleaded for my life, and then I negotiated and made a deal with God. "Please let me live!" I cried out. "I promise to write a book on Jewish meditation." I intuitively felt that God would want such a book to be written because I had witnessed so much spiritual growth and joy unfolding in many of my students during my meditation classes.

Because I lacked confidence and had never written anything before, I had procrastinated with many foolish excuses. Who am I? Who do I think I am? And, I do not have time or the talent to write a book. That night I promised God I would write a book in spite of my own insecurities.

The very next morning after a sleepless night, another friend called me with the name of a leading specialist in exotic diseases. She assured me that this famous doctor, who had worked with celebrities and dignitaries from all over the world, would surely be able to heal me.

Upon immediately calling his office I was miraculously able to see him in an hour's time. As quickly as possible, I dressed and took a taxi to a fancy East Side doctor's office from my humble West Side apartment. This doctor prescribed a different, powerful and more expensive medication and explained to me that the suffering I had experienced was due to the previous medication given to me the day before. I instantly began to feel better. My full recovery was however not instant. It took additional months, involving many different kinds of doctors and healers, but it was a start. Most importantly, I now had hope I would live.

As I began to recover from my long illness, a girlfriend and I visited the grave of the Lubavitcher Rebbe, on July 7th, 1995, which is my English birthday. We engaged in what I call Jewish ICHING. Since the Rebbi's passing, some Lubavitchers adapted the practice of using the Rebbe's previous correspondence to receive answers to personal questions. This was possible for me because my friend read and understood Yiddish. As I opened a book of letters written by the Rebbi, I was wondering about my next step, considering whether or how I could write the spiritual book on Jewish meditation I promised God I would write. Was I really worthy or capable of doing this?

The letter I looked at was written by a person requesting the Rebbe's permission to write a book on Chabad. It was even addressed to a person with my married name. That itself was quite a Divine coincidence that really caught my attention. The Rebbe not only gave this man a blessing, he pledged to help him. I took this as a blessing to me and a sign that I should begin to write a book.

Several months later, a free-lance literary agent contacted me to suggest that I write a book on Jewish meditation as she had become aware of my teaching Jewish meditation. Ultimately, she did not like my writing style and rejected me. With a proposal in hand, I soon connected with the Vice President of William Morris Agency, one of the most famous and prestigious talent agencies in America. He happened to be in the beginning of a personal Jewish soul awakening and was interested in me and a book on Jewish meditation. In a few weeks time, he obtained a book contract with royalties for me for my first book that was followed with the publishing of two additional books also with royalties while serving again as my agent.

Through many miracles and Divine assistance, I was blessed to write and publish three books on Jewish meditation and spiritual growth in the next five years along with two CD's of music and meditation while also maintaining a busy practice as a therapist and meditation teacher. And most importantly I regained my health.

Upon reflection I seriously doubt that had I not gone through the hell that I did and called out for Divine partnership and assistance, I would not have written or published the books that I did. Because of my prayer to God, I let go of my insecurities to do what I knew in my heart God wanted me to do and I was Divinely supported.

Please understand that this personal account was not ultimately about bribing God, though it may appear that on the surface. Rather, it was a testimony to how sometimes life humbles us enough, for our own good so we have no other choice but to call out for Divine assistance. When we can get out of our own way, I have found and seen repeatedly that we are supported and empowered to do what our soul came into this world to do.

Finally, I can not underestimate the power of the posthumous blessing of the Lubavitcher Rebbe. Blessings from a righteous person who is alive or even from one who is not even physically embodied like the Lubavitcher Rebbe also makes a difference.

In summary, what I want to say is that I have come to see that the secret to having one's prayers answered is to align our personal will with Divine Will so as to want what God wants for us and to get out of our own way. Our prayers will then have greater likelihood of a positive response.

Energy: Opening to Newness

The month of Tishrei signals the beginning of the Hebrew calendar year. Its hallmarks are the willingness to be vulnerable, to be in the state of not knowing, to let go of the past, and open to new possibilities.

Tishrei is the headquarters for receiving blessings for the entire year for every human being, not just Jews. Learning to receive is a very important skill and even a spiritual practice to heighten this month. The guidelines, meditations and teachings in this chapter will help you to create and receive a new order for you personally that will transform your life this year and in years to come.

The Bible starts with the words: *In the beginning* to teach us that wherever we are in life, we can begin anew. There is always a new beginning. No matter how spiritually connected or disconnected we may feel, we can always grow. We are not limited nor bound to our past. What we chose in the past does not mean that we will have to make the same choices in the future. The past is past and does not have to contaminate the present.

We are taught that the Torah starts with a *bet*, the second letter in the

Hebrew alphabet rather than the first letter, *Aleph*. *Bet* is the first letter of the word *berakah* which means blessing to teach us that this world is a blessing. The numerical value of *bet* is two, to teach us about the emergence of duality. Prior to creation, there was only *Ein Sof*, limitless light, and now there is a world.

The name Tishrei contains most of the same Hebrew letters as the word *Bereshit* which means In the Beginning. The month of Tishrei begins with the holiday of Rosh Hashanah that is held on the new moon of this month. In Hebrew, Rosh Hashanah means *head of the year* as Tishrei is considered the beginning of the new year.

Rosh Hashanah is a holiday celebrating the creation of the human being by the one and only unique Being often referred to as God. God has many names in common usage such as Infinite Being, True Reality, Supreme Consciousness, The Universe, The Source of All Life and so many more. Even in Judaism, there are many Hebrew names for God. Regardless of the multiplicity of the names of God, there is only One God. During this month, it is important to internalize the idea of the existence of One Creator for all of life regardless of what the Divine is called, regardless of what is happening in the external world.

The energy of newness is flowing in Tishrei for those who are ready to receive. Be particularly open to new ideas, new experiences, new people, a new place to live, new work, or anything new this month. Newness brings joy. Tishrei is a joyous month. If we are willing to begin thinking and acting differently in the coming year, Tishrei is an amazing and unique spiritual opportunity to open to newness and take leaps forward in our lives. Many people will initiate life enhancing choices and changes to support their new vision for the upcoming year. As the first month of the year, Tishrei sets the tone for what will happen during the upcoming year.

This month of Tishrei is a powerful time to expand our spiritual awareness and transform our lives in the ways we have always wanted. This month is an optimal time to listen to our inner guidance. There is much heavenly support for this transformation but yet it will still require a great deal of personal inner work on our part. There must always be a balance between personal effort and grace. The astrological sign corresponding to the month of Tishrei is Libra, which is represented by scales. Libra is known as a sign of balancing and weighing everything carefully. As the first month of the year, Tishrei teaches us that everything begins from a place of balance within ourselves.

In Tishrei, balance is reflected in nature in most places in the world. The autumnal equinox approaches; the days and nights are now of equal length. The weather is also generally balanced, not too hot, and not too cold in most parts of the world. The rainy season has not yet begun. This balance in Tishrei is represented by the astrological sign of the scales of Libra. As the first month of the year, Tishrei teaches us that everything begins from a place of balance. To begin anew, we must first find this place of balance within ourselves.

In Judaism, Tishrei is considered both the seventh month as well as the first. Certain sections of the Torah call Tishrei the seventh month because the new year begins with the new month of Nissan—March-April—yet Tishrei is widely known and celebrated as the first month of the Jewish calendar and is considered so according to Jewish law and calendar.

The numbers one and seven are considered the most beloved in Kabbalah. As the seventh month, the midpoint of the year, and as the first month, the beginning of an entirely new year, Tishrei is the time of harvesting and also the time of beginning new projects. Schools reopen and people return to work after the summer holidays. No other month has as many Jewish holidays as Tishrei does. Some of them are among the most important Jewish holidays of the entire year.

It is no coincidence that there are so many Jewish holidays this month. As the seasons change in many places throughout the world, people feel particularly vulnerable at this time. The holidays are given for us to bathe, shelter, protect, and fortify ourselves during this time of vulnerability and transition. During this month, practicing Jews live in a spiritual bubble—they are either celebrating a holiday, in the interim days, or preparing for the next one.

The month of Tishrei may be likened to a spiritual shopping center where we have the opportunity to fill our baskets with blessings for the next year. The various holidays are each particular stores where we receive different spiritual gifts. In olden times, the granaries were stocked up at this time to sustain people through the cold winters. So, similarly, during Tishrei, we stock up on blessings to sustain us for the year ahead.

During this month we will receive the blessing of Divine Revelation to the extent we have the vessels to receive. The more refined our spiritual vessels are, the more Godliness we will receive, contain, and embody. The more ego-identified we are, the more anger and resentment we hold in our consciousness, the more limited will our revelation of Godliness be. In this month, we must realize more than ever that we pray not for ourselves and our loved ones but for the whole world. The key to receiving blessings for oneself is to pray for others, for the Jewish people and for the world.

During this month, our appreciation of the bonds with family and friends is heightened. All the holidays bring people together. The energy of this month supports the establishment and deepening of relationships with others. A sign that we are becoming closer to God is that we love others for no reason and feel connected to our family and our lineage.

> The energy of this month supports the establishment and deepening of relationships with others.

As a general rule, be mindful this month to not assume that people know that they are loved by you. Take advantage of opportunities to tell people they are loved by you, and remind them also that they are, more importantly, loved by God. It is good to express love frequently to others. Expressing love dissolves barriers and brings people closer to each other and to their own souls.

This month is considered the headquarters for sexual healing. In Judaism, sex is acknowledged as important, essential, and even holy. Sexual relations are the foundation of life. According to Kabbalah, the genitals correspond to the *sephira*, the Divine emanation of yesod, which means *foundation*. Because Tishrei is the foundation for the rest of the year, similarly, sex is the beginning of life and the foundation of all relationships whether they are sexual in nature or not. It is sexual energy that is the source of all creativity as well as our actual physical life.

It is no accident that life begins through the sexual act. Sex is God's gift to us and it is a way that we can draw close to God as well as to another person. God could have chosen to perpetuate the species in another way, but instead chose to involve us as partners in the most intimate and deep way. Sexual relations bring unity with another person on the spiritual, emotional, and physical levels, and through unity with this one person, unity with all of creation.

According to the Ramban—Nachmanides—sexual relations brings blessings of spiritual healing not only to the people who are engaging in the act, but also to the world. Performed with the proper intentions in the appropriate manner, sexual relations become a vehicle for experiencing Godliness. As such, sex is a most pleasurable human experience.

Too often, people experience sex in a negative or limited way and feel guilty, anxious, or ashamed about it. As a therapist, I often deal with sexuality issues. Rather than experiencing sex as a source of pleasure or holiness, many people find sex a source of anxiety, shame, guilt or obligation.

It is a shame that God's gift to the human race is not fully honored. And even worse that rape, sexual abuse, and exploitation are so rampant in the world. Our appreciation of sex needs to be elevated in general and particularly during this holy month. Sexual dysfunction issues between partners should be addressed this month.

General Guidelines, Goals, and Spiritual Practices

The following guidelines, goals and spiritual practices enable us to direct our energies in the way that are optimal for our growth and transformation this month. It is recommended that you read and meditate upon them often in the course of the month. Reflect on their applicability to you, and allow them to inspire you often throughout the month.

1. KNOW HOW AND WHY YOU WERE CREATED.

On the first day of this month of Tishrei, we celebrate the creation of the human being. Understanding how and why we were created guides us to live more meaningful lives. Here is a most important fundamental teaching, paraphrased straight from one of the deepest Kabbalistic texts, *Etz Hayim, Tree of Life*, based on teachings by Rabbi Yitzchak Luria.

> Before there was time and space, there was only *Ain Sof* (Limitless Light). Kabbalah teaches us that there arose a desire within Ain Sof, to bestow love and to be known. To create space for something else to exist, Ain Sof created a void, withdrew its light, and then re-entered the void in a lesser and more differentiated expression than what was previously.

The Torah uses the word *Elohim* in the seven day creation story. The Divine Name of Elohim is associated with the feminine *sephira*—Divine emanation—of *Gevurah* that sets boundaries. This is a most important point to understand: Creation was not a revelation of light but an actual expression of the concealment of Divine Light.

According to Kabbalah, Ain Sof created five worlds yet it is in our most dense physical world where the Light of Ain Sof is most concealed that the Divine purpose is most realized. According to Divine Will, human beings were created to reside in this lower dimension of physical reality only for a limited period of time because residing in the most dense world allows God a greater opportunity to bestow goodness, to be known and loved by something that feels itself separate from Ain Sof. In our world of seeming duality, God is often experienced as physically hidden to us.

Nevertheless, it is God who is animating, sustaining, and guiding our very existence on all levels of our being through the agency of our own souls. Even though only a part of our Divine soul actually incarnates into this dense physical reality, most of us do not usually have full access to this Divine soul nor do we know her full purpose for our unique physical incarnation. In the course of our lifetime, many of us are blessed to have glimpses of the love and wisdom of our souls and her purpose for this incarnation.

By way of a general understanding, we have to appreciate that we came into this physical reality to be human beings because being human offers our souls and even God opportunities and experiences that are not available to our souls in the higher more unified planes of existence.

Prior to our incarnation, Kabbalah tells us our souls reside in the Palace of Love and Kisses, enthralled to varying degrees in Divine Light and Love. Our souls re-enter into this physical reality for the opportunities to grow spiritually, to love, heal, and to make amends for actions taken in previous lifetimes. What we do here in this current incarnation will impact our standing in the next world and in our next incarnation if that is Divine Will that we be incarnated again. Yes, Judaism does believe in reincarnation.

Always remember, God created this world and each of us for love and joy. Life is not a punishment but rather an opportunity to learn, grow, and share in the short period of time we are physically embodied. It is up to each of us to align with Divine Will, to do good so as to be brought close to God, the Ultimate Giver while in this physical world. Though we may sometimes take our lives for granted, being a physical human being is a time limited experience that was said to be even envied by the angels who are not embodied in the way we as human beings are.

2. KNOW THERE IS ONE GOD AT ALL TIMES.

It is basic to know and accept that God is not a figment of our imagination nor a projection of one's own thinking. GOD IS REAL. It is fundamental Jewish principle to know that each of us is alive only because we are sustained and supported by this wondrous Infinite Divine Being with many names who breathes us and everyone into existence. No one is here on our own. No one has been abandoned by God, though some of us have chosen to not align ourselves with God or Divine Will. Nevertheless, that does not negate our connection to the Creator.

To experience the power of God in our lives, we do not have to look further than our own breath. Our very breath is a testament to our Divine connection. We do not breathe on our own, rather, we are breathed by God.

Each breath is a Divine message that we matter, we are loved, and we are supposed to be here now in a physical body.

It is a wonderful daily practice to take time each day to be consciously aware of the miraculous gift of life experienced in the breath. Every breath is precious. Conscious awareness of the breath helps us to better receive the love and support contained within each breath.

Be grateful for the simple, awesome and yet amazing gift of life. This cannot be overstated. It is a great privilege to be physically embodied. Knowing that it is only for a limited period of time makes our life even more precious.

The Tanya, the mystical book of Lubavitch Chassidism, explains the use of the metaphor of breath in the creation of the human being. When the Bible says, God made man of dust from the ground and He breathed into his nostrils the breath of life and he became a living being, in Genesis 2:7, *The Tanya* explains that it does so to convey a primary idea that souls come from the depths of the Divine. *The Tanya* explains this metaphor further comparing the difference between the breath which flows when one is speaking to that of forceful breathing. It says:

> When speaking, there is embodied within the breath only the smallest amount of the speaker's power and life force, … But when he blows forcefully, he blows from deep within Himself. The breath embodies the internal power and life force of the vivifying soul.

To say that God breathed into man a pure soul shows that there is no separation or obstruction between God and man. *For if there were an obstruction, the exhaled breath of the Supreme One would not reach the human body.* Breath means that there is a direct connection between the Divine and the soul.

My teacher, Reb Shlomo Carlebach of blessed memory, once said to me that meditation is the experience of God being even closer to us than our own breath. The soul of a human being is not separate from God but a part of God. Study this teaching deeply for this is a foundation for accelerated spiritual growth.

Beyond our awareness of the breath, every Torah mitzvah—good deed or commandment prescribed by the Torah—is designed to deepen our awareness of our Divine connection. This is the month to take on another mitzvah to deepen your awareness of your intrinsic Divine connection. It will change your energy and bring additional blessing into your life.

3. SET A VISION FOR THE NEW YEAR.

As the first month of a new year, Tishrei is an opportunity for a new beginning. Every year brings with it new blessings, new opportunities, and new possibilities. What we open to during this month sets the course for the entire year.

During the days of this month, particularly when you engage in the celebration of the holidays, take time to envision what you want for yourself. Ask yourself, *Am I living a life worthy of who I am?* For example, are you living where you want to live? Do you do the kind of work you love and get paid what you want? Do you have the kind of relationships you want in your life? Do you support your physical well-being with nourishing, healthy foods and exercise? Do you have outlets for creative expression? Do you have times for recreation and play? Do you have a vibrant prayer or meditation practice? If the answer is no, or not entirely, to any of these questions, you need to open to newness. What adjustments do you need to make life-affirming choices to better open one to receive the blessings of a new year. Prayer can help.

Remember that we are not bound by the limitations of the past. If we keep doing what we have done in the past, it is likely we will get the results we have in the past. The energy of this month proclaims that we can change. We can be the people we want to be and have lives more reflective of who we really are.

Now is the time to let go of old excuses of the ego mind to justify not having what we want in our lives. Let go of the past for it is over. It is safe to let go of the past. Holding on to the past is a kind of bondage keeping us hostage to what is familiar to us. This is the month to welcome the wondrous unknown and open to a new more expanded soul-embodied life.

As we move away from ego-based limiting thinking and reacting, we raise our consciousness and gain the capacity to make new choices. Our lives are a reflection of our consciousness. Commit to changing your energy and consciousness this month. Loving and accepting ourselves increases our capacity to receive blessings in our lives. Loving the Divine gift of life opens gates for blessing.

Visualize yourself living the life you want—vibrant, joyful, healthy, and loving. You are embodying the wonder of who you really are. Know that the Creator of the universe and all enlightened and holy beings are rooting for you to live a more joyous and purposeful life. Your ancestors in your personal family lineage are also rooting for you to complete the work that they have done.

Speak to the Creator about your desires and needs. Ask for guidance and blessing. God is your partner to help you live your life more consciously and meaningfully. Remember that you do not and cannot change on your own. When you accept that you are blessed and loved by the Creator, you will allow God to work through you more consciously. In so doing, you will open to receive more of life's blessings.

4. AFFIRM YOURSELF AND WHAT YOU WANT IN LIFE.

Affirmations are powerful tools for manifesting what we want in our lives. See yourself healthy, happy, radiant, fulfilled, and engaged in meaningful work and relationships, enjoying your life on all levels. Affirm that this is your true self and that you are committed to living on this level of truth.

Write powerful affirmations for yourself and repeat them often during the course of the month. For example, *I am a radiant spiritual being who enjoys life fully* or, *I am loving and lovable*. Affirmations may not be what you experience currently but that possibility of the affirmation is present within all of us, and is an expression of who we really are, and who we were created to be.

Take note of the negative voice within, the inner critic or ego mind, which in the guise of self-protection and rational thinking, is self-deprecating. This is the voice that tells you are not enough, you are not worthy, you are inadequate—you are basically flawed and deficient. This negative voice is a product of your fears. It is not who you really are.

The human being is created in the image and likeness of God. Do not waste time indulging in negative thinking or actions. This does not honor you, nor God, our Creator. Continue the repetition of your positive affirmations until they resonate deeply within you as the truth and you naturally begin to live from them.

5. TRY TO MAINTAIN SILENCE DURING THE HOLIDAYS.

Taking care with speech is a beneficial and powerful spiritual practice at any time of the year, but is particularly potent during this month and on Rosh Hashanah itself. This entire month is a time of judgment. As we judge others, so we are judged. Be watchful of your words and make an effort not to speak badly about other people, particularly on Rosh Hashanah. It is so easy to be careless and judgmental in our speech.

When we speak badly about others our spiritual energy is actually diminished and the negative inclination—known as the *yetzer hara*—is strengthened. The negativity we project onto others returns to us manifold. Guarding our tongue is a most important spiritual practice in Judaism. We extend our life by speaking words of prayers, and we diminish our life by speaking badly about others. It does not matter if the words we speak are true or not. They still hurt us.

6. MAKE AN EFFORT TO BE HAPPY, EVEN IF YOU FEEL SAD.

The great Rebbe Reb Nachman of Breslov (1772-1810), used to say that it is a great mitzvah to always be happy. Being happy demonstrates our faith in the goodness of God.

Being happy means that even when we are sad or heartbroken, we are still in touch with this place of inner happiness inside us, because we trust in God. When we trust God, we know that all things are happening in our lives to support us to move us closer to God. Though we have free will and are responsible for the choices we make, we must always remember that God is running the world.

Being happy does not mean that we are always jovial and smiling. It does not mean that we repress our real feelings and not allow ourselves to be sad when it is appropriate. It is good to love and accept all of your feelings whatever they are. It is good to let go of judging yourself and making yourself wrong for the feelings you have.

You are a beautiful sensitive being. Your sensitivity may not have always been fully appreciated by others nor even by yourself. Welcome and love all the feelings that take place within you. Be compassionate towards yourself. You do not have to numb or distract yourself to feel safe. That is not loving yourself. When we allow ourselves to feel and accept our feelings without judgment we can release the hold they have had in blocking the flow of blessing in our lives.

> Welcome and love all the feelings that take place within you. Be compassionate towards yourself.

My rebbe, Reb Shlomo Carlebach of blessed memory, used to encourage his students to dance and be happy on Rosh Hashanah for by doing so we demonstrate our trust and faith in the goodness of God. And if God forbid it were decreed that we were not going to live to see the completion of the next year, we could actually change our fate by the joy we open up to on Rosh Hashanah. This is true for the entire month. When we are joyful for no reason other than being gifted with the privilege of being alive as a human being, we raise our vibration and thereby attract more blessings into our lives and reasons to be joyful.

7. LISTEN TO YOUR SOUL GUIDANCE THIS MONTH.

We each have been bestowed with a Divine soul that is our God Protection System, a kind of GPS. When we quiet the mind, we let go of trying to figure out life with our minds, and we let go of trying to be better people than we think we are. We learn to trust life and God and hear our own soul's guidance.

In the stillness of the mind, the soul shines a holy message to you: *You are beautiful. You are precious. You are loved. You are good enough as you are.* It does not matter whether you are suffering physically, emotionally, or mentally. Allow these soul messages to soak deeply into you. Repeat these love messages to yourself until they are internalized, authentic and true to you. These messages will empower you to go forward. Loving yourself as you are is the most important foundation for your growth and blessing this year.

Tishrei is a most auspicious time to live more authentically in accordance to the guidance of the soul within us. It is the time to let go of the internal voices from the ego mind of fear, guilt, shame, or feeling not good enough that have blocked the flow of blessing in our lives. When we are honoring and loving ourselves, we receive greater guidance and blessing to go forward in our lives.

8. CHERISH AND HEAL YOUR RELATIONSHIPS WITH FAMILY.

Cherish your family members. Nothing is an accident. No one is in your life as a family member by chance. Family is a special Divine appointment. Kabbalistic wisdom believes in reincarnation and reminds us that people are connected to present family members because they were connected to them in former lifetimes, especially true of our parents.

Consider this possibility. Everyone has the perfect parents and siblings needed for them to fulfill their soul purpose and soul correction for this lifetime. Everything that has happened to us in this lifetime has been Divinely choreographed and perfect for what we need to learn and grow at that time. We may resist this premise or embrace it. It is our choice. When we embrace this possibility, we let go of resistance and move into greater acceptance and empowerment.

Embracing ourselves and totality of our life experiences allows us to proceed forward and receive blessings and support. There is a Divine gift and spiritual opportunity within all the challenges we have faced and will face in our lives. If you like, write for yourself or share with someone the learning opportunities in your relationships with family and friends in the last year. What are you envisioning for the upcoming year?

If you like, take a few breaths to center yourself and begin writing a stream of consciousness such as, *Now is a time in my life when I ...*

Continue writing until you feel complete. This writing is for you alone, unless you choose to share it with others.

Astrological Sign: Libra

The astrological sign for the month of Tishrei is Libra, represented by scales. The energy of this month is one of deliberation, balancing, and weighing everything carefully. There is an inherent desire to find equanimity. These qualities are often characteristic of people born under the sign of Libra. The time period between Rosh Hashanah and Yom Kippur is also considered a time for deliberation, balancing and judgment.

Tishrei retains its position as the seventh month also in astrology. According to astrology, the first six months focus on the development of the individual. Now in Tishrei, a balance is found between the individual and the community, along with a new capacity and desire to bring harmony into the world.

Libra rules over the seventh house, which is that of marriage and relationships. Relationships are very important this month. Libra is ruled by the planet Venus, the goddess of Love. Love is the primary force in the creation and sustains the world. Love is the primary force within us and it is what attracts and binds people together in harmony. This month of Tishrei brings people together to renew and strengthen their relationships with each other.

Hebrew Letter: Lamed

The Hebrew letter for this month is *lamed*, the tallest of all the Hebrew letters. Its height reflects the tremendous spiritual heights possible during this month. Jews refer to the lamed as *a tower*

soaring in air. The lamed, the tallest letter and the *yud*, which represents the month of Elul, the month immediately preceding Tishrei, together spell out *Le*, which means *to Me*. This indicates that Tishrei builds on the previous month, Elul, and is devoted to God. The significance of this word is taken from the high point of the wedding ceremony when the groom says to the bride: *Harei at mekudesht le*, which means: *You are holy to me*. The joining of a husband and wife is symbolic of joining of God and people. The energy of this month is one of coming together, unifying in love. As mentioned earlier, the area of healing for this month is sexual relations.

Looking at the size and shape of the *Lamed*, we see a channel connecting the higher worlds to the lower worlds. The lamed, whose name literally means *to learn*, reflects the human aspiration to ascend in knowledge. The lamed also means *to teach*, which, according to Kabbalah as discussed by Rabbi Yitzchok Ginsburg in his book, *Aleph Beit*, reflects the hovering mother who offers protection and inspiration to those who truly aspire to know God. Energies of both learning and teaching are active this month. We also see an allusion to the healing of sexuality in the letter *lamed*. Sex in the Bible is called *knowing*. When the Bible says that *Adam knew Eve*, it is referring to sexual relations.

Lamed is the first letter of the Hebrew word *lev* which means heart. The word *lev* consists of the letters *lamed* and *beit* which has a numerical value of two. We could read *lev* as two *lameds*. If we put two *lameds* face to face, we see a heart. Tishrei is the heart of the year. Like the heart, it distributes the energies for the entire year. Tishrei is the headquarters for the opening of the heart.

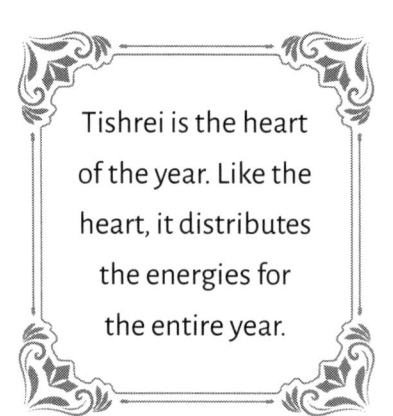

> Tishrei is the heart of the year. Like the heart, it distributes the energies for the entire year.

The *lamed* is also the heart of the Hebrew alphabet. The first half of the alphabet from aleph to *lamed* spells out *El*, which is a name of God associated with the Divine emanation of love, *hesed*. From the letters *men* to *tet*, the second half of the alphabet spells out *met*, which means *death*. Tishrei marks the end of the first half of the year that begins in Nissan and the beginning of the second half of the year.

Hebrew Tribe: Ephraim

The tribe associated with the month of Tishrei is Ephraim, from the younger son born to Joseph while he ruled in Egypt. About the naming of this son, the Torah says: *and the name of the second son called Ephraim, for God has caused me to be fruitful in the land of my affliction."* Gen.41:52.

When Jacob, the father of Joseph, sees his grandsons, he says, 'And now your two sons, Ephraim and Menashah, who were born to you in the land of Egypt before I came to you into Egypt, are mine, as Rueven and Shimon, they shall be mine." Gen 48:5. Jacob's adoption of Ephraim and Menashah elevated them to the level of his other sons. The tribes named after them were thereby placed on equal footing with the other tribes of Israel.

Before his death, Jacob blessed Ephraim and Menashah, his brother, his other sons for whom the tribes were named. He blessed Ephraim, who was the youngest, with his right hand and Menashah, with his left. Thinking that Jacob had made a mistake in blessing his younger son over the firstborn, Joseph attempted to correct his father only to find out that Jacob was insistent on blessing Ephraim over Menashah.

Ephraim was beloved of God. *"Is Ephraim my dear son? Is he a darling child? For whenever I speak of him, I remember him still."* Jer. 31-20. This reminds us of the beloved energy of this month of Tishrei.

Divine Name Permutation: VHYH

The Divine permutation is one of the most important indicators for understanding the flow of spiritual energy into the world each month. The letter positions correspond to the different spiritual worlds. The first and third positions are considered lights and the second and fourth positions are vessels. In examining the permutation for this month, we note that the letter *hay*, (H), is in its usual position for YHVH. The *hay* is in the world of Assiyah, the fourth position, indicating an abundant flow of Divine energy into this physical world. The *hay* in the second position is in the world of Beriyah, indicating expansiveness in the mind.

The *yud*, (Y), is in the world of Yetzirah, the third position, indicating that one should concentrate the heart into a *yud*, a small point. To receive the energy of this month, one must be very internally focused, directing the heart upward toward the higher worlds. The *vav*, (V), in the world of Atzilut, the first place, indicates that there is a great and direct flow of light from *Ain Sof,* the term for the Infinite unknowable Being, generally called God. This heightened flow of light this month is evidenced by all the holidays taking place this month.

Torah Portions

Special portions of the Torah highlighting the energy of the month are read during the holidays of this month. On the first day of Rosh Hashanah, we read the Torah story of Sarah giving birth to Yitzhak, Isaac in English. Gen.21. And we read the Haftorah of the first day, we read of Hannah giving birth to Samuel after much prayer in Samuel I:1-2:10. Both women have difficulty conceiving naturally and God intervenes. Both stories testify to the Divine role in the birthing experience, reminding us that we need God and prayer to begin our lives anew.

On the second day of Rosh Hashanah, we read about the binding of Isaac and the willingness of Abraham and Isaac to sacrifice themselves to Divine Will. Gen. 22. It is said that this even actually took place on Rosh Hashanah, and the blowing of the shofar on Rosh Hashanah reminds us of the ram who was sacrificed instead of Isaac. We read this story not only to remind us of God, but to remind ourselves of the spiritual merit of Abraham and Isaac. And more importantly, to recognize that our personal will should always be subordinate to the Divine Will. In the coming year, we will be tested and we will each have to make different kinds of sacrifices—how we respond is a demonstration of our faith.

The Torah portion for Yom Kippur is Leviticus 16:1-34, which recounts the death of the sons of Aaron and the service offered by Aaron, the high priest, to obtain atonement for the people. We read in this Torah portion, God's establishing of this very day as a Day of Atonement for eternity. Yom Kippur is the day Moses returned from Mount Sinai having obtained forgiveness for the Jewish people for the building of the Golden Calf.

There are two interesting Haftorah portions that are read on Yom Kippur. The morning one is from Isaiah 57:14-58. Although the Torah tells us to fast and afflict ourselves on Yom Kippur, and people generally do so, we read in the Haftorah that God does not really want this: God wants us to dissolve groups that pervert justice, share our riches with the poor, and free the oppressed. If we do these things, God will be pleased with us.

During the afternoon service, we read about the prophet Jonah, who was unwilling to share God's prophecy with the non-Jewish city of Nineveh. Escaping this mission on a boat that experienced turbulence, Jonah was thrown into the water and swallowed by a whale. While inside of the whale, when he had no other choice, Jonah prayed to God and agreed to carry out God's Will. As Jonah feared, the people of Nineveh repented and were spared destruction.

Many of us can identify with Jonah because we have also resisted what we were called to do with many excuses or reasons. It is possible that we could lose the opportunity to do something important. Other times, like Jonah, we will be placed in situations where we will have no choice but to call out to God, and do what we felt we were asked to do.

The book of Jonah also offers a most important teaching for the Jewish people. Sometimes the Jewish people tend to be insular and reluctant to spread the beautiful holy teachings of Judaism to the world. In the beginning of the year, we need to recognize that sharing the spiritual light of the Torah with people of other nations is an important part of the mission of the Jewish people. We have one God, and God wants each of us to share God's love and wisdom with all who would like to receive. In the upcoming year, we each can make sincere efforts to be ambassadors of God's love and light and share with people. It is certain that we will be given opportunities to give more this year than previously.

On Sukkot we read Leviticus 23:33-44, the Biblical commandment to observe the holiday of Sukkot. We also read the Haftorah of Zechariah.

Zech.14:1-24, and the Haftorah of Ezekiel Ezek. 38-39:16. Both interestingly forecast the war of Gog and Magog and the cataclysmic series of battles that bring about the messianic era. It seemed like a Divine sign we were reading these Torah portions at the very time during Sukkot, when the United States began its war on terrorism by bombing Afghanistan after September 11th. Some of the details related in scripture about this event seem quite gruesome and frightening, but ultimately a good and happy ending is forecast. It is important to note that these doomsday prophecies are not written in stone. We can change our destinies.

In the remaining days of the month, when all the holidays within the month of Tishrei have ended, the Jewish people begin a new cycle of Torah reading from the beginning with the chapter *Bereshit*, which means, *In the beginning*. The chapters, in a storytelling format, contain the most mystical secrets about the nature of reality such as the Divine purpose for creation of the world and the purpose for every human being. So much is revealed and hidden in the story of Adam and Eve. My book *The Secret Legacy of Biblical Women: Revealing the Divine Feminine*, offers further insight into these secrets.

Holiday: Rosh Hashanah

Rosh Hashanah marks the beginning of the new year and is the most universal of all the Jewish holidays. Considered the birthday of humanity, Rosh Hashanah commemorates the creation of the human being by a Divine Being who is One, but with many, many names, even within Judaism. On Rosh Hashanah, when we acknowledge that God is the Creator of the world and that the world continues to exist only because Divine Will that it do so, we can tap into the original vision that God had in creating the world. Kabbalah teachings quite succinctly tell us that this world was created by God to bestow goodness and to be known.

Through the special prayers, songs, and melodies of Rosh Hashanah, we may be blessed with a vision of this Divine intention and be bathed in Divine love. The celebration of Rosh Hashanah makes us grateful for life itself, and reminds us that we cannot take life or this world for granted. Life is ultimately a Divine gift.

Unlike most holidays, which occur at the full moon, Rosh Hashanah occurs on the new moon and consequently embodies the energies and mysteries of this phase of the moon. Just as what we open to at the time of the new moon shapes the entire month, what we open to during Rosh Hashanah shapes the entire year.

Rosh Hashanah is a time of tremendous blessing. On Rosh Hashanah we receive visions of new possibilities for ourselves. These visions empower us to go forward in our lives and to let go of what has kept us stuck or limited. In a passage in which Tishrei is numbered as the seventh month, the Torah instructs us: *In the seventh month on the first day, you shall do no laborious work, it shall be a day of shofar blowing for you.* Num: 29:1 and Lev 23:24. Other than this reference to Rosh Hashanah, the Torah does not provide much information about the holiday. Most of what we know about the holiday comes from the oral tradition.

Rosh Hashanah is traditionally known also as a day of judgment. We say repeatedly in the Rosh Hashanah prayers: *Today is the birthday of the world. Today all creatures of the world stand in judgment, whether as children or as servants …* We stand on this day with humility, not knowing what the upcoming year will bring. Jewish liturgy affirms that the destiny for each person, Jew and non-Jew alike, is determined on Rosh Hashanah and sealed on Yom Kippur, though some say it extends to the end of Sukkot or even Chanukkah. Whatever our destiny may be, we are told that we can change it through *teshuvah,* which means, *returning to God,* by *tefila* prayer, and *tzedekah*—charity.

As we see from the Torah reference, the main event of Rosh Hashanah is the blowing of the shofar, which is a bent ram's horn. Oral tradition stipulates that we should hear one hundred blasts of the shofar each day of Rosh Hashanah. The shofar blasts import the essence and teachings of the holiday more directly and powerfully than words could ever do. The Zohar, an ancient book of Jewish mysticism, says, *Happy is the people who know the teruah,* the shofar blasts.

The shofar blasts help us access the deepest places within ourselves where we know there is a God. The sounds of the shofar emulate the cry of our souls and enable us to turn inward to our deepest core. As a basic and primal sound issuing from the horn of the ram, the shofar blasts puts us in touch with what is true and real. It awakens our spiritual potential and inspires us to change and become better people.

When we hear the shofar blasts, some of us may find ourselves crying to God, *Here I am. I made mistakes, I am not complete. Please help me to be a better person. Please help me to be all I can be. Please guide me in Your ways.* The shofar blasts help us to feel and release all these feelings of sadness, guilt, and fear that have blocked the flow of blessing in our lives.

Other people may hear the shofar as God talking to us, saying, *I made a world for love and joy, not for pain and suffering. Please take care of my world. Please take care of the holy soul within you. Wake up to Me, your Creator, and all that is true and real. I am real and present right now.*

According to Saadia Gaon, a great rabbi of the ninth century, one of the main reasons for blowing the shofar on Rosh Hashanah is to coronate God as King. On Rosh Hashanah all the prayers and shofar blasts are to acknowledge that God as the Creator and King of the world. Just as trumpets are blown to announce the arrival of an earthly king, so the shofar is blown to testify that God is King—in Hebrew, *melech*—on the anniversary of God's creation of humanity. As we listen to the shofar blasts, we may reflect upon the questions such as how do I make God king over myself? What would the world be like if everyone recognized God as King?

In my humble opinion, it would be wonderful if the blowing of the shofar on this day would take place all over the world so all of humanity would recognize that there is one God and God is our King and Creator. Let's blow the shofar not just in the synagogues, but in the city parks, city streets and in other places where people gather and even worship, all over the world. Would that not be wonderful?

Many people have difficulty with the metaphor of God as King and feel it is patriarchal, outdated, and alienating. However, when we say God is King, we do not mean God is a white-haired elderly man sitting on a throne making judgments about our fate. That image may have been sufficient for us as children, but it is limiting and false to us as adults. Even though we may recognize this intellectually, it is sometimes emotionally challenging to rid ourselves of childish images of God.

Even though I am a woman, I experience the metaphor of God as King as empowering. It awakens devotion and reassures me that in essence there is a unified underlying Divine order beyond what appears on the surface. There is Divine Reality. God is real, and not a product of our imagination. People may have their own interpretations and projections about who God, but that often reinforces their own limitations in experiencing the truth of Divine Reality, and Divine Oneness.

When I acknowledge God as King, I feel empowered and strengthened. I am transported to a higher spiritual consciousness. I see the Divine order underlying all the events in my life and in the world that may otherwise seem unconnected. My life and everyone's life as well is not a series of random unrelated events, there is order, purpose and meaning in my life and in the world. This realization brings joy and blessing.

God as King is the metaphor for this higher spiritual awareness. At the deepest most mystical level, on Rosh Hashanah we have glimpses of a deeper truth, that only God has true existence and only God has real dominion and power in this world and in my life. There is a Divine plan underlying all of reality and all is unfolding according to Divine wisdom. This profound realization brings more than a simple joy but the experience of bliss and ecstasy. When I am totally absorbed in the Oneness of the Divine, I know that only God is truly real, and I am a part of God, or a reflection, of that Divine Reality.

The essence of the holiday of Rosh Hashanah is all about the proclamation of the kingship of God. What this really means is that there is Divine order in the world. Even though there is free will, there is also Divine providence and paradoxically everything is unfolding according to the Divine Plan.

ON ROSH HASHANAH AND THROUGHOUT THIS MONTH, REPEAT THIS AFFIRMATION:

I open to receive a new vision of my life and my service. I rejoice and trust that the power of God that flows through me will empower and guide me to do what I am to do, to meet the people who I need to

> meet to express more fully who I am. I have faith that God's kingdom will be established on this Earth. There will be peace, a true peace, and this makes me very happy and peaceful.

OBSERVANCE OF ROSH HASHANAH: Ritual observances and customs associated with Rosh Hashanah include lighting candles, saying prayers, and eating festive meals with friends and fallibly. People eat round challah bread—the circle signifying endless and continuing of life—with honey rather than the usual salt, to bless everyone with a sweet year. Apples with honey are eaten as well. Before the main meal, some may eat many different kinds of fruits, including pomegranates and dates, and vegetables such as carrots and cabbage as well as a fish head at their Rosh Hashanah table to confirm special blessings. Prayer books such as an *Art Scroll* outline the order and significance for the eating of these special foods.

It is strongly recommended that every Jew hear hundred blasts of the shofar if possible. Often there will even be a shofar blower to visit homes of homebound Jews, or synagogues will do a later shofar blowing for people who missed the shofar blowing during services for a variety of reasons. If you are homebound, contact a nearby synagogue and ask that someone come to your home to blow shofar for you.

In one custom known as *tashlich,* which occurs on Rosh Hashanah afternoon but can be done until Yom Kippur, people go to a natural body of water and symbolically cast their sins into the water. This ritual is designed to help people let go of the particular ways they have blocked themselves. This letting go prepares us to receive the blessing of Yom Kippur.

Ten Days of Teshuvah

Rosh Hashanah is the first day of what is known as *The Ten Days of Teshuvah.* Teshuvah literally means, *to return,* often translated as repentance or to turn in a new direction. Teshuvah has many facets to it. The teshuvah process opens us to fuller expression of our essential self along with a deeper connection and experience of God. In its most common usage, Teshuvah notes a return to or an acceptance of a greater level of Jewish observance. It also refers to an acknowledgment of an error, the resultant feelings of regret and the commitment to correct a situation and do differently in the future. On the deepest most mystical level, teshuvah is the return to inner wholeness, beauty, and potential—a return to the soul and the memory and the experience of oneness with the Divine.

> On the deepest most mystical level, teshuvah is the return to inner wholeness, beauty, and potential—a return to the soul and the memory and the experience of oneness with the Divine.

My beloved holy teacher of blessed memory, Rabbi Yitzchok Kirzner, raised the question of why Rosh Hashanah comes before Yom Kippur. One would naturally think that first we should be cleansed on Yom Kippur before opening to the newness of Rosh Hashanah. It is true that the entire month before Rosh Hashanah is earmarked for teshuvah, but the teshuvah between Rosh Hashanah and Yom Kippur is called the Ten Days of Teshuvah. Why? He explained that Rosh Hashanah gives a person the strength and the possibility to do a deeper kind of teshuvah.

I have included the following section with a variety of teachings, meditations and spiritual practices for the Ten Days of Teshuvah to facilitate a deeper introspection and springboard for inner and external changes. These ten days between Rosh Hashanah and Yom Kippur are devoted to healing our relationships with others as well as with ourselves. These activities can be done at other times of the year as well. They are not in any specific order, so each day, select one that you would feel most drawn to do. Understandably, it may not be easy for many of us, yet those who do all or most of these exercises will find great benefit. Do your best to address as many exercises as you can easily.

Suggested Activities for the Ten Days of Teshuvah

(Does not have to be done in any order.)

1. SEEK FORGIVENESS.

In the course of life, particularly in this last year, we may have been hurt or hurt people close to us. We may even be unaware of how we have hurt others and we may not have shared with others how they have hurt us.

On Yom Kippur, we ask God for forgiveness. Before Yom Kippur we are expected to make efforts to both forgive and seek forgiveness from people. It may be hard to make ourselves vulnerable, especially when we have been deeply hurt. Be gentle with yourself, but stretch yourself in the beginning of this month. Try to forgive others, even if they have not asked for forgiveness.

It is a common practice to approach people and ask for forgiveness in the time period between Rosh Hashanah and Yom Kippur. In The Carlebach synagogue when Reb Shlomo was alive, it was common for people to ask almost everyone for forgiveness. There may be someone who is carrying resentment or hurt that you were unaware that you hurt them. So it is good to ask for forgiveness of everyone.

If you like, you can prepare for the asking of forgiveness from someone who you know holds resentment and anger towards you prior to actually doing it. Perhaps it is a person to whom you committed an action you now regret. See this person on your inner screen, and say, *I ask for your forgiveness. I ask that you open your heart to me and that you forgive me for how I hurt you in the past, through my words, my actions, or my thoughts.* Speak about what you specifically did. Visualize that the person is forgiving you. And forgive yourself. Extend a blessing to them, and visualize them surrounded by Divine light and love. If you feel it would be helpful, reflect on something you could offer them for the pain you have caused.

If it is possible, it is important to do this in person. For some, a letter might be more comfortable for both of you. For example, you might write something like, *Please forgive me for anything I might have done to you or not done for you this last year. I love you, my relationship with you is important to me and I want to start anew to strengthen it in this coming year.* It is not necessary to stipulate specific offenses unless the person asks you, because doing so often causes pain and greater harm. Let's say you gossiped about a friend and your friend did not know. Because learning of your indiscretion would cause additional pain, it may be best to not reveal it.

In other scenarios, it may be quite clear to all parties what was done. Obtaining forgiveness might mandate some financial compensation or a commitment to act differently in the future. And it is possible that, when we ask for forgiveness, others might not be willing to give it to us. Our sages advise us to try three times, and even use intermediaries if necessary. The Rambam—Maimonides—recommended that you bring three friends with you when you approach a person you have deeply hurt. But what happens if you have tried in all possible ways and are still unsuccessful? You may have to give the person some time and space and be patient. Pray for the person's welfare and forgive yourself. Forgiveness is a process, and it is also a heavenly gift that comes through prayer and personal growth.

2. FORGIVE OTHERS.

Letting go of anger and forgiving others is an act of compassion to ourselves. Forgiveness is a gift you give to yourself. Blaming others keeps you stuck in a victim role and prevents you from opening to new possibilities available in the coming year. Being angry is a waste of your precious vital energy. We cannot embrace fully the newness of this coming year if we are carrying the jealousy, anger and resentments of past years. We cannot expect to receive God's forgiveness without first trying to forgive and receive the forgiveness of other people. The anger we carry inside hurts us more than anyone else. It keeps us bound to limiting ideas of who we are, unable to access the growth opportunity of this relationship.

Make a list of people to whom you continue to hold feelings of anger and resentment. Do this preparatory meditation with every person to prepare you to request forgiveness directly from a person who has hurt you. Ask God to help you have love and compassion for them and for yourself. Reflect on the pain that the person must have felt inside when he mistreated you in the way he or she did. Consider how you may have contributed to the pain you experienced. Forgiving others is an act of liberating yourself from being at the effect of other people.

Take a few breaths, and say silently and out loud, *I forgive you*, as you see an image of the person on your inner screen. Allow your heart to open and breathe out and let go of feelings of anger and resentment. Compassionately accept those angry feelings within you and then release them. This anger was from something that happened in the past. The past no longer exists. Do not allow feelings of anger and resentment to contaminate your present moment.

If you are ready to forgive a person, and if you want, you can tell the person of your forgiveness. Your forgiveness is a wonderful gift you give to others as well as to yourself.

Joseph in the Bible forgave his brothers who sold him into slavery. Though he ended up as the ruler in Egypt he spent twelve years in a terrible disgusting dungeon, yet he forgave. More recently, a mother of a hostage who was mistakenly killed by an Israeli soldier expressed forgiveness and love to the soldier who killed her son. She knew he must be feeling very guilty and terrible, so she extended an invitation to visit her and her family so she and the entire family can hug and express their forgiveness to him. If these people can forgive, can we not also forgive and move on with our lives?

3. FACE YOUR MORTALITY.

Imagine for a moment that the future of the world and the fate of each person are to be decided during the High Holiday period. Imagine that the words in the liturgy—who shall live and who shall die—are to be taken literally. Can we take our personal existence for granted? Sometimes a person may have to have a close call with death to realize how precious life is, how vulnerable each of us is, and how every moment is a gift.

What happens when you consider your own mortality and the mortality of others? Most of the time, we live in denial of the inevitability of our death. Some of us will die without warning, some gently, some violently, some with great pain. Most of us do not know how and when we will die. The *Gemara*, the book recording the oral tradition within Judaism recommends that each day of our life be considered as our last day.

How do we live our life differently when we really understand and accept that our time in this world is finite and that we could die at any time? Imagine that you have only a few days to live or even just one day as the Gemara suggests. What would you do? What do you need or want to complete or say before you depart from your bodily form?

Take a journal and write the following into your journal. Take deep breaths and write stream of consciousness as long as you feel drawn to write. Imagine that today is your last day on earth. What would you say or do? If you like, take time to write a response.

If someone else were to talk or write about your life, what would be said about you? If you like, write about your life in the third person. This act will be very interesting and even informative to you.

4. CHANGE YOUR ENERGY AND YOUR LIFE.

Judaism offers a prescription to significantly alter the quality of your life in the coming year and even possibly actually change the decree of whether you would live or die as well. In High Holiday liturgy, we affirm that *tefilla*—prayer, *tzedekah*—giving charity, and *Teshuvah*—repentance, can transform us into better people, people with a larger capacity to receive greater blessings. Reflect on how you might use these spiritual *weapons* for personal transformation. When you feel ready, write down your commitment to grow in each of these areas such as prayer, giving, and repentance. It would

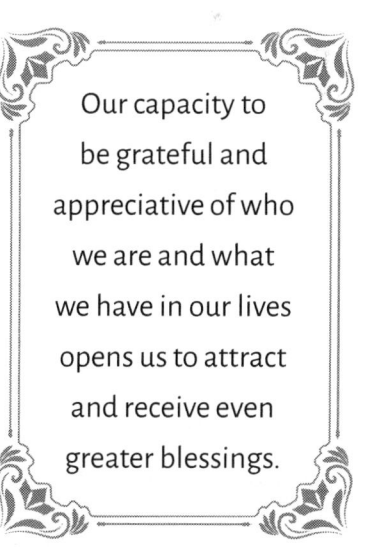

> Our capacity to be grateful and appreciative of who we are and what we have in our lives opens us to attract and receive even greater blessings.

be helpful to write this down in a journal that can easily be available to you during the year.

5. EXPRESS GRATITUDE.

Remembering that life in a physical body is finite increases our appreciation for each day. Take time to feel grateful for the gifts you have in your life right now. Our capacity to be grateful and appreciative of who we are and what we have in our lives opens us to attract and receive even greater blessings. Gratitude also promotes a deep feeling of well being, inner joy and actually strengthens our capacity to engage in positive life enhancing behaviors. What do you appreciate having in your life right now? List at least fifteen things, and after you have completed your list, take time to savor them.

6. EXPRESS APPRECIATION DIRECTLY TO PEOPLE.

What people do you appreciate having in your life? Have you told them or shown them your appreciation recently? Contact these important people in your life in the days before Yom Kippur if possible. Share with them some of the experiences you had with them that were particularly meaningful to you and bless everyone with a happy, healthy and joyful new year.

7. APPRECIATE YOUR WONDERFUL GOOD POINTS.

What do you appreciate about yourself? Here are some options: List your own good qualities. Or write yourself a love letter to win over your own heart. Or write a love letter to the inner child within you on how you love your inner child and plan to take better care of him or her in the upcoming year. If you want to embody more of your soul purpose, it is important that you love and honor yourself.

8. CELEBRATE YOUR BLESSINGS.

How do you celebrate the blessings in your life? Make a plan to celebrate your life and a plan to support the unfolding of the best you in the coming year. Make a plan to bless others in all ways you feel guided to do so.

9. OPEN TO GREATER LOVE.

God is the source of goodness yet we hold ourselves back, we sabotage, deny, and we limit our capacity to give and receive this goodness. Write your personal confession. Allow yourself to write stream of consciousness in any or all of these areas.

> I regret …
> I feel guilty about …
> I feel sad about …
> I am fearful of…

After taking several deep breaths to center yourself, love and accept yourself totally with great compassion for all the feelings you have felt during these exercises. Through love and acceptance of yourself, you can release limiting feelings, and appreciate how they may have even contributed to your growth.

10. BECOME A MORE COMPASSIONATE PERSON.

Write a plan to live a more meaningful and compassionate life towards yourself and others. How will you deepen your Divine connection in the upcoming year? How will you express compassion in the upcoming year? What actions will you do to fulfill your plan?

Holiday: Yom Kippur

HISTORY: Yom Kippur, the holiest day of the Jewish calendar, is known as the Day of Atonement. The Torah says, *On the tenth day of the month of Tishrei, it is a day of atonement, a holy convocation and you shall afflict yourselves, you shall not do any work on this very day for it is the Day of Atonement to provide you atonement before God. It is a day of complete rest* *for you and you shall afflict yourselves.* Lev 23:26. Up until Yom Kippur, we have done what we could do on our own to purify ourselves. On Yom Kippur we receive Divine grace, love and compassion and are cleansed, forgiven and liberated in a way we could never be on our own. As the Torah says, on Yom Kippur, *You shall be purified from all your sins.* Lev 16: 30.

Yom Kippur commemorates the day when Moses descended from Mount Sinai with the second set of tablets and a message of forgiveness for the Jewish people after the sin of the Golden Calf. Yom Kippur is the culmination of the forty-day period of teshuvah that began on the first day of the previous month of Elul. Yom Kippur is the tenth day of the more intensive period of teshuvah that began on Rosh Hashanah.

In the days of the Holy Temple in Jerusalem, Yom Kippur was the one day when the High Priest entered into the Holy of Holies in the Temple and uttered a particular name of God that ushered in forgiveness for the people. The service the High Priest engaged in on Yom Kippur is recounted in detail during the Mussaf service on Yom Kippur day.

OBSERVANCE: Yom Kippur is a day for meditation and prayer. As the Torah instructs, we *afflict ourselves* on this day. We do not eat, drink, wash, cook, have sexual relations, or engage in worldly activities. In today's world, we turn off the computer, radio, and the television. We wear white clothes if possible and do not wear leather shoes. These restrictions enable us to attune to the heavenly transmission of love, forgiveness, and grace given on this holiest of days. The Torah tells us: *On the tenth day of the month of Tishrei it is a day of atonement, a holy convocation, and you shall afflict yourselves.* Lev.23. And, the Torah tells us that on Yom Kippur: *You shall be purified from all your sins.* Lev 6:30.

It is a tremendous gift to pray in a congregation on Yom Kippur, for what we can do together is greater than what we can do alone. To be in the company of people who are strong enough to acknowledge that they are vulnerable human beings and as people have all made mistakes is an inspirational and powerful bonding experience. We also receive much more Divine Light and grace when we feel responsible for the community than praying alone as isolated individuals.

Yom Kippur offers us a special opportunity to attune to the experience of *at-one-ment* with the Divine in the most direct way. Because there are no distractions on Yom Kippur and the day is spent in prayer and meditation, it is easier to release all the ways we have blocked the flow of goodness into our lives. We do this in part by confessing our sins communally.

During the entire day of Yom Kippur, there are repeated requests for forgiveness and recitations of individual and communal sins. The requests are said in the communal rather than the singular to teach us about our interdependence and responsibility for each other. On Yom Kippur, we are constantly reminded of our unity and connection with each other.

In Hebrew, to sin literally means to miss the mark. In Judaism, because people are made in the image of God, there is no doctrine of original sin, as in some forms of Christianity. Human beings are not considered inherently sinful; rather, they may think, feel and do things that are not in keeping with their true nature—that is what is meant by *sin*. Because sin does not emanate from the true essence of the human being, but rather from a false identification with the ego mind, it is easy to relinquish what is not attached to our true essence.

Everything on Yom Kippur is designed to facilitate this kind of psychological and emotional release to open us to the clarity of who we really are and who God is. Being willing to feel and let go of fear, sadness, and anger underlying our negative and reactive choices allows us to experience God's love for us, for the Jewish people and for all of humanity.

> Everything on Yom Kippur is designed to facilitate a psychological and emotional release to open us to the clarity of who we really are and who God is.

Out of our willingness to feel our brokenness and vulnerability, we become stronger and more whole. We are in essence holy beings with pure shining loving souls. We simply need to let go of limiting, illusory, and false concepts of the ego self that we have misidentified as ourselves. We can then trust ourselves, life and God in a deeper way.

On Yom Kippur we repeat the *Thirteen Attributes of Compassion* many times as they were revealed to Moses. Sung like a mantra, these words are said to be a formula for invoking Divine compassion. As important as it is to reflect on the sins we have committed, to feel regret, and make rectification, it is more important to take refuge in the reservoirs of Divine compassion, to allow ourselves to experience forgiveness and unconditional love.

On Yom Kippur we pray in community, we embrace our humanity, and feel love for each other. We are all vulnerable human beings, we have all made mistakes and we all want to grow and be better and happier people. On Yom Kippur we pray for ourselves and for each other.

May we each be blessed with such a joyful holy Yom Kippur that we feel so full from receiving the heavenly manna of love and revelation of the Shechinah, which is the Divine Feminine, on this holy day that we have no desire for anything else.

May we feel washed clean of all the inner and external barriers that have limited us in the past and claim ourselves as the pure holy souls and wonderful beings that we really are.

May we love ourselves and each other more. May our prayers also help remove some of the impurities and negativities in the world.

May we each create such a powerful vortex of light around us that everyone in our path is lifted up by our radiance and love.

Holiday: Sukkot

HISTORY: The Torah tells us: *You shall dwell in booths* [Sukkot] *for a seven day period, in order that your generations shall know that I caused the children of Israel to dwell in booths when I brought them forth from the land of Egypt.* Lev 23-42.

Other Biblical references to the holiday include Leviticus 23: 33-36: On the fifteenth of the seventh month shall be the festival of Sukkot to God, lasting for seven days. *The first day shall be a sacred holiday when you may not do any work. For seven days then you shall present an offering. The eighth day is a sacred holiday ... a time of retreat when you may do no work.*

In addition to being a holiday commemorating the Jewish people's dwelling in a little sukkah, a hut, Sukkot is an agricultural holiday replete with prayers for rain, nature, rituals, and gratitude for the harvest. The Torah tells us, *Celebrate to God for seven days in the place that God will choose, since God will then bless you in all your agricultural and other endeavors ... so that you will be only happy.* Deut 16:16. Though all Jewish holidays are times of joy, Sukkot is the one holiday that is called the time of rejoicing.

The Torah instructs: *On the first day, you must take for yourself an* etrog—*fruit of the citron tree, a* lulav—*palm branches,* hadasim—*myrtle branches, and* aravah—*willows that grow near a brook. During the seven days each year, you shall celebrate to God.* Lev. 23:40-41.

When the Holy Temple stood in Jerusalem, the Jewish people brought offerings during the seven days of Sukkot in honor of the seventy nations of the world. According to the Torah, there are seventy ancient nations that are the soul roots of all diverse national groups and cultures. The number is derived from Genesis 10, which recounts seventy as the number of descendants of Noah.

Rashi, the primary commentator of the Bible, explains that the purpose of these offerings was to seek atonement on behalf of the seventy nations, so that the entire world would merit rain during the coming year. *Rain* means actual rain, but it is also a metaphor for all that is needed for continued physical life and sustenance. These blessings are said even today for all nations, regardless of how they have treated Jews. How elevated and beautiful that the Jewish people pray and seek atonement even for their enemies. The Jewish people pray for all nations to be able to receive the flow of blessings from the Holy One. Perhaps if the nations understood that the Jewish people pray and work for the perfection of the world for the benefit of everyone, for all nations, they would better support them.

The sages have asked why we observe the holiday of Sukkot after Yom Kippur. The Israelites lived in these dwelling after the Exodus, which occurred in the Spring. Why are Jews commanded to live in these dwellings in Tishrei, during the fall? One of the main reasons is that if the Jews lived in the huts in the Spring, it would be experienced as a communion with nature, rather than a testimony to faith in the Divine protection during the wanderings in the desert.

Another reason is that the Sukkot commemorates the clouds of glory that surrounded the Jewish people after the Exodus. The clouds of glory departed after the sin of the Golden Calf and returned after Yom Kippur, when forgiveness had been received. The clouds of glory then remained with the Jewish people for the entire time in the desert. It was the most visible sign that God was with them.

As we learn about the energy of this month, we understand that it is most appropriate for the holiday of Sukkot to be placed in Tishrei as instructed in the Bible. The month of Tishrei is a time to experience one's vulnerability and need for Divine protection, which is best done in the fall when the weather is changing, when it is not too cold, but getting colder. Because a little sukkah provides shelter from the natural elements to some extent, it engenders a feeling of Divine protection.

OBSERVANCE: The holiday of Sukkot is replete with many rituals and spiritual practices. Through these various rituals, the deepest teachings of Sukkot are transmitted kinesthetically, for the entire body, mind, heart, and soul are engaged. As soon as Yom Kippur is over, Jews begin to construct hut like dwellings reminiscent of the dwelling the Jewish people lived in the desert. During the seven days, we sit, eat, drink and even sleep in these huts. This is the main commandment for the holiday. Not everyone these days sleeps in a sukkah, however, most Jews will make an effort to eat in one as best as they can.

Being in the sukkah is a total body experience. People can talk a lot about God's loving protection but when we are actually in the sukkah itself we feel it almost magically. When we sit in the sukkah we experience our vulnerability, but we feel safe because we sense God's surrounding presence. Life is simple and joyous. We learn directly that all the external structures we build in our lives to protect ourselves from the experience of our vulnerability are unnecessary. Furthermore, they separate us from our true selves, from other people and from God. Being vulnerable before God is the best and safest place to be.

Being in the sukkah is a time of intimacy. The sukkah extends an invitation to be real, totally and authentically oneself and to welcome others to be fully themselves as well. This intimacy with self and others brings happiness and awakens the child within each of us. Sitting in the sukkah is fun, yet also profound and mystical. The sukkah imparts a deep teaching more powerful than words alone could ever convey. In truth, all human beings are children of the One God and the world is God's home.

The holiday of Sukkot occurs during the harvesting time, when we rejoice in the plentiful we have been given. We draw to us many blessings during the time of Sukkot that will set the tone for the entire year. We sing special songs of praise every day during Sukkot. If sung in the proper spirit, these songs fill people's hearts with great joy.

We also read Koheleth, Ecclesiastes, during Sukkot to remind us of the temporal nature of human existence. In this book, King Solomon of ancient Israel, who had wealth, women, power, and knowledge, reviews all these things and concludes that none of them really matter. He tells us: *All is vanity*. We read this book as we reap our bounty, when it might be easy for us to be full of pride and arrogance and attribute our harvest to our own efforts. Even though this is a time of bounty, it is also a time when we sense that the cold and barrenness of winter, whether we like it or not, will soon be upon us. There is a pervasive sense of impermanence of life during this month that is reflected in this book.

We might think that the book of Koheleth is fatalistic and depressing but King Solomon concludes it with uplifting and empowering instruction. He tells us that: *In the end of the matter, all is heard, you shall fear God, observe His mitzvah, for this is the whole of man.* It is the God connection that is the most important possession we must acquire and earn during out brief time on earth. That is the main lesson of this holiday and the source of its joy.

During the holiday of Sukkot, Jews wave the *lulav*, the branches of date palm, the *hadas*, the myrtle leaf, the *aravah*, the willow leaves, and the *etrog*, the lemon like fruit, all together in all directions. These four species are said to represent the four personality types of people who are brought together at this time. The *etrog* is edible, fragrant, and represents the refined person who is learned and charitable. The *lulav* is odorless but produces nourishing food. It represents the learned person who is not very sweet because he is not doing beautiful things in the world. The *hadas* is fragrant, but tasteless, so this person does good things but is not very knowledgeable.

The *aravah* branch is neither fragrant more edible: it represents the ordinary person undistinguished by knowledge or good deeds.

Others say these species represent parts of a single person. The *lulav* is the spine, the *hadas* is the eyes, the *aravah* is the mouth, and the *etrog* is the heart. By shaking these branches together, each person brings these parts of the body into alignment and they are permeated with the joy of Sukkot.

Various meditations are to be undertaken when one is waving these four species in all six directions. Reb Shlomo Carlebach of blessed memory, would say that we are bringing God's holy energy into the world. For example, when we shake to the right, we are drawing down God's loving kindness, *hesed*, and when we go to the left, we are drawing down Divine strength, *gevurah*. We wave and shake in all six directions, each one bringing down different blessings, clearing the path for a greater connection with the Divine for ourselves and the world. It is an ancient shamanistic, wonderful, magical practice.

Reb Nachman of Breslov said that the mitzvah of waving these four species brings about a revelation of Godliness so we can recognize that the whole world was and is filled with Godliness. He said that simply sitting in a sukkah brings purity of heart. Ref: Likuty Moharan 33.

Holiday: Shemini Atzeret and Simchat Torah

HISTORY: Shemini Artzeret, the eighth day following the seven days of Sukkot, is considered a separate holiday. The Torah tells us: *On the eighth day shall be an atzeret* [cessation] *for you.* Num 29-35. It is a day of stopping that allows us to make the most direct connection with God. In Israel, Shemini Artzeret and Simchat Torah, which literally means Happiness of the Torah, are observed together on one day. Outside of the Land of Israel, they are celebrated on two separate days. We do not find any reference to the celebration of Simchat Torah in the written Torah, but much of Torah is not written down and many customs have been practiced for so long that they seem to have the same status as what is prescribed in the written Torah.

OBSERVANCE: Shemini Atzeret And Simchat Torah enjoy the usual rituals associated with a holiday such as candle lighting, Kiddush—a blessing over the wine—and the prohibition of work. The She-hechi-yo-nu blessing is also said at candle lighting or Kiddush.

During Sukkot, the Jewish people pray for the whole world: the sukkah is open to anyone. Shemini Atzeret is a day for the Jewish people to be alone in their love and connection to the Holy One. As joyous as the holiday of Sukkot is, Shemini Atzeret is usually even more so. A special powerful energy and blessings are given to those who celebrate this holiday. Though Shemini Atzeret is one of the most joyous times of the year, unfortunately, it is one of the least known or celebrated of Jewish holidays.

There is a question whether people should eat in the sukkah during Shemini Atzeret. Most people do not, but my teacher Reb Shlomo would make Kiddush one last time in the sukkah for Shemini Atzeret. There are special prayers and practices for this holiday. At the time of the Mussaf service, we do a most beautiful prayer for rain. When Jews pray for rain, it is never simply for rain. Rain is a symbol of all of God's blessings.

On Shemini Atzeret and Simchat Torah, the yearly reading of the Torah is completed. The Torahs of the synagogue are all taken out and danced within seven circling known as the Seven Haffakot. These circling are reminiscent of the circling of the bride around the groom at the traditional Jewish wedding. There is the feeling of a wedding between God and the Jewish people.

Meditations

Here is an affirmation that I wrote many years ago for Rosh Hashanah. If it speaks to you, I suggest that you repeat it frequently during the month. Say it out loud and silently to yourself. Share it with others as well.

AFFIRMATION FOR THE MONTH OF TISHREI

I so much want to experience God as King because God is the source of compassion, love, ecstasy, wisdom, beauty, and all that is good. When I experience God as King, the negative limiting thoughts of the *yetzer hara*, the voice of doubt, fear and judgment have no domain in my consciousness and the wonderful qualities of God are active and supreme in my life. Who I am is more than enough. I do not judge myself. I relinquish self criticism. God is my judge. God is kind, compassionate and loving and seeks my highest good.

I am surrendered to God. I do not experience myself as a victim but rather I experience myself as a part of God. I know that on some level, whether it is conscious or not, my soul has chosen the challenges that I have experienced in my life because these are the ways for me to grow. I accept the lessons I have learned in life with love and gratitude even though I may not understand with my mind the reasons for the choices I have made in my life. I am committed to learning, growing, and living in the coming year.

I am committed to living authentically, to give voice to my dreams, my heart and soul for I know that these all come from God. It is God's will that I be free, that I be loving, that I be holy, that I be joyful, that I be creative, that I be who I truly am.

I trust that through Divine grace all will be revealed. I will be all who I am and all who God wants me to be. The creator of the world is the God of Israel, *Yud-Hay-Vav-Hay*, the God of compassion. This God is my King and I am God's holy servant.

I do not fear and I do not hate for God is my King. I know that my true and lasting happiness rests in doing God's will. Through serving God on the inside and outside of my being, I serve the whole of myself and the good of the universe.

IMAGINED MESSAGE FROM THE HOLY ONE FOR ROSH HASHANAH

(To be read this month)

On Rosh Hashanah, we commemorate the creation of the soul. On Rosh Hashanah and throughout this month, God is speaking to us on the level of our soul.

"I created this world to be known and to bestow love and goodness. I contracted My Light to allow a world to be created that would experience itself as separate from Me so I could love its inhabitants and they might love and know Me so they would experience themselves as a part of Me.

Contrary to what many people may experience or believe, I did not create this world for suffering or even for struggle. In the end after much struggle, you will understand that I created this world for love and joy. Every year on Rosh Hashanah and the holidays of this month, I make Myself available to every soul in the most direct way. I ask that you ready yourself to receive My revelation on the holy days I have set for you.

Spend the holy days immersed in prayer, meditation and be in a loving community so you will be better able to experience Who I am, and what I want of you in this coming year. Ask yourself often, what does God want of me? Quiet your mind, open your heart, listen deeply and you will hear Me. I will reveal Myself to you.

In creating this world, know that I have made you my partner. Do not ever think of yourself to be small or insignificant. You are made in My image. Always remember that. You are important to Me and My creation. Some of you may have received a message from your parents that you were not important. You may have been abused or even exploited. You were not heard nor did you feel loved. I am so sorry that your parents were not My best representatives. And that you have suffered. Cry to Me. I will wipe your tears and I will take away your pain.

You are beautiful, lovable and capable of being the person I created you to be. No one can take this away from you. You can always go directly to Me. You are My child. Call on Me at any time. Your prayers make a difference to Me. Meditation, prayers, learning Torah and doing mitzvot and good deeds make a difference to Me. And more importantly, they will help you to be able to receive the vibrations of My love that will guide and protect you during the awareness times. I believe in you, whether you believe in Me or not.

Know that you have entered into a time of great revelation for those who are connected to Me. In this time, the dark forces, those who oppose the revelation of My oneness may appear to get stronger, they will seek to confuse you, to frighten you, disempowering you. They will masquerade as holy or loving, they may even claim to be from Me.

As the opponents of My light have done throughout the ages, they will attack the Jewish people, My people and seek to destroy them because they know, whether you know it or not, that you are My representative. Be careful to use the discernment I gave you so you will have clarity to determine what is good and what is not good. Cling to what is good, what is true. Read My scriptures, My prophets and the psalms of David.

Most importantly, do not be afraid. Trust in Me. I have given you the power to obliterate the evil within and outside of you. Whether you know it or not, you control the flow of Godliness in this creation.

As a member of the Jewish people, I have made a covenant with you, available to you through the many times you may visit this planet Earth. I am your God and I will always protect you, I will guide you, I will provide for you. My deepest desire is for you to know Me and reveal My oneness in this world. It is for this purpose that I created you.

Always remember wherever you go that you are My representative.

I made covenant with your ancestors in ancient times and I renew it with you on Rosh Hashanah and throughout all the holidays this month.

Will you do your part? Will you do what I sent you to do in this world? If you do not know what you need to do in this lifetime, tune into Me. Quiet your mind, open your heart, and I will guide you. Always remember you do not do this alone. Align your will with My Will and I will pour down all the blessings you need so as to empower you to fulfill your soul purpose. This Rosh Hashanah and throughout this month, say Yes, I choose life. I choose to be connected to what is good and what is holy.

On Rosh Hashanah, more than any other time in the year. I will reveal My *Malchus*, My Kingship, to you. When you will know Me as Melech—King—you will have a glimpse into the Divine Plan. You will see the Divine Order underlying all of creation and you will be filled with love and joy. I love you more than you can fathom."

Practical Recommendations

1. BLESS PEOPLE EVEN MORE THIS MONTH.

Beginning on Rosh Hashanah and extending until Yom Kippur, it is a common practice to bless people with a happy and healthy new year. This can be done in a perfunctory way or it can be done with sincere feeling and focused intention. Our words are powerful. Just as God created the world with words, so we can change our reality with our positive words. Our blessings make a difference. As you bless others, so you are blessed. The more you bless others, the more blessings you will receive from others and God.

Here is some guidance on the harnessing the power to bless others. As we bless, so we are blessed, as the saying goes.

It is a great pleasure to allow Divine energy to be expressed through you in a blessing. Just get out of the way, nullify yourself and allow the Divine energy to be channeled through you. You know how to do this. Imagine that the light of the Shechinah, the Divine Presence, is above your head, entering you and surrounding you. We are each channels of blessing. You can do this in the person's physical presence or you can do it to a person physically away from you by visualizing him or her on your inner screen. Reflect on what this person wants and needs and then open to bless him or her in ways even beyond what he or she might request. Formulate a blessing in your mind and then pronounce it. *May God bless you with …* or, *You are blessed with …* visualize the person happy to receive your blessing. Say Amen to the blessing.

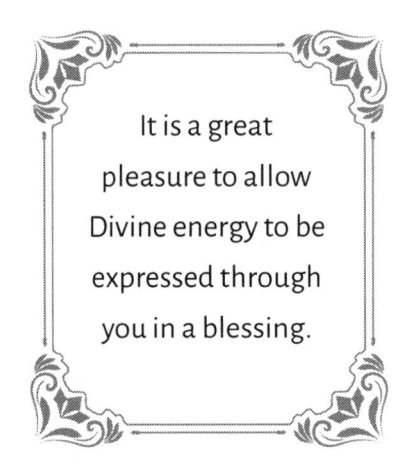

> It is a great pleasure to allow Divine energy to be expressed through you in a blessing.

Be sure to bless the people closest to you, but also extend blessings to people not in your immediate circle. Extend blessings to people who need them. Think of all the people you know who need blessing in their lives. Bring these people into your mind and take time to bless them in your meditations and prayers. Bless those who are childless and want to be fruitful with children. Bless those who are without a partner with meeting their soul mate. Bless people who are poor with the means to earn a good living. Bless those who are sick with a speedy and complete recovery. If you really want to be empowered by the practice of blessings, bless people for whom you may still harbor negative feelings.

2. LOVE, LOVE, AND LOVE.

Because we were created in the image and likeness of God, we all have an intrinsic desire to love and be known like our Creator does. Deep within each of us is the desire to love and also to know we are loved for the human beings we are. Mistakenly, some of us think that we have to earn this love from God and others rather than accept that we are loved by God for just being here in this physical reality. This love is implanted within our very being.

You were created to love and be loved. When we love and allow ourselves to be loved, we are aligned with Divine Will. Love dissolves barriers and illusions of separation from God and others. Fear and judgment creates separation and blocks our receptivity to Divine blessings. So always remember to love, rather than judge particularly during this month. If you do not feel loved by someone whose love you want, let that inspire you to love yourself more. We cannot make other people love us. Usually when people love themselves, they will love the people who are in their lives. Similarly, when people are unable to love those around them, it is often because they do not love themselves.

Remember that when we leave this physical world, we will be unable to take with us any of the physical possessions we have acquired. We will however take with us the love that we have shared in the world. So love and love some more. Love without expectation.

3. GIVE CHARITY OR DO A SERVICE PROJECT.

We say repeatedly during this month that *tzedekah*, charity, can literally change our destiny. Giving charity atones for negative actions. Charity is always considered an antidote for suffering. It is a known spiritual principle that the more you give, the more you receive.

Charity is important year round, but it especially important this month, prior to Yom Kippur. Giving charity places one in the flow of blessing and expands one's capacity to receive. *Tzedekah* in Hebrew means *to bring into order*. This is the month to not only give *tzedekah* but to make a plan of what you can and will give in the coming year. Many organizations know this and that is why they solicit funds for the coming year during this month.

Also consider what you can do directly in the coming year to help other people. Giving to other people without thinking about what you will receive back from them places you in the Divine flow of abundant blessings. Envision yourself as a channel for God. When we give joyfully to others because it is a gift to give and we give without expectation of what we will receive back for our giving, we are renewed and blessed rather than depleted.

4. IMMERSE YOURSELF IN A MIKVAH.

The mikvah is a ritual bath used for purification. There is a mikvah in most Jewish communities. A natural body of water may be used in lieu of a constructed mikvah. The great Jewish prophets and heads of ancient Torah academies obligated people to purify themselves in a mikvah either before Rosh Hashanah or Yom Kippur or both. It is a common spiritual practice for both men and women even today.

Prior to the immersion in the waters of mikvah, one showers or bathes and removes all make-up or nail polish. When entering into the mikvah, a person focuses on his or her intention and then dunks, fully immersing the entire body under the water several times. One can read about the mikvah, but reading about something cannot compare with the actual experience. Do not deprive yourself of this wonderful and powerful ancient ritual, especially before the holidays when dunking in the mikvah is more accessible to people.

A Tale to Live By

One day the Baal Shem Tov, the founder of the Chassidic movement, called some of his followers to accompany him on a trip to the home of a poor innkeeper. When the innkeeper greeted the Baal Shem Tov, he was aware that he was in the presence of a great and holy person. He welcomed the Baal Shem Tov into his home and provided generously and joyfully for all his needs as well as those of his followers. To do this, the poor innkeeper sold his horse and his goat, and he slaughtered all his chickens. The innkeeper recognized that he had never been in the presence of such a holy person before and he could not do enough for him. The Chassidim were aware that they were imposing on this poor person but do not feel comfortable to say anything to their rebbe—spiritual master—so they kept quiet.

The Baal Shem Tov informed that innkeeper of his plans to stay with him for Shabbat and made a long list of food that was needed such as twelve loaves of challah, the finest meat, chicken, fish, the finest wine and other delicacies. Without blinking, as if in a trance, the innkeeper sold his humble home to obtain the money to purchase these items for the Baal Shem Tov and his followers. And they had a very beautiful Shabbat.

As soon as Shabbat was over, the Baal Shem Tov boarded his carriage. He shouted to the innkeeper, *I am the Baal Shem Tov of Mezeritch*. And he was off. He did not even thank the innkeeper for all the kindness and generosity the innkeeper had displayed to him.

Sunday morning, the spell lifted and the innkeeper realized what he had done. How could he tell his wife and children that they would not have a home Monday afternoon? He was overwhelmed and went into the forest and began to cry. He cried for all the poverty he had experienced in his life. He poured out his heart to God. He soon heard himself yelling at the top of his voice, "Make me rich. Make me rich. If I were rich, I would know what to do with the money. I would take care of poor people. Make me rich."

When the innkeeper had no more tears to cry and was gathering himself together, Moshe, the town drunkard, appeared to him in the forest. Every town had such a person as Moshe who was generally ridiculed and held in low regard by most of the people. Moshe spoke to the innkeeper and expressed his gratitude for the friendship and respect the innkeeper had always showed him. Because of this, Moshe told him that he was not truly poor but that he had a treasure chest buried in the forest that he wanted the innkeeper to have at his passing. He showed him exactly where it was buried. That night, quite unexpectedly, Moshe took off to the next world.

Early the next morning, the town was talking about the mysterious death of Moshe. Our innkeeper ran immediately into the forest to claim the treasure of riches. He was now a very wealthy man. He kept his promise to take care of poor people, and still he had a great deal of money left. After several months, his wife suggested to him that they go to see the holy man who had visited them before they became wealthy, perhaps he could explain what happened to them The boarded their carriage and rode to

Mezeritch to find the Baal Shem Tov. They were quickly escorted to the synagogue where the Baal Shem Tov taught and to his personal study to meet directly with him. The Chassidim, the followers, recognized them and were a little embarrassed to see the inn keeper and his wife again. They had not understood why their master had acted as he had. But they also noticed that something had changed. The couple now wore the clothes of very wealthy people.

The innkeeper and his wife were ushered in to see the Baal Shem Tov. The innkeeper said to the Baal Shem Tov: *Before you visited me, I was a very poor man. Now I am a very rich man. What happened?*

The Baal Shem Tov responded: *It was decreed in heaven that you should be rich. But you never asked God for it. I had to eat you out of house and home to get you to the point that you would ask God for what you wanted and needed.*

This month is the time that we ask God for what we need. It is good to know that if we are challenged, if we suffer, it might be that we need to humble ourselves and call out to God for guidance, assistance, and blessing. We are not alone and we can change our destiny with Divine support. God listens to our cries.

2

Cheshvan

OCTOBER – NOVEMBER

ENERGY
The Inner Work of Personal Transformation

AREA OF HEALING
Smell

ASTROLOGICAL SIGN
Scorpio

HEBREW LETTER
Nun נ

HEBREW TRIBE
Menashah

DIVINE NAME PERMUTATION
VHHY

HOLIDAY
Reserved for the establishment of the Third Holy Temple in a future time

A Personal Story

The month of Cheshvan offers an invitation to enter the depths of who we are and reclaim our inner riches. In the month of Cheshvan, we each may be challenged to let go of what does not support our well being and integrate more deeply into our life what does support living more purposefully and joyfully.

Though our life journey may be challenging this month, it is helpful and important to know that everything that takes place during this month is choreographed for our growth. Loss is a common theme this month as it is often a necessary step in growth. The challenges we face in Cheshvan take us forward towards living a more authentic life more in accordance with our soul purpose. Here is a true story of a friend written long ago. Her name has been changed.

Susan was excited to return to Israel after many years of living in America. She had been in contact with her college friend and she was excited to fulfill a dream they both shared of living together in Israel. Since college, they both had married, had children who were now mostly grown. Now, once again, as single women, they looked forward to reclaim their friendship in this next chapter in their lives.

When Susan returned to Israel before the Jewish holidays, she entered into the beautiful furnished house that Dina secured for the two of them. Her entry into the Land of Israel was busy with holiday prayer services, celebratory meal gatherings, meeting new people and settling into a new living situation.

Once the month of Cheshvan arrived, Susan had to admit to herself that her living situation with Dina felt more like a nightmare rather than the fulfillment of a dream. In so many ways, Dina imposed her will on Susan, expecting that Susan tolerate many things that were not agreed upon or not even known about in their initial discussions about living together.

For example, Dina began to rent out the extra room in the house for

Air-BNB and received additional money that she did not share with Susan, even though Susan was sharing all the expenses of the living space. While Dina took frequent vacations to the Dead Sea during Cheshvan, Susan was expected to take over the responsibilities for the visitors to their home as well as attend to the needs of Dina's troubled son. There were so many more examples of Dina exploiting her friendship with Susan.

During the month of Cheshvan, Susan had to acknowledge to herself that she did not embark on this new journey of life in Israel to feel disrespected by a close friend. With my guidance, Susan saw that what was taking place in her relationship with Dina was a mirror of an internal process. Rather than blaming Dina for her selfishness, Susan began to take responsibility for the ways she had been unable to set respectable boundaries between Dina and herself. Even though she had changed her living situation in her move to Israel, she realized that nothing would really change for her unless she did the inner work of personal transformation.

Too often in the past, Susan had tolerated relationships and work situations for security and approval. Like many of us, Susan would frequently try to please others to avoid conflict with them. Over the years, Susan stuffed her feelings of resentment for having to give herself up in her personal relationships and in her work environment into a weight gain of twenty five pounds. Food, alcohol, drugs, shopping, television, are common ways that people numb themselves from the anger and resentment they feel inside so they can stay in unhealthy relationships.

With my encouragement, Susan took responsibility for her situation and was then able to take steps to explore ways she could move out of this apartment quickly. It was clear that there was no point in spending time and effort to work out this living relationship with Dina. If possible, she wanted to maintain a relationship with Dina but not live with her. Once Susan made her decision, she was Divinely supported and found another reasonably priced housing situation with women she did not know. This house was run by a woman who had very specific rules for the household that honored her and the tenants. It was a business contract, so expectations were very clear. It may not be an ideal situation for the long term, but it was a welcome change for Susan.

Energy: The Inner Work of Personal Transformation

In Cheshvan, the hard inner work of spiritual and personal transformation becomes our primary focus. As we begin to translate and integrate the blessings we received during the month of Tishrei, we need to let go of the old, of what is no longer essential and purify ourselves so we are really able to contain the new. We do this letting go, this purifying, and integrating work during this month of Cheshvan.

In many places in the world, the leaves have now mostly turned beautiful colors and fallen to the ground, and the temperature is becoming colder. As we view the barren trees, we become aware of the cycles of life and of the cycles in our own lives and we find that our attention is naturally directed inward, to the life that is below the surface reality.

Because there are currently no holidays in Cheshvan, it is sometimes called Mar Cheshvan, which means Bitter Cheshvan. There are no holidays so as to not distract us from settling into the normal routine of life.

We must remember the month of Cheshvan as bitter for the impact of October 7th and the challenging aftermath it has had on the land of Israel during this month. As Israel rose to defend itself during this month, the reality of life in Israel changed dramatically much in keeping with the intensity of the month of Cheshvan.

It is, however, said that Cheshvan has no holiday because it will be the month when the Jewish people will inaugurate the Third Temple at the time of the Messiah. This signifies that ultimately this month will be transformed into a very joyous time in the future. So it is also important to remember that when we go through hard times individually or communally blessing will come out of it in the end.

If we celebrated the holidays of Tishrei in their true spirit and depth, we have opened and received many blessings. We have been inspired to make changes within ourselves. As we begin to implement these changes during this month of Cheshvan, we may encounter our resistance to change. As much as we may want to change, forces within us are frightened of change and want things to remain the same. Because they are familiar, it feels safe to us. This month we have to ask ourselves if holding on to the past really makes us safe or do we just feel safe because it is familiar to us.

As we come up against these ego defenses and resistances, we also become more aware of deep-seated beliefs that shape our emotions and make it hard for us to change in the way we want. We may become discouraged and even question our capacity for real change during this month.

We may find ourselves becoming more aware of the shadowy parts within ourselves more this month than other months. Remember that what we know about, what is in our awareness, will change solely by virtue of our simple awareness and acceptance of it. When we allow ourselves to feel without resistance, what is within us, everything will simply move through us. As it is frequently said, emotion is only energy in motion. What we resist, what we deny, what we avoid will continue to occupy psychic space within us and we will continue to be at the mercy of our own unconsciousness.

To go consciously forward in our lives, we will each need to confront our resistance: the ways we have played it safe, the ways we have betrayed and sabotaged ourselves from living joyful fulfilling lives regardless of what is happening around us. To play it safe is to deprive ourselves of the spiritual opportunity of expressing our soul potential and mission for being in this world. When we take responsibility for the choices we have made consciously or even unconsciously, we will no longer blame others for the ways we have abandoned ourselves often to receive their approval and validation. The transformation we seek comes when we love ourselves on a soul level more than we need to be loved and validated by others on an ego level.

As the previous month of Tishrei is considered the optimal time to set the direction for the upcoming year, this month of Cheshvan is the month to let go of what does not support well being in the new year. Much like a caterpillar shedding his skin to emerge as a butterfly, we let go this month of what is no longer true or needed for our growth this month. We may do this consciously or it may be done to us for our benefit. It is all good. This kind of transformation is what the month of Cheshvan is all about. With every ending, there is a new and a better beginning. Even death is a new chapter and not a finality. We are always growing and evolving.

Cheshvan is the month to let go of fantasies, illusions, and falsehood so as to see more clearly what is true. It is a time to have moral clarity as well as be with all our feelings, whatever they are. What enables us to go through fear, anger, grief and sadness within us is faith. Faith is not the passive belief in an external Being we call God, but the direct experience of this Being within us. The challenges of this month offer an invitation to enter the depths of who we are and reclaim our inner riches.

> The challenges of this month offer an invitation to enter the depths of who we are and reclaim our inner riches.

It is helpful to remember that we do not do this work of inner transformation alone. There are heavenly angelic forces available to help move us forward when we courageously take our first steps out of our comfort zone. When we employ our faith and trust in God, we experience firsthand that God is in control and we can let go of the illusion that we control life.

Some of us will make the commitment to go forward in our lives only when we realize that we are up against the wall. We are so unhappy in the way we are living that we are ready to do whatever it takes to change and move forward. This level of suffering is a blessing for it serves as a needed catalyst to move us forward. When we recognize that there is no escape, nowhere to run, there are not even any holidays to help us transcend, we will settle down to do the inner work of this month. This is the spiritual opportunity and challenge of this month.

Without the anchor of holidays, there is a general sense of falling in this month of Cheshvan. We identify with the leaves that have fallen from the trees this month when we feel that we are also shedding parts of ourselves. Spending time in nature particularly this month is spiritual medicine. We learn so much about trust by watching the grace of change embodied within nature.

Loss is a theme this month. There is often a noticeable increase in the breakup of marriages and relationships, the loss of employment and life during this month. Do not be alarmed. This is not necessarily negative if we realize that falling is part of going forward. Each ascent is often preceded by a descent. Be peaceful, let go and trust that everything, even the challenges you face this month, is unfolding for your benefit and growth.

This month healing is through the sense of smell. The sense of smell is the one sense that was not involved in the sin of Adam and Eve in the Garden of Eden. They saw, they touched, and they ate from the tree, but it does not say that they smelled the tree. The sense of smell is the most refined and spiritual of all the senses. The sense of smell is likened to the intuition of the soul. It is this sense that needs to be heightened during this month.

In purifying the sense of smell, we become sensitized to the inner essence of things. And when we do this, everything becomes clear. We need to develop and trust our capacity to *smell* to penetrate to the essence of what is before us. Our minds tell us many things, our emotions tell us more, but the sense of smell informs us about the true essence of things. This intuitive gift is what we need to access this month.

Kabbalah teaches us that fragrance is not really a physical thing, but it connected to the soul. The more alive, the purer something is, the better its fragrance. That is true for food, but also true for people. People who embody a deep and real connection with God are vibrant and attracting. We are purified and feel energetically uplifted just by being in their presence. Seek to connect with people who inspire and mirror to you the best qualities within yourself.

Cheshvan is also called *Chodesh Bul*. Bul is taken from the word *mabul* which means flood. The Flood that we read about in the Bible began on the seventeenth of Cheshvan and continued to the twenty seventh of Cheshvan in the following year. It is said that every year until the time of the building of the First Temple in Jerusalem by King Solomon, which was completed in this month, it rained for a forty day period that included the whole month of Cheshvan.

Even today, it rains a lot during this month in Israel, New York, and Florida, all places I have resided in during the month of Cheshvan. Water is a prominent element in the cleansing and preparing of the environment for the upcoming winter. The astrological sign of this month is Scorpio, a water sign. Water is the purifier and cleanser. Water removes what is not essential. And that is the essence of this month of Cheshvan.

General Guidelines and Goals

The following guidelines, spiritual practices, and goals enable us to direct our energies in the ways that are optimal for our growth and transformation in accordance with the energy of this month. It is recommended that you read and meditate upon them often in the course of the month. Reflect on their applicability to you and allow them to direct and inspire you often this month.

1. YOU ARE NOT YOUR NEGATIVE THOUGHTS.

Upon observation and inquiry, become aware of the thoughts that you focus on during the day. What is the frequent conversation that you have with yourself? The negative thoughts repeated in our minds reflect false beliefs about ourselves. Negative thoughts are not the truth of who we are. Too often people feel that they are not lovable, adequate, nothing will ever change for them, and they are doomed for failure.

Sometimes, these ego-based thoughts try to justify unhappiness such as you are a failure because you do not possess the material prosperity you see that others have. You must not be lovable because you do not have the kind of loving intimate relationships that others seem to have. These ego-based thoughts are not rooted in truth. Yet, our egos will faithfully fight to defend them as the truth and thereby rob ourselves of the experience of inner peace and happiness. Take note when negative thoughts are triggered within you.

Negative thinking will neither empower you nor motivate you. Rather, it will keep you bound to a limited expression of yourself, feeling alone, disconnected from others, and from God. These negative patterns will lessen and change with spiritual practice and the grace of a Divine connection. Please know that you can liberate your beautiful precious soul from the hold of the negativity of the tyrannical ego.

There is a battle within every person between the *yetzer hara*, the evil inclination aligned with the ego mind, and the *yetzer tov*, the good inclination aligned with the Divine soul. This battle is part of the human experience for most everyone. When our sense of self is determined by external factors, we are distracted and become disconnected from our own soul. We will too often compare ourselves and feel inadequate in relation to others. The need to be right rather than to be kind and loving to ourselves and others is prominent within people who define themselves and value their lives on the level of ego.

Remember joy and happiness, and our vitality on all levels of being comes from within us, from the experience of our intrinsic connection with God. It is not true that we need to have personal achievements, prosperity, possessions, or fame to be happy or feel fulfilled. That may be the desire of the ego but it is not that of the soul. The deeper truth is that you have what you want and what you are able to receive in your life right now.

The path to our freedom lies in expanding our awareness, liberating ourselves from our identification with the ego. When we break through the walls of ego identity, we access the pure soul within us and we receive the blessings of our innate Divine connection. Once we raise our vibration to access our Divine soul, the negativity of the ego mind has no threshold to reside within us.

Who we really are on the level of our souls cannot be defined externally or artificially with anything in this material world. Make it a spiritual practice to discern and differentiate between the needs of the ego and those of the soul. Choose to listen to the wisdom and peace of your own soul rather than the unhappiness of your ego.

If there is a strong battle between the soul who wants to give and the ego who only wants to receive for itself, call out sincerely to God for assistance. God is free, God is whole, God is loving. When you are attached to God, you will be uplifted to the experience of these same qualities.

2. OWN YOUR OWN PROJECTIONS.

If we see something we do not like in someone else, we often need to rectify that quality within ourselves. The world is our mirror, and our relationships are mirrors of who we are, and reflect to us often what we do not want to acknowledge within ourselves.

For example, if we are angry at others for not loving us the way we want to be loved, we need to look at whether we are loving ourselves the way we need to be loved. If we see others as judgmental and critical of us, we need to practice loving and accepting ourselves as we are right now.

Generally, people waste a lot of energy blaming other people for the internal experience they have of themselves. We foolishly want others to change, so they will meet our needs, rather than be willing to change ourselves to meet our own needs. When we blame others, we are weakened, and we are unable to truly move forward. We need to focus on ourselves, loving and embracing ourselves, and not blaming others.

3. LOVE YOURSELF UNCONDITIONALLY.

Loving ourselves unconditionally means accepting ourselves as we are right now, with all our imperfections and shortcomings. Unconditional love is the willingness to be with ourselves fully and compassionately without having to change our feelings or do something about them.

Too often people want to rid themselves of their uncomfortable negative feelings rather than simply allow themselves to feel them. By feeling our emotions, we can actually release the hold negativity has in our lives. By resisting or avoiding our feelings they continue to remain within us affecting us both consciously and unconsciously. What we resist and avoid persists within us.

Loving ourselves unconditionally is new for many of us because we received negative messages and internalized them as children. We did not feel worthy to be loved as we were as children and we continue to judge ourselves, others, and even God harshly. Too often we compare ourselves to others and fall short in our estimation or we project our shortcomings onto others and blame them for the feelings we have inside ourselves. We fail to turn to God because we feel that God will not find us worthy of love and may even punish us. Take note of this tendency this month and be gentle with yourself. Many shadow parts of ourselves and others will surface this month asking to be loved and redeemed. Practice unconditional love this month for yourself and others.

Be aware of the choices you make on a daily basis. Are these choices loving to yourself? Do these choices support your well being? Or do your choices strengthen your ego identity?

4. LET GO OF THE "SHOULD'S" IN LIFE.

When we are not in touch with the beauty and purpose of our souls, we often seek validation from others, frequently at the expense of our well-being. Too often, we are governed by *should* in life. We *should* be a certain way to please other people and be loved by them, or people *should* behave in a certain way toward us in order for us to feel loved and validated. These tendencies will only lead to unhappiness.

Many people who come to me for therapy have this very common problem. They find themselves in relationships with people where their needs are not met or they are employed in work positions where they feel unappreciated or even belittled or they do not feel that their work is connected to their soul purpose. To remain in these kinds of situations or relationships, the person engages in a familiar pattern of giving oneself up to avoid conflict and maintain peace and the relationship.

When we give ourselves up too many times and for too long a period of time, resentment naturally builds. Sometimes, a person's anger will explode or be internalized. Addictions may rise as a way to avoid feeling painful feelings. When the ego's need for validation and approval from others is too great, a person will ignore the guidance of the soul. And there is a price that we each pay by not attuning to what is opening up within us.

At a certain future point there will likely be a clash between the soul's needs for her unique expression and the agenda of the ego identity for security and validation from others. If we fail to listen to the soul, she will often speak to us through sensations in our bodies such as illness, and challenging life circumstances. She will be heard! She cannot be ignored.

She came to this physical world for a holy purpose. She will be heard! So please take time to listen!

Be aware of what you do and have done in order to feel safe. Often people will be manipulative, controlling, experience oneself as a victim, or a doormat when they do not feel safe. Wake up from a fearful life of giving oneself up to receive love and approval from others and claim a life of loving and honoring yourself and your Creator.

In the therapeutic process, therapy clients begin to appreciate that giving oneself up to meet the needs of other people is a familiar pattern they learned in their first five years of life when they were very vulnerable and dependent on others for survival. The healing journey often requires a revisiting of early childhood experiences to learn how to feel compassionately the feelings that they previously covered up and avoided. Through the therapeutic process, people learn to love themselves enough to take responsibility for the feelings of shame, guilt, fear, anger and emptiness they may feel inside. One of the most important things we can do as adults is to make the inner child within us feel safe, loved and even joyful.

When we let go of blaming ourselves or others, we can then begin to make choices that are more honoring of the beautiful loving beings we really are. Transformation really begins when we learn to love ourselves more than we need to be loved or validated by others.

5. DEVELOP GREATER TRUST AND FAITH.

Many of life occurrences on an individual and collective level do not seem to be within our control. Did we choose the Corona virus? Do we choose war? Do we choose illness? Do we choose a financial crisis?

The great and holy Rebbe Rabbi Nachman, who was no stranger to terrible suffering, in one of the pamphlets of his teachings reminds us in all that *Everything is under God's unflagging supervision, for God oversees each of the infinite details which comprise our universe.* Just because we have all kinds of challenges does not necessarily mean that there is something wrong with us. Consider the life of Rabbi Nachman and other righteous people for confirmation.

Every day, we must fill ourselves with the faith that God is alive and in control of whatever is generally happening in the world and in particular in our personal lives, regardless of whether we can attribute our experiences directly to our actions or not.

When we affirm that God is in control, we trust that what is meant to happen for us will happen. Life may be challenging but we know that whatever is happening to us is for our benefit and our growth. Many of us can attest that we do our greatest learning through the challenges we faced. On some level we must need these challenges to wake us up to God and to our very own souls.

Faith in God is not just a passive belief in a Being who is external to us, rather, faith is the experience of this Being within us. Faith is not blind as people often say, but it is a higher level of knowing that is actually hardwired into the core of our being. Faith reveals to us that we are always connected to the Source of all, God, regardless of what is happening externally. With faith, we can let go of the fears of the ego mind and access our awesome soul potential, always present within us.

Rabbi Nachman reminds us that *the more we run to God, the more we will draw God's light to us ...* and, *If your desire is to cling to God, you will taste the world to come while you are still living in this world.* This teaching is from a pamphlet entitled, *A Simple Faith: Teachings of Reb Nachman and his student Reb Nason.*

Astrological Sign: Scorpio

Cheshvan corresponds to the astrological sign of Scorpio. Pluto, the ruler of Scorpio, was known in mythology as the lord of hidden wealth. Many of the earth's important resources, such as iron, gold, silver, oil, and minerals, are hidden below the ground. To find the resources one needs is to be willing to dig deeply, to get down in the dirt and mud to uncover and sort out the inner riches. This is what the energy of this month of going beneath the surface is all about.

In the inward journey to the depths that occurs this month, be aware that the energy of Scorpio is sometimes intense and often ruthless, forcing us to let go of attachments, sometimes those we hold most dear. We are often thrown out of our comfort zone this month.

Scorpio is a water sign. Unlike the astrological sign for Cancer, which is also a water sign, whose emotions ride the waves and tides of the moon, the emotions of Scorpio are intense, underground and steady. The sign of Scorpio is associated with the scorpion, the eagle, and the phoenix, the mythological bird that rose from the ashes of destruction. The scorpion is dangerous, the eagle soars high, and the phoenix renews itself from death—this is the emotional range of Scorpio reflecting the energy of this month.

As we witness the workings of the mind this month, we may become aware of the destructive thoughts of the poisonous scorpion within us and we feel its sting. It is generally known that you do not want to hurt a person born under the sign of Scorpio because he or she will seek revenge and not easily forgive when slighted.

Scorpio is also represented by an eagle. This month our consciousness can soar upward to new heights and it can also swoop down to new depths as an eagle. The deeper we go inside, the more we will uncover and the more expanded we will feel.

And most importantly, what was destroyed will take new inner and outer forms like the phoenix. Cheshvan is the month of transformation. As the ruler of the dead, Pluto symbolizes the transcendent forces that cause death to the old and life to visions of the future.

People born under the sign of Scorpio are said to have an extremely emotionally sensitive disposition. If emotions are channeled positively, they have the potential to penetrate the depths of life like few others. If not, they can easily fall into depravity and addiction. Such ultra-sensitivity may also cause them to be withdrawn and hidden.

Hebrew Letter: Nun

The Hebrew letter for Cheshvan is the *nun*. In Aramaic, the word *nun* means fish. In Kabbalah, fish have great significance.

Tzaddkim—totally righteous people—are said to reincarnate as fish. One of the explanations is that fish swim in water with their eyes open. All their needs are met, and they are considered pure with no self-consciousness. The nun directs us to acquire the attributes of fish, particularly this month. Interestingly enough, according to Jewish law, fish are *parve*, meaning fish can be eaten with dairy and with meat.

Kabbalah divides souls into two categories: *leviathan*—fish, and *behamot*—animal. Through gematria, the Kabbalistic practice of assigning numerical value to letters and making connections between words having the same numerical value to letters, we discover that the words *leviathan* and *malchut*, which means kingdom, have the same numerical value. That informs us that there is a connection between these words. Understanding the connection between these words sheds light on the energy of this month. The sephira, or Divine emanation of *malchut,* is represented by King David. This is an allusion to the Messiah, for the Messiah comes from the House of David. This is further corroborated by the fact that the *nun* is the fourteenth letter of the Hebrew alphabet and the numerical value for the letters in the name David equal fourteen. As mentioned, it is said that the Third Temple, in which the Messiah will be revealed, will be established in this month.

The *nun* is associated with the word *nefilah*, which means falling. Kabbalah teaches the concept of descent for the purpose of ascent. Because of a descent, a person can rise higher than before. We see this principle demonstrated in the way people grow and become better people through the mistakes they make and the challenges they confront. It is also true ontologically. The soul's entry into the physical world is a descent for the purpose of ascent. The soul enters into a physical body to raise itself up, to purify, to do good, and make rectification in a way that can only be done in the physical world. In so doing, the soul can go higher than if it remained solely in the spiritual world.

Interestingly enough, the Messiah, the highest person, the redeemer of the Jewish people and the world, is said to come from lowly and impure origins. We learn from the Torah and Kabbalah that the Messianic lineage began with the illicit affair of Yehudah—Hebrew for Judah—the fourth son of Jacob had with his daughter-in-law Tamar who was disguised as a prostitute, and also from the incestuous affair of Lot and his daughters. Given the emphasis that Judaism places on sexual purity, you might not expect the redeemer of the world to have these soul roots. This is, however, in line with the energy of this month and the Jewish perspective that negativity will ultimately be transformed and redeemed. Because the Messiah represents the highest form of spiritual evaluation, his origins are in the lowest place.

Hebrew Tribe: Menashah

Menashah was the first born son of Joseph, born to him when he was in Egypt. When Joseph named him, he said: *For God said He has made me forget all my toil and all my father's house.* Gen 41: 51. The birth of Menashah gave Joseph perspective and the ability to release the pain and suffering he had experienced earlier in his life.

Having been born in Egypt, a word translated to mean narrow straits, a place of impurity and limitation, Menashah had the unique ability to uproot negativity and evil, characteristic of the energy of this month. The unique capacity to defeat evil within oneself and in the world was demonstrated by Menashah's descendant Gideon, who led a victorious battle against the Midianites. Judg.6-8. The Midianites had posed a threat to the integrity of the Jewish people. The word *midian* relates to the word *madon*, which means strife. It refers to the psychic force within us that causes strife and disunity.

The army of Gideon circled the Midian nation, carrying shofar and earthen jugs with torches with them. They blew the shofar, broke their jugs, and waved their torches, lighting up the sky, overwhelming and defeating the Midianites, and winning the battle without even raising a sword.

Though Menashah was the firstborn of Joseph, he did not receive the blessing of the firstborn. That blessing was given to the younger brother, Ephraim, who represents the previous month of Tishrei. Unlike the animosity that occurred between Jacob and Esau over the blessings of the first born, there was no jealousy or anger on the part of Menashah. This represented a tremendous fixing of the jealousy between Esau and Jacob and between Joseph and his brothers, who sold him into slavery.

The letters of Menashah, when rearranged, spell *neshama*, which means soul, or *neshima*, which means breath. Breath and soul are bound up with each other: As the Torah says, *God breathes into us a pure soul.* Both are connected with the sense of smell, the area of healing for this month. Though we smell by breathing through the nose, smell refers to the sense of the soul, to our intuition, and ability to discern the essence of the matter. This kind of discernment is a primary mode of transformation for this month. We learn to trust our intuition and capacity to discern this month.

Divine Name Permutation: VHHY

In reviewing the Divine Name permutation for this month, we see that the *yud* (Y) occupies the position of the world of Assiyah, this physical world, as an indication that activity in this physical world is reduced. This month is not particularly a time to go forward in many or new ways. It may be difficult to do so now, so be patient. The work must first take place more internally, in the mind and heart. The two *hays* in the worlds of Yetzirah and Beriyah indicates that the flow of light is greatest in these worlds. So the focus this month is for an expansion in one's thinking, in one's mind, in one's emotions, and one's heart. The *vav* (V), in the world of Atzilut, the first position, indicates that there is a direct influx of Divine energy from the highest world of Atzilut, the spiritual world closest to Ain Sof, the Kabbalist term for the unknowable, limitless Divine Light. Indicators from this permutation align with what has been said about the energy of this month: This is a time to focus on working with one's thinking and feelings.

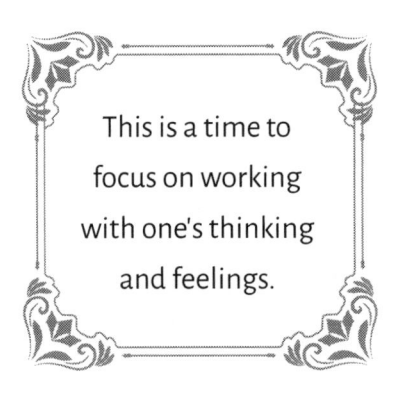

> This is a time to focus on working with one's thinking and feelings.

Torah Portions

The Torah portions for the month of Cheshvan begin with Noah and the Flood in Genesis 6:9-11:32. This Flood was believed to cause the destruction of the entire world except for Noah, his family, and representatives of the animal species who would begin the world anew. Even though the story of creation was just related in the first and previous Torah portion, human beings engaged in such wicked behavior that it was necessary for the world to be purified. As we read about Noah and the Flood, we are reminded to find that we need to let go and be cleansed of the parts of ourselves not in alignment with our true nature and what we opened to in the previous month of Tishrei.

It is interesting to note that God told Noah to build an ark, which took time to do. People had an opportunity to investigate what was happening and be included in the ark if they so desired. The ark provided the sanctuary for maintaining the purity of the Divine Intention. Similarly, during this month, we must build an ark for ourselves to afford us safety and security. We must go deep inside ourselves to find refuge by consciously accessing the purity of our own soul.

There will be many floods in the forms of challenges in the course of a person's life, and particularly during this month. Our internal ark will serve us through these times. Through our challenges, we let go of negativity. We are humbled, purified and strengthened.

The Hebrew word for ark is *teva* which also means *word*. The arks we build in our lives are the words of prayer, affirmation and blessing. Positive words provide a sanctuary for us and we need to fortify ourselves with them. We need to be aware of the conversations we have with ourselves and with others this month. Many thoughts may enter the mind, but they do not gain a foothold in ourselves unless we give them energy and express them. If people realize the damage they do to themselves by speaking negatively to others, they would make a greater effort to practice holy silence.

The next Torah portion, *Lech Lecha* from Genesis 12, offers a most important message for this month. Lech Lecha literally means *Come to your Self.* These were the first instructions Avraham received from God. He was told: *Leave your land, your family and your father's house to the land that I will show you.* Gen. 12:1. These words contain important instructions for those who are committed to a spiritual journey as well.

People have to leave a place or situation either physically or gain objectivity about the impact of the external influences on their ego identities if they are to discover and embody their true selves, their own souls. Unless we inquire into the impact of those influences, exercise discernment, and know how to tune into our inner calling and soul purpose, it is quite possible we will live the life that other people want for us and not the life that expresses our potential and soul essence. The ego identity, unlike the soul, of a person is always looking to be validated and approved of by others.

For example, people sometimes marry or choose a profession not because of their personal desire, but rather because they think it will give them the parental love and approval they so much want. Though this choice may not have been a conscious one at the time, sometimes later in life people come to realize that they are living a life script written for them by someone else.

Abraham in these Torah portions models the steps a person takes on the spiritual journey. When our Patriarch Abraham was told by God to leave *his land, family, and father's house*, he was essentially asked to let go of all the attachments that previously shaped his sense of ego identity and enter into the vulnerable state of not knowing to become a true servant of God. We also need to be comfortable in the not knowing, and let go of the physical and emotional attachments that do not support our true essence. Like Abraham, we need to contact the soul within and trust our own inner voice to guide us forward in our lives to new possibilities. This takes great faith because there is not always clarity. We have to transcend the mind, what we already know, and open to living more in the heart. From the inner knowing of the heart and soul, we will receive direction. This is not always easy, but that does not make it impossible or inessential.

If the journey outlined by God for Abraham was intended to be a purely physical one, the instructions would have been phrased differently. Abraham would have first been told to leave his parent's home, then his birthplace, and finally the land. In fact it was reverse: Abraham was first told to leave the land, then the birthplace, and then his father's home. The journey God directed Abraham to take was essentially a spiritual journey, one that mirrors the journey we each must try to be responsible for our own subjectivity.

It is easier to leave the external influences of one's land or one's culture than to leave the influences of one's family. Because we were so impressionable and vulnerable as infants and children, the imprint of the family upon us is the greatest. This level of subjectivity is much more difficult to separate ourselves from because we often associate it mistakenly with our intrinsic selves. Too often we believe the messages we received about who we were as children and continue to live from them. As a therapist, I see that often these messages are limiting and negative and not essentially true. Much of therapy and spiritual practice involves discernment and insight into our true nature through separating ourselves from the influences that have externally and internally affected our experience of ourselves. With this insight comes greater objectivity. With objectivity, comes freedom and choice.

When we access our own soul, we have that direct connection to the Source, to the Creator, to the experience of the limitless Divine Love within ourselves, so there is little need to be afraid or give oneself up to be validated by others.

In the next chapter of the Torah, Veyara, Abraham is worthy to receive the visitation of three angels in Genesis 18. Interestingly, the Torah portion begins with, *God appeared to him*. It does not even mention Abraham's name. This indicates that Abraham had entered a state known as *bittul*, meaning a nullification of ego self, which is what made it possible to have the kind of revelation of God that Avraham had. Similarly, we also must have moments when we *bittul* ourselves to experience spiritual revelation and guidance.

Each angel who visits Abraham has its own mission. One heals him from his circumcision. Another angel reveals the prophecy of the birth of Isaac. The third angel informs him of the pending destruction of Sodom and Gomorrah. This Torah portion also recounts in detail the pleading and bargaining Abraham engages in on behalf of the people of these towns. This is a powerful demonstration of the *hesed*, the loving kindness, of Abraham, who prays for the wicked people.

Throughout these Torah portions, Abraham continues to grow through many tests. He has to send his son, Ishmael, and Hagar, the mother of his child, away, but his hardest test was the sacrifice of his son Isaac. This act went against everything Abraham stood for, yet he was willing to do it because it was what he thought God wanted. It is interesting that he pleaded for the lives of the evil people of Sodom and Gomorrah, and not for his own son. Did he not know the impact of this act on his wife Sarah?

The Zohar tells us that Sarah had a vision of the sacrifice and her soul departed her body with cries and whimpers. Her last words may have been, *Take me and not my son*. She was Abraham's sacrifice. I wrote two books, *The Secret Legacy of Biblical Women: Revealing the Divine Feminine* and *Biblical Women Who Changed the World*, to provide a voice for Sarah in this story as well as in the untold stories of Biblical women that are also not well known.

The last Torah portion of this month is "Chaya Sarah" the Life of Sarah, which is really an account of her death. In the midst of this Torah portion that begins with the death of Sarah and concludes with the death of Abraham Gen 23:1-25:17 is the marriage of Isaac. The Torah describes in much detail the selection of Rebecca as well as their meeting. The Torah tells us that Isaac married her, loved her and that he was comforted in the loss of his mother. Here the cycle of life continues. The parents Abraham and Sarah die, the son Isaac marries and a new generation will come into being.

> It is helpful to remember that we often do our greatest growth through the challenges we face.

In summary, Cheshvan is the month that we may each have our own tests, probably not as dramatic as Abraham, but nevertheless, we are challenged. It is helpful to remember that we often do our greatest growth through the challenges we face. Whatever tests you are facing this month, know that you will grow through them. Let that be a comfort for you.

Meditation

SELF OBSERVATION WITHOUT JUDGEMENT

Take a few minutes to center yourself with long conscious deep breaths inhaling through the nostrils and exhaling through the mouth, letting go of tension and stress with each exhalation, allowing yourself to go deeper inside with each exhalation. Then, change the breathing to inhalations and exhalations through the nostrils. Take conscious, long, slow breaths as you allow yourself to move into a more meditative state of awareness.

This meditation is a time for you to be present with yourself, as an observer, quieting the mind of judgment and constant chatter of the mind. As you focus on the gift of every breath, your mind will become more quiet. Receive each breath with gratitude, then hold it to your comfort level and when you exhale, let go, relax, and go deeper inside. It is safe to relax. Give yourself the gift of deep relaxation. For a slightly different kind of experience, if you like, you can repeat to yourself, *Henini*, which means *Here I am*. Let this take you to the state of being present to yourself in this moment, ready to serve.

Begin by focusing on your physical body. Scan the body and be compassionately aware of the tensions, sensation and pain present in your body. Be aware that the body is speaking to you in the form of sensations. Take time to be compassionately present with your body. Then affirm to yourself, you may have sensations in your body but you are not your body. You are the soul who is witnessing the body, for this body is a temporary residence for you. Affirm that you will honor and nourish this body temple for your soul for however long you are granted to be embodied.

Now take a few moments to become compassionately aware of what emotions or feelings are present within you right now. There are no good or bad feelings. Allow yourself time to be with whatever feelings are present for you. There may be feelings of sadness, anger, guilt, shame, jealousy, etc. All your feelings are beautiful. Breathe and allow yourself to feel what is present for you without judgment. Then affirm to yourself that you have many emotions, but you are the not the emotions or feelings that you experience. You are the one who is aware of these emotions. You can welcome the wide expression of these emotions without judgment, but with compassion, for they only reflect your human experience, not your soul essence.

Now, become aware of the thoughts that travel through your mind. There may be thoughts of the past, or of the future, judging thoughts, anxiety thoughts, or simply distracting thoughts that keep you from being present with yourself in the moment. Just become compassionately aware of the thoughts that travel through the mind. Then affirm to yourself that you are not the mind. You can let go of trying to figure out life on the level of your mind. You are not your mind. You are not your thoughts. You are the soul who is witnessing the thoughts. You are the pure holy eternal soul who is contained in the body-time continuum having a human experience for a precious limited amount of time.

As we affirm greater identification with the witness, the soul, we can easily let go of limiting ideas of the ego mind. We are able to embrace and embody more of our soul potential. We become more identified with the Divine, for our soul is a part of God. We may likely experience glimpses of true freedom and limitless love. Conclude this meditation by bringing your attention to the breath, taking a few minutes to internalize and integrate what you opened to during meditation. When it is your time to conclude, just open your eyes.

Practical Recommendations

1. REVIEW THE GOALS SET FOR THE PREVIOUS MONTH.

In Cheshvan we begin to implement the vision received during the month of Tishrei. What progress have you made towards realizing the goals set for yourself? What resistances have you encountered within yourself or in the external world? Make a note of this and share it with a friend or write it in your journal.

2. UPDATE YOUR PLAN TO GO FORWARD IN YOUR LIFE.

You may now have greater clarity in this month of Cheshvan to formulate goals and strategies for the new year than you did in the previous month of Tishrei. During the challenges of Cheshvan you have gained greater insight into what you truly want to express and embody this year and you now have a greater capacity to articulate this to yourself and others. Give yourself more permission to express yourself to others.

3. MEDITATE TO FIND A PLACE OF REFUGE WITHIN YOURSELF.

Finding a place of quiet and healing within yourself is important at all times, but it is even more so now during this month. It is easier to go forward in your life when you are centered and relaxed. Relaxation is the greatest gift you can give yourself if you want to go forward in life. Make a schedule and commit to a daily practice of meditation. A meditation can be very brief or extended. You can also meditate as you go about your

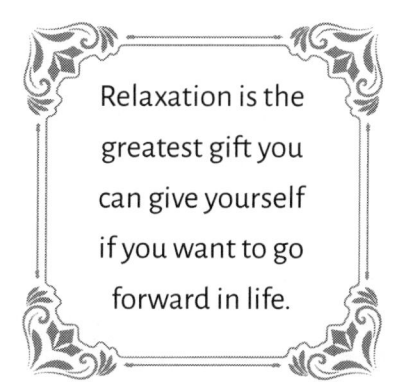

> Relaxation is the greatest gift you can give yourself if you want to go forward in life.

errands. Simply take deep breaths, quiet your mind, allow yourself to be open and present. The Divine Presence surrounds you and is within you at all times.

4. TALK TO GOD.

Talking to God is a powerful practice. This cathartic experience helps people uncover broken and wounded parts of self and bring them into greater awareness. This is a potent practice any time of the year, but now, as we are shedding the old and not clear about the new, we need to receive higher guidance. When we make a God connection, our consciousness is lifted upward in ways that we might not have even imagined possible. Talk to God, then quiet your mind and listen deeply.

5. SPEND TIME IN NATURE.

Spending time in nature aides us in learning how to let go and flow with the cycles of life. In some places this month, you will observe how leaves gracefully shed their leaves and how trees stand tall and barren. Trees may inspire us to accept changes that occur within us at this time of year. Being connected to nature opens to receive greater blessings as well.

A Tale to Live By

One day a very wealthy man came to a rebbe and asked him, *How can a person be happy in the midst of suffering? I have all the wealth I need and more, and I am still not happy.* The rebbe said to him that to learn the answer to this question, he would have to see Reb Zusya [an eighteenth-century mystic who is a beloved character in many Chassidic stories]. The rebbe gave him the direction to Reb Zusya's home.
The rich man traveled there and came upon a disheveled broken-down house. He thought, *This can't be the home of Reb Zusya. How could a person*

live in such a dwelling? Yet it must be, so he knocked at the door. Reb Zusya answered and identified himself. The rich man explained that he was sent by the rebbe to find out how a person can be happy in the midst of suffering. Reb Zusya replied that he did not know why the rebbe sent him, saying: *I never had a bad day in my life.*

This story reminds us that true happiness and vitality on all levels of being comes from within us from the experience of our connection with God. It is not true that we need to have personal achievements, possessions or fame to be happy or fulfilled. That may be the desire of the ego but it is not that of the soul. Reb Zusya was a very humble person. He never referred to himself as I, but was known to say, Zusya, when talking about himself. There are many stories of his humility and modesty. His consciousness was said to be always in a state of *dveykut*, meaning clinging to God. As such, he often said that he never had a bad day in his life, and was always grateful and joyful.

3

Kislev

NOVEMBER – DECEMBER

ENERGY
Rekindling and Fulfilling Dreams

AREA OF HEALING
Sleep

ASTROLOGICAL SIGN
Sagittarius

HEBREW LETTER
Samech ס

HEBREW TRIBE
Benjamin

DIVINE PERMUTATION
VYHH

HOLIDAY
Chanukkah

A Personal Story

The month of Kislev is a month to leave your comfort zone and to actualize some of your dreams and go forward in your life with faith. Here is one of my own personal stories about when I gratefully substituted fear for faith and trust in God.

After receiving a Master's degree in social work and having worked as a social worker in two previous positions, I was blessed to be hired as the Manhattan Borough Coordinator for Mental Retardation and Developmental Disabilities for New York City. This position resembled much of the dream job I envisioned for myself in graduate school while also offering me the security of a government position with a wonderful pension.

After several years however, when I had mastered the challenges of the position, the job lost its luster and became routine and even boring to me. I also became repulsed by the politics I witnessed and I resented all the unnecessary paperwork of a government bureaucracy that took so much of my time.

I knew in my heart that this job was no longer connected to my soul purpose and I wanted to leave. A rabbi and a few others told me that it was foolish to leave the security of a high paying government job with a good pension. I lived in New York City at the time. How did I expect to support myself?

What a blessing that I substituted fear with faith at that time. I somehow knew in my heart of hearts that I would be taken care of by the Divine Hand. So I quit. Within a short amount of time, I began to teach Jewish meditation and work as a psychotherapist in private practice with individuals and couples. I actually loved the not knowing where my livelihood would come from each month. Some months, my livelihood came mostly from my private practice as a therapist. Other months, it came from the meditation classes. I experienced God as a partner in my life, never fearing that I would not be provided for.

I also began to attend a new women's *yeshivah*, a place to Jewish learning, daily that had recently opened. When I left my job, I did not know that I would be blessed to be a student of the most awesome and holiest of teachers, Rabbi Yitzchak Kirzner of blessed memory, who was teaching there for what turned out to be the last few years of his life. From the first time I heard him speak, I knew I was in the presence of a great and lofty soul. Learning with him each time was actually thrilling to me. He also made himself available for private counsel for his devoted students like myself.

Rabbi Kirzner gave me a solid foundation in Judaism. He introduced me to the classics of Jewish philosophy, books written by the Rambam, the Ramchal, Rabbenu Yonah, and more. For years I studied with him the book, *Duties of the Heart*, by Ibn Paquda. This book, which I had stumbled upon while browsing in a Jewish bookstore years before, had placed me on the path of religious observance. I literally could not put this book down, reading it every possible waking moment. This book spoke to my heart and soul like no other book had ever done. After I completed reading it, I was a new and different person.

After years of learning with Rabbi Kirzner, I discovered, much to my surprise, that I had had a dream about him several years before I met him. I had not even heard of Rabbi Kirzner previously. In my dream, he was named Isaac Kirzner, and he worked as an interior decorator for the Salvation Army. He was working in a neighbor's apartment, advising him on what to keep and what to throw away. In my dream, I invited him to help me. I asked him if he would be my interior decorator. Then we had a deep discussion about what it meant to really trust in God.

As I was in Jungian analysis at the time and the therapist was only interested in my dream life and not in what was actually happening in my life, I recorded the dream in detail. I was grateful that I had the opportunity to read to Rabbi Kirzner this dream from my dream book, and tell him that he was indeed my interior decorator two months before he passed away at the age of forty in 1991. He was as astonished as I was that I had had this dream about him years before I met him or even heard his name.

My life would not have been same had I not had the courage to leave the security of a government position and go for what my soul wanted and needed. If I had not done so, I would not have been able to study with Rabbi Kirzner as I did. Being a student of Rabbi Kirzner remains a great blessing to me to this very day so many years after he departed from this earthly plane. Now, I understand learning with him as part of my soul destiny. It was why I dreamt of him before I even heard his name. My life would not have been the same otherwise.

Energy: Rekindling and Fulfilling Dreams

The days are getting shorter and the nights longer. It is one of the darkest times of the year physically, yet Kislev is a time of expansiveness, travel, and going forward in life. The energy of this month is about acting on trust and faith to actualize your dreams and visions. This is the month of miracles and redemption. Optimism, hope, confidence, and faith are easily accessible this month to support you in actualizing your dreams.

Though the name Kislev itself is Babylonian in origin, the word *kis* in Hebrew means *pocket* and *lev* means *heart*. This has been said to refer to the capacity to be a vessel for what our hearts desire. Very often people want but they do not know how to receive what they want in their lives. They therefore stay in a place of wanting, unable to receive what they want. During this month we have a greater capacity to actually receive what we want by just a small allowing within ourselves. By the way, according to the Talmud, Kislev has also been known as a time to receive unexpected money.

The spiritual energy of Kislev is very different than the previous month of Cheshvan, While Cheshvan is known for the purification and the hard inner work of the transmutation of what is limiting in our lives, Kislev is all about transcending what is logical, actualizing our dreams and visions and going forward. The month of Kislev is the time to rekindle our deepest dreams, embrace possibilities before us, and be empowered to go for what we want.

We gain focus and are able of go forward and take risks this month because the month of Kislev is a time of deepening faith and trust. Living with faith enables us to not be bound by the reasoning powers and limits of the mind. When we are limited by the mind, we are always tied down to what is known and familiar and we only seek to understand why and how.

Faith by definition is beyond the reasoning powers of the mind. Faith enables us to be present, to not dwell in the past or worry about the future, but to live life moment to moment fully with trust and fearlessness. It is faith, not the mind, which opens us up to new possibilities and new dimensions enabling us to go forward in ways we could not do solely on our own.

As we deepen our faith this month, we come to understand that what is happening in our lives and in the world is for our benefit and growth, even if it may be very challenging, seemingly disagreeable, and uncomfortable. Nothing is an accident in our personal lives and in the collective. To believe that everything is happening randomly by chance or due to the free will of human beings is to not believe in God.

During the month of Kislev, we become increasingly aware of Divine synchronicity. We are not here on our own, and during this month we are aware that God is very much alive and active in our lives and in the world. When we can see the Divine Hand in what is happening in our life, we are happier, we are spiritually aligned, we accept life more peacefully and we spiritually grow through the challenges we face more easily. Wonderful and even miraculous opportunities emerge unexpectedly to take us forward.

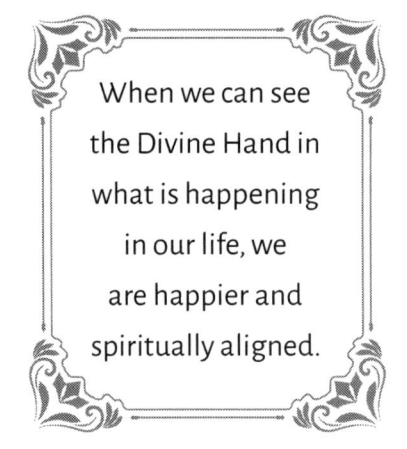

> When we can see the Divine Hand in what is happening in our life, we are happier and spiritually aligned.

One of the signs that we are living in accordance with our life purpose and Divine Will is that we will experience more synchronicity and abundance in life. Small miracles seem commonplace, an everyday occurrence. This awareness fills us with gratitude. The whole month of Kislev is a time of thanksgiving. It is no accident that the secular American holiday of Thanksgiving occurs during this month.

The whole month is shaped by the holiday of Chanukkah, the holiday of miracles that occurs at the end of the month, the darkest time of the year. As we celebrate the holiday with the lighting of candles, we learn experientially a most important and deep truth about life: There is light amidst the darkness. At the darkest time there is light and there will be light. Actually, the light in the darkness shines even more brightly because of the darkness that surrounds it. Darkness is a cover for the light too great to be openly revealed, according to Kabbalistic teachings.

Chanukkah is the celebration of the rededication of the Holy Temple in Jerusalem in 164 BCE. The Temple, the site of the most holy, intimate place of Divine connection, had been violated by the Syrian-Greeks. Foreign practices and influence infiltrated the psyche of the Jewish people, threatening belief in the Divinity of God. The Greeks, rulers of the Syrian-Greek Empire, believed in the reasoning powers of the mind, what is logical and rational, and used this philosophy to undermine the intrinsic faith of the Jewish people in the Divine.

Like the Maccabees, who redeemed the Temple in ancient times during this month, we redeem the Holy Temple within us. Much more than a physical place, the Holy Temple represents the holiest and most pure dimension within us. It is the seat of our deepest hopes and our visions of life, which are beyond the mind, not bound by the laws of reason and logic. The oil used for the rededication of the Temple was pure and undefiled, reminding us of the possibility of returning to a state of original purity. The miracle of the rededication was that, although, there was only enough oil to burn for one day, it lasted for eight days. It was not logical, but God is beyond logic.

This month is the time when we go beyond what is rational and go for what we really want. This may be different than what we think or feel we want. In determining what we really want, we may still need to sift and distill our visions to make sure that they are not contaminated by the ego mind and come from the purest place within us. To know what we really want inside, we have to listen to what God wants for us.

During this month, we try to stop the tendency of trying to figure out life with our minds. Give up any excuses you may have to rationalize not going for what you want this month. It is usually only fear wanting us to remain in our comfort zones, even if we are unhappy doing so. When you go forward, know that it is natural to be afraid. But do not let fear stop you from going forward. This month learn to simply let go, relax and more deeply trust in the Source of Life.

Kislev is an auspicious time to meditate on one's life purpose and receive important guidance. Kislev is a time of clarity. Give yourself time this month to tune into your intuition and listen to the guidance of your own soul.

The healing area of this month is sleep. Though we sleep every night, it is still a mystery how we sleep and what occurs to us during sleep. Though we have some choice about when and how we sleep, we all have to sleep whether we want to or not. Just as we trust in God to go forward in our lives this month, we also demonstrate our trust in God through sleep. When we can let go into the mystery of sleep and sleep deeply, we emerge rested and renewed. So much healing occurs during a sleep state. Though sleep is likened to one-sixtieth of death, it is also a time of vision. When we sleep, we are told, our soul is able to ascend to the higher worlds. Those who have purified their consciousness may receive true vision and understanding through dreams. Many dreams may be prophetic.

As the nights get longer and it gets colder outside, you may find yourself wanting to sleep a little longer, which is fine. It is even good to allow yourself to sleep longer than usual. Sleep is not a waste of time, but provides an opportunity to live in another dimension.

The healing of sleep also means that this is a time when we should wake up from the sleepy dimension that we usually live in. When we sleep, we should sleep deeply. When we are awake, we should not be sleeping.

General Guidelines and Goals

The following guidelines and goals enable us to direct our energies in the ways that are optimal for our growth and transformation in accordance with the energy of this month. It is recommended that you read and meditate upon them often in the course of the month. Reflect on their applicability to you and allow them to direct and inspire you often this month.

1. GIVE YOURSELF TIME TO DREAM YOUR DREAMS.

You have a right to dream. Your dreams speak the message of the soul. They need not be logical. This is the month to pay attention to your dreams, listening to the part of yourself beyond the rational mind. During this month, we reclaim the pure faith of the child within who believes in dreams and miracles.

Close your eyes and allow images and visions to emerge about yourself and your life. Focus on the breath to quiet the chatter of your mind. When the mind is more still than usual, be with these following questions and listen to what opens up within you. Who are you? How do you want to live your life? What kind of work do you do or want to do? What kinds of relationships do you have or want to have? What do you really want in your life now? If you want, give yourself time to be with these questions and journal the thoughts awakened within you.

As a child you may have had many dreams for yourself. What were they? Some of these dreams you may have realized and some you may have abandoned as you thought they were not practical or possible. And other dreams you may have partially fulfilled. Some of these dreams you may now want to revisit in a different form. Give yourself time to pay attention to your dreams and hopes.

This is the month to love and listen deeply to the inner child within you. Allowing your inner child to have fun is the key to being happy and successful. When your inner child is having fun, you are beloved and gates to success on every level of your being open for you. The magic in life comes from your inner child. So come out and play this month whenever you can.

2. SEEK TO GO FORWARD IN YOUR LIFE.

The mind always wants to understand, it seeks answers, reasons, and justifications. This is not often a fruitful inquiry. Understanding does not change things. It may be interesting but it does not make a difference.

Note the tendency of your mind to try to understand, explain, and justify why you are not living your dreams. Assert now that you will not be limited by the mind. As human beings we cannot fully know the reasons why certain things have happened in our lives nor why other things did not happen. The effort to understand is often futile.

We do not have access to the whole picture of the karma we accrued in past lives as well as in our current life. So it is important to leave the past in the past and trust that everything in our lives has been unfolding according to Divine Will. Breathe, and connect with God. When we align our intentions with Divine Will, we are empowered. It will become clear what our next move in life will be.

3. STRENGTHEN A *CAN DO* ATTITUDE WITHIN YOURSELF.

This is the month to go forward. As much as we want change, as much as we want more light and joy, we are resistant and frightened by change. This is natural. Be mindful to not allow fear or resistance to stop or limit you this month.

Always remember, particularly this month, that you are created with a soul purpose to offer something new and wonderful in this world. Whatever you do with your life let it be an embodiment of who you are on a soul level and what your soul purpose is for this incarnation.

Sometimes when we do not love and trust ourselves enough, we give up our dreams, we hide to play it safe. This is the month to restore our self confidence and courage to be ourselves and live in accordance with our soul purpose. This month, be particularly mindful to not give up on your dreams in order to please other people and to receive their approval and validation. Do not accept fear projected towards you by others, supposedly on your behalf, who may be afraid to live out their own dreams.

Do not wait for others to give you permission to fulfill your soul purpose. When we stay with what is known, it may feel safer to us than venturing into the unknown. But does that really make us safer?

We pay a great toll on ourselves when we stay in work situations, or relationships that are stifling, toxic or even abusive to us. Sometimes the safest place is to be with what is not known and be totally vulnerable before

God. Your soul is your GPS, your God Protection System, so listen to her guidance. What you need to know now is within you.

4. MEDITATE ON DIVINE LIGHT EACH DAY.

In Kislev, we celebrate the miracle of light in darkness. We meditate on the lights during Chanukkah and Shabbat, but the practice of meditating on Divine Light is not to be confined to just those times. God's light is always present for those who yearn for it. Divine Light will illuminate you to the truth and will cleanse you of negativity and impurity.

Meditating on Divine Light is a foundational practice of Jewish meditation. When we connect with Divine Light, the light changes our energy. We do not try to change other people but the Divine Light we radiate will change them for the better.

When you sit down for meditation, open yourself as if you were a vessel and ask to be filled with Divine Light. Ask to be aware of the Divine Light that surrounds you all the time. The experience of Divine Light is accessible, but you must want it sincerely. No matter what you are going through at any given time, Divine Light and love is available to flow through you.

When you find that your mind is filled with negative thoughts, wherever you are, even if you are out on the street doing your errands, stop for a moment, take a few deep breaths, and be aware that God's Light is everywhere. Breathe in God's Light. It is available to flow to you and through you anywhere, any time.

5. HONOR THE HOLY TEMPLES IN YOUR LIFE.

There are many holy temples, those places where the Divine Presence is experienced in our lives. For example, our body is a holy temple for the soul. Our intimate relationships with our spouses, our parents, our children, and our friends are holy temples. Our synagogues, our places of communal worship, are holy temples. This month is a time to purify these places. Relationships may easily be strengthened at this time.

With all that being said, Torah Judaism is awaiting and preparing for the Third Holy Temple in Jerusalem. The Third Temple will be a source of blessing for all the nations of the world. Whether you know it or not, there are Jews who will not eat a piece of bread without praying for this Third Holy Temple. Ancient prophecies have told us that the Third Temple will change the world for the better. Its establishment will bring peace and foster Divine Revelation throughout the world.

6. PRACTICE GRATITUDE.

The whole month of Kislev is a time for thanksgiving and praising God. Sometimes we experience God's hand very directly, and at other times it is very subtle and we may take for granted or be unaware of all the miracles, growth opportunities, and blessings we are given each day. Make a conscious effort to practice gratitude this month. Savor all the blessings that are part of your life each day. Keep a journal to record insights and experiences of gratitude on a daily or weekly basis.

Astrological Sign: Sagittarius

Sagittarius is represented by the centaur, a mythological creature that is half man and half horse. The horse portion represents animal energy and the drive for freedom; the human portion poised with a bow indicates the ability to direct consciousness above the instinctual animal level. Sometimes Sagittarius is represented by an archer. The glyph for Sagittarius is also plainly an arrow. The arrow expresses the desire to go forward, to explore and reach beyond what you know of yourself. A new vision often emerges in the month of Sagittarius.

Sagittarius is a fire sign. The energy of the month and the people who are born this month are fiery, inspirational, and expressive. Enthusiasm and passion are directed upward and outward in a way that did not occur in the previous months.

Sagittarius is ruled by the planet Jupiter. In mythology, Jupiter, also called Jove or Zeus, was the king of the gods. The energy of Jupiter is expansive, beneficent, and optimistic. Jupiter sees the larger vision and opens doors to new plans, aspirations, and growth opportunities. There is an adventurous and freedom-loving spirit and the willingness to take risks this month. Travel is often indicated.

The energy of Sagittarius encourages us to explore other cultures, to pursue advanced studies, and be inspired by ethical, philosophical, and religious principles to build a beautiful life upon. Sagittarius rules the ninth house, the house of philosophy, religion, and high education. People born under this sign are generally exuberant, positive thinking, and good humored. I am happy that at least my moon is in Sagittarius.

Hebrew Letter: Samech

The *samech* looks like a circle and is one of two letters that are totally closed. The shape of a circle has important properties.

First, a circle is a closed system. One feels protected in a circle.

Second, a circle reminds us of the transcendence and immanence of God, for each point on the circle is equidistant from the center. All souls are in essence equidistant from or equally close to God.

Third, a circle is continuous. You can't tell the beginning from the end of the circle. Every point in the circle is both a beginning and an end. The *samech*, through its circular shape, reminds us that life is a cycle. Things may seem to be breaking down, but they are really continuing in another form, and this form will change yet again. This symbol has particular meaning during this month when there continue to be so many changes occurring on the physical plane.

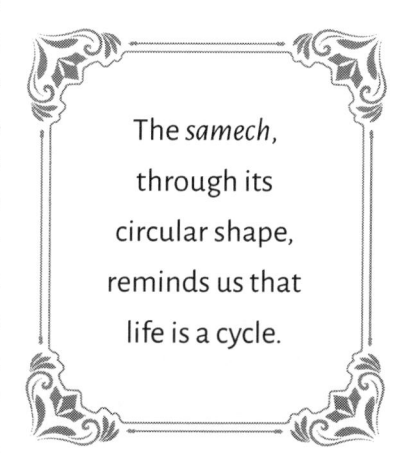

> The *samech*, through its circular shape, reminds us that life is a cycle.

The *samech* is also likened to a wedding ring, reminding us of the covenant between God and the Jewish people.

The word *samech* means *to support*. Significance is found in the fact that the *samech* follows the *nun*, the letter for last month which means *falling*. In King David's psalm of Ashrei in Psalms 145, it says, *Samech HaShem l'col hanoflim*, meaning, God supports those who fall. Support means being with or descending with so as to lift upward. Everything in life goes through a cycle of falling and being lifted upward. Kislev lifts up the month of Cheshvan. The word *semicha* begins with a *samech*. *Semicha* is a support whereby the teacher lifts the student to become a teacher.

Together the *nun* and the *samech* spell out *neis*, which means miracle. This month is truly a month of Divine support to go forward and experience miracles.

Sefer Yetzirah, an ancient book of Jewish mysticism from which much of this material derives, says that: *God coronated the samech with the attribute of sleep*. The *samech* of this month helps us to overcome our spiritual slumber and awaken to realize our dreams. The healing of this month is through sleep. The numerical equivalent of *samech* is sixty. It is said that sleep is one-sixtieth of death, and a dream is one-sixtieth of prophecy. This is also an allusion to the importance of dreams this month.

Hebrew Tribe: Benjamin

After many years of infertility, Rachel gave birth to a second son, her first son being Joseph. Knowing that she was dying during the birth, she cried out his name, Ben oni, which means son of affliction. Gen.35:18. Though she died, her son lived on, echoing the theme of light in the darkness of this month.

Not wanting his son to bear such a negative name, Jacob changed it to Benyamin, which means son of the south, or, son of the right, or son of the days. South refers to the energy of love for the emanation of *hesed*, meaning loving kindness emerges from the south, according to the holy Kabbalistic text *Sefer Yetzirah*. Right also refers to *hesed* as on the right side in the Tree of Life.

Benjamin was the only son of Jacob born in the Land of Israel. Just as Israel is associated with a higher level of Divine providence than any other place, Kislev receives a higher level of Divine providence than any other month. The way the Torah speaks of Benjamin informs us about the energy of this month: *And of Benjamin he said, the Beloved of the Eternal shall dwell safely by him. He hovers over him all day long and rests between his shoulders*. Deut. 33:12. The Torah is telling us that this month of Kislev is a beloved month, and there is a special sense of Divine providence available this month.

The land of Benjamin included the Temple Mount, the location of the Holy Temple. The Temple, rededicated in this month, was the site of the greatest vision and dreams for humanity, ultimately to be a place of worship for all nations. Benjamin was seen to be a tribe of great vision worthy of this holiest site, bestowing preciousness for this month of Kislev.

Divine Name Permutation: VYHH

In examining the permutation for this month, we see that there is expansiveness in the world of Assiyah, this physical world and in Yetzirah, the world of the heart and angels, by the positioning of the letter *hay* (H). This is a time of action in the physical world as well as a time of opening and allowing the heart to guide you. The *yud* (Y), which is a small letter, in the world of Beriyah, indicates that the mind must be contracted, focused and made small, so the light of the Divine can shine through with less obstruction. This is the month to not figure out life with your mind at all. The *vav* (V), the letter that makes connection between things, in the position of the world of Atzilut, indicates that there is abundant light being drawn through the higher worlds. The drawing of abundant light initially this month comes from the world of Assiyah which is a larger container and vessel for Divine Light. This explains why this month is a time for miracles.

Torah Portions

The themes of this month are echoed in the Torah portions which provide important and relevant spiritual guidance for this month. The Torah portions for this month often begin with Vayetze in Genesis 28:10-29:35, which recounts Jacob's departure from the home of his parents after stealing the blessings from his brother, Esau. In keeping with Kislev as the month of dreams and visions, the Torah portions includes Jacob's dream vision of a ladder, standing on the ground, and reaching into heaven, with angels ascending and descending it. Through this vision, Jacob receives a prophecy about the future of the Jewish people, how long and how many times they will be exiled from the Land of Israel and how they will ultimately return. He is assured that God is with him and that he will be blessed to continue in the lineage of his grandfather, Abraham, and his father, Isaac. Jacob says, *God is truly in this place. How awe-inspiring this place is. It is a gateway to heaven.* Gen.28:16-17. This is the consciousness that we need to receive blessing and guidance to go forward in our lives, wherever we are in our lives.

Representative of the energy of this month, Jacob goes forward and soon marries. His wives, Leah and Rachel, and their maid servants, Bilhah and Zilpah, all bear him children. He also works hard and his business thrives. Abundance is a theme of this month.

Jacob had wanted to marry Rachel whom he loved upon seeing her, but he is deceived into marrying her twin sister Leah first. Just as he had deceived his father in order to receive the blessings of the first born, so he was similarly deceived. The *Midrash* tells us that Leah told him when he learned that he had been tricked to marry her: *Just like you deceived your brother, so it was necessary that you be deceived. When you lied to your brother and to your father, you showed me that it is permissible to lie for a good cause. I am merely following your example.* There is always karma in all our actions, but that does not mitigate the blessings.

In the next Torah portion, Va Yishlach in Genesis 32:4-37, Jacob is returning to Israel and is afraid that his brother Esau will kill him. Even though he is afraid, he does not let fear stop him. He prays, but he is also practical and makes various contingency plans for dealing with Esau. He will bribe him or fight him if necessary. This is seen to be a model of how to deal with a possible enemy: pray, bribe, and prepare for war. In a life transformational struggle with an angel Jacob's name is changed to Israel. The Torah will refer to him as both Jacob and Israel from that day on. It has been said that Jacob married Rachel and Israel married Leah. In this way, he earns the blessings he originally stole. As a result of his preparation, the meeting with Esau was positive and healing.

The next Torah portion, Vayeishev, focuses on Joseph, the first son of Rachel in Genesis 37:1-40:23. Again we see the theme of dreams, for Joseph's prophetic dreams so enrage his brothers that they conspire to kill him. Ultimately, they sell Joseph into slavery, but the brothers take Joseph's tunic and dip it in blood so it looks like Joseph was killed. The brothers sell Joseph to the Midianites who sell him to Egypt, to Potiphar, the Chamberlain of the Butchers. Joseph has to undergo many tests. When he resists the efforts of Potiphar's wife to seduce him, she falsely accuses him of trying to rape her and he ends up in prison.

This month usually concludes with Joseph in prison interpreting correctly the dreams of the baker and the cupbearer. Though Joseph asks the cupbearer whose dream he interpreted accurately to remember and speak highly of him to Pharaoh, the cupbearer forgets, and Joseph remains in prison another two years. My teacher, Reb Shlomo, told us that Joseph needed to learn in those two years to rely only on God for his liberation. Two years later, the cupbearer remembers Joseph when Pharaoh has a dream that no one can interrupt for him.

In the next Torah portion of Miketz which straddles both months of Kislev and Tevet, the cupbearer informs Pharaoh of Joseph's skill in dream interpretation. When Joseph is brought out of prison to interpret the dream, Pharaoh tells him that he has heard that he can interpret dreams. Joseph answers Pharaoh by saying: *This is beyond me, it is God who will respond to Pharaoh's welfare.* Joseph then interprets Pharaoh's dream in such a powerful and authoritative way that Joseph is lifted up to a high government position in Egypt also demonstrating the miraculous energy of this month. One day he is a prisoner living in a dungeon. In a few moments, Joseph is elevated to be second only to Pharaoh, now responsible for administering the distribution of food during a famine. It was the famine that causes the brothers of Joseph to travel into Egypt and soon, they are in front of Joseph, who recognizes them.

People may wonder why Joseph does not reveal his identity to his brothers at this time. Why does he put them through so many tests? The Rambam, Maimonides, tells us that Joseph understood that his initial dreams that made his brothers so jealous of him had to be fulfilled and he would have to let things happen unfold in a more hidden way. He also probably wanted to see if his brothers regretted selling him into slavery and whether they had changed. Would they still be jealous and hate him? He knows that they have changed when Yehudah, Judah, offers his own life to replace Benjamin as a captive.

The theme of redemption is found in the Torah portions of this month in two interesting stories that provide the antecedents of the prophecies of the two messiahs: Messiah Ben Dovid and Messiah Ben Joseph. Both Yehudah and Joseph faced the test of sexual temptation. Joseph resisted the temptations of the wife of Potiphar and ended up in prison. Joseph represents the *tzaddik*, the pure righteous person who suffers on behalf of others. He has moral clarity. Yehudah succumbs to his daughter-in-law, Tamar, who was disguised as a prostitute and even fathered a child with her. Yehudah has the courage to admit publicly that he had sexual relations with his daughter-in-law. She tricked him because he refused to allow her to marry his third son when two of his other sons died while being married to her. Yehudah represents the Baal Teshuva, the person who does wrong, but acknowledges his or her guilt and repents. The archetypes of Messiah ben Dovid and Messiah ben Yoseph both have important roles to play in the final redemption.

Holiday: Chanukkah

HISTORY: The conquest of Israel by Alexander the Great in the fourth century BCE brought with it a blending of Eastern traditions and Greek culture that was called Hellenism. Hellenism was a very revolutionary, cosmopolitan, and intellectual movement that attracted many Jews. A century later, Israel was captured by the Seleucids of Syria.

By the second century, the divisions within the Jewish community about how it wanted to relate to the Seleucid Empire—the Syrian Greek Empire—became delineated. The Hellenists, who favored assimilation, were generally educated, wealthy and powerful. The Chassidim, who favored separation so as to protect religious piety, were the poor farmers who chose not to mix with the Greeks.

When Antiochus IV became the ruler of the Syrian-Greek Empire, he did not want to murder Jews but make them more like Greeks. He forbade the study of Torah as a Divine Revelation as well as other ritual practices like circumcision, Sabbath observance, and sanctification of the new moon. He did not necessarily even want Jews to convert to his religion but only that they not take Judaism so seriously as a religion; rather, Jews should be rational, and the Bible should be viewed and studied as literature rather than Divine Revelation.

Needing more for his military campaign against Egypt, he sold the position of the High Priest in the Jerusalem Holy Temple, installed a Jew sympathetic to himself, introduced idols into the Holy Temple and instituted foreign practices like pig sacrifice and sacred prostitution. These practices spread throughout the entire empire. The Chassidim accepted those violations as evidence of Divine punishment, believing that martyrdom was preferable to disobeying the Torah: They were fervent pacifists. A much smaller third group began to emerge, the Maccabees, who were also religiously observant like the Chassidim, but believed that human beings should be active partners with God, even fighting on Shabbat if necessary to protect the covenant between the Jewish people and God.

What spurred the Maccabees into battle was not, interestingly enough, the religious violations, but an ordinance stipulating that Jewish virgins had to have sexual relations with the (Syrian-Greek) Seleucid governor prior to marriage. Though most people got married secretly, the story I heard is that the upcoming marriage of Yehudit, the daughter of Yehudah, the High Priest, became public. When she was told she had to have sexual relations with the governor, she challenged the Maccabees to defend her honor. She called them hypocrites who thought they were so holy because of their study of Torah but were not really holy because they allowed Jewish women to be sexually violated. She told them that she was prepared to die rather than submit herself to the Greek general. Her arguments hit home provoking them to battle.

Initially small in number, the Maccabees engaged in guerrilla war. They knew the terrain well. Soon their numbers swelled as moderate Hellenists and militant Chassidim joined their ranks. The Jewish people for the most part were sympathetic to the cause of the Maccabees. Another Jewish woman named Yehudit, a shy, beautiful widow, played a significant role in the military victory by seducing the Greek general, Holofernes, and then beheading him. When the armies saw their general beheaded, they retreated. Though it is not talked about much, this war was also a civil war between the Jews. Devoted Hellenists sided with the Seleucids and Jews fought against other Jews.

The holiday of Chanukkah celebrates the military victory of the Maccabees. Previously a day of cult sacrifice, the twenty fifth of Kislev was chosen as the most appropriate day to re-dedicate the Holy Temple by lighting the menorah, the symbol of the Light of the Divine Presence. Any oil could have been used in the menorah, but the Maccabees wanted a vial of oil that had not been defiled, and quite surprisingly, they found a buried one. Looking for a vial of oil that had not been contaminated was an expression of their desire to return to the original purity of their connection with God. And as the story goes, the oil burned miraculously for eight days rather than the expected one day. Eight is a symbol of Infinity, beyond the natural order.

The Maccabees ruled in the Holy Temple for only one year, and afterward, they were defeated by the Hellenists led by Lysias. King Antiochus then appointed a new regent over his kingdom, and a new agreement was negotiated that allowed the Jews to maintain control of the Holy Temple and freely practice their religion as they wanted.

When Israel was occupied by Rome many years later, the holiday of Chanukkah became more important and gave hope and inspiration to the masses. Even today, the story of Chanukkah offers much hope and inspiration to Jews all over the world. Israel has had to continually confront national and terrorist group enemies much larger than her who unrelentingly seek her destruction. Miraculously, Israel has continued to defeat her enemies seeking her destruction numerous times.

OBSERVANCE: The holiday of Chanukkah begins on the twenty-fifth of Kislev and continues until the second of Tevet. The main observance of Chanukkah is the lighting of the menorah. At this time we receive the blessings to remind ourselves of the military victory as well as the miracle of the oil burning for eight days. There was a debate between Rabbis Hillel and Shammai about whether one candle should be added each day so eight candles are lit on the last day or whether eight candles should be lit of the first day and one extinguished each night. Hillel's position won.

In lighting the menorah one begins on the first night by lighting the candle on the extreme right. The next night an additional candle is placed immediately to the left and lit first. Then the candle to the right from the previous night is lit. This procedure is repeated for the eight days. In the case of Shabbat, the Chanukkah candles are lit first. At the conclusion of Shabbat, the Havdalah candle that marks the end of Shabbat is lit first and then the Chanukkah candles.

The purpose of the candle lighting today is to publicize the miracle, so it is recommended that the candles be placed near a window so people on the street can see them. One menorah may be lit for an entire family or individuals may have their own. It is suggested that the candles be lit as early as possible after the appearance of stars, but it is not prohibited to do it later.

In the course of the holiday thirty six candles are lit. The Talmud says that there were thirty six hours when Adam and Eve could see from one end of the world to another. There were also said to be thirty six elevated souls in every generation that sustain and guard Divine creation. Special Halleh prayers of praise and thanksgiving are sung in synagogue every day.

Chanukkah is a joyous holiday with great mass appeal. It does not have the restrictions associated with Biblical holidays. The holidays prescribed in the Torah have things we must do and not do, which acts like a container for the light of Divine Revelation. On Chanukkah, there are no restrictions for as my teacher, Reb Shlomo Carlebach said that on Chanukkah we get both the vessels and the light together. It is a complete gift. One simply lights the Chanukkah candles and one is plugged into Divine Light.

Chanukkah is often considered a holiday for children. Whether you are an adult or a child, Chanukkah is a delight, awakening the inner child within us to play. Chanukkah parties are many, gifts are exchanged, and children spin dreidels. On the dreidel are written the Hebrew letters of *nun, gimmel, hay,* and *shin* for: *Nes gadol hayah sham,* to proclaim that a *Great miracle happened here.* People eat donuts and potato latkes made with oil to commemorate the miracle of oil.

The holiday of Chanukkah has increasing relevance for the Jewish people in modern times. Once again, the Jewish people, such a small group of people and the state of Israel, such a small, almost miniature state, have such large enemies both inside and outside of its boundaries that threaten its integrity, and its very existence.

Chanukkah reminds us that, though we may suffer, the Jewish people will always prevail. We are frequently reminded that the Jewish people live on the level of miracles. Our survival from antiquity may not be logical because Jews have faced the kinds of persecution from enemies more numerous and powerful than they have been in almost every generation. The holiday of Chanukkah and the energy of this month teach us that life is miraculous. When we light candles, we are also saying that we believe in miracles. With faith and trust in God, we know we can go forward in our lives in ways that transcend what is logical.

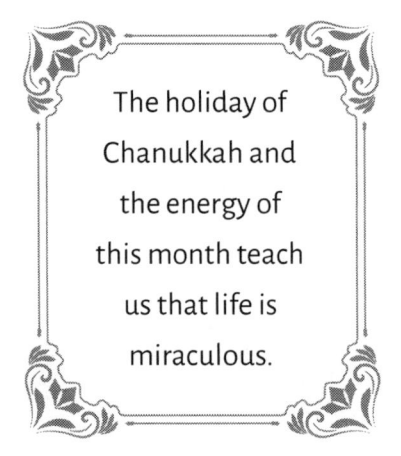

> The holiday of Chanukkah and the energy of this month teach us that life is miraculous.

Meditation

The meditation this month is for lighting candles for Chanukkah. It can be modified for Shabbat candle lighting or even for a weekday candle meditation. The light of the candle provides a glimpse into the light of God and the light of one's own soul. This holy light enables a person to see the miraculous nature of life, to experience the holiness and purity of God and the human soul.

In lighting the Chanukkah menorah, read slowly the Al Nissim blessing, found in Jewish prayer books, in which we praise God for all the miracles. Then we light the candles and say the following blessings.

> *Baruch Atah, Adonai Eloheinu Melech ha-Olam, asher kidshanu b'mitzvotav v'tzivanu l'hadlik near shel Chanukkah.* This means: Blessed are You, Adonai, our God, King of the universe, Who makes us holy through the commandments and commanded us to light the Chanukkah light.
>
> *Baruch Atah Adonai Eloheinu Melech ha'Olam, shah nissum la'avotenu ba'yamin ha'heim ha'zeman has zeh.* This means: Blessed are You, Adonai, our God, King of the universe, Who performed wondrous deeds for our ancestors in those days and at this season.
>
> On the first day only: *Baruch Atah Adonai Eloheinu Melech ha-Olam, she-Hecht-yo-nu v-ki-y'manu v'higiyanu la-z'man ha zeh.* This means: *Blessed are You, Adonai, our God, King of the universe Who has kept us alive, sustained us and brought us to this season.*

After you have said the blessings slowly and consciously, stay in front of the menorah or Shabbat candles. Gaze at the light. Be with the light. Let it enter deeply into your heart.

Although it may be a little uncomfortable, keep your eyes open as much as you can and let the light fill your screen of vision. This light has the power to purify and transform us. We each have varying degrees of resistance to change or to experiencing ourselves in new ways.

Be gentle and loving with yourself, allowing space for any internal discomfort without running away or distracting yourself. Just simply be with the light and with yourself. Imagine that you can cast into the light anything you want to release. The more you are able to let go, the brighter the light is. Allow yourself to be present, continue to let go of distractions and steadily focus on your breath.

This candlelight provides a glimpse into the eternal light of God, the hidden light, the holy light. This light has burned forever and will burn eternally. This is the light of creation, light present before creation. This is the light of God made manifest. Repeat these phrases silently to yourself and meditate upon them.

Allow your eyes to close and visualize yourself as a Chanukkah or Shabbat candle. Your body is the candle and your soul is the light. Our soul is God's candle in the world. On Chanukkah, the light of our very soul is being kindled. Visualize the light of your soul radiating and shining brightly in this world. Stay with this as long as possible and alternate between keeping your eyes open and closed.

> Our soul is God's candle in the world.

Every night the candles will dance before you in unique ways as they tell the story of life in general, and particularly your life before you. For example, sometimes the *shamash*, the head candle, will go out first, sometimes last. Sometimes a few candles will hug each other and be diminished. I love reflecting on the message of the dance of the candles each night.

If you like, consider doing a writing meditation while the candles burn. Imagine that the candles could talk to you, God is talking to you.

Begin by writing in your journal: *This is what I want to say to you …* And continue writing a stream of consciousness about messages you receive while gazing at the Chanukkah candles. This is just for you.

It is no necessary to share it with anyone. Every night the candles have a precious message for you.

Affirmations and Prayers for Chanukkah

(Best said out loud when the candles are burning.)

This Chanukkah, I stand with my little candles and declare that I believe in miracles. God performed miracles for the Jewish people in the past and God will perform miracles for the Jewish people in the present and in the future.

God is active in this world and in my life. The light of God sustains me and the world.

The Holy One blesses me to do what only I can do in this world to make this world more beautiful and peaceful.

The holy light of Chanukkah removes the psychic debris I have allowed to enter my body mind temple, cleansing me of doubt, anger, fear, and sadness.

I am immensely grateful for the privilege of being embodied and alive at this time.

May I more fully embody the human being God intended me to be.

May I shine the light and love God entrusted within me to shine.

May I see the Divine hand active in my life and know that everything is happening for the good.

May I always be aware of how miraculous and holy life is.

May the world wake up to see more clearly and support what is good and not support what is not good nor true.

May the world reject the rise of anti-Semitism and anti-Zionism and see through all lies promulgated against the Jewish people and Israel.

May the world see what an awesome holy light and blessing the Jewish people are and Israel is to the world.

May I stand up for Israel at all opportunities granted to me to do so and may I support those who are standing up to support Israel at this time.

May God bless the holy soldiers of the IDF and all the beautiful citizens of Israel. May all hostages be released and heal from the trauma they have experienced. May there never be hostages ever again.

May the Jewish people be united and victorious against all the forces that seek their annihilation, the destruction of the State of Israel, and ultimately, the destruction of all Western civilization.

I pray for the soul of America. May America, for its own protection and blessing, return to its democratic spiritual roots that made it such a powerful force in the world.

May America fully support Israel for the Bible has told us that those who support Israel are blessed and those who curse Israel are cursed. May America be worthy of God's love and support.

May the Jewish people defeat once again the tyranny of Persia, now

> called Iran, in our day just as the Jewish people did during the reign of Queen Esther in ancient times.
>
> May there be peace in the world. May everyone come to know the love and awesomeness of the Infinite Light and Love of our Creator.

Practical Recommendations

1. PAY ATTENTION TO YOUR DREAMS THIS MONTH.

When you take time to read spiritual books, meditate or pray before sleep, you will transform your consciousness during your dream life during your nightly sleep. Your sleep will be deeper and your dreams will be a source of inspiration and guidance. Keep a journal by the bed and record your dreams. Recording your dreams sends a message to your subconscious mind that your dream life is important. As you pay attention to your dreams and record them, your dreams will become richer, more vibrant and you will remember more and more detail.

2. PRAY FOR THE HEALING OF THE SICK.

When people are ill, it is often hard for them to dream, to vision, or be free to do what they want. Illness can be a prison. This is the month of liberation. When you pray for someone who is ill, you send the ill person love and surround him or her with light and blessings. See the person as healthy and strong. Remember God is the true healer and God is not confined to the laws of cause and effect. When we are attached to God, we are also not confined to the laws of cause and effect. Miracles are possible whenever we make a true God connection. There is much blessing available this month that may be channeled for healing. When you pray for others, more Divine Light flows through you.

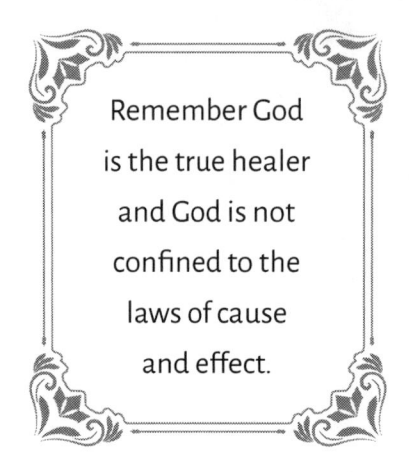

> Remember God is the true healer and God is not confined to the laws of cause and effect.

A few months ago, without going into details, I was hospitalized for a few weeks. During this challenging time, there were even a few moments when I feared for my life. I can tell you, from my personal experience, that every visitor, every call, every prayer uttered on my behalf was very precious and helpful to me.

My recovery was truly miraculous. I came out of the hospital unable to walk on my own. I was fearful that I would be unable to manage living on my own. When a friend who had been staying with me when I returned home from the hospital decided to leave, several people recommended that I look into assisted living facilities. But a miracle happened. In just a few weeks, I was walking on my own, driving and shopping for myself. Soon I even began to exercise. After much prayer, I gratefully returned to writing this book. So remember that it is important to call, visit and pray for sick people. Your kindness makes a difference.

3. PRAISE GOD AND YOURSELF FOR YOUR VICTORIES.

On Chanukkah, we celebrate the victory of the Maccabees. Reflect on your current life, your work, and your relationships, and acknowledge the growth and victories you have had in your life in recent years. What are you able to do now that you could not have seen yourself doing years ago? What challenges have you overcome? Praise God for the growth that has occurred in your life. Celebrate your victories with a friend who loves you. In our lives we are constantly challenged and we wage many battles. We need to pause to savor our victories and celebrate them with others. This helps give us strength and courage for the battles ahead.

A Tale to Live By

There was a king who, by magic, one day decided to construct walls and place obstacles around his palace to make entry into the palace difficult. He even placed wild serpents and lions to guard the palace. Hidden within the palace, the king issued a proclamation that whomever made it through the obstacles and reached the palace would be richly rewarded.

Some people tried, but when they encountered the serpents and scorpions at the first gate, they retreated. They were unwilling to risk their lives. To those with courage capable to overcome the first gate, the king appointed servants to stand behind some of the walls to give riches to those who were able to overcome some of the challenges. A few of these brave souls were sufficiently rewarded and then retreated, not willing to risk what they had accumulated so far.

The king had a son who had been separated from him who had a great desire to see his father again. His desire and yearning were so great that he was unconcerned about the risks and perils of the journey. When he saw the wild animals, he wept, and said: *Father, please be compassionate. I so much want to see you.* His longing to see his father was so great that he had no interest in the rewards offered him along the way as well.

When the king heard the cries of his son and saw his great desire and courage, he removed all the obstacles. In a moment they vanished as if they never existed. The king, the father, was right before him. Everything was suddenly beautiful and peaceful. The experience of being in the presence of the king was so deep that all the former obstacles were now seen as an illusion. The obstacles were not real but served only a test to see who really loved the king.

Similarly, this month, through our yearning to experience God, to be close to God, we can access the faith within to confront all the challenges we face. It is faith that God is with us that opens the gates before us to go forward in ways beyond what we could imagine. We can then see that the walls and obstacles that seemingly separated ourselves from God are illusory. We have a direct glimpse beyond the veil of physicality and limits of our personal ego existence and see that only God is the True Reality. By our attachment to God, we feel ourselves free in a new expanded way. We know that we do not belong solely to this physical world. We are also eternally attached to the transcendent world.

4

Tevet

DECEMBER – JANUARY

ENERGY
Purification and Transformation of Negative Emotions

AREA OF HEALING
Anger

ASTROLOGICAL SIGN
Capricorn

HEBREW LETTER
Ayin ע

HEBREW TRIBE
Dan

DIVINE NAME PERMUTATION
HYHV

HOLIDAY
Last Days of Chanukkah
The Tenth of Tevet

A Personal Story

Tevet is one of the darkest and coldest times of the year and those qualities are often reflected in our personal lives as well. For example, Cindy, a client and student of mine, was mistreated in her marriage. After Cindy's divorce, the abuse from her husband actually escalated. Because of her ex-husband's ability to hire a powerful lawyer and his connections to wealthy and influential people in the legal system, he gained custody of their only daughter. With only a court appointed defense attorney to defend her, Cindy was deprived custody of her daughter, even though she had been the primary care provider for her daughter prior to the divorce.

The judge even ordered Cindy to undergo numerous drug and mental health tests, all proving negative, and permitted her with only a few hours of supervised visitation one day a week with her beloved daughter. To top it off, Cindy had to pay for travel experiences and supervision out of her own pocket. Having not worked in a long time, Cindy had to ask her parents for financial help. Needless to say, the ex-husband paid no alimony to Cindy. Even though Cindy had worked as a licensed physician prior to being a mother and had received many testimonies as to her good character and job performance competence from former colleagues, this was not enough to move the judge to reconsider her plight and pain for being denied custody of her daughter.

Depressed and angry at the injustice of what had happened to her and her daughter, Cindy, as a physician, volunteered to work on the front lines to help patients suffering with COVID. During the time of her employment, Cindy contracted COVID, having been denied proper protective equipment at her place of employment. She even was forced to continue to work, as ill as she was. Cindy survived COVID, yet years later she continues to endure painful health consequences including expensive dental treatment.

After Cindy completed this work on the front lines, she appeared once again before the judge who now lifted the restriction for supervised visitation allowing for unsupervised weekend visitation. The judge told her that he was impressed that Cindy had served the citizens of New York so courageously. The court agreement was updated, but because of COVID in New York City, there was often no legal recourse during the quarantine for enforcement of the new updated contract when her husband violated the agreement and withheld visitation from Cindy. The husband frequently took away the phone from his daughter so Cindy was deprived of daily telephone contact with her daughter as stipulated in the court agreement.

At this point, Cindy began to work with me as a spiritual psychotherapist and as a meditation teacher. In the spirit of the month of Tevet, I advised her that the best recourse to overcome these challenges is to find, extract, and amplify the Divine light hidden within them. To fight the challenges directly with limited physical resources is often unwise. But aligned with the Infinite Power of the universe, that we call God, nothing is impossible.

Guided and supported to connect and align with the Divine, Cindy began to let go of her ego identity as a victim. She understood very quickly when identified as a victim she would not be able to go forward in her life. She would continue to feel helpless and angry. As Cindy let go of her anger as well as the underlying feelings of unworthiness, feeling herself as a loser, she began to open to the experience of accessing God's unconditional love for her. Guided to love and accept herself more fully, she could feel and release a range of her feelings, including her sadness and her anger. She now was able to be more available for the flow of positive blessing in her life.

Through therapy, she began to understand that by speaking badly about the father to her daughter, she had placed the daughter in an uncomfortable situation. Heartbroken by the separation from her daughter for so long, Cindy needed her daughter in ways that caused strain in their relationship. Cindy began to understand that her daughter was not there to comfort her but she as the mother was there to provide love, comfort, and guidance to her daughter. Cindy learned to reclaim and love the inner child within herself so as to be better able to give love to her daughter rather than only need her. Her relationship with her daughter improved.

Unable to defeat her ex-husband in court, I guided Cindy to send healing light to him rather than anger. Miraculously, he softened and began to be more accepting of allowing Cindy time with her daughter.

No longer experiencing herself as a helpless victim, Cindy was empowered. Excited about the opportunities now in front of her, Cindy wrote a proposal for a research project with a nearby university hospital to educate children about COVID. She began to look for employment as a physician. I connected Cindy with two lawyers who filed criminal suits with Cindy's employer for failing to provide her with adequate PPE and denying her treatment for the COVID she experienced. She eventually received more than a hundred thousand dollars for the suffering she had endured.

Energy: Purification and Transformation of Negative Emotions

Tevet, the darkest month of the year, brings challenges that force us to tap into our inner resources and become stronger. The winter solstice occurs during Tevet. Though the days begin to grow longer and the nights shorter in our part of the world, in many places in the world, it is still very cold, with frost or snow covering the trees and the ground, and the sky is gray, making us spend more time inside than outside. These physical conditions reflect the spiritual themes of this month.

Kabbalah divides the calendar months between Jacob and Esau. Tevet is one of the three months that belong to the other side, that of Esau. In Jewish history, Tevet has been a time of great trial to the Jewish people. As the darkest and often the coldest month of the year, Tevet brings challenges that force us to tap into our inner resources and become stronger as individuals and as a people.

Unlike the expansiveness of the month of Kislev, when we contact our dreams and our visions to go forward, in Tevet, we uproot the remaining negative forces within us that keep us contracted and limited. There is a natural tendency to be cautious, prudent, and focused during Tevet. This is an optimal month to establish and strengthen a routine that supports your well being.

According to Kabbalah, the month of Tevet is devoted to the purification of negative emotions—particularly anger and jealousy. Jealousy, the root of so much suffering and anger, personally, communally, and globally, comes from the incorrect perception that someone can have something that is meant for you. This is not possible. People can only have what they have the vessels to receive.

The month of Tevet is a time for spiritual transformation, regardless of what is happening externally around us. During the month of Tevet we process deep feelings and purify our consciousness. What we can witness, acknowledge, and release during this month will provide the openings and opportunities that will be available for us during the remainder of the year.

Tevet is the time when we awaken to the futility of anger. Blaming ourselves and others keeps us tied to the past and does not serve us in going forward in our lives. When we can accept that the past is over, we can move forward. In the month of Tevet, we have an amazing opportunity to heal the anger we often carry inside that limits us. It may not be an easy process but working through it will bring greater well-being, freedom, and joy in our lives. Awareness is our first step. It does not matter whether the anger is directed toward ourselves, or toward other people. Blaming oneself or others is disempowering and disconnects us from the Source of all love.

When we can be with the feelings of anger inside us without becoming reactive and we can embrace the feelings of sadness and sorrow often underlying our anger, we will open to the deeper more authentic and more vulnerable experience of being a human being.

Anger and resentment only remains present within people who have not learned to love and accept themselves as they are. Deep within, many of us feel unlovable. Many of us may feel that we have not ever been loved for who we are. When we were very small children, even infants, we were programmed or conditioned to be good, cute, and polite in order to be loved and have our needs met. The fear of abandonment or annihilation is a real fear for young children and may remain within us even into our sunset years.

As we grow up into adults, we look for love and validation from others often in the very ways we were programmed to do as children. Unless, we have matured, we are bound to be disappointed and pained when we look for love and validation from others who have a similar difficulty as we do in loving themselves and others. How can we realistically expect to be loved by others when they do not love themselves?

Many of us may feel that we have to be different than we are in order to be loved and validated by others. Some of us are driven to be very successful materially in the eyes of the world to feel lovable. Yet regardless of our external success, inwardly we still feel unlovable if this love depends on other people. If we do not feel that we have been loved for who we really are, we must learn how to love ourselves.

As the month of Tevet is devoted to the healing and transformation of anger, most likely there will be numerous opportunities for you to acknowledge and explore the many different forms of anger within yourself and others during this month. It is the energy of the month. When it is cold outside, people get heated up inside. Even knowing about the energy of the month of Tevet, I am still surprised to witness how anger becomes prominent in so many people's lives during this month.

During this month, many things may trigger your anger. Most likely there will be challenges in the world or in personal relationships. Nothing happens by accident. Accept life as gracefully as you can. There is goodness and spiritual opportunity within every challenge you confront. This month you may find that people appear unexpectedly from your past and you now have an opportunity to heal unresolved conflicts and let go of anger you may have been carrying.

Forgiveness is a gift you give to yourself as well as to others. During these meetings, make a conscious effort to let go of the need to be right and attempt to see everything and everyone in the best light. You will know how you are progressing spiritually by overcoming your anger. Becoming angered easily is a sign of the need for purification on your part.

Our sages tell us in *Ethics of the Fathers*, that, *Anger, jealousy, and idolatry drive a person out of this world*. These three things are each connected to the others. If we are honest, we have to admit that jealousy is often the root of anger. Anger is likened to idolatry in Judaism. Idolatry is the belief in forces other than God. God is the True Reality, yet because of our ego's subjectivity, we often distort reality with illusions and become angry when reality does not conform to our needs and desires. It is like worshiping idols: we want life and God to be in our image.

The inward tone of this month forces us to see reality at it is. Though the process may feel painful and disillusioning, we are actually strengthened through it. This kind of introspection puts us in touch the essence of truth, which in itself brings inner joy and goodness. In this month, we can come more easily to experience God as God is, and accept life more as life is. As we humbly let go of our projections of what we want life or God to be, we become more peaceful and empowered. This process of surrender is also one of moral clarity. We more clearly understand who we are as human beings and who God is.

We each must make a decision to work on anger, because being stuck in anger has so many negative consequences. Reb Nachman of Breslov used to say that illness comes from a lack of joy in one's life. Kabbalah tells us that the body receives its spiritual nourishment from the soul through its good thoughts, feelings, and deeds.

Rabbi Hayim Vital, the principal student of Rabbi YItzchak Luria, wrote in his book *Shaare Kedusha, Gates of Holiness,* that, *Through our emotional qualities we connect our souls and Godliness to our physical bodies. Or we disconnect. If we are overcome with anger and jealousy, the soul begins to depart. Due to our negative angry speech and actions, we set up blocks, barriers between the flow of soul energy into the body.* If we want to heal from illness, we have to dissolve and transform the anger we feel inside of ourselves.

When we are angry, we are not free. We are slaves to our emotions, and we are out of control. We lose our center when we blame other people or events for our unhappiness. That is why during this month of Tevet, the Torah portions we read are all about slavery.

As we go through life challenges this month and throughout the year, it is important to remember that nothing is coincidental, things don't just happen, and that the deepest pain often precedes the greatest awakening. Sometimes, the pain that we experience in life is so overwhelming that we are brought to our knees forcing us to surrender and call out to God in a new way and for a new way. Take heart. God does answer the sincere calls of the heart and soul. Our greatest growth comes from our surrender to Divine Will.

> As we go through life challenges this month and throughout the year, it is important to remember that nothing is coincidental, things don't just happen, and that the deepest pain often precedes the greatest awakening.

On the inside level, this month of Tevet is a time of great light for the greatest light is hidden in darkness. We can dispel the darkness of this month when we know with certainty that God is always present, even when hidden in darkness and challenge.

General Guidelines and Goals

The following guidelines and goals enable us to direct our energies in the ways that are optimal for our growth and transformation in accordance with the energy of this month. It is recommended that you read and meditate upon them often in the course of the month. Reflect on their applicability to you and allow them to direct and inspire you this month.

1. EXPLORE THE NATURE OF YOUR ANGER.

In the course of this month, you may find yourself becoming angry. Allow yourself to feel your anger without judgment. Feeling anger is different than expressing it. As you open to the feeling of anger, observe it, accept it and consider the following questions: Does this anger come from the ego or the soul? Does this anger empower me to make positive changes or does it actually weaken me?

Anger is usually derived from arrogance and pride, from the ego mind demanding that we be treated better or honored more. We may become angry when we do not have what we perceive others having. When we are angry we often fail to take responsibility for what we have created or allowed to occur in our lives. We blame others, we blame God, and we even blame ourselves. In so doing, we become paralyzed, unable to change in the ways we want.

Sometimes, people think that if they are angry enough towards themselves, they will change and become better people. It does not work that way in the long run. Anger may enable a person to make changes that are reactive but not integrative nor sustainable. Real change occurs only through love and self-acceptance. We may regret certain behaviors, but be careful not to identify these behaviors with the self—that we must love unconditionally.

If you find that the anger you are experiencing is resulting from the ego mind, its source is the wounding of the inner child. The child within is vulnerable and may be easily hurt. This inner child within your being needs your love and compassion. When we are angry at others for not nurturing us the way we want, it is a sign that we need to nurture ourselves more.

There is however a kind of anger that has a positive side—righteous anger that comes from the soul. This anger enables us to take back our power. The expression of this anger actually liberates, motivates, and inspires us to make positive changes within ourselves and in the world.

For example, Susan was in a relationship with a man who imposed himself on her in ways that were not comfortable for her. She found herself becoming angry at him. Not the kind of person who easily expresses anger, Susan initially stuffed those feelings inside herself. She ate more than normal. She was depressed and often tired. Owning and expressing her feelings of anger in a therapeutic context enabled her to leave this relationship and regain her physical vitality and well-being. She could terminate the relationship with this man, not from anger but from a place of loving herself.

During the month of Tevet, we learn that the sadness and the anger we may feel inside will not decrease by looking for love and validation outside of ourselves. Only by learning to listen and being with the underlying feelings of anger and sadness, can we begin to release them energetically. Remind yourself frequently this month: *it is safe to feel the depth of my feelings.*

In the month of Tevet, we open to the experience of loving and accepting ourselves as we are. That means giving ourselves permission to accept ourselves with whatever we feel with love and compassion.

The challenging nature of life during the month of Tevet provides many opportunities for inward reflection and purification. When you find yourselves becoming angry in your relationships with others or if you are confronted with negative events that naturally make you angry, remember to take conscious deep breaths, relax, and find your inner stillness. It is always there.

Accessing inner stillness brings peace and well being. Being angry keeps you trapped in the past. When we can come to acceptance about what has happened in our lives, we are then free to move forward in our lives.

2. ASSUME RESPONSIBILITY FOR YOUR FEELINGS.

Transformation begins with the recognition that we are largely responsible for what happens in our lives and most definitely responsible for the responses we have as a result. No one can trigger something within anyone that is not already within that person that is calling out for healing and acceptance. It is disempowering to blame others for what has been triggered within you.

When we take responsibility for the ways we have been triggered, we are empowered and able to forgive others. For example, if we are hurt, we need to recognize that we are hurt because we were available to be hurt. If we feel betrayed by others, often it is because we have betrayed ourselves. We also need to recognize that God is behind and within everything taking place in our lives. Nothing happens by chance. Divine Will is ever present, so there is good to extract and learn from everything.

Trying to understand why bad things happen to us is futile. We may ask questions such as why does God make it so hard for me? Why did this person hurt me so much? Why do bad things keep happening to me? Why me?

Do these kinds of questions sound familiar to you? These kinds of questions are basically disempowering. They make us feel helpless. What would be more helpful and honest is to be compassionate with ourselves, allowing ourselves to feel our feelings, and ask how we can grow through the challenges we are now facing.

Our angry or sad feelings result directly from our own thinking and actions. Too often people give up what they want and what they need to placate others and avoid conflict with them. Being validated by others is more important for many than being authentic and honest. Be aware of this tendency within yourself. When this tendency to give oneself up to please others is a primary mode in our relationships with others, resentment mounts within us. As a coping mechanism, we may stuff our angry feelings with food, drugs, watching television, or we shut down and make ourselves numb to keep the peace. The anger eventually explodes, often during the month of Tevet.

Give up a tendency you may have of trying to fit in with others. Too often, doing so requires you to diminish your own light. Remember, no one can give you anything you are unwilling to give to yourself. For example, if we do not love ourselves, we will be unable to receive love from others.

3. PRACTICE HUMILITY.

The great Kabbalist Rabbi Yitzchok Luria in his book, *The Gates of Holiness,* tells us that when we refrain from anger, we engender in ourselves a spirit of humility. The spirit of Shechinah rests upon us only when we are humble. The more we negate our anger and our sense of self-importance, the more Godliness is revealed within us. Humility actually expands our consciousness. Humility is very different from low self-esteem or self deprecation. In our tradition, we are taught that the greatest man, like Moses, was the most humble. Be grateful for opportunities to practice humility.

In Jewish liturgy, the following silent prayer is included to limit the expression of anger. *My God, guard my tongue from evil and my lips from speaking deceitfully. To those who curse me, let my soul be silent. And let my soul be like dust to everyone.* These words imply that you no longer identify with your ego identity. It is the ego within us who seeks approval and validation from others and is hurt when that is not forthcoming. Becoming indifferent to praise and insult is considered a prerequisite for entering higher states of spiritual attainment. Make this your goal. Here in lies your freedom and joy.

Another important and inspiring teaching about humility comes from the Jewish classic, *Duties of the Heart*. A sage was asked how he came to be the head of his contemporaries. He answered that he had never met any person in his whole life that he did not detect a superior quality than himself. *If he was more learned than me, I felt that he must be more God fearing than me. If he was older than me, I would reason that his merits must exceed mine. If he was younger than me, I thought his demerits were less than mine. If he was richer, his wealth would enable to him to serve the Creator and give more charity than I could do. If he was poorer than me, I saw that he had more humility than I did. Thus I always humbled myself before everyone and honored them.* A humble person lifts up everyone he meets and is loved by all. His humility allows him to always learn from everyone and all of life experiences. Only a humble person can truly live in the Divine Flow.

4. SEE THE GOOD IN EVERYONE AND IN EVERYTHING.

We each have the ability to penetrate and transform darkness with the light of our awareness. The Baal Shem Tov says that the power of God's light requires concealment. Tevet begins with the letter *tet*, and is also the first letter of tov which means good. This is a code to tell us that light and goodness can be experienced this month.

In this dark month of Tevet, it is important to see the light within every person and every event. In this way, we remove the concealment of darkness. Whatever we see is reflected back to us. Everything is a mirror. If we see good, the good is reflected back to us. If we see the negative, the

> Make an effort to suspend judgment about yourself and other people.

negative is reflected back. Make an effort to see good in everyone and everything. Make an effort to suspend judgment about yourself and other people. God is the true judge, so stop judging yourself and others.

5. ACCEPT THE PAST AND MOVE FORWARD.

Fully accept the past because it is over. It is done, let it go and let go of wishing life should have been different than it was. Let go of any suffering associated with a past event. Know that everything that happened to you contributed to making who you are today. If you feel you need to make amends or ask for amends from another person you can do so, but do not give another person the responsibility for your state of consciousness. That is your responsibility alone.

If you have difficulty letting go of anger because of something someone said or did that hurt you, it may be helpful to speak to the person directly about what happened and share with this person how you feel. But keep it limited to what is happening in the present and do not bring up dirty laundry from the past.

Do not waste the preciousness of life today by dwelling too much on what happened in the past. Everything was designed to take you forward in life, especially negative events. You are not a victim.

6. DO NOT JUDGE OTHER PEOPLE.

We are repeatedly told not to judge other people. How we judge other people will be how we will be judged. This point is illustrated in a saying from *Ethics of the Fathers*. Akiva Ben Mahalel wrote, *Consider three things and you will not come into the grip of sin. Know from where you came, to where you are going, and before whom you will give justification and reckoning.*

The Hebrew words for justification and reckoning are *din v' chesbbon*, which translates as judgment and accounting. One would expect that it would say that first one makes an accounting then one is judged. It is taught that when a person dies he will be requested to make a judgment about someone else who has a similar situation to his own. He thinks it is about someone else but it is really about himself. How he judges the person will be how he is judged. For one's own self interest, it is best to get into the habit of demonstrating compassion.

Astrological Sign: Capricorn

The sign of Capricorn is named for the goat constellation. Like the goat climbing the mountain, according to astrology, this is the month to be focused and methodical. Capricorn is an earth sign, indicating that the physical world is the arena of focus and challenge. Capricorns are said to be focused on their career and have a desire to amass great material wealth.

In ancient times the sins of the Jewish people were symbolically placed on the goat. Lev:16:20-22. The Talmud says that the goat is brazen, always wanting to be first. This trait can be positive if it is directed toward holiness or negative if directed toward impurity.

While Jupiter, the planet that ruled the previous month of Sagittarius, is about expansion, largeness of vision, optimism and faith, Saturn, the ruler of Capricorn, is about restriction, establishing boundaries, discipline and pragmatism. Saturn is a taskmaster, also a teacher, who forces us to do our greatest learning through challenges.

Saturn also rules over Saturday, the Sabbath. The Sabbath is a time of restriction. When restrictions of the Sabbath are embraced as a spiritual practice, this time can be a time of transcendence and contemplation. The inward and restrictive focus of Saturday and the entire month of Tevet supports us to go more deeply inside and transcend external limitations.

In Roman mythology, Saturn was the god of agriculture, yet Capricorn, the sign it rules over, is in the winter when the growing season is over. Saturn is depicted as holding a sickle used for cutting grain and corn. He represents the physical work that we must do on our own, the organization, all the hard efforts, all the toiling that does not show immediate fruits.

Those born in Capricorn are generally thought to be hard workers, serious and disciplined yet could have a tendency for loneliness, depression, and isolation according to astrological teachings. But remember that no one is totally defined or limited by the astrological teachings or readings.

The ancient Greeks called Saturn Kronos. Kronos was a father figure who, unlike Jupiter, did not encourage his children to grow. His jealousy of his children kept them confined and restricted. Saturn is known as Father Time or the Grim Reaper, reflecting the seriousness and darkness of this month.

Hebrew Letter: Ayin

The name of the letter *ayin* means eye. *Ayin* is associated with perception, insight, discernment, and understanding. When we say *we see*, we mean that we understand. According to *Ethics of the Fathers*, a good eye is one of the greatest human achievements. The ability to see the good in every person and in everything is a worthy goal for this month and one that offers protection. When we can see God's hand, or God's signature, in all of creation, we are more peaceful. The letter *ayin* seeks to teach us to see God in everyone and everything. Meditate on the letter *ayin* this month.

In the Mishnah it is written: *Whoever has the following attributes is a disciple of Abraham. The disciples of Abraham have a good eye, a humble soul, and humble spirit.* A good eye means that one is not jealous of others and is as considerate of a friend's honor as one's own. According to Rambam, a good eye means one is satisfied with what one has and does not pursue excesses. The *evil eye* is the opposite of the *good eye*. The evil eye is jealous, haughty and demanding.

> According to Rambam, a good eye means one is satisfied with what one has and does not pursue excesses.

Cultivate a good eye this month. Before we judge ourselves and others we must be aware that our eyes may deceive us and what we see may not be true. People may become jealous of others because they only see externalities. They mistakenly think that if they had the material possessions or external achievements of another, they would be happier than they are. This is most likely not true.

When we judge others in a negative light, we see only the *klippah*, the negative shell of a person or event, and not the underlying Godliness. We are sometimes projecting our own negative qualities onto a person whom we judge harshly. Projection is an ego defense mechanism we use to protect ourselves from the experience of our own vulnerability. Even when projection is not involved, when others have qualities of their own that we are rightly critical of, we can still take a cue that the reason those qualities bother us so much may be that they are mirroring something within ourselves needing healing.

The numerical value of ayin is seventy, an important number. The Torah tells us that there are seventy nations that are the root of all the nations in the world. Seventy elders received the Divine Revelation, described in Exodus 24:9. This is the only recorded mystical experience in the Bible. Also, in Numbers 11:16, God asks for seventy elders to receive the Holy Spirit to ease the burden of Moses because the people were complaining and Moses felt that the burden of leadership was too great for him. There are seventy faces to the Torah. Seventy was the number of Jews who originally entered Egypt escaping the famine in Canaan. There are seventy names of God. There are seventy holy days in the year, including Shabbat and festivals.

Hebrew Tribe: Dan

When Rachel was unable to become pregnant and her sister, Leah, had already borne Jacob several sons, Rachel became jealous and angry and decided to give her handmaid, Bilhah, to Jacob, as was the custom at that time. Through her handmaid, Rachel would bear a child. When Bilhah gave birth to a son, Rachel named him Dan, and said: *God has judged me and has also heard my prayer. He has given me a son.* Gen.30:6. The name Dan has the same letters as the Hebrew word *din*, which means judgment. From this name, we see the attribute of judgment that is so prevalent this month.

Perhaps because of the negative energy underlying Dan's birth and the loss of Rachel, the tribe of Dan was most vulnerable to idolatry, sorcery, and forbidden sexual relations. When the Jewish people traveled in the desert, the tribe of Dan marched in the rear, on the periphery of the clouds of glory that protected the Jewish people. They were known to find and return the lost objects left before them, which is reflected in the blessing that Jacob gave to Dan. On his deathbed, Jacob blesses him. *Dan will be a serpent on the highway, a rattlesnake on the path, that bites the hoof of the horse and the rider falls backwards.* Gen. 49:17. A horse in Kabbalah represents licentiousness. Though the snake is usually associated with the evil inclination, Dan is the holy snake that is viewed to weaken the power of the evil inclination.

The tribe of Dan produced the famous Samson, who single-handedly fought against the Philistines. Samson was considered a forerunner of the Messiah. Samson took a Nazirite vow, which meant that he did not cut his hair or drink wine. Samson's strength was compromised, however, by his intense and overwhelming attraction and marriage to Delilah, a Philistine woman who was bent on undermining him. His eyes deceived him. He told her his secrets and she betrayed him.

According to the Kabbalist, Rabbenu Bachaya, the nation representing this month is the Philistines. The Philistines are said to be associated with the sexual desire that seeks to wound the holiness of Israel. This is a month of tests, particularly in the sexual arena. The eyes make one particularly vulnerable this month, and one must make an effort to guard against this tendency.

The enemies of the Jewish people will do their best to seduce, exploit, and compromise the sexual purity of Jewish people because they know that infidelity and promiscuity weaken the Jewish people. Remember how Balak, the King of Moab, hired Bilaam to curse the Jewish people? Though Balak tried to curse the Jewish people three times, he was unable to do so because the Jewish people maintained sexual purity. Ultimately, Bilaam even gave the blessing to Israel that is used in Jewish prayer books to this day. *How goodly are your tents, Jacob, your dwelling places O Israel*. Sexual purity maintains the holiness of the Jewish people and that of the individual. Improper sexual relationships weaken the Jewish people, and the individual. Even today, Iran, the chief sponsor of terrorism against Israel, hires beautiful prostitutes who attempt to seduce Israeli soldiers on social media platforms.

The tribe of Dan occupied the north of Israel. According to the ancient Kabbalistic text, *Sefer Yetzirah*, the energy of *gevurah* emanates from the north. Gevurah is the energy of judgment, strength, and discipline. The north was also the place of material wealth, enabling the tribe to amass much gold. There is a rabbinic teaching that anyone who wants wealth should face north. Many people place their beds facing north for this reason.

Divine Name Permutation: HYHV

The Divine Name permutation for this month is a little more challenging to understand. The reversal of the first two letters, *yud hay* (YH) to *hay yud*, (HY) is indicative of judgment and tests, which is reflected in the energy of this month.

The *hay* in the worlds of Atzilut, the first position, and in Yetzirah, the third position, indicates that there is expansiveness and blessing in these worlds. The *hay* in the first position indicates that there is a great influx of Divine Light in the higher worlds during this month. The letter *yud* (Y) in the world of Beriyah indicates that one should be focused mentally. The *hay* (H) in the world of Yetzirah indicates that the focus is on the heart opening this month. The *vav* (V) in the final position, the world of Assiyah, corresponds to the physical world. We may not see expansiveness immediately this month but we set the stage for it in the future by what we do this month.

Torah Portions

It is in the Torah portions for this month that Joseph reveals his true identity to his brothers. Gen. 45:1-46. The brothers are beginning to understand that all the challenging events they underwent in Egypt were Divine punishment for selling Joseph into slavery. They are now full of regret and pleading for mercy on behalf of their father who continues to suffer over the loss of his son Joseph. When Yehudah, Judah, offers himself in place of his brother, Benjamin, it is a sign to Joseph that the brothers have done teshuvah, repentance, for selling him into slavery so long ago. When Joseph hears this conversation, he can no long bear concealing his identity and reveals his true identity to his brothers. Forgiving his brothers, Joseph tells them not to feel bad about selling him into slavery. He says, *God sent me ahead of you to insure that you survive in the land. It is not you, but God.* Gen.45:7-8.

Joseph is a powerful model for the transformation of anger this month. When we really understand that everything that happens in life is according to the Divine Plan, our anger is diminished and replaced with compassion and forgiveness. God is talking directly to us through everything in our lives so there is goodness to be extracted from everything unfolding in our lives.

The Torah portions for this month include the descent of the Jewish people into Egypt and Jacob's blessings to his sons in Gen: 46-49. Even though the descent into Egypt was part of the prophecy received by Abraham, Jacob is frightened to leave Israel. When he receives a vision that God will be with him, he is reassured. This is itself an important teaching, reminding us that God is with us in the midst of whatever is happening in our lives. Before his death, Jacob blesses his sons, as well as the children of Joseph, whose descendants became tribes in their own right. Jacob states what he sees and feels about each tribe, even if it is sometimes critical.

In this month we open to a new book of Torah that in Hebrew is called *Shemot*, which means, Names. Why is this book called the Book of Names? A name is considered a definition of a person's potential. This book is a journey towards uncovering and embodying the potential of the Jewish people and of ourselves. In English, this book is called Exodus because it traces the Jewish people's departure from Egypt. According to Jewish teaching, Egypt in Hebrew means a place of constraints, limitation, and impurity.

While Joseph lived, the Jewish people enjoyed a special status in Egypt, prosperous in wealth and multiplying greatly in numbers. But with the book of Exodus, after the death of Joseph, the Jewish people are now seen as a threat. Over time, a new Pharaoh emerges who fears their power and seeks to weaken the Jewish people. The plight of the Jews becomes dismal, they become enslaved and persecuted.

As we read these Torah portions this month, the energy of the month invites us to revisit what it means to be in our personal Egypt, what it means to be in exile from fulfilling our soul potential and to feel un-free. The concept of being in exile has not only national ramifications, but existential overtones as well.

It is painful to live in a tyrannical regime that does not honor and respect personal rights and liberty. It is however even more painful to feel cut off from your own soul. When people are aligned with their Divine soul, they can feel peaceful regardless of what is taking place externally. When people are not consciously in touch with their Divine connection, they suffer. They are confused, unhappy, and frightened. All emotional problems—disorders, anxiety, and depression—come from this sense of separation within ourselves to our Creator.

> Revisit what it means to be in our personal Egypt, what it means to be in exile from fulfilling our soul potential and to feel un-free.

This kind of exile is self-imposed by one's own ego. People exile themselves from their soul potential and God when they see only the worst in themselves, the worst in others, and the worst in life. When they cannot access their own intrinsic goodness, they become trapped in their own negativity. This is truly a most harsh exile. Such people try to escape the inner pain they feel by looking outside for the feeling of aliveness, for reassurance, for power, and for identity. Whatever comfort we may experience is temporary when we are comforted only by what is outside of ourselves.

People continue to reinforce their experience of personal exile by not believing in Divine Providence. When people believe only in what they can see, what they can understand or control, they do not believe that God is running the world or that they can call out to God in times of crisis. This is a very dark form of exile plaguing many people today. As my teacher, Reb Shlomo Carlebach of blessed memory, would say, we have to admit that we are all still a little bit in Egypt but we must have hope because there is a God who is continually pouring love and compassion to take us out of our personal and collective places of limitation and restriction. When we really wake up to our intrinsic Divine connection, we live in the Divine Flow and are freed of suffering.

There are many great teachings about how to meet challenges that are imparted in the Torah portions of this month. The redemption of the Jewish people from Egypt reflects our own redemption from our personal exiles. The birth of Moses is read in the Torah portion read this month. In Exodus 2, Moses is saved from the water where all Jewish male infants were placed to drown. Ironically Moses is rescued and even raised by Batya, the adopted daughter of the Pharaoh, in the very house of Pharaoh. The birth of Moses is an important reminder that during times of the greatest darkness, there is light and goodness. There will be redemption.

The strength of the Jewish people in Egypt came when they saw that God was talking to them through the adversity they faced. Their suffering was not random nor without meaning. They called out to God and God heard their cry. All the hardships, all the challenges were then viewed as opportunities for purification and growth. This is also true on a personal level as well. This perspective is empowering.

In the following Torah portions of this month, we see the development of Moses as a leader and prophet in Exodus 3-5. Though initially reluctant, Moses assumes leadership of the Jewish people. Moses meets with Pharaoh and many plagues take place where God's power is demonstrated, and yet Pharaoh's heart was continually hardened. Reality is shattering before their eyes and the Jewish people are forced to remain in slavery. With each plague there is a deeper revelation of Godliness. From the Torah portions of this month, we see that this month is more about purification and cleansing, rather than moving forward.

Holiday: Last Days of Chanukkah

Much has been said about Chanukkah in the previous chapter on Kislev. Chanukkah is the one holiday that occupies two months, Kislev and Tevet.

The last night of Chanukkah is the beginning of the month of Tevet. Since Chanukkah is about revealing light in the midst of darkness, it radiates its light into the month of Tevet, the darkest month. The light of Chanukkah brings clarity, hope and strength into the month of Tevet enabling us to more easily release the hold that anger and jealousy has had in our lives.

On the first days of Tevet and the last days of Chanukkah, when we are still lighting Chanukkah lights, we have a unique and precious opportunity to consciously shine the Chanukkah light, the light of unconditional love, the light of eternal truth, into those places within us and the world that call out for healing, light and love.

These days also offer us the most healing and transformational blessing of teshuva that began in Tishrei. Teshuva means to return, to return to who we really are, to the experience of our most glorious loving beautiful souls we can experience within our own bodies. On these precious last days, take time to gaze and be with the light of the Chanukkah candles to more fully experience the Infinite light of your own soul. When you have experienced this love and light within yourself you will want to share this light with your families,

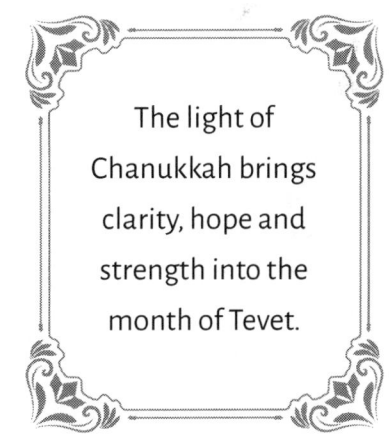

> The light of Chanukkah brings clarity, hope and strength into the month of Tevet.

friends, communities, and to all those who so need to experience the light of their own souls.

Holiday: The Tenth of Tevet

HISTORY: The Tenth of Tevet commemorates the breeching of the walls of Jerusalem by the Babylonian King Nebuchadnezzar that resulted in the exile of Jews from Jerusalem in the month of Av. Jer. 52. Beginning on the day the Jewish people entered the Land of Israel under the leadership of Yehousha, Joshua, the Jewish people inhabited the Land for over 850 years. When the Jews were exiled from the land and their Holy Temple destroyed, they understood that this was not a random act. They took responsibility for what happened. The prophets of Israel had told them that they would be exiled if they did not follow the commandments of God that had been given to them earlier. They were particularly admonished for the practice of idolatry. In Leviticus 18:24, they were warned, *and you shall observe all my statues and all my judgments and you shall do them ... so that the land may not spit you out, wherein I bring you to dwell in it.*

OBSERVANCE: The Tenth of Tevet is observed as a fast day, although it does not have the same mandate or restrictions as the fasts of Yom Kippur or Tisha B'Av. One can wash, wear leather shoes, and eat until daybreak. Those who do not fast easily or are weak or ill need not fast on this day. People are, however, asked to refrain from eating in public or over-indulging; only moderate portions of healthy food are recommended. Fasting is recommended for a community undergoing a hardship, such as a drought, or for individuals undergoing personal trials. Fasting is viewed as a powerful spiritual practice if done with the proper intention.

From this day, we learn that suffering takes place when we are not in alignment with Divine Will. By fasting and introspection, we seek to bring ourselves in greater alignment with the Divine flow of blessing.

Meditation

In accordance with the energy of the month, the following meditation is offered to transmute the negative feelings stemming from hurt, anger, or regret that may still be stuck within you.

> Take a few minutes to center yourself by taking long slow conscious breaths. Focus on letting go and deepening on the exhalation. It is safe to let go and go deep inside. When you feel centered and present take a few moments to scan the physical body and take note of any sensations, tensions, discomfort, or numbness in the body. Imagine that you can direct the breath to those places. Continue to take slow deep breaths and breathe into any sensations or discomfort. Continue to relax with the exhalation. Any painful sensations you may be experiencing will dissipate.
>
> Now begin gently to open to the feelings that are buried within the tensions in the body. The body speaks to us in the form of sensations or discomfort. Give yourself permission to feel and be with any feelings that are present for you without judgment but with love and compassion. Too often, people try to distract themselves or admonish themselves for the feelings they have. All feelings are valid and acceptable so it is safe to relax and accept whatever feelings are present for you.
>
> Stay with the breath, and continue to take slow deep breaths. It is good to feel your feelings. It is safe to feel your feelings. Embrace and accept your feelings with love and compassion. Stay with the feelings that are present for you as fully as you can. When we feel, embrace, accept our feelings, the hold that they have had on us dissolves.
>
> Often anger and sadness we experience as adults have their source

> in the wounding we experienced as young children. Access the inner child who continues to reside within you. See yourself as a small child around five years of age. What does this inner child really need to feel safe and happy? Give yourself a hug, and apologize to this inner child for not taking better care of her or him. Affirm your love and commitment to be there for this inner child. What does this inner child need from you now? What can you do for this inner child today or even right now as you read these words?
>
> Take a few breaths to internalize what you released and opened to during this time of meditation. If you like, conclude this meditation with a writing meditation. On a piece of paper, write the following and allow the words to flow: *Now is a time in my life when …* Keep writing a stream of consciousness. This is for you. You do not have to share this with anyone unless you choose to do so. You may even be surprised if you allow yourself to write stream of consciousness without too much thought.

Practical Recommendations

1. BE MINDFUL OF YOUR SPEECH.

In the midst of anger, people say things they regret, words that can never be taken back. When you are angry, always make an effort to calm yourself and not speak or act impulsively. Speaking loudly will only escalate the situation. Before you speak, consider whether your words will contribute to the other person's growth and healing. It is not that you should repress your thoughts and feelings; rather, you should express them in a way that loves, honors, and is of service to others as well as yourself.

Train yourself to take long deep breaths and visualize the release of tension through the breath. Think before your speak. Make a habit of speaking in a soft, gentle voice so even when you are angry you will not raise your voice too much. When you do speak, as much as possible, make *I* statements such as, *I feel this when you do this*, rather than accusatory *you* statements such as, *You did that ...* or, *Why do you always do that?*

Be careful to not drag old dirty laundry into the conversation about something that has hurt you currently. Be specific about a particular current event that has angered or hurt you. This allows a person to better respond to your hurt or anger without being overwhelmed or accused of things way in the past.

2. DILUTE YOUR ANGER.

When you are angry, it may be helpful for you to vent your anger, but not directly to the person you are angry with. Be mindful to not be reactive. Give yourself time to process and release anger before talking. Processing your anger by talking to a supportive friend or therapist may be helpful. Or you can write an imaginary letter to the person you are angry with and read it aloud only to yourself many times.

Rabbi Kalonymous Kalman Shapiro of Piaseczno, known as Rebbe of the Warsaw Ghetto, suggested that a person write such a letter and read it out loud frequently for an entire month. As you do this, take time to breathe and be with your feelings. Get in touch with the needs of the wounded child within you. Be compassionate with yourself. When the hurt wounded part of yourself feels heard, you will become calm. When you are calm, you can more easily speak to a person about how you were hurt by something they said or did if you choose to do so. By then, you will most likely no longer need anything from that person. You may choose to share it with the other person as a way to help him to be a better more compassionate and sensitive person in the future.

3. PROTECT YOURSELF FROM THE ANGER OF OTHERS.

When you are confronted with the rage of another, you may need to place yourself in a protective bumble of white light or imagine yourself behind the shield of Abraham, the first patriarch, who defended all people as mentioned in the first blessing of the Silent Amidah prayer in the standardized Jewish prayer book.

In most cases, you are not responsible for the anger directed towards you. This anger is often not even really about what is happening in the present. Usually, it is an expression of early wounding and is indicative of an unresolved problem within the person who is angry. The most helpful quality to call forth is compassion.

When a person is angry or raging, it is not hard to see the two-year-old child within him or her who felt ignored, and learned to make a lot of noise to be noticed. As two year olds need limits for their own protection, an angry or even raging person also needs to have a limited space in which to ventilate his or her feelings but under no circumstances should physical or emotional abuse be tolerated. If a person is screaming at you with uncontrollable anger, it may be necessary to excuse yourself from this scene. You do not have to subject yourself to this experience if it is challenging for you to do. You can tell the person you can listen to them if they do not yell at you. Once the rage has been released, the person may be spoken to calmly and firmly and instructed in more effective ways of communication. I always instruct my clients to make I statements and to tell others to make I statements rather than accusatory you statements.

To acquire a feeling of detachment and objectivity in a heated situation, imagine yourself on a mountain top looking down. How does this change your perspective? To avoid being pulled in by the anger and becoming angry yourself, raise or heighten your own vibration by doing something nurturing or enjoyable. When we are happy in ourselves, we are less vulnerable to becoming angry. Though angry individuals may be presenting a very unattractive side of themselves to you, look to see the good in them and remind them that the good person you see is who they really are.

> Gratitude is the key to joy, the antidote to anger.

4. BE HAPPY FOR WHAT YOU HAVE.

Gratitude is the key to joy, the antidote to anger. Make a list of what you are grateful for in your life. Be sure to include even your own breath. When we are grateful, our anger is reduced. Look at your list often. Take moments each day to acknowledge the gift of life and all the blessings you often take for granted.

5. NURTURE YOURSELF.

When we get angry, it is a sign that we need to nurture ourselves. We are often angry at another for not giving us what we can give ourselves. During this month particularly it is important to give yourself time and energy. I often instruct clients to literally give themselves a hug, speak sweetly to themselves, and open to the experience of being embraced and accepted fully. You can say, *I love you*, silently and even out loud.

A Tale to Live By

This popular story attributed to Rabbi Nachman provides an important teaching for this month. A man named Moshe from the city of Chernovitz had a recurrent dream that a treasure chest of riches was buried near the steps to a particular bridge in St. Petersburg. He initially dismissed the dream, however, when the dream persisted for more than a week, he decided to journey there. As he was not a rich man, the journey posed a great hardship for him. Still he went.

When he finally arrived in St. Petersburg, he soon saw the very bridge that was in his dream. Next to the steps to the bridge stood a policeman. At that time, Jews were not allowed in St. Petersburg without a special business permit. Moshe waited for the officer to leave. The officer, noticing him loitering in the area, asked him why he was in St. Petersburg. Moshe then told him about his dream, how he saw this very bridge, and that a treasure was buried under it. He even offered to share the treasure with him. The officer laughed and laughed, telling him that he was a fool to follow crazy dreams. *Do you know*, he told the Jew, *I also have a dream that keeps coming back to me every night. In my dream there is a Jew named Moshe from the city of Chernowitz, and under his stove, there is buried a treasure.* The officer smirked. *You do not see me running there.* Moshe was startled, and then quickly excused himself, and sped home. He found the buried treasure he was seeking under his own stove.

Everything that has happened to us has contributed to where we are in the present. Every experience served its purpose. Many of us traveled to many places and had adventures only to finally discover that everything we were seeking could be found within us, right where we are. If we are angry about previous life events, we are denying the role that God has played in bringing us forward to grow and we block the flow of blessing in our lives. Whatever we are seeking, we can find within ourselves.

5

Shevat

JANUARY – FEBRUARY

ENERGY
Inner Renewal

AREA OF HEALING
Eating

HEBREW LETTER
Tzaddi צ

HEBREW TRIBE
Asher

DIVINE NAME PERMUTATION
HYVH

HOLIDAY
Tu B'Shevat

A Personal Story

In the month of Shevat, we plant the seeds to open to a new beginning. Sometimes in Shevat, we feel that we are at the end and there is no choice but to let go. Once we let go, we become aware of something new opening up within us. What we open to during this month of Shevat will have long lasting consequences for many years to come. Here is a personal Shevat story.

It may have been in the month of Shevat when I came out of the closet as a Jew in college and began to wear a Jewish star. When I did, I was not connected to any synagogue. I was not learning Torah. I knew lots of Jews but I did not know anyone who affiliated as a Jew or wore a Jewish star. Choosing to visibly wear a Jewish star when I did was actually a demonstration of considerable courage and faith on my part. Yet, at the time, I also felt that I had no choice but to wear my Jewish star so the world could see me as a Jew.

The New York state universities I attended in the late 1960s and early 1970s for undergraduate and graduate school were basically government left-wing indoctrination institutions. They were not quite as tyrannical and left-leaning as schools are today; nevertheless, they were definitely progressive. We had our share of rallies against the Vietnam War, along with tear gas bombings, and wild parties by most standards even today.

When I first arrived in college, I remember feeling like a farm girl from Idaho next to the sophisticated Jews from New York City I met in my first days. I grew up very sheltered, attending a high school with only sixty people in my grade, and I was primarily involved in Jewish extra-curriculum activities. My father would not allow me to stay out past 10:00 p.m. when I did have a rare date.

Now here I was in college living on my own. My college roommate for my freshman year was a beautiful woman from the Five Towns in New

York with a bleached-blonde Cleopatra hair style who sported mini-skirts, pearls, and other beautiful jewelry. She looked more like a model or a movie star than a college freshman. To me, she seemed like a wise sage who clearly knew more about life than I surely did. Unfortunately, she only spent three or four nights in the room with me. Occasionally she returned to the room for a change of clothing. During her absences, I never knew where she was. She never once confided in me. By January, she dropped out of college to travel with a graduate student to South America as he completed his doctorate work in archeology. I basically had a private room.

In those first months of college, my values were challenged. I was for the first time confronted with promiscuity, drugs, nude-ins, tear gas, and a variety of alternative lifestyles, and ideologies. I so much wanted to belong and participate in the spiritual awakening taking place on the college campus. Initially I was attracted to the universality, expansiveness, and spirit of egalitarianism of left wing ideology being promulgated in and out of classes. I was excited, even thrilled, to meet and dialogue with the kinds of people I never would have met in my small semi-private high school. I was amazed that I even had conversations with charismatic white and black leaders of communist, socialist, anti-American revolutionary movements right in the college cafeteria. When these radical socialists began to denounce Israel, I knew that I could no longer associate with them. That was a red line then and now that I will never cross.

Why did I care so much about Israel? I did not really know. I never had been to Israel yet caring about Israel was a part of who I really was as a person. Though I was not brought up religious, I always had a strong identity as a Jew, a pride and deep love for Israel even as a child. In high school, I hoped to move to Israel after college. When confronted with a university culture that was promoting anti-Israel ideas and values so opposite of how I was brought up, I became confused about who I really was.

Was I simply a product of my parental, societal, or peer values, or did I have a more transcendental, more essential inner self. Who was I really? Why was I born? What was my purpose? Why was this world created? What existed before creation? Who and what was God? Who created God? I was haunted by deep existential questions. My life itself felt like an existential question. Even though I was very popular in my first year of college—I had a date every night—I was lonely and troubled. Taking courses in sociology and philosophy only added to my anxiety and discomfort. Therapy offered me no relief. In my despair and loneliness, I called out to God and began to meditate on my own. I wrote poetry to God in a journal I still have to this very day.

In the midst of my existential despair, I sought out the campus Hillel rabbi to talk to about God. This rabbi listened to me and then told me to not think so much and take up swimming. He, however, told me to read Abraham Heschel's book, *Between Man and God*. This book was a life saver for me. Rabbi Heschel addressed the very existential questions that had troubled me so deeply. I even became ecstatic reading and meditating on his teachings on radical amazement. This book was the soul tonic I desperately needed. I no longer felt so alone. Over the years when in college and graduate school, I tried to go to a few synagogues hoping to find the kind of spiritual transcendental experiences Heschel wrote about and to also find people I could talk to about God and Heschel's ideas. I was disappointed and pained each time I went to synagogue by the emptiness and the lack of joy I experienced there. The spiritual conversations I so yearned for were not to be found there. My loneliness seemed only magnified in the synagogue.

One day, I listened to a folk song by Buffy St. Marie in which she implied in the song that it was cowardice to not tell the world that God is your healer. It was then I was called to wear my Jewish star. I knew that I had to let the world know that I believed in God as a Jew. I clearly knew and experienced directly on my own by then that it was only God who was sustaining and supporting me. It would be an act of cowardice and be inauthentic of me to pretend otherwise.

The Jewish star was my signal to God, to myself, and to others that I believed and trusted in God. No matter what has happened to me, and I have experienced many extraordinary challenges and great hardships, the Jewish star has always reminded me that God was and is my strength and my refuge. Little did I know when I first chose to wear a Jewish star in college that years later, my life would be devoted to learning, teaching Torah, and living a Jewish lifestyle.

Throughout the years, some days when I wore the star, it was not easy. It felt like the yellow star forced to be worn by Jews in Nazi-occupied countries before and during World War Two. It felt even dangerous to expose it during job interviews, at some social gatherings, and even walking in certain neighborhoods in New York City where I visited as a social worker. I would hide it under my blouse, but I nevertheless continued to wear it. I still wear it today. Now I wear it openly for everyone to see at all times.

Energy: Inner Renewal

It may still be the heart of winter in many places but Shevat marks a hidden and mystical time of new beginnings and rebirth. This month is a time of new inspiration and creativity. It is time when it is easier to come close to God. The first part of the month may still feel dark and harsh, but that all changes according to Kabbalistic teachings after the fifteenth of the month.

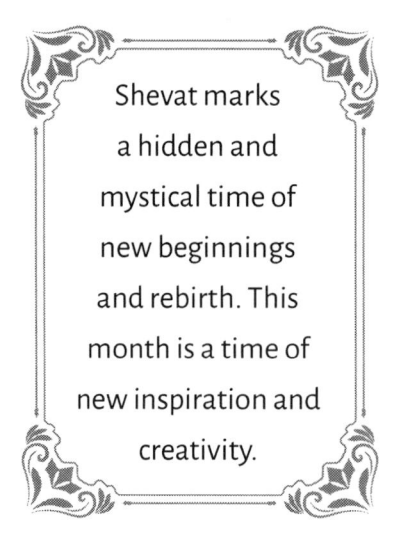

> Shevat marks a hidden and mystical time of new beginnings and rebirth. This month is a time of new inspiration and creativity.

The renewal occurring in the month of Shevat may not be manifest on the physical plane but the process has begun and is occurring on the inner and hidden planes. This month is pregnant with new possibilities. We may have lived through a cold and challenging winter this year in our lives, but spring is coming. As a metaphor, winter represents the time when it is not always easy to see the fruit of one's labor; indeed, in our lives there may have even been long periods of time when it felt like winter. But be patient and never lose hope. Shevat is here!

In the previous month of Tevet, we overcame many of the negative forces that had been limiting and keeping us from realizing our vision and dreams. Even though the purpose of the challenges we faced may not have been clear to us, the work we have done to meet and overcome them has not been in vain. The seeds of our expanded potential have been planted deeper within us this month and we have been strengthened.

Know that now, in Shevat, the seed is sprouting. Something new is going to come forth within you. A little more patience is needed. Believe that you will bear new fruit and you will. We will bring forth our visions into reality. Open to a new beginning. Say yes to newness of life once again and open to the new life force energy stirring within you this month. The month of Shevat is an optimal time for conceiving new projects, planting new seeds, and opening to a new direction in life. Like the sap of the trees, our creative juices begin flowing this month, so we too will bear new fruit and flowers in the spring.

The energy of this month is best represented by the holiday of Tu B'Shevat, which is the fifteenth day of Shevat, the time of the full moon. Though not widely known or celebrated, like the renewal energy of this month that is not yet manifest, Tu B'Shevat, the New Year for the Trees, is considered one of the most spiritual and joyous days of the year according to Kabbalistic teachings. At this point, the trees are mostly still barren, yet we are told that the sap has begun to flow, and we trust in the cycle of life to produce new leaves, fruits, and flowers in the spring.

The Torah tells us that the human being is likened to a tree, so we can think of this day as another Rosh Hashanah for us, but a more spiritual and hidden one than the one we celebrated in September. Tu B'Shevat is a celebration and opening to the infinite potential within the human being.

By honoring trees this month, we are reminded of the theme of the cycles of life. Many trees go from barren in the winter to full and vibrant in the spring and summer, and then to leafless again in the fall. Similar changes occur within the individual and within the Jewish people as a whole. There are times in our personal lives and in the life of the Jewish people when we are shining and expressing ourselves fully, when our branches are full; and there are times when we are emptying ourselves, we are humbled and appear leafless. Knowing that there is a cycle to life enables us to flow with and accept these changes gracefully.

In the creative process there are also cycles. Inspiration for a new creation often occurs after a period of emptying. Creation usually begins first in the spiritual plane, then to the mind, to the heart before it manifests on the physical plane. For example, an author empties her mind and is inspired and conceives of a new book. As the vision becomes clear, the strategy for translating this vision into reality becomes apparent, but there is not yet a book. This is what Shevat is about. The internal process begins, but it is not yet visible on the physical plane.

This month the area of healing is eating. Eating is also a mysterious inner process of renewal. How we eat, digest, and gain energy to animate, sustain, and heal our bodies and souls is still a great mystery. We do not eat just physical food, we ingest all kinds of *food*. What we do for recreation, the movies and television we watch, the books we read, the music we listen to, the friends and acquaintances we associate with, the work we do—everything we take into ourselves is food and has the ability to strengthen or weaken us. This month asks us to become more conscious of what we take within us. Awareness is the first step for change.

The redemptive energy of this month has shown itself historically. Zerach, the daughter of Asher, the ancestor of the tribe representing this month, informed Jacob that his son Joseph was alive on Rosh Chodesh Shevat, the first day of the month of Shevat. What a joy that must have been for him. Not only had he suffered the loss of his favored son, but because of his depression, he no longer experienced the presence of the Shechinah. This gift was restored to him when he found out that Joseph was alive. This month is associated with the Oral Torah, which is the fruit, the blossoming, of the written Torah. Moses began to explain the Torah he had received in his own words on the first day of Shevat as well.

The energy of Shevat connects to the energy of Nissan (March-April), a time of newness and freedom. Not only do we read the Torah portions relating to the Exodus in Shevat, both Tu B'Shevat and Passover, in Nissan, have a Seder with four cups of wine. Passover is the most outwardly celebrated of Jewish holidays and Tu B'Shevat is the least known. As wonderful and transformational as Passover is, Tu B'Shevat is a more hidden celebration of the potential within life. Because the potential within us is infinite, the celebration of Tu B' Shevat is very awesome and particularly wonderful. Interestingly enough, there are forty-five days from Rosh Chodesh, the first day of Shevat until Purim, and forty-five days from Tu B' Shevat until the month of Nissan.

General Guidelines and Goals

The following guidelines and goals enable us to direct our energies in the ways that are optimal for our growth and transformation in accordance with the energy of this month. It is recommended that you read and meditate upon them often in the course of the month, Reflect on their applicability to you, and allow them to direct and inspire you often this month.

1. OPEN TO NEWNESS.

This is an optimal time to conceive of new projects, to open to newness in your life in general. It may not be clear what the new is for you, but simply agree to open to the process of renewal in your life. Say YES in your heart of hearts to the process of renewal. Be open to surprises, meeting new people, and doing new things. It is good and wonderful to give yourself time to be with not-knowing and allow something new to be birthed within you.

Give yourself time this month to relax and open to receive new inspiration. Paradoxically, we open to newness in life by accepting our life as it is and trusting that life is unfolding for our highest good. As we relax, we open to something new and more in alignment with who you really are on a soul level.

Know that you have come into this life to be a portal for love and blessing in this world. Do not allow fear and doubt to limit you. Believe and trust the future holds hope and joy for you. Whether you consciously know this or not, the Creator of all of life to whom we refer with many names is supporting you this month to be more fully who you are and to fulfill more of the soul purpose you came into this life to demonstrate. Say YES to whatever is unfolding

> We open to newness in life by accepting our life as it is and trusting that life is unfolding for our highest good.

for you this month. There is much blessing available this month. Know that God believes in you, whether you believe in God or not. The Creator believes in you more than you believe in yourself.

2. EAT TO SUPPORT YOUR WELL-BEING.

This month is devoted to healing through eating. As human beings we need to eat to sustain our lives. What and how we eat is an expression of who we are and what our relationship is to God. Food is a contraction of Divine Light. By eating with the proper consciousness the Godly sparks within the foods are elevated and returned to their source. Eating provides an interface between the spiritual and the material. When our spiritual and physical dimensions of our being are unified, there is balance and joy.

We need to reflect on whether what we eat and how we eat supports our well being. Reflect on the following questions: Is my diet filled with fresh, organic foods including lots of vegetables and fruits or is my diet filled with processed foods, heavy on carbohydrates and laden with chemicals and hormones like those found in milk products and meat? Do I eat when I am hungry or do I eat to stuff down negative feelings? Do I eat slowly, chewing my food carefully, blessing food before and after, or do I eat on the run, gulping my food down unconsciously, sometimes even standing?

Our physical bodies have been Divinely designed and we inhabit them for a limited period of time, so it behooves us to take excellent care of our physical bodies. Make a commitment to eat more consciously this month so as to support your well being on all levels.

3. DEVELOP A PLAN TO NURTURE YOURSELF.

In addition to looking at the quality of our physical food, we need to look at the quality of love and work in our lives—the main areas that either nurture or deplete us. For example, we may find that relationships we have with some people are literally draining. These people seem to eat off of us, demanding and taking whatever they can with little thought to what they can give. Other relationships are healing and life affirming. Choose to let go of draining relationships and strengthen life-affirming and nurturing ones.

In previous months, we have worked hard to heal, transform and redeem negative relationships, but sometimes we simply have to let go. There is no need to feel guilty about this or to continue to allow ourselves to be manipulated by others. We may feel we cannot let go of such relationships because we have to take care of others but there are times in our caregiving when we are simply enabling others to be dependent, so we are not serving them or ourselves by maintaining the relationship. This month asks us to be discerning.

Take time this month to also look at the work you do. Is your work meaningful, life affirming, expressive of who you are? Or do you spend your days toiling for money, feeling alienated, doing work that is disconnected from who you are and what you hold as important in life? If you do not love your work, what kinds of work do you love and would prefer to do? If you cannot change your work, how can you change your attitude and find joy in what you do?

Remember that you came into this world with a soul mission, so it is important to spend at least some time each day doing what resonates with your soul purpose. *Do what you love and the money will follow* was a popular book title years ago. You are here to love. You are here to fulfill your soul purpose. You are not here to accumulate material wealth but that may happen but it is not the primary goal. When you are aligned with your soul purpose, the physical world will be brought into alignment with your soul. It is possible and even likely you will be rewarded with physical wealth.

4. GUARD THE ENVIRONMENT.

This month we should be mindful of the *mitzvah* of *shomrei adamah* which means guarding the environment As we celebrate the New Year of the Trees, Tu B' Shevat, this month, we extend our acknowledgment and caring to the whole physical environment. God created a beautiful world with everything in harmony.

In a powerful story, a *midrash,* from the Oral Torah tradition that is relevant today, God shows man the trees in the Garden of Eden and says to him, *See My works, how beautiful they are. Now all that I have created,*

I created for your benefit. Think upon this, do not corrupt or destroy My world, for if you destroy it there is no one to restore it after you.

Because of our greed, we currently face threats to our survival. The purity of our air, our water, our oceans, our forests, and various species are endangered. Even many foods we eat have been tampered with. Who knows what the outcome of genetically engineered food will be?

During this month, make a commitment to learn more about the problems affecting the health of our environment.

Astrological Sign: Aquarius

Aquarius is ruled by the planet Uranus. Uranus was only discovered in 1781 which coincided with a time of great social change. Until Uranus was discovered, Aquarius, along with Capricorn, was thought to be governed by Saturn. Kabbalah suggests seeing Capricorn—Tevet, and Aquarius—Shevat, as two eyes. With the eye of Capricorn, we see the past and the negative, and with the eye of Aquarius, we see the future and the positive.

In astrology, Uranus is associated with new directions, inventions, independence, and sudden change. Under the influence of Uranus, one suddenly sees things in a new way, and new possibilities and vistas are available. One also sees the larger picture. There is a waking up to greater consciousness, along with the desire to translate this inner vision into action during this month.

In mythology, Uranus is associated with Ouranos, a primeval god who stole fire from the gods to enable humans to grow in knowledge. This planet shows itself in the willingness this month to break down rigid and old structures that do not serve the higher good. Much like the energy of this month, people born in this sign are said to be the most unconventional and open-minded of people.

Aquarius is an air sign that has the capacity to be both objective and expanded, reflecting the expansive nature of the energy of this month. Uranus is also known in astrology as the planet of the higher mind.

Aquarius is represented by the water pitcher, a symbol indicating a willingness to contain and share blessings with other. This month is surely a water pitcher that is pouring out blessings for the entire year. Water in Kabbalah is a symbol of Torah, Written and Oral. In the Torah are several stories illustrating the worthiness as a mate determined by their willingness to offer water. We see how Rebecca was selected to be the wife of Isaac by her willingness to fetch water for Eliezer and even for his camels. Moses also draws water for the daughters of Jethro and he marries the eldest. Moses is also associated with this month, for he is seen as the water pitcher giving spiritual nourishment to the people.

Hebrew Letter: Tzaddi

This month's letter, the *tzaddi,* represents the *tzaddik,* the righteous, perfected one. Though often hidden, the tzaddik is considered the foundation and conduit of blessing for the world. Similarly, also hidden, the month of Shevat is also a foundation and source of blessing for the entire year. Like the water pitcher representing the astrological sign of this month, the tzaddik and the month of Shevat brings down the blessings from the highest world. The tzaddik represents the hidden potential of every Jew as it says several times in the Torah, *all of Israel are tzaddikim.*

The word *tzaddi* means *to hunt.* The tzaddik *hunts* in order to redeem and elevate fallen sparks. In Kabbalah, this is referred to as the act of eating for the tzaddik. According to Kabbalah, in the act of eating there is the raising of the fallen sparks of Godliness. So similarly, the tzaddik raises the fallen Godly sparks within a person as he connects this person to God. These redeemed sparks elevate the tzaddik even more. This is an allusion to *eating* as the area of healing prominent this month.

The letter *tzaddi* is the first letter of the work *tzelem,* which refers to the Divine Image in which God created humankind, and is the second letter in the Hebrew word *etz* which means *tree.* The tzaddik mirrors the Divine Image and is also compared to a tree. Like a tree, the tzaddik, planted firmly on the ground, extends into the heavens and provides shelter from the sun. We refer to the Torah as *Etz Hayim,* a Tree of Life. We will learn more about the mystical significance of trees in the holiday section of this chapter, for in this month, we celebrate the holiday referred to as t*he New Year of the Trees* in the month of Shevat.

Hebrew Tribe: Asher

Asher was born to Zilpah, the handmaid of Leah. When Asher was born, Leah proclaimed, *Happy am I, for the young girls will call me blessed*, and she called him Asher. Gen.30:13. Asher was born after Leah had already given birth to four sons. Her first sons were born when Leah felt the pain of being loved less than her sister, Rachel, and these sons carried the scars of her pain. This pain is reflected in the months the tribes her sons represent. As Leah develops spiritually, she emerges as a powerful woman in her own right. By the time she gives birth to her fourth son, Yehudah, Judah, she no longer begs for her husband's love with each new son, but praises and thanks God.

When Leah stops bearing children, she offers Jacob her handmaid Zilpah, who first bears the son Gad and then the second son Asher. It is significant to note that Leah is now strong and self-confident enough to share her place with another woman. She is more interested in expanding her role as a matriarch of the Jewish people by having more sons. Asher is a source of great joy; he was not born out of pain, but out of the joy of bringing forth more life.

The Torah offers additional things about Asher that sheds light on the wonderful energy of this month. When Jacob blesses him he says, *Out of Asher shall come the richest foods and he shall provide the king's delights.* Gen.49:20. Moses also blesses Asher, and says: *Blessed among sons is Asher. Let him be acceptable to his brothers and let him dip his foot in oil. Your shoes shall be iron and brass and as your days, so shall your strength be.* Deut.33:24-25. What powerful affirmations and blessings for this month!

The land Asher inherited was rich and full of oil from olives. Oil is said to represent the Oral Torah, which gives a special blessing to the Jewish people and to this month. Although most, if not all, of the Oral Torah has now been written down, it is still considered more hidden than the written Torah. The Oral Torah is the flowering of the written Torah. Oil represents purity, for oil never blends with another liquid, but always rises to the top. Oil is made from pressing the olives. There is a similar pressing within us that puts us in touch with the oil within us, which represents what is pure and cannot be contaminated. This pressing most likely will occur during the first part of the month.

According to Oral Torah, the members of the Tribe of Asher never showed their age. I have noticed that righteous people have a spiritual radiance that keeps them looking young, no matter how old they are. It is also said that the tribe of Asher never wandered in search of what they did not have. There were happy with their portion. They also had the most children. All these qualities of Asher, the youthfulness, the contentment, the abundance, and the productivity are expressive of the energy of this month.

Divine Name Permutation: HYVH

At the first glance, we note that the first two letters are in an inverted order and the last two letters are in their natural placement in the Tetragrammaton YHVH. From this we are told that the month is divided between judgment and grace, judgment for the first part of the month and grace for the second. The placement of the first *hay* (H) in the world of Atzilut indicates a great heavenly influx of light this month, and the *yud* (Y) in the second position indicates that the mind must be contracted and concentrated so as to receive this flow of grace. This Divine influx can then be best channeled through the heart into the physical world.

It is interesting to note that when the work of transformation relates primarily to consciousness, as during the months of Cheshvan and Tevet, the *hay* appears in the second position, in the world of Beriyah, corresponding to the mind. In this month of Shevat the *yud* occupies the world of Beriyah. When the spiritual energy for the month is more about manifesting in the physical world, the letter *hay* will be in the fourth placement, in the world of Assiyah, the world of action in the physical world as it is now in the month of Shevat.

To experience this flow more consciously, meditate on the Divine Name permutation for this month, HYVH. After a few breaths, visualize the *hay* above the head, the *yud* in the head, the *vav* in the heart and the final *hay* in the waist and legs. Meditate particularly on the *hay* guiding manifestation into the physical world. Meditate on the Divine Permutation for this month so as to open to receive the downpour of blessings unique to this month.

Torah Portions

The Torah portion for Shevat usually begins with Bo in the Book of Exodus, in Exodus10, recounting the story of the Exodus of the Jewish people from Egypt. This event is very much in line with the energy of this month, a time of breaking free from the past and beginning anew. In this Torah portion, we see the final plaques given to demonstrate God's power and finally take the Jews out of Egypt.

This Torah portion of Bo begins with God telling us that Pharaoh's heart would be hardened in order *that I lay (put) these miracles of Mine in his midst*. Exodus 10.1. As much as these plagues were for the benefit of the Jewish people, they were also performed for the Pharaoh and the Egyptian people to give them an opportunity to choose to accept God as God. The plagues demonstrated that God's power was greater than Egyptian magic, and that there was a difference between the Jewish people and the Egyptian people. For example, in one plague, the Jewish people had light while the Egyptians had only darkness.

The Jews were instructed to place the blood of the slaughtered ram on their doorposts and this protected them from the final plague. The Oral Tradition tells us that twenty percent of the Jewish people failed to do this act and were consequently not protected and perished. This failure to do so was either because they did not want to leave Egypt or the sacrifice of the ram was considered an Egyptian god. They had assimilated to such a degree that the call to serve the God of the Jewish people did not resonate with them.

When the Jewish people finally did depart, they did not go empty-handed. The children of Israel followed the order of Moses and they requested from the Egyptians, silver objects, gold objects and robes. *God granted the people favor in the eyes of the Egyptians and they granted their request. They emptied out Egypt.* Exodus 35-37. This departure from Egypt was the fulfillment of the earlier prophecy received by Abraham about his descendants before he had any descendants. The laws of Passover are also given in this Torah portion in the month of Shevat.

Interestingly, there are Ten Plagues, Ten Commandments, Ten Sayings used in creation and Ten Sefirot. These are all connected to each other. As we study the text on the literal level, we only see the plagues. When we understand the connection of the plagues to the Sefirot or to the Commandments, we see clearly that with each plague God is revealing the deepest secrets of creation to the entire world.

Sometimes, the month of Shevat begins with the Torah portion of *Beshallach* in Exodus 13:17. In this Torah portion, the Jews cross the Red Sea in the most miraculous way. The Jews have left Egypt, but they now find that the Red Sea is in front of them, making it impossible for them to go forward, and Pharaoh's army is quickly approaching from behind. There is confusion about what to do.

Should they return to Egypt, should they fight the Egyptians, or should they drown themselves in the sea and so commit suicide? They cry to God and God tells Moshe in so many words, *Do not cry to Me. Go forward into the sea. Raise your staff and I will split the sea.* God offers them a solution they never would have imagined possible. The key here is to pray, lift up your consciousness, move forward, and trust in God, an important teaching for us in our lives in general and particularly for this month. In the month of Shevat, we begin opening to new ways of being in our lives.

When we are faced with what appears to be insurmountable challenges this month, we must tune into the wisdom of our soul; that is, tune into the higher knowing within us beyond our rational mind. If we fight negativity, we often become mired in it. If we retreat, we lose and deny a part of ourselves and to some extent we will deaden and numb ourselves to accept retreat.

When the Jews moved across the Red Sea, the Sea magically parts. Moses sings and Miriam sings. The connection and revelation of God was so strong that it has been said even the consciousness of the simplest person was said to be beyond that of the level of a great prophet. Crossing the Red Sea was very unique and powerful because the body of every person was immersed in this experience. This Divine Revelation manifested within nature offered a direct experience to everyone from even babies to adults.

Remembrance of the Crossing of the Red Sea continues to be a source of great joy for people even today because in this miraculous experience God was not hidden in nature, but revealed through it. To experience Godliness fully expressed in this physical world is a taste of messianic consciousness promised for the End of Days.

Further on, we read about the complaints of the Jewish people for water and then for meat. Again the concern about food reminds us about the energy of healing through eating of this month. God gives them the manna in these Torah portions affording the Jewish people an opportunity of a very close relationship with God, which is reflected in the energy of this month. God is literally feeding and sustaining us with manna.

In the next Torah portion, Yitro, in Exodus 18-20, the Jewish people receive the Ten Commandments. By this time, the Jewish people have reached such a high level of God consciousness that they declare a willingness to do whatever God asks of them, even prior to understanding. This is indicative of the kind of surrender of the need to figure out or understand what life is asking of us with our minds. This is a prerequisite for Divine Revelation and its internalization.

In the following Torah portion, Mishpatim, in Exodus 21-24, the Jewish people receive the laws by which the holiness of the nation would be maintained. The laws regarding slavery are discussed in detail. In Judaism, slavery was an act of kindness given to an unfortunate person who may have committed a crime and needed rehabilitation. God reminds us in this Torah portion to cry out to God when a person is wronged or hurt because God will hear these cries. All the Torah laws protect the human soul, enabling a person to realize his or her awesome potential and purpose for being embodied. For this reason, we read about this during Shevat.

The only recorded mystical experience is written in this Torah portion of Mishpatim. The Torah describes: *Moses, Aaron, Nadah, and Abihu and the seventy elders ascended. They saw the God of Israel and under His feet was the likeness of sapphire brickwork, and it was the essence of heaven's purity.* Genesis 24. 8-11. This also speaks to the holiness of this month. This extraordinary experience is still available to people today through Divine grace. It is often said that subsequent generations were not on the high level that Biblical people were in ancient times, yet my beloved teacher, Reb Shlomo of blessed memory, told us and showed us that this is not always true. People today have opportunities to evolve their consciousness in exciting ways that may not have been available previously.

According to the Zohar, the Torah portion of Mishpatim is all about the secrets of reincarnation. The Torah descries the laws regarding slavery, yet the Zohar states that slavery refers to the laws regarding the transmigration of souls. Being in the physical body is equated to slavery. The Torah portion starts: *If you buy a Hebrew slave, six years shall he serve.* This means that the soul may come back to this world six times to correct its deficiencies. As an aside, there is another option that says that the soul comes back, three or four times, derived from the Biblical verse in Exodus 20:5. The sins of the fathers are revisited to the third and fourth generation because it is the same soul who comes back in the third and fourth generation to correct its deficiencies.

The Torah portions read during the month of Shevat connect us to Passover, the Exodus from Egypt which occurs in Nissan, the receiving of manna which occurs in the month of Iyar, and the receiving of the Torah which occurs in the month of Sivan. Even though Shevat occurs in the winter, we are reading about the spring in these Torah portions. These Torah portions support us in opening to a vision of freedom and newness that is characteristic of the month of Shevat.

Holiday: Tu B'Shevat

HISTORY: The holiday of Tu B'Shevat, the fifteenth of the month of Shevat, the time of the full moon, is biblically a *halachic* demarcation, formerly used to determine which year a crop belonged to for the purposes of *smittah*, the practice of allowing the land to rest every seven years. If a tree began to flower before the fifteenth of Shevat, it was included in the tithe for the previous year; if after the fifteenth of Shevat, it was counted in the following year. One explanation for this date was that in the Land of Israel most of the annual rain has fallen by the fifteenth of Shevat, the sap has risen in the trees, and the process of bearing fruit has begun. Another opinion was that a tree that blossomed before Tu B'Shevat did so with the rainwater of the previous year, before Rosh Hashanah, so it should be counted in the last year's tithe. At the time of the Holy Temple, Tu B'Shevat was a date to regulate the giving of tithes.

The Talmud calls Tu B'Shevat *The New Year's Day for the Trees*. Much like our Rosh Hashanah, it becomes a day marking a new beginning for the trees as well as a day of gratitude for the fruits available in the Land of Israel. There is much testimony in Jewish writing regarding our appreciation of the benefits we receive from trees. Kabbalists in Safed recognized the mystical connection between trees and humanity and celebrated Tu B'Shevat as a spiritual and mystical Rosh Hashanah for us, a time of new beginnings, even a day for ushering in the redemption for the world.

In the Mishnah, Tu B'Shevat is actually called the New Year of The Tree, rather than Trees which is a reference to the original Tree of Good and Evil that Adam and Eve ate in the Garden of Eden story in Genesis. Because eating of this particular tree was forbidden, humanity was said to have been cast out of the Garden of Eden. Adam was initially commanded to eat from all the fruit bearing trees with the exception of this one tree. The eating of this one tree was considered a sin.

After Eve, who was seduced by the snake to eat from the forbidden tree, gave the fruit to Adam, their consciousness changed dramatically.

Now they could no longer remain in the Garden of Eden. Cast out of the Garden, Adam was told that he now would have to eat the grasses of the fields like animals and toil working the ground to grow vegetables. This was originally a curse and humiliation for him. The fruit of the tree was the most perfect food. To live solely eating simply fruit was the original intention. Because the tree surrenders its fruit gracefully, when we eat it, the integrity of the tree is not compromised. The tree is planted once, and then it goes through cycles and bears fruits every year with little or no effort on our part. Vegetables, however, have to be planted every year, requiring continual effort from people.

The eating of fruit on Tu B'Shevat is a symbolic rectification of this first original sin offering us a glimpse of a return to the consciousness of being in the Garden of Eden, the place of the original and total connection of humanity with God. The Kabbalists developed the custom of holding a Kabbalistic Seder, modeled and comparable to the Passover Seder, to reveal the deepest secrets of creation and bring down a flow of new blessings to participants and to the world. Interestingly enough, Tu B'Av is forty five days before Rosh Hashanah and Tu B'Shevat is forty five days before the month of Nissan. Forty five is a Kabbalistic secret code to a particular permutation of the Divine Name.

OBSERVANCE: The way the holiday of Tu B' Shevat is celebrated has developed over time and varies in different communities. The most popular form is as a day of gratitude for all the fruits of the Land of Israel, which helps to deepen one's connection to the Land of Israel. Tu B'Shevat is often a day for picnics, a time to be outdoors surrounded by trees and feel blessed for God's beautiful creation. For some, it is a day to focus on ecology, celebrating our partnership with God, and remembering our responsibilities to take care of the land. In Israel, it is Jewish Arbor Day, when trees are planted.

For most of my adult life, I celebrated Tu B' Shevat in a Kabbalistic format and found it to be one of the most joyous even ecstatic experiences of the entire year. Since the 1980s until this past year, I conducted almost every year a Tu B'Shevat Seder with my students. During this Seder, we drink four cups of wine and eat more than fifteen kinds of fruits. In a kinesthetic way we experience the Kabbalistic secrets of Divine creation. We also experience the application of the creative process as outlined in the Seder to our personal lives as well.

It is hard to outline the Seder in detail here, because there are no scripts in the way I conduct a Tu B' Shevat Seder. Through teachings, songs, and stories in addition to the eating of the fruit, and drinking of wine associated with each spiritual world, the secrets of creation are transmitted. Because this kind of Seder is a living transmission it is always new and exciting. There is a book written to help guide a person through a Tu B'Shevat enjoying wide circulation that was actually written by a dear friend of mine, Yitzchok Buxbaum of blessed memory. The order of the Seder is totally different than mine because this Seder is not based on Kabbalah teachings. So for me, it is not as meaningful, powerful, or fun. But it is excellent guide for the general public not so interested in meditation or Kabbalah.

My Kabbalistic Seder begins with a journey in our imagination to the consciousness before there was time and space. We can't really imagine such a place, but we are taught that before there was time and space, there was only Ain Sof, Limitless Light, a name often used for God in Kabbalah teachings. It is important to know that Ain Sof was never created and as such can never be destroyed.

One of the deepest Kabbalistic books, *Etz Hayim*, teachings of Rabbi Yitzchak Luria, compiled by his principal disciple, Rabbi Hayim Vital, tells us that in the first chapters there arose a desire within Ain Sof to bestow goodness, to love and be known. We know this desire because it is the deepest desire within us because we are created in Divine Image. As there was only Ain Sof, there was nothing to give to, nothing to be known by. Ain Sof withdrew, so to speak, to create an empty space where worlds would be brought into being. The Tu B Shevat Seder is a journey through these spiritual worlds that ends in a meditation on our physical world. By drinking different colors of wine and eating different kinds of fruit, representing various worlds, we gain insight into the nature of these worlds, their purpose and gifts to humanity. Needless to say, the drinking of wine and the eating of the fruits takes place in silence, at least in my Seders.

The first cup poured of totally white wine is for the world called *Atzilut*, the world of nearness. We say the blessing over the wine, drink it and meditate on the world of *Atzilut*, the world of the most intimate connection with Ain Sof. This reminds us that the highest level of our soul is outside our physical world, outside our physical body, and resides in the world we call Atzilut. Though many people may be unable to actually sense this world, they must be reminded that this world does exist.

Atzilut is in such proximity to Ain Sof that it is absorbed in the domain of the *sefirot*. In the world of Atzilut, we meditate on the Ten Sefirot, for it is through the sefirot that we may experience and interact with the light of Ain Sof. We meditate on the letter *yud,* the point where infinity meets the finite. We expand our awareness to the loving pure energy that surrounds our physical body. There is no fruit in this world, only the absorption in Oneness with Ain Sof.

The second cup is for the world known as *Beriyah*, the world of Creation. In this world, creation is seemingly separate or outside of Ain Sof, though nothing is really outside of Ain Sof. This world is the beginning of the appearance of the separation between Ain Sof and the human being. Here we drink a second cup of wine, white wine with a little red wine mixed in it. We say the blessing over the fruit associated with this spiritual world. These fruits are completely edible, such as grapes, figs, carob, orange, and blueberries. This world corresponds to the level of soul that is known as *neshamah,* the seat of our Higher Self, our witness consciousness. This level of our soul is totally pure and cannot be contaminated by any impurity within the physical world. This is the seat of our essential self, the part of us which remains always present through and in between our various incarnations. We know we access this level of our soul when we are filled with peace, love, and wisdom. This world is also the world of the Archangels like Michael, Gabriel, Uriel, and Rafael. When we enter this world in our Seder, we drink the wine, eat the fruit and meditate on the Hebrew letter *hay.* We welcome these highest angels and open to the level of our soul known as *neshama* at the top of our head.

The third cup is poured for the world of *Yetzirah,* the world of formation. Here we drink a cup of red wine with some white wine mixed into it. In this world, there is increasing differentiation because it is further removed from the direct light of Ain Sof. The fruits corresponding to this world are olives, dates, peaches, cherries, and pears. The fruits are edible on the outside but have a protective covering for the inside seed, which is not edible. This world corresponds to the level of soul of *ruach*, which is seated in the heart.

The heart feels more fragile and delicate to people so there is often a protective shield around it. We meditate of the letter *vav* in the heart and we open the heart to the blessings of the angels of this world to receive the unconditional love and light of Ain Sof.

The fourth cup is poured for the world of *Assiyah,* the world of action, corresponding to our physical world. Here we drink a cup of completely red wine. The fruits of this world—pomegranates, almonds, avocado, walnuts, mangos and so on—are the most vulnerable. They have an outside protective covering and in some cases an inside covering as well. We often have to work hard to eat the fruits of this world. We have to crack the nuts ourselves, and we have to peel the fruits ourselves. This is our physical world in which we do things, and what we do makes a difference to us. We meditate on the final *hay* of the tetragrammaton.

As creative human beings, our consciousness inhabits each of these worlds. We receive vision, inspiration and guidance from the higher worlds, translate that powerful reservoir of love and light into the heart that empowers us to express our unique purpose for being in a physical body into our physical world in the time and space we now occupy.

During the Seder, we meditate on the letters constituting the Divine Name as we travel through the worlds associated with each letter. We meditate on the *yud* (visualized outside of the body, six to twelve inches above the heart), the *hay* (visualized close to the top of the head), the *vav* (visualized in the heart), and the final *hay* (visualized in the waist and legs). Always seek to align with these spiritual worlds. Repeat the meditation on the letters of the Divine Name, carving out the letters deeper and deeper when you are not sitting at a Seder.

(Please note: I have a guided meditation through these spiritual worlds in a video entitled *Touching Eternity in the Midst of Daily Life*, as well as several meditations on the Divine Name YHVH on the Melinda Ribner You Tube channel.)

Meditation

Begin by focusing on the breath. Place your hands below your navel, and breathe into this part of the body. Let go of concerns of the day and simply be with the breath as it enters this part of your body. As you inhale the abdomen expands and as you exhale, the abdomen contracts. Hold the part of the body below the navel gently and compassionately as this is where we digest our food and store our deepest emotions.

Now leave one hand below the navel and bring the other hand to the chest. Allow the breath to deepen, from the belly to the chest and hold the breath in the space between the breaths and focus on the top of the head, the seat of the soul.

Continue to take long deep conscious breaths, making a connection between our belly—our physicality, our heart—our emotions, and the top of our head—our soul. Visualize a line connecting these powerful centers. Embrace yourself as a multi-dimensional being. You are a physical being, an emotional being, and a spiritual being. Sit in meditation for five to fifteen minutes.

Now come to a standing position. Imagine yourself as a tree. Your legs are rooted into the ground. Through roots are usually hidden, they are strong and dig very deep into the earth. Now allow your hands to lift upwards to the earth. Your arms are the branches of the tree but they are now barren at this time.

Go deep inside and open to the new creative energy that is stirring within you right now. Breathe slowly and deeply and open to a new flow of blessing. Open to a new beginning. Keep breathing deeply as you do this simple opening to the new. Your legs are rooted and your arms are lifted upward. Say *Yes* silently and even out loud to awaken yourself to be a creative channel for birthing something

> new in your life. You will bring forth new fruits and beautiful flowers in the coming months.
>
> When you are ready, allow the arms to open to your sides and float downward slowly, almost as if you were not even seen moving your arms. When we slow down the breath and we slow down the movement, we are more able to be in the present moment and experience the Divine Presence. When your hands have returned to your sides, take a few moments to breathe, to internalize, and to integrate what you opened to during this time of meditation.

Practical Recommendations

1. DO NEW THINGS.

This is the month of creativity, so add new activities to your life that will open you, nurture you and enable you to be creative and expressive. Much to my surprise, my brother began writing beautiful awesome poems and walking miles each day during this month. Both activities he had never done previously and they have added much joy to his life. When we do new things, we stimulate our creative juices, and this adds enjoyment to our lives. It is a joy to be creative and allow oneself to be a channel for the wisdom, love and beauty of God to be expressed through you.

2. LEARN TORAH.

According to Kabbalah, the water pitcher in the sign of Aquarius is a symbol of Torah, as water refers to Torah. The oil of the tribe of Asher for this month is symbolic of the Oral Torah. This is also the month of New Year of the Trees and Torah is called the Tree of Life. Learning Torah will open your mind and heart to newness and inspiration. Give yourself time to learn Torah this month. Go to a Torah class, find inspiring books to read, and meditate. Even on You Tube one can easily find many wonderful Torah teachers to listen to and learn with.

3. BE MINDFUL AS YOU EAT.

The area of healing for this month is eating. In selecting foods for a meal, take a moment to get in touch with what your body wants right now. This may be hard to discern at first, but as you listen to your body more, you will have greater insight into what your body really needs. Be very mindful that you eat only to support the well being of your physical body and not eat to stuff down or assuage painful or negative feelings.

Before you eat, take a moment to breathe, say the appropriate blessings, and then breathe again for a moment or two. Be aware that this food has been given to nurture you in the ways that you need right now. Eat slowly and consciously, chewing each bite of food many times so it becomes liquid. Be present with your eating as much as possible. Delight in the sense and taste sensation in all the foods that are on your plate. After you complete eating, take a moment to relax, to allow the food to digest, and say the appropriate blessings after the meal.

4. EAT HEALTHY IN A KOSHER OR VEGETARIAN DIET.

Our consciousness is influenced by the foods we eat. The Torah provides clear instructions regarding the kinds of foods that will nurture us spiritually. We may not understand the reasons behind the rules, but if we want to grow in the Jewish path, we will need to accept this higher wisdom. For example, the Torah prohibits the eating of milk with meat. There is no logical reason why we should not mix the two, but the Torah is very clear about this. It must mean we cannot easily digest the energies of these two foods together. When we do eat these foods together, we may become spiritually blocked and unable to receive the influx of Divine energy in these foods.

Although many Jews may like to eat foods like pork, lobster, or scallops, the Torah forbids it. Some food items prohibited in the past may have had actual hygienic reasons that were not known at the time of the writing of the Torah. These prohibitions protected observant Jews from illness and disease. Now that may not be the case, but they are still prohibited, so we have to assume and accept that these prohibited foods do not support us spiritually. One of the reasons that Jews did not suffer as much as others in previous plagues historically was because the Torah instructed Jews to wash their hands prior to eating long before people were aware of the hygienic importance of hand washing.

I personally recommend that people become vegetarians or vegan, including eating lots of all kinds of sprouts. If that is not possible, good, or appropriate for them, it is best to eat kosher organic free range chicken or meat. At least with kosher meat, one is assured that the animal was healthy when it was slaughtered and it was slaughtered in a way to minimize pain of the animal. However today even in kosher factories, animals are given antibiotics and hormones and the long term health hazards of such practices are not yet known. Also, even kosher animals are often locked up in cages and not allowed to roam and get the exercise needed to maintain health. This is not in keeping with the Torah rules of compassion towards animals. Therefore, it is best to limit the intake of meat and buy organic free range kosher meat when possible. Trader Joe's with stores all over America has organic free range kosher chicken and meat at reasonable prices.

Eating lots of fresh vegetables and fruits brings more life and nutrition to people. Foods that are processed and dead do not have the same life giving properties within them. Feed your body with life giving foods as much as possible. It is best to eat most of our foods the way God prepared them for us, natural and organic.

As a diabetic, I was encouraged to eat high protein foods and low carbohydrate foods by many doctors. And I did so for many years. Today as I write this chapter, I have returned to a vegan diet that I had prior to my diabetes diagnosis. What is new today with my vegan diet is that I am now eating sunflower sprouts, pea greens, broccoli, and clover sprouts in salads, juices, and smoothies. In this way, I feel more assured that my body is getting needed nutrition. I just returned from a three week vacation eating entirely raw foods and drinking wheat grass and green juice once or twice a day. I saw a few miracles among participants when I was there.

Since my return I have done my best to continue eating lots of salads, drinking wheat grass, and green juices daily. This regimen feels fortifying.

A Tale To Live By

Since the month of Shevat is all about accessing visions of what we want to manifest, I share this favorite story highlighting the power of intention, the power of love. Though it was originally a Hindu story, the message of the story seems very Jewish to me. So, I have given the characters in this story Hebrew names.

A man called Yehudah falls in love with a princess, the king's daughter, called, Yekera Kadisha, which means precious and holy. Yehudah is constantly reciting her name, Yekera Kadisha, while meditating on her beauty and opening his heart to love her even more. Entering into states of bliss while thinking of her, chanting her name, and yearning for her, he can do nothing else. The king has compassion on him and tells the people to feed and care for this man, Yehudah, who calls out the name of his daughter wherever he roams, and to send him the bill for the supplies they offer to this man.

Soon dozens of men claim to be Yehudah, each calling out the name Yekera Kadisha. Not able to distinguish who is the real Yehudah, the people feed all the men. The number of Yehudahs in the kingdom increase dramatically with each day. With great yearning and love, they each passionately call out the name of the king's daughter, entering into states of intoxication, and they are all fed by the people of the kingdom who then send the king the bills for what they offered.

Upon hearing of this situation, the king becomes aware that these men are taking advantage of his goodness. He then issues a decree that anyone calling out the name of his daughter will be killed. All of a sudden, there is only one Yehudah calling out the name. This Yehudah is the one who truly loves the princess. All the others were just imposters who faked love because of the material benefits they received. The real Yehudah loves the princess, not because of what he receives from her, but simply because he loves her.

The story has a happy ending for the power of true love is great. Because Yehudah loves the princess so truly, she begins to feel love for him. Yekera Kadisha begins to wander through the palace crying out, Yehudah, Yehudah, Yehudah. The king tries to distract her but whenever he suggests something, all the princess can say is, *Will Yehudah be there?* The king realizes that these lovers should be together. Because of his great love, Yehudah attains Yekera Kadisha.

This story illustrates the power of true love to support the manifestation and fulfillment of our desires in the physical world. Ultimately, this tale is really about a love story between a human being and God reminding us that pure devotion to God is richly rewarded. If we are sincere and truly want to love and be close to God, we will be. Though our sincerity may be tested, when we remain faithful, we will be supremely rewarded.

May our deepest yearnings be pure and may we find Divine portals within our lives and within our very own being to receive the love, wisdom, and light that our souls so yearn to embody and share in this world.

6

Adar

FEBRUARY – MARCH

ENERGY
The Joy of Oneness

AREA OF HEALING
Joy and Laughter

ASTROLOGICAL SIGN
Pisces

HEBREW LETTER
Kuf ק

HEBREW TRIBE
Naftali

DIVINE PERMUTATION
HHYV

HOLIDAY
Purim

A Personal Story

I will never forget the day when I had an awesome realization about God and Judaism which I feel captures the essence of the spiritual opportunity of Adar. At the time, in the mid 1970s, I was living in an ashram that was just a few blocks from the Carlebach Shul on the Upper West Side of Manhattan. Every other weekend the ashram would hold wonderful, awesome retreats where we would chant and meditate several hours each day and listen to brilliant inspirational talks. As I lived full time in the ashram, these retreats were available free for me to attend. That was a great blessing for me at the time.

One Saturday I had a particularly powerful meditation. I felt myself burning up with intense internal holy fire that was initiating me to a higher level of God consciousness beyond what I had known previously. It was an absolutely thrilling event, though I doubted I would be able maintain and internalize this experience. It was just too awesome.

During the lunch break, I stepped outside to enjoy the fresh air. It may have been the first time I happened to notice Jews returning from synagogue wearing their prayer shawls, walking with their families. Even though I had just experienced an intensity of ecstasy beyond whatever I had previously, I cried. Immediately, I understood that Judaism was about living a holy life in this world as a human being, while my yoga meditative experiences were about transcending the human experience to be rooted in the Divine, beyond this physical world. Judaism seemed to me to be more about bringing Godliness into this physical world. And that attracted me deeply. I was in my twenty's and I wanted experiences in this world.

My exit from living in the ashram and my immersion into a Torah observant lifestyle took more months. The death of a beloved grandfather, and a few other catalysts were needed to get me out of the ashram both physically, emotionally, and spiritually. When I did leave, I became observant on the next following Shabbat. I knew the power of a disciplined spiritual practice from living in an ashram, so I was *all in* from the very beginning.

When I first became observant, Yom Kippur was my favorite holiday. I dressed in white and even covered my hair, and I felt bathed in Divine love and compassion the entire day. I loved Yom Kippur! I did not struggle with fasting as I knew how to transcend my body so my soul could soar upwards in great joy. I particularly loved the melody and chant of the Kohanim in the Holy Temple recited during the Mussaf service. These prayers and melodies transported me to the experience of the holiness of that unique time when the Jewish people had the Holy Temple in Jerusalem. I was in bliss!

For many years, I was puzzled by the teaching that Purim was considered spiritually higher than Yom Kippur. Sure, Purim was fun, lots of music and alcohol, but I did not experience it as holy. How could it be even compared to Yom Kippur? Yom Kippur is said to be a day like Purim. What could that possibly mean?

It took entering Studio 54 with my teacher and rebbe, Reb Shlomo Carlebach, my guru replacement, to awaken me to the holiness of Purim and the holiness of this world. Studio 54 was one of the most trendy discotheques in Manhattan at this time. People used to wait in line for hours to get in and then they still had to be chosen. It had a wild reputation even for New York standards and was eventually closed by the police or the FBI years later for a combination of drugs, sex orgies, and tax evasion.

Reb Shlomo invited two male disciples, in addition to me, to accompany him to Studio 54 for a thirty-minute performance on Purim night. The atmosphere was a bit overwhelming to me as I was in my most religious period in my life, wearing long skirts, praying three times a day, not doing mixed dancing, and not even listening to secular music. I had moved from years of living in an ashram to an immediate total Torah observance, so Studio 54 was a bit of a shock to my nervous system.

Needless to say the people attending Studio 54 were not attending synagogue on a regular basis, many were not Jewish. Most did not know it was Purim or even what Purim was. How would they respond to Reb Shlomo? I was not concerned. By that time, I had witnessed how Reb

Shlomo transformed all kinds of people with the power of his melodies and words.

In the few minutes allotted to Reb Shlomo, the loud music stopped and Reb Shlomo took the microphone and soon all that was heard was the strumming of his guitar and his soft sweet voice singing and telling stories. In a short time, everyone was dancing in circles, wishing each other *Good Purim* and there was such a heavenly holy energy in the air. As I handed out flyers I had prepared to invite people to come to the synagogue, I told people that at Reb Shlomo's synagogue, we sing and dance, and get high naturally there. God is one. I was a bit of a missionary in those times.

For those few moments in Studio 54, I tasted such exquisite holiness that felt even higher than that of Yom Kippur. It was one thing to experience the holiness beyond this world on Yom Kippur but so much fun to experience the holiness within this world on this Purim night. Here in Studio 54 were people from all walks of life dancing with so much love and joy together. I saw clearly how the density and limitation of physicality could easily be lifted in a single moment of Divine Revelation. In a moment Divine Oneness and Love could suddenly be revealed. What a holy privilege it was for me to be a human being living in the midst of other human beings! Because our time inhabiting human physical bodies is limited, life is so very precious.

Before we even left Studio 54, the loud music resumed, and the strop lights were once again flashing. As we exited, I looked at the discotheque and it looked like everything had quickly reverted back to what it had been before Reb Shlomo's concert. But I now knew a secret that I did not know before. The physical world is transient but ultimately it is only a cover for a most profound holiness of the True Reality, that is God. Because ultimately the Divine Will is for God to be known in this physical world by all people, I knew on that Purim night that this Divine Revelation will happen quickly in the right time according to Divine Wisdom.

On that night, the holiness of this Purim event was carved into my soul. I finally understood the holiness of Purim and why the month of Adar is considered the culmination of the calendar year according to the Torah. As I left Studio 54, I laughed with Divine joy.

Energy: The Joy of Oneness

The sages in the *Gemara*, the commentary on the Torah, have said, *Joy is increased in the month of Adar*. There is a heavenly flow of joy this month but we must do our part to claim it as well as increase it. In the other months of Tammuz and Av, we talk about the growth and healing that occurs through pain and suffering. According to Kabbalah, joy is the greatest healer. Reb Nachman of Breslov said it quite simply, that sickness comes from a lack of joy and healing comes from joy.

Joy is not trivial but is actually a powerful spiritual weapon. The joy of Adar defeats sadness, depression, jealousy and anger. It is possible for each of us to access the kind of joy that comes not from acquiring external things but rather from tapping into what is within us at all times. When we are in alignment with our Divine connection and soul purpose, our spiritual vibration is lifted and we lift up the vibrations of those around us as well. This month is a time to commit to increasing joy in our lives.

The joy of this month comes from fully embracing the Divine gift of our humanity. When we recognize that life itself in a physical body is both a gift and privilege we can rejoice regardless of what is happening in our lives. As challenging as life can be for us at times, there are also wonderful spiritual opportunities that are available to us only when we are physically embodied. As we accept all of our life experiences, we find that they each has served as an avenue through which we may be of future service to others. Because we underwent certain experiences, we can be of greater service to others who are going through similar experiences. We can better appreciate the role of Divine providence in our lives, even when life is challenging.

Everything that has taken place in our lives has been designed for our highest good. Nothing is an accident. God is within us and running this world. It may not always be possible for us to see this at the time when we have suffered a trauma or tragedy. Over time, we may come to see and appreciate our growth. Surely in the next world we will see everything in life more clearly. As we love and accept ourselves more and our life experiences as vulnerable human beings, we better access and experience the light of our soul shining through us. This is redemptive.

The joy of this month comes when we see that the physical and spiritual dimensions of life are not separate from each other but unified and together. This joy is epitomized in this month's holiday Purim, when we are told to feast, drink to the point of becoming drunk, wear costumes, play and be happy. The holiness we experience on Purim is considered even greater than that of Yom Kippur. As holy as Yom Kippur is, it is a day compared to Purim.

The heroine of this month is Queen Esther. Through her innate power as a beautiful woman, Queen Esther was able to unify the Jewish people. As so often in our history, the Jewish people were again divided into groups favoring assimilation and those opposed to it. Queen Esther helped the Jewish people to awaken and experience their intrinsic unity with each other. Once they realized they had the same enemy threatening their annihilation, they were willing to engage in an arduous fast and prayer with Queen Esther. Together they brought forth and awakened a revelation of God that is referred to in Kabbalistic teachings as the Divine Mother.

Under the feminine leadership of Queen Esther, the enemy seeking to annihilate the Jewish people was defeated. Queen Esther modeled the power of the revelation of the Divine Feminine. In her scroll, Queen Esther taught us how to protect ourselves from enemies in future times. Jewish unity is the key. The month of Adar is ultimately about the heart and wisdom of the Feminine. The revelation of the Divine Feminine means that this month is about experiencing the inner Divinity within the physicality of life. God is not only in heaven, transcendent, but God is imminent, animating and sustaining all of creation.

In Adar, we are told to destroy Amalek. *Remember what Amalek did to you … You shall erase the memory of Amalek from beneath the heavens, you shall not forget."* Debt. 25:17-19. Jews read this in a Torah portion on the Shabbat before Purim, and the rabbis have asked that everyone be present to hear it. The scripture sounds very heavy, and one might naturally wonder what it has to do with the joy of this month.

Historically, Amalek was a descendent of Esau who had sworn to hate and kill the Jewish people. His tribe, the Amalekites, waged war on the Jewish people as they wandered in the desert. Though the Jewish people posed no direct physical threat to them, these people identified as Amalek at the time went out of their way to battle the Jewish people because they could simply not bear that the Jewish people had a special connection with God.

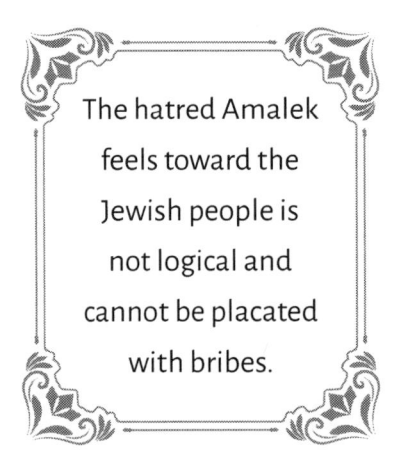

> The hatred Amalek feels toward the Jewish people is not logical and cannot be placated with bribes.

No longer confined to a specific Bedouin tribe, the faces of Amalek have changed but the energy of Amalek has remained consistent throughout history. The energy of Amalek is so bent on the destruction of what is positive and good, on destroying the spiritual integrity of the Jewish people, even if its proponents receive no benefit from Israel's destruction and it costs them their lives. The hatred Amalek feels toward the Jewish people is not logical and cannot be placated with bribes. You cannot negotiate with them. They will not keep their promises or commitments. The Bible tells us clearly what to do with Amalek. *Wipe them out*! This statement is not politically correct to many, but the Bible is clear.

Haman in the Purim story was considered a descendent of Amalek. Hitler may be considered the Amalek of the last generation. In this generation it has become clear that the faces of Amalek today are the various terrorist entitles of radical Islam which are mostly sponsored and supported by Iran, which was ancient Persia. The atrocities that happened on October 7th, along with the kidnapping, abuse, and holding hostage of innocent people from babies to elderly is a clear demonstration of the evil of Amalek. Caring more about destroying the Jewish people than helping their own people is a primary way to identify Amalek. Hamas clearly fulfills this definition. Rather than use donated millions and billions of dollars to care for their own people and develop a thriving economy, Hamas used its financial resources to build an elaborate underground system of tunnels and place weaponry amidst population centers.

Amalek's battle is really a war against God more than it is about the Jewish people. They hate the Jewish people so much because the existence of the Jewish people is a testament to God being alive and active in this world. Such Islamists also hate Christians, other God centered people, and even Moslems who are not as radical as they are. They have already stated numerous times, that they will kill: *First the Saturday people and then the Sunday people.* These current day battles we see against Israel today have been forecasted in Biblical prophecies such as Ezekiel, Zachariah, Isaiah and others.

The final destruction of Amalek will take place in the messianic time. Each year, during the month of Adar, the energy of Amalek is erased a little more by the power of joy that we open to this month. On Purim when we feast, drink, wear costumes, and give gifts to each other, we wipe out the impact of Amalek (evil) in the world in the most fun way. Joy and faith are powerful spiritual weapons to weaken the power of evil in the world.

Adar is a very positive time for good for things to happen on the material plane. The *Gemara* says if a Jew has to go to court, he should go during the month of Adar. The *Gemara* also says: *Someone who wants a fortune should plant it in Adar.* Sounds like a good time to invest in the stock market.

According to Torah and astrology, Adar is considered the twelfth month, the last month of the year. Adar is therefore less a time to start new projects and more advantageous attending to existing projects to complete them as quickly as possible. The energy of Adar is about the fulfillment of the original Divine Intention; that is, to create a dwelling place for the Divine Presence in this physical world.

The joy of Adar comes from the revelation of the Divine Feminine when we experience the immanence of the Divine in ourselves, within everyone and within everything happening. If we count Tishrei as the first month of the year, as is often done, Adar is the sixth month. Six in Kabbalah is indicative of the weekday, the material world, So we see that Adar is the revelation in the inner Divinity within the physical world.

The joy of Adar is increased every seven years with an additional month of Adar. In those years, Purim is celebrated in the second month of Adar as to link it with Passover. In this way, by adding an additional month of

Adar, the Jewish calendar assures that Passover will occur in the spring as mandated in the Torah.

As an aside, it is interesting to highlight that the Jewish calendar is unique. Though the Chinese and Moslems also use a lunar calendar, they do not add an additional month as the Jews do every seven years. Consequently, their holidays take place at varying seasons during the calendar year. The calendars of western civilizations revolve exclusively around the sun so holidays are always on the same day each year. The Jewish calendar is unique and offers the perfect balance between the forces of materialism represented by the sun and spirituality represented by the moon. This balance is another reason why Israel, the homeland of the Jewish people, resides in the Middle East, the center between the West and the East.

General Guidelines and Goals

The following guidelines and goals enable us to direct our energies in the ways that are optimal for our growth and transformation in accordance with the energy of this month. It is recommended that you read and meditate upon them often during the course of this month. Reflect on their applicability to you and allow them to direct and inspire you often this month.

1. COMMIT TO INCREASING JOY IN YOUR LIFE.

Make time to contact what brings joy in your life and commit to increasing joy in your life this month. God created this world for love and joy, not for suffering. Though we learn many things through the challenges we face, it is only when we experience joy and love that we feel most alive. The main reason we have come into this world is to experience and teach joy. If we understand that this is what God wants and what we really want in our heart of hearts, we can be joyful even when we are challenged, because we are learning what we need to learn. It is important to not be too serious or analytical. See to see the humor in life—it is always there.

Give yourself time to play, to enjoy nature, dance, to sing, meditate, and to do whatever brings you joy. Within each of us is an inner child who absolutely loves to play and have fun. Let the inner child come out to play. Affirm that every moment is an opportunity to love and connect with your inner child and your higher self and with God. Just remembering this will fill you with joy.

2. ELIMINATE OR REDUCE WHAT DOES NOT GENERATE JOY..

Review the way you live your life on a daily basis, and see whether your time is filled with things that you do not want to do but feel that you should do. If you find that you are the kind of person who spends more time listening to others talking about their problems or venting their anger than you would like to do, remember that you can diplomatically end conversations with such people without hurting them. Be mindful not to waste your time.

Sometimes people feel so obligated to do for others that they forget about their own needs and may even hurt themselves in the process. Being there for other people at your own expense generates resentment. Be honest about what your underlying motivations are when you do for other people. For example, you may find that the real reason is that you are seeking validation for being a good person and not because you really want to give to that person.

If you are honest, you will admit that most things you do, you do for yourself. If you know that clearly, you should not resent other people. Simply ask yourself if you need to continue to prove to them or yourself that you are worthwhile or lovable in ways that do not make you feel happy. If you find yourself spending time resenting other people, remember that you do not serve yourself, other people and God when you engage in activities or in relationships that drain you of your life force energy.

If you are in a job, in a relationship, or in anything that does not bring your joy, take responsibility for creating this in your life, forgive yourself, and know that you can now choose differently. It is not necessary for you to know why you allowed yourself to be unhappy or suffer in the way that you have.

You can let go of the past for the past is over. You can let go of the stories you have told yourself of being victimized and why. Do not keep alive your interpretation of past events so they interfere with your capacity to be present in real time. How do you let go of the past?

Be with the breath. As you inhale open to receive a new influx of energy and blessing. God is sustaining you with each breath. As you exhale, consciously let go of the stronghold that past events have on your life today. Whatever happened to you in the past is over. Let go of what you have been taught to dislike or reject about yourself. When we let go of negative self talk, we quiet the mind, tune into inner stillness, and we naturally open to the love that has been implanted within us.

Being happy is a natural authentic state of being for everyone. Within each of us is an inner child who loves to play and have fun. When our inner child feels safe and loved, we feel joyful. For example, a client with a terribly abusive childhood attempted to justify his unhappiness because of the kind of parents he had. I asked him if he wanted to be right or if he wanted to be happy. We all need to ask ourselves this question at various times in our lives. Will I allow myself to be happy even when I can easily justify the reasons to be unhappy? To be happy requires us to stop blaming other people, God, or even ourselves. It means making a commitment to love ourselves unconditionally. You may not have felt loved unconditionally by your parents, but that is no reason why can not learn to love yourself unconditionally.

If you are willing to open to living a more joyful life, begin by saying YES to yourself and inwardly agree to open to the kind of work and relationships that will allow you to express more of who you really are. Remember that thoughts, feelings, and even our bodies change all the time so try not to identify with them. They are not who you really are. You are the unchanging holy eternal soul within. Access to our own souls is the primary source of joy for us that is not dependent on externalities or on aspects of yourself that are changeable. Attune to the soul within and allow your life to be brought into alignment with your soul purpose. We are naturally happy when we are fulfilling our soul purpose.

You may not be able to let go of your victim stories about your life immediately so be patient with yourself. Yet, when you clearly realize these victim stories mostly reflect outdated programming you previously received, the hold that these stories have on your life will dissipate.

Increase your access to the soul within by doing joyful activities, praying, meditating and doing good deeds. Be patient and compassionate with yourself. When the chatter of the mind quiets, you will more easily tune into your intuition and be guided from within. Your inner guidance will support you to be joyful for no reason at all. The best reason for love and joy is for no reason. That which is not dependent on anything in this world is sourced in the Divine and is free.

> Increase your access to the soul within by doing joyful activities, praying, meditating and doing good deeds.

3. WIPE OUT YOUR PERSONAL AMALEK.

People search for happiness in many ways. We look towards a variety of experiences, possessions, relationships, and accomplishments for happiness. When we reach our goals or obtain what we want, we may be happy momentarily, but the happiness does not last. Rather, we often feel a sense of loss or the fear of loss. It is frustrating not to be able to hold on to our happiness. It is not easy to be in a constant state of joy as Reb Nachman so strongly recommends. Yet when we experience joy, it feels so natural that we wonder why we are not able to maintain it all the time.

As we grow in love and acceptance of who we are, we are in a state of joy more of the time. This is because we are better able to access the joy that is integral to who we are, not dependent on anything external to us. Happiness has to be found within ourselves. It is our ego that often robs us of joy and pushes us to pursue joy outside of ourselves. It tells us that we are not enough in ourselves and that we need to have more in order to be happy with ourselves. This is the internal voice of Amalek. Be mindful of the voices within you that take you away from the experience of the joy of simply being alive.

In common usage today, Amalek also refers to the negative inclination (*yetzer hara*) within human beings. Amalek has the same numerical value as the Hebrew word for doubt which is *safek*. The energy of Amalek causes us to doubt ourselves and our capacity to accomplish what we feel called to do, especially in regard to spiritual growth. It is the evil inclination that makes us self-critical, judgmental, and vulnerable to depression.

Amalek is anti-God. It is the energy of Amalek within us that says *things just happen*, or *everything is random*. Amalek is that negative inclination within people that is spiteful, jealous, and willing to do harm to oneself or to others even though it serves no purpose and will bring no benefits. Amalek is the root of drug addiction. Amalek is not the voice of the soul, not the voice of who you really are. You can recognize the voice of the soul for the soul is full of love, peacefulness, and wisdom, Amalek is the opposite. It is full of drama, intensity, and stress. Do not give it more energy or credibility.

The final destruction of Amalek is anticipated for the messianic time in a battle that asks each of us to participate in our unique ways. Though we all may not be called to the frontline to physically fight Amalek, we all have an important role to play in this upcoming messianic war against Amalek. We each must utilize our spiritual weapons of faith, love, joy, and possibly a little holy wine to cut off the evil of Amalek at its root. Evil feeds on fear, doubt, illusion, lies, and confusion. Evil does not have any real substance and only has power that we give it. When we affirm that *HaShem Melech* (God is King), we affirm that God is running the world and we need not fear. When evil fulfills its purpose of strengthening our connection to the Creator, evil will dissipate. Without fear, evil dissolves because it does not have real substance but only what we give it out of fear.

Some Chabad congregations say the following after the Mussaf Amidah prayer: *Do not fear sudden terror or the holocaust of the wicked when it comes. Plan a conspiracy and it will be annulled, speak your piece and it shall not stand, for God is with us ... I remain unchanged and even till your ripe old age, I shall endure. I created you, I shall bear you. I shall endure and rescue.* These verses seem more meaningful today than they did even ten years ago.

4. SEE THE DIVINE HAND IN YOUR LIFE.

During this month, it is so important to remember that things do not happen randomly. God is communicating with us through everything that is happening in our lives and in the world. Listen closely to what is being said, read between the lines. Remember God has a sense of humor, so we should too. Seek to see the humor in life—it is always there. Everything is part of the Divine Plan. Do not personally take credit or blame for what God is unfolding in your life.

> Remember God has a sense of humor, so we should too. Seek to see the humor in life—it is always there.

As we see from the Purim story, life is full of irony. Esther might have been criticized for living with a non-Jewish king, but through a turn of events she becomes the savior of the Jewish people. Everything that happened previously to Esther set her up to fulfill this awesome destiny. Like Esther, we may never know all the reasons for the challenges we face in life but know that they were all necessary and have prepared us for the unique contribution we can make in our lives. We never know when we will be called to do something absolutely amazing. Like Esther, we each will have opportunities in small and possibly big ways to bring love and redemption to other people and experience it within our own lives as well.

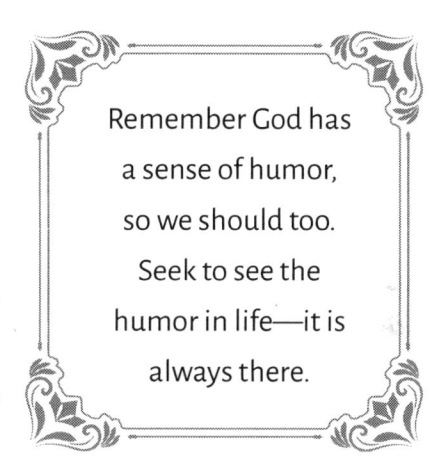

5. GIVE CHARITY.

According to Jewish law, people are obliged to give to the poor on Purim and during the month of Adar more than at other times of the year. On Purim we are asked to give directly to at least two poor people. Even poor people are required to give charity to other poor people. Charity does not have to be money; it can be clothes, food, other items, or even acts of service. It can be small—even one penny or a single piece of fruit—but everyone has to give. As God is the ultimate giver, when we become givers we become like God, and we are more able to receive the Divine flow of blessing in our lives.

Astrological Sign: Pisces

Pisces, according to astrology, is the twelfth month of the year, representing the final stage of human development. In Pisces, we complete what we have worked on all year. We let go of ego limitation to connect and embody the Divine. In Aquarius, the previous month, we looked outward and conceived new projects. In Pisces, we look inward, visualizing a place of God consciousness in this human world. As the last month of year in the astrological calendar, Pisces is a time when the soul longs to bring heaven to earth on all planes of consciousness.

Pisces was traditionally ruled by Jupiter and acclaimed to embody more of its spiritual elements such as faith and surrender of the ego. Pisces is a time of letting go of the illusion of separateness and opening to unconditional love. Jupiter rules over Sagittarius and Kislev, which hosts the holiday of Chanukkah. Purim and Chanukkah are connected. They are both rabbinical holidays in which evil against the Jewish people was destroyed in miraculous ways.

When Neptune was discovered, Pisces was assigned to Neptune. Neptune was the Roman god of the sea. The prophet Isaiah spoke of the time of the messiah *when at that time the earth will be filled with the knowledge of God as the waters cover the sea.* Isa.11:9. Torah is compared to the sea. According to kabbalah, Pisces is the water sign representing the messianic time when Godliness is fully revealed on Earth. The Vilna Gaon said Adar, the sixth of the winter months, corresponds to the sixth millennium when Amalek will be destroyed.

As a water sign, Pisces operates in the realm of feelings. Like those born under other water signs of Cancer and Scorpio, Pisces connects through deep feelings. For the most part, Pisceans are deeply sensitive, intuitive, feeling-oriented people. Sometimes Pisceans try to absorb and transmute the negative energy around them and may think of themselves as martyrs. They may become too sensitive for their good. People born under the sign of Pisces are said to be the most compassionate and loving of people. These characteristics are also expressive of the loving, sensitive, and compassionate energy of this month.

Pisces, from the Latin word for *fish*, is represented by two fish swimming in opposite directions. One fish is looking towards Aquarius and the other towards Aries. Fish are known to have spiritual properties. Other animals were destroyed at the time of the Flood, however, the fish were not. Fish swim with their eyes open at all times, and Kabbalah likens fish to *tzaddikim—righteous people*—who swim the waters of Torah with their eyes open, always alert. According to Kabbalah, the two fish in Pisces represent Mordecai and Esther who saved the Jewish people this month.

Hebrew Letter: Kuf

The *kuf* is the first letter of the word *kedusha*, which means holiness. It is the first letter of *korban,* which means sacrifice, and of *kabbail,* which means to receive. Of course, there is a connection between these words and the energy of this month. The sacrifice of the ego allows for the receiving of holiness. Participating in the joy of this month is the easiest way to let go of the ego and open to greater holiness. Interestingly enough, the *kuf* is a letter that descends below the line reflecting the spirituality that enters into the material realm. It signifies the unification of the physical and spiritual worlds that gives this month a very special feeling of joy and holiness.

The word *kuf* means monkey, which is a symbol of laughter for this month. We sometimes use the expression, *to monkey around*, to mean to play or joke. We see the play of the monkey in the celebration of the holiday of Purim. Monkeys are said to be the animal most like human beings and they are great imitators. Monkeys imitate humans and humans imitate God. This letter representing the monkey reminds us that reality is not what it appears to be. God and holiness are often hidden, but they are revealed naturally during this month.

Hebrew Tribe: Naftali

When Rachel lent her handmaid, Bilhah, to Jacob a second time, Bilhah bore a son whom Rachel names Naftali, saying, *With God wrestling, I wrestled with my sister and I have been able to do it.* Gen. 30:8. The Torah commentator, Rashi, explains that Rachel did many things to be equal to her sister. She tried exceedingly, and Naftali represents her zeal. With the birth of Naftali, Rachel is now happy and feels she has been successful in participating in the building of Israel by having sons, even if they were through her handmaid. Rachel's accomplishment and joy are characteristic of the energy of this month.

When on his deathbed, Jacob blesses Naftali, he says that *Naftali is a deer like messenger and one who gives beautiful speeches*. Gen. 49:21. As a deer like messenger, Naftali does things swiftly. Rabbi Samuel Hirsch, in his commentary on Naftali, says that this blessing implies that Naftali may not be particularly productive or creative but he knows how to express himself in beautiful words and carries out what needs to be done efficiently and quickly. The energy of Naftali reminds us to complete things as quickly as possible and to be mindful to speak good words as we do what we need to do. When we hesitate or procrastinate, we become vulnerable to doubt and possibly depression. Naftali did everything quickly so he was said to always

> The energy of Naftali reminds us to complete things as quickly as possible and to be mindful to speak good words as we do what we need to do.

be joyous. Naftali's good words also protected him and were reflected back to him. Our good words are mirrored back to us and protect us as well.

Interestingly, Esther, the heroine of the Purim story of this month is called a feminine deer in the Talmud, as described in Psalm 22. The Talmud explains that a deer is always attractive to its mate, as Esther was always appealing to Achasheveirosh. It is said that Esther recited this psalm in preparation for her meeting with the king.

The blessing Moses gives to Naftali sums up the highest potential for this month. Moses says: *Naftali is fully satisfied with what he wished for and is full of God's blessings. He shall occupy the sea and the south.* Deut 33:23. Moses actually commands him to occupy the area around Lake Kinneret. The seas Kabbalah refers to is the Torah. In Koheleth, in Ecclesiastes 1:7, we read: *All rivers lead to the sea.* Sefer Bahir, an ancient Kabbalah text, says that the sea is an allusion to God. Because the sea is so vast, it is also a Kabbalistic allusion to the *World To Come*. The energy of Naftali represents the blessing of this world as well as in the world to come, which comes though the inheritance of Torah.

Ethics of the Fathers provides an important teaching about happiness. It asks, *Who is happy? He who rejoices in his portion.* This is the energy of Naftali. Naftali was satisfied with the will of HaShem, another name for God, and it was this that gave him the strength to do things quickly. The *Sfzat Emet*, the work of the Gerer Rebbe, said that when people are happy, they can be zealous because they know and feel that their actions can reach heaven. When we know we can make a difference, we are happy, and we will work quickly.

Even though Naftali was known as the quickest of the tribes, Naftali was often listed last. When it came to the dedication of the Mishkon, the portable tabernacle constructed for the Shechinah—the Divine Presence, Naftali was last, which was a sign of humility. Naftali represents a kind of humility that believes that even though one is far away from God, one can come close to God and this brings joy to a person. In a similar fashion, Naftali represents Adar, which is the last month according to the reckoning that begins the year with Nissan. As such, Adar is not an optimal time to create new projects, but a great time to complete them. Naftali signifies a blessing for abundance in this month, but we must also access the energy and zeal of Naftali.

Divine Name Permutation: HHYV

The letter *hay* occupying the first and second position indicates a great flow from above, from the higher worlds of Atzilut and Beriyah. This is indicative of expansiveness in the soul and the mind. Often it is said that on Purim we should be in the *I do not know* consciousness. Not knowing is often a higher form of knowing. By not knowing, our consciousness is open to the experience of a new revelation of the awesomeness of life itself. This revelation lifts our consciousness up to trust that life is unfolding according to the Divine Plan. *Vav* in the fourth placement indicates that the events in this physical world are the instruments, the channels, to express what is above. The letter *hay* in this position would indicate that the physical world is a vessel, but the *vav* informs us that it is a conduit. Everything in this world is a conduit for God's light.

Torah Portions

The Torah portions for Adar are mostly about the building of the Mishkon, the special place where God could be most directly experienced. Exod.36-40. The Mishkon was a physical testimony of the renewed relationship of the Jewish people with God after the sin of the Golden Calf. The Torah reports that the people gave from the heart with great joy and were so happy to have an opportunity to contribute in the building of the Mishkon. Exod.35:21-29. This reminds us of the joy of giving this month.

It is interesting to note that the Hebrew Scriptures, the Bible, give just a few lines explaining the creation of the world, but the creation of the

Mishkon is told in great detail and repeated in varying versions seven times. Even though Jews were told to build the Mishkon so God could dwell within them, much attention is given to the actual structure of the building. One might wonder why the Torah spends so much time on these details when the Mishkon only stood for forty years while the Jews were in the desert, and then for a few hundred years before the first Holy Temple was built.

As we read all these details in varying accounts, it is natural to wonder their relevance to us today. Kabbalah teaches us that the Mishkon was a miniature universe, a replication of our physical universe as well as that of the human being. Many secrets were encoded in all these details, the study of which goes beyond what we can explore here. The details of the construction of the Mishkon, however, have important implications according to Jewish law today. On the most basic level, the thirty-nine categories of work prohibited according to the laws of Shabbat are derived from the definition of work on the Mishkon. The laws of Shabbat are given this month as well.

The Torah portions of this month as a whole reflect the energy of this month. As Adar is about the joy of experiencing Godliness in the physical world, the Torah directs attention to the construction of a physical building. The reporting of all the details is to remind us of Godliness. For example, in the chapter of Tetzaveh in Exodus 27:20-30, Jews are commanded to bring pure olive oil to light the menorah so it will burn continually. It was not that God needed this service, but the people needed to be reminded of the light of God that was within them at all times. The clothes worn by the high priest also gets much attention. The garments are important because they also reveal aspects of Godliness. Every article of clothing expressed a different spiritual attribute and provided atonement for a different character trait.

The Torah portion of Ki Tisa in Exodus 30:11 begins with the census and the requirement for every man to give a half shekel, no more and no less. Counting is an uplifting process, communication that each person is important. The fact that everyone gave the same half shekel equally brought a feeling of unity among the people. That it was one half of a shekel teaches that a person is incomplete in himself. This section is read before Purim. The *Gemara* says that because the Jewish people were so zealous in the giving of the half shekel and were unified, they were saved from Haman's future decree. The giving of the half shekel expiated for the sin of the Golden Calf.

The main event reported in the Torah portion of Ki Tisa is the story of the sin of the Golden Calf. Even though the Jewish people had witnessed so many miracles, a portion of the people, mainly the mixed multitudes, the Egyptians who joined the Jewish people departing from Egypt, were frightened when Moses did not return as expected. They left Egypt because of their attachment to Moses whose magic was superior to their own. They could not relate to an invisible and unknowable God and felt incapable and unwilling to live life on a supernatural level now required. Being the magicians of Egypt, they used their magic to build a Golden Calf to act as an intermediary for them in the absence of Moses, who had been an intermediary for them. They needed to relate to something physical. God recognized this need and thereby commissioned Moses to build the Mishkon as a physical place for the Divine Presence to be concentrated. A pillar of cloud stood before them by day and a column of fire at night as they lived in the desert.

In the next portion, Vayakhel, in Exodus 35, the people are instructed to give what their heart inspires them to give. The Torah does not discuss what exactly was given, but is concerned with highlighting the intention in giving. Intention is what is important. The people were exceedingly generous.

Holiday: Purim

HISTORY: The events that form the basis of Purim holiday took place in Shushan, the capital city of Persia, in about the fourth century BCE. At this time, Jews lived in prosperity under the rule of King Achashveirosh At a banquet, King Achashveirosh orders his wife, Vashti, to dance naked before him and all who were present, but she refuses. Vashti is banished and murdered. It has also been said that there were many Jews in attendance at this feast who had assimilated sufficiently into Persian culture, and kosher food was even arranged for those who kept kosher. This was a wonderful renaissance time for many Jews to finally feel accepted in the host country where they were living.

In search for a new queen, the king stages a series of beauty contests across the region. Whether Esther entered the contest willingly or not is subject to debate. Nevertheless, she is selected to be a finalist. After many months of preparation, she is ultimately selected to be the next queen. Esther keeps her Jewish identity and her real name, Hadassah, hidden. Esther, in fact, means *hidden* in Hebrew.

Haman, newly appointed as prime minister, demands that people bow down to him and is incensed when Mordecai, known as Mordecai The Jew, refuses to do so. Haman then convinces the king to annihilate the Jewish people in the land on the day chosen by the drawing of lots. Purim is the Hebrew word for *lots*.

At this time, the Persian Empire encompassed 127 provinces extending from India to Ethiopia, so Jews all over the known world were targeted by Haman's decree. Because Haman tells the king that there is no unity, no brotherhood among the Jews, he feels confident that the king will accept this plan for their extermination. It would appear that the enemies of the Jewish people seem to know intuitively that when the Jewish people are not unified they are vulnerable to attack.

Mordecai persuades an initially reluctant Esther to plead for the lives of the Jews before the king. It was known that it was dangerous to appear before the king without an invitation. Mordecai tells her: *Do not imagine that you will escape in the king's palace any more than the rest of the Jews. If you persist in keeping silent at a time like this, relief and deliverance will come to the Jewish people from some other place, while you and your father's house will perish. Who knows whether it was just for such a time as this that you attained the royal position.*

Esther realizes that it was Divine

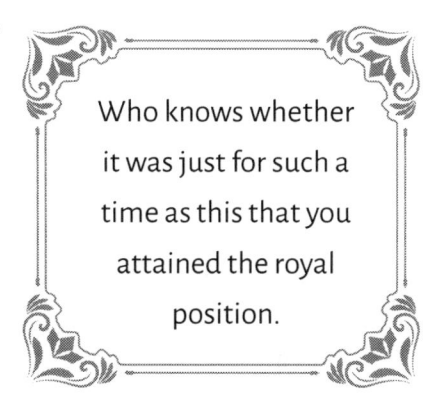

> Who knows whether it was just for such a time as this that you attained the royal position.

Providence that led her to the throne and that she has a certain responsibility to use this position now to save her people, even if it means risking her life. To prepare for this meeting, Esther undertakes three days of prayer and fasting, and asks the Jewish people to join her in this arduous undertaking. Esther intuitively knew that the key to saving the Jewish people was through strengthening their connection to God, and to their chosen people-hood. Though prayer, fasting and unity with the Jewish people, Esther contacts a greater strength inside herself to enable her to carry out her mission. That so many Jews participated in this fast was itself considered miraculous.

After the fast, Esther appears before the king uninvited, and the king is overwhelmed by her spiritual beauty and power. He asks: *What is your petition? Even if it be half the kingdom it shall be granted to you.* Rather than making her request directly, Esther invites the king and Haman to a party. Esther intuited that it would not be effective to make her request directly to the king when he was so enamored by her beauty. That decision would not stand the test of time. She knows it is best to use her sexuality to arouse the king, to flirt with him, and even with Haman, and through this, she will demonstrate to the king that Haman is not to be trusted. The king could not be told what to do but Queen Esther could create an environment so the king would see clearly who Haman really was.

After the first party, Esther invited them both to another party for the next night. The king, not able to sleep that night, is reviewing his records and discovers that Mordecai has done him a great favor and was not rewarded. At the next party, the king asks Haman what he should do to show favor to someone. Haman, thinking he is the one that king wants to show favor to, describes all kinds of wonderful honors.

He is later quite surprised when he learns that it is Mordecai whom the king wants to honor. Mordecai is awarded all the honors envisioned by Haman. Esther then reveals her identity as a Jew and informs the king that Haman wants to kill her and her people. The king is furious and orders Haman to hang on the very gallows he had earlier prepared for Mordecai. The king, seemingly unable to rescind the earlier decree, issues another edict empowering the Jews to defend themselves with military power from the king's own arsenal. There is a terrible war, but the Jews are victorious and celebrate their victory on the fourteenth of Adar. The fighting continued in the walled city of Shushan until the fifteenth of Adar, so that became the date of Shushan Purim.

The events of the story occurred over a nine-year-period of time. God is hidden in this story. There is no voice from heaven speaking through a prophet telling the people what to do, as with other Biblical holidays. In the Megillah (the scroll) of Esther, God's name is not even mentioned.

According to the teachings of one of the greatest Kabbalah teachers of all time, Rabbi Shlomo Elyahiv (1814-1926), Rabbi Avraham Sutton records in his profound book, *Purim Light*, that for six thousand years, the light of *Arch Anpin* (the higher face of God), called *Abba* (Divine Father) and *E'ma* (Divine Mother), flowed directly into *Zer Anpin* (the small face), known as *Hakodesh Borech Hu* and then to *Nukva* (the Divine Feminine) known as the Shechinah, that is received only in accord with our limited capacity to receive in this world. It is in this sense that Zeir Anpin (Hakodesh Borech Hu) and Nukva (*malkut*) are said to dominate during the entire six thousand years of the world through the six *sefirot—chesed, gevurah, tiferet, netzach, hod*, and *yesod*. The Shechinah through the agency of Malkut receives from these six *sefirot*. She governs and oversees all that transpires in the lower worlds. Everything that Ain Sof (the Infinite Light) does in our world, it does through the agency of Nukva, also known as the Shechinah. Nukva descends into the realm of evil to return Divine sparks from the realm of evil allowing them to be rectified.

There are however times when the higher modes of Abba and E'ma are revealed directly to us in this physical world in the form of Divine Revelation or miracles. These times are exceptional because when the higher revelations of Abba and E'ma are revealed directly to us, there can be no free choice. Infinite mercy and love pours down gloriously upon us, regardless of our merit. In these kinds of miraculous times, the face of God known such as Ha Kodesh Baruch Hu is hidden because now we receive directly from E'ma, the Divine Mother.

This revelation of Abba and E'ma directly to Malkut is said to be what happened in the story of Purim. This is a Kabbalistic explanation of why HaKodesh Boruch Hu (the Holy One Blessed be He) was not even mentioned in the *Megillah Esther* read on Purim. This revelation on Purim is

> Purim is a taste of the rise and revelation of the Feminine, both human and Divine, that will restore harmony and balance between the masculine and feminine in the messianic time.

a taste of the upcoming Messianic age when the unconditional love and light of Divine Mother will pour directly into the Shechinah to be fully revealed in the world. Purim is a taste of the rise and revelation of the Feminine, both human and Divine, that will restore harmony and balance between the masculine and feminine in the messianic time.

In this fantastic Purim story, a Jewish woman who by winning a beauty contest and marrying a non-Jewish king rises to become the savior of the Jewish people. God's deliverance comes during the Purim story in the midst of feasting, drinking, and sexual intrigue, revealing a most important teaching that God is everywhere and in everything. There is no split between the material and spiritual. The miracle of Purim demonstrates that God occupies all realms equally.

My teacher, Reb Shlomo Carlebach of blessed memory, taught that Kabbalah sees in the name, Haman, a reference to eating of the fruit of the Tree of Knowledge of Good and Evil. When God asked Adam: *Did you eat from the Tree of Knowledge?* (Gen. 3:11) Adam answered: *Ha-meem ha etz*. The *Gemara* says *ha-meem* refers to Haman. It is the power of evil, the power of Amalek, which the original snake represented.

Going beyond the knowledge of good and evil may be one reason for the recommendation to drink a great deal on Purim. Purim is about transcending the rational mind and being in the *I do not know* consciousness. This brings joy and a sense of wonderment to life.

The Gemara says that in the messianic time, all the holidays will be abolished except for Purim. I think that is because Purim embodies the consciousness of the messianic time, a time when we fully experience Godliness revealed in the physical world. Purim offers us a glimpse to the deeper truth that this physical world is a dwelling place of God which was the original intention for God in creating the world. Purim also represents a return to the unity consciousness of the Garden of Eden that existed prior to the Eating of the Tree of Good and Evil.

OBSERVANCE: On the thirteenth day of Adar, the Fast of Esther is observed in memory of the fast called for by Esther. It is not observed with the same frequency as many other fasts, but still many people do observe this day as a fast day. Fasting was a traditional spiritual practice observed by the Jews when confronted with war or a pogrom. The Jews were instructed to fast before they battled Amalek in the desert.

On the fourteenth of Adar, the holiday of Purim commences with the reading in its entirety of the Megillah of Esther. In cities that were walled, the Megillah is read on the fifteenth of Adar. Reb Shlomo insisted that the Megillah be read quickly. Many come to synagogue dressed in costumes and the Megillah is read in an atmosphere of merriment amidst cheering at the mention of Mordecai, booing at the mention of Haman and sometimes even whistling at the mention of Esther.

The holiday of Purim is a rabbinical holiday and does not have the restrictions according to Jewish law that biblical holidays do. For example, people may handle money, cook, turn lights on and off, and even go to the movies. According to Jewish law, people are supposed to have a feast on Purim and drink so much alcohol that they do not know the difference between *Cursed be Haman* and *Blessed is Mordecai*. These phrases actually have the same gematria so as to indicate their equivalency. By the way, many people actually take this rabbinical recommendation very seriously. By encouraging alcohol, the rabbis wanted people to become so intoxicated and joyful that they would experience everything as God. Good and evil are Divine disguises. When we can see through the masks of reality and see God underlying all of reality, we are very happy. People dress up in costumes to demonstrate that life is full of masks but it is fun because we know that God is behind them all.

Purim reminds us of a very important spiritual practice needed to transform our lives and the world. To defeat the illusion of separation, falsehood, and evil is to know and accept that God is running the world. When see God in everyone and everything that happens in the world and in our life as a spiritual practice we are given a taste of Divine Oneness. It is not necessary nor is it possible to understand this revelation only with your mind. We need Purim with all its customs and celebrations to open us to this level of ecstatic experience.

Since the miracle of Purim took place through parties and alcohol, Purim is party time. There are concerts, spoofs, and a tremendous spirit of joy and open-heartedness that is enhanced though the widespread use of alcohol. Purim is not complete without eating hamantasch, those delicious three-cornered pastries filled with prunes or jelly, supposedly reminding us of the hat worn by Haman. It is somewhat silly, but it is in keeping with the fun spirit of the holiday.

> Usually these gifts are not given directly to the person but through a third party, so the giver is hidden and it feels like God is giving to each person.

People are also told to give *shalochmonis* (gifts) to at least two friends. Some make elaborate baskets with fruit, cakes, and wine. Others make simple bags and pass out quite a few. It is fine to simply give two pieces of fruit, or fruit with a cookie. The great Rebbe Levi Yitzchok of Berditzov was said to kiss every banana, every apple, and everything he gave for Shalach Manot. It is definitely a heart-opening experience to prepare these gifts. Usually these gifts are not given directly to the person but through a third party, so the giver is hidden and it feels like God is giving to each person. So much fun to give and receive in this way.

Additionally, giving to the poor is encouraged at all times, but especially on Purim. *It is preferable to increase gifts to the poor rather than to increase shalach manot.* From: Kitzur Shulchan Aruch on the laws of *mishloach manot*.

When we give to other people, we are uplifted and feel closer and more bonded with these people. And most importantly, we feel closer to God, the ultimate giver. *God gives through us. We are God's hands and legs.* **So know if you see opportunities to give, it is because God wants you to**

use you to give on God's behalf. You will only be enriched through these acts of giving.

Holiday: Fast of Esther

In honor of Queen Esther, a fast is held on her fast day, which is the day preceding the holiday of Purim. Look at the Jewish calendar for exactly what day that will be when you are reading this chapter. It is good to make an effort to fast, at least part of the day and spiritually connect with the holy Jewish people who are fasting on this very day and to the tradition of Jewish people who have been fasting for thousands of years on this day.

Dedicate your fast and prayer for your own purification and for the elimination of evil in the world. Join with the Jewish people and all people who are praying that the consciousness of the wicked will wake up and be turned away from evil and towards the Divine and all that is good.

Meditation

Many Jewish books tell us that the Divine Names are the keys to receive anything a person needs in the world. In the great Kabbalah text, *Sharre Orah, Gates of Light,* we are instructed to ask anything from God by focusing on the Divine Name associated with that need. *Not only will this request by granted but this person will be loved in the heavens and beloved in the world, and will inherit both this world and the next.* From: *Share Orah,* First gate: The Tenth Sphere.

Just as we respond when our name is called, so does God. Though we can call on different names of God to better access unique qualities within ourselves, it's fine and often best to not be so specific. When Jews see the

Divine Name of YHVH in their prayer book or in their meditations, they do not pronounce the Divine Name itself; rather they say *Adonai* instead. The blessings of Adonai is considered the name most available to the masses of people and is honored as a treasure chest of blessings.

When we see the YHVH, the Tetragrammaton, in the prayer book or in our meditation and we say the Divine Name, Adonai, which is the Hebrew name associated with the sephira of Malkut, we are actually making a unification between Zer Anpin, which is the Divine Masculine, known as Hakodesh Borechu, with Malkut, which is the Divine Feminine known as the Shechinah. In so doing, this meditation is revealing the experience of the Oneness of God.

> Place yourself in a meditative state by taking at least five or six long conscious inhalations and exhalations. As you exhale, breathe out any tension, stress, anxiety, anything keeping you feeling limited or stuck that you may be experiencing. Focus first on the exhalation and letting go. The more you let go, the more you can open.
>
> Then focus on the inhalation. As you inhale, become aware that you do not breathe by your own will, but by Divine Will. Open to receive the breath. Open to the experience of being breathed. Every part of the body, every cell within your body receives the breath. Scan the body and allow yourself to identify areas of tensions or discomfort and direct the breath to those particular places. It is safe to relax and let go. Now focus on breathing into the heart and consciously open your heart as you inhale. Allow yourself to be with whatever feelings are present for you with love and compassion. Be aware that everyone and everything is breathed and sustained by the very same power that breathes you.
>
> Now carve out the letters of the Divine Name, one letter at a time, and place the letters on your inner screen with your eyes closed. See the letters of the Divine Name. See the yud, the hay, the vav and the

hay on your inner screen. As you visualize the Divine Name, repeat silently the Divine Name of Adonai. Now you are making unification and increasing your receptivity to the revelation of Divine Oneness. Stay with this meditation as long as you are comfortable.

You can also repeat, *Ribboneh Shel Olam*, Master of the World, which also means, Master of That Which is Hidden. As your consciousness deepens in this meditation, take time to listen to the stirrings within your own soul. What is your internal experience? What is your heart and soul yearning for? During this time, you can also ask to be blessed with anything you need or want. Do this for a minimum of five minutes. The longer you do this meditation with your heart, the deeper and powerful your experience will be.

A KABBALISTIC CONTEMPLATION FOR ADAR

Upon being inseminated by Abba, the Divine Father, Chochmah, E'ma, the Divine Mother, Binah, went through contractions to birth you and this entire magnificent, awesome, beyond beautiful and amazing physical reality as a garden of delight for all Her creation. She created you and everything for love and through love. Abba and E'ma are our Divine parents. It was for the sake of love and out of an act of love were you created. You have also been gifted with the capacity to emulate Her, that is, to create and give birth like She did and does with so much love, joy and ecstasy.

Repeat and meditate on this affirmation until you internalize the vibrations of this truth: *I was created out of love and for love. Only out of love. The Divine Mother never forsakes me and never forgets me because I am a part of Her.*

From: A contemplation from my book, *The Secret Legacy of Biblical Women: Revealing the Divine Feminine.*

Practical Recommendations

1. MAKE TIME FOR YOURSELF.

Sometimes we are so busy fulfilling all our responsibilities that we do not take time for experiences that bring joy into our lives. For example, if you enjoy being in nature because you feel most connected to yourself and to God in nature, give yourself time to be in nature. Wherever you live, you can find beautiful parks and nature settings. Even in New York City, it is not hard to do.

One simply needs to make a commitment to do activities that bring joy into one's life. Make a list of at least five activities and experiences that are joyful to you. Make a plan and commit to do at least two of these things this month and two other things in the next few months. It is important to give yourself permission to be joyful. When you are joyful, you are aligned with Divine Will, so let go of any thoughts you may have that you are wasting time by enjoying yourself.

2. DRESS UP IN A COSTUME FOR PURIM.

Dressing up in a costume increases joy during the Purim holiday. It is not just for children. It is fun to get out of the usual roles we play in life and pretend to be someone else and be seen in a different way. Choosing a costume that keeps people from recognizing you at all is great fun. You will be hidden like God. And people will be wondering the whole night who you are. That is most fun. Purim is a time when it is permissible to be absolutely outrageous. Men often dress up as women and women even dress up as Chassidic rebbes.

Get out of your thinking, analytic, rational mind, and get into your inner child. Your fun-loving inner child connects you directly to your soul. Fulfill some of your fantasies. Purim is a wonderful time for play and having fun. As adults we have a responsibility to make our inner child feel safe and joyful.

3. TRY TO BE AS HAPPY AS YOU CAN.

One of Reb Nachman of Breslov's important teachings is that it is a great mitzvah to always be happy. Though this may perhaps be an unattainable goal, still we can strive to be happy regardless of what is happening around us. In order to be happy, Reb Nachman advises us to always think about all our good qualities and blessings. Another most direct way to be joyous is to pray and meditate. There is a kind of extraordinary joy that is beyond this world that can be found in prayer and meditation, so do not deprive yourself of this experience. For a deepening experience of prayer and meditation, it is most helpful to be guided by someone who knows how to ignite access to the soul and/or be in a minyan with others who have also gathered together for this experience.

Always, make an effort to be happy especially if you feel sad. Even when you are sad, you can feel those sad feelings, without judging yourself wrong for feeling sadness. You can be happy even in your sadness if you remember that you are not alone and God is with you. If you have your health, there is nothing that is so important to be unhappy about. If you do not have your health, you still always have your soul and you have God. It is said that Shechinah rests on the bed of a sick person. You are never alone, even when you feel most alone.

Reb Nachman advises the depressed to read the passages in the prayer books that deal with the daily incense offering with great concentration. The incense in the Holy Temple had the power to remove negative energies. Today we can easily buy incense or essential oils to bring a feeling of joy into our space. They really help alleviate depression and anxiety. Avraham Sand, who lives on Reb Shlomo's *moshav* in Israel, has developed essential oils that approximate the contents of the oils used in the Holy Temple. You can contact him for this most special set of oils as well as easily purchase essential oils wherever you live to lift up your spirits.

Music is always very helpful. The prophets of old were always surrounded with music to keep them in a state of joy. Along with music is dance. Moving the body and allowing the body to be moved by music brings joy and connection between the body and soul.

Watching funny movies is also a way to be more joyful. Dr. Norman

Cousins popularized the importance of humor when he checked himself out of a hospital and watched comedies as a way to heal himself. Tell jokes to other people to get them to laugh so you can laugh with other people. That is also very healing. I recently watched a Netflix comedy series entitled, *Young Sheldon*. I laughed so hysterically for the first few episodes it was almost painful. I do not recall ever laughing so much as I did during those first few episodes. Now, I just chuckle but still enjoy the series almost nightly.

4. GIVE GIFTS TO FRIENDS AND THOSE LESS FORTUNATE.

Reb Shlomo used to say that on Purim we give to poor people in the same way we give to our friends. In this way, the poor people who receive a gift from you may think you are giving it to them not because they are poor but because they are your friends.

A wonderful service project for the holiday of Purim is to make many bags of *shalach manot* and distribute them to the homeless, elderly, homebound, or those in hospitals and nursing homes. Also give *shalach manot* to your friends, family, and acquaintances in your neighborhood or synagogue. Greet each person with a strong greeting of *Good Purim* in order to communicate strength, love, and hope. You will have much fun doing this, so do not deprive yourself of this joy.

5. LET QUEEN ESTHER BE A MODEL FOR YOU.

As a therapist I frequently hear frustration expressed by women about their inability to get their husbands to do what they want them to do for them, for himself, and for their children, Too often a woman will speak to her husband in a way that is demeaning, complaining, and demanding. That kind of speech is ineffective in motivating her husband to do what she wants. On the contrary, he resents and resists all of her suggestions, and tensions between them often increase. When I guide them to speak like Queen Esther did, not necessarily verbatim, but in the spirit of Queen Esther, they become successful and are able to get what they want.

What do we learn from Queen Esther from how she spoke? Even though Queen Esther was married to a most unsavory disgusting man, not by her choice, she transformed him by building him up in the way she spoke to him, saying, *If it pleases the king …* Esther spoke calmly and with great respect to her husband. She did not make requests of him, rather she skillfully guided him to come to the conclusions she wanted him to reach rather than telling him what he should do. Most women have to wake up to this reality. If they want a good relationship with their partner, they must know that men do not like to be told what to do. Criticizing them, crying, and begging them to do what you want often breeds resentment and accomplishes nothing positive.

A Tale to Live By

This Reb Nachman tale in the short book of teachings, *Restore My Soul*, reminds us that God gives us everything that is meant to be ours in this physical world. If we do not have it or if we lost something we must know that it was not meant for us now. There is no benefit in blaming ourselves for not having what we thought we wanted or should have. This tale shared in this section reminds us to trust in God and know that God is in charge of our lives and the world. To me, this teaching is a great comfort. We all do our best, but if we do not have what we thought we wanted, it may simply not be our destiny. It is not because we failed. Here is a Reb Nachman story illustrating this very point.

> One day a young man found a very large diamond in his digging for clay. He knew that only in a city like London would he receive the optimal value for such a jewel. Because he did not have money to travel to London, he merely showed the captain of the ship this diamond, and told him he would pay him for this trip upon reaching the destination.
>
> The captain impressed with this man gave him a first class cabin. Whenever he ate, he placed the diamond on the table and gazed lovingly upon it. One day, he fell asleep after eating and

the steward cleaned off the table and shook everything on the tablecloth into the sea, including the diamond.

When he woke up, he immediately realized what had happened. He was afraid to tell the captain what happened, because who knows what his response would be. So he maintained his spirit of optimism and joy as if nothing had happened. He trusted in God that somehow it would work out.

Meanwhile, the captain had a problem. He was carrying a cargo of wheat in his boat but he learned that he would suffer severe legal difficulties if it was listed it in his name. He asked this man to do him a favor and sign a bill placing all the wheat in his name. And the young man agreed.

The ship continued its journey. But shortly, before its arrival in England, the captain suddenly died. Now this young man had an entire shipload of wheat in his name that was more valuable than the single diamond he originally had.

Rabbi Nachman concluded this story by saying: The diamond did not belong to the man; the proof is that it did not remain with him. The wheat was meant to be his for the proof is that it did remain with him. He had good fortune only because he did not let his misfortune overwhelm him.

He trusted in God that harm would not come upon him even it looked like he faced a dismal fate. The lesson here is that we will have what is our destiny in the material world if we trust in Divine Will, so let's be happy.

Two of my favorite mantras of Reb Nachman are the following, *Gevalt! Never give up hope!* And, *If you believe you can break something, also believe you can fix it.*

7

Nissan

MARCH – APRIL

ENERGY
Moving towards Freedom

AREA OF HEALING
Speech

ASTROLOGICAL SIGN
Aries

HEBREW LETTER
Hay ה

HEBREW TRIBE
Yehudah (Judah)

DIVINE PERMUTATION
YHVH

HOLIDAY
Passover

A Personal Story

My friend, Rose, is my neighbor and a Holocaust survivor. When she meets new people, she usually introduces herself in this way, even though she is reluctant to share details of her story unless she knows a person is really interested. Like most other Holocaust survivors, Rose has a powerful story of hell and redemption.

As this is the month we celebrate the Exodus of the Jewish people from the bondage of Egypt, I felt it appropriate to share a little bit about the miracles and redemption that accompanied Rose's descent in Nazi controlled Poland followed by an ascent to freedom to Israel, New York, and ultimately to Florida. Rose's story is relevant to us because even if we were not personally challenged by the Holocaust, we each have had our own trials in varying degrees and many of us have similarly felt the Divine Hand protecting us. There is clearly often no other explanation for our survival and ascent than that.

Rose was born in Lodz in Poland, which is now Lviv in Ukraine. Before the Holocaust, Rose's early childhood was in a loving nuclear family with her life filled with Shabbat and holiday celebrations. The safety of her childhood was dramatically interrupted when she was seven years old by pogroms and eventually the Holocaust. In 1939, when Rose was seven years of age, her father was taken in Auschwitz. She never saw him again. Her brother was murdered by the Germans in 1941. Cold and hungry, Rose and her mother survived on their own in the Jewish ghetto. As a young child, Rose rummaged daily through garbage cans for food for her mother and herself. Starvation was rampant in the ghetto.

Her mother had been an observant Jew in the early years of Rose's life. When she and Rose both witnessed Nazis throwing beautiful Jewish babies and young children into a nearby synagogue set ablaze by them, Rose's mother told her to give up believing in God and to be street smart. Her mother said to her very definitively: *Do not pray to God. There is no*

God who will rescue you. Be strong. Be smart. And you will survive. Those words were carved into the heart of Rose until she reached her late 80s.

A few years later while still living in the ghetto, Rose and her mother were forced to board a train to Belzec, which was only a crematorium, as opposed to a concentration camp where there was a possibility of working and surviving. Her mother knew exactly the destination of this train and what it meant. With little notice, she unexpectedly threw Rose off the train. Her mother's last and only words to her were: *You are going to survive.* Rose had just turned eleven years old. It was a miracle that Rose survived, as the Nazis were shooting to kill Jews who jumped from the train. Many Jews did not survive the jump.

Soon, Rose found a woman in her early twenties with a young infant from the same ghetto who had also survived the jump from the train. Together they walked without food or water for two days to return to the ghetto. Rose returned to the only real home that she had known, now empty. Another miracle was that her uncle was still alive and quickly arranged false identity papers for Rose. With money and family jewels, he bribed a former maid to take care of Rose, not knowing that this former maid was now a prostitute for German soldiers. When German solders frequented the prostitution services of her supposed caretaker, Rose hid under a bed, quiet and fearful that she herself would be raped, and her Jewish identity would be discovered. It was not very long until this woman forced Rose to leave her home.

With nowhere to go, Rose went to stay in the cemetery by herself, a place she intuitively felt was safe from Germans. Cold, hungry, and depressed, Rose confessed to me that she no longer wanted to live but she was not going to kill herself. Everyone she had loved was no longer in this world. Why should she live? Her mother's last words, *you will survive,* resounded within her and gave her strength and fortitude.

Then one day, Rose left the cemetery to look through garbage cans for food when someone recognized her and called her name. How someone recognized Rose at that time was another miracle to Rose. She had not showered nor changed her clothes in a very long time. A Catholic lady who had been married to a Jewish man invited Rose to stay with her. She promised Rose that she would feed her, wash her, take care of her, and shelter her from Nazis. The woman had been a friend of her mother's so Rose knew her and trusted her. It turned out that this woman was already hiding seven Jews besides her husband in her home behind a wall. Rose had false identity papers, spoke very good Polish, and was eleven years old so she was able to go outside of the group hiding place of the other Jews. She stayed with this woman and seven other Jews until 1944.

After the war, Rose worked in an orphanage for several years. In 1947, she was fifteen years old, when she met her future husband. She initially refused his marital proposal saying: *I am just a child*. But he pursued her for two years and she married him when she was seventeen years old. Rose had wanted to make Aliyah and soon they moved to Israel and she bore two children there. Life was not very easy in the early days of Israeli statehood.

Rose was fortunate that her husband worked hard and was able to make a very good livelihood. They left Israel, moved to Paris, Canada, Brooklyn, New York, and finally ended up in Florida living in a fifty-five-plus community in a large and beautiful home. Rose's trials did not end with her marriage. Though Rose had a good marriage, her husband was very ill for many years. Rose nursed him until he left this world when he was only sixty years old, and Rose was fifty.

When asked, Rose speaks about her Holocaust experiences because she feels it is important that people know what the Holocaust was about. Many people ask her to tell them why and how she survived. She always confesses that she does not know.

Upon reflection, over time, Rose has come to realize that her survival was a miracle. It must be that *God wanted me to live*, she now says. She has no other explanation. Rose can now appreciate that she had been protected by a series of miracles. Subsequently, in her late 80s, Rose developed a personal relationship with God. She also dated a wonderful man who was also rabbi for a few years before he also left the world. That relationship may have helped to soften her to open to God.

Rose, now at the age of ninety-four, will tell you today that she is grateful for all of her life experiences, even for her personal health challenges and parenting challenges with her children. She claims to be in a continual conversation with God at all times. *God was with me in the past and God is with me today.* This mantra gives Rose the strength and courage to live her life with faith and integrity.

How Rose learned to speak, read, and write six languages without ever going to school is another miraculous story. Rose has told me she is street smart. I appreciate that about Rose. Rose sees life clearly. She does not entertain fantasies or illusions. I very much like that we can have frank and honest conversations about all kinds of matters. As a Holocaust survivor, she is quite alarmed by what is happening in the world today.

We frequently take walks together in the evening when it is not too cold or too hot. On Shabbat sometimes we sing Shabbat songs and I give over words of Torah. When she wishes me *Gut Shabbos,* sounding like a religious Jew with that old European accent, her eyes twinkle and she has a most beautiful smile. I can see that she is experiencing within herself the place of gratitude and Divine connection that sustains her each day.

Energy: Moving to Greater Freedom

Nissan is the month to leave personal restrictions and limitations and move to greater freedom. It is a time of miracles and redemption. This was the month when the Jewish people were redeemed from Egypt, it will be the month in the future when the final redemption will take place and in every Nissan, there is the hope and expectation that something new and wonderful will happen. Nissan is also called *Chodesh Ha'Aviv,* the Month of Spring. The scent of spring in the air makes us aware of the new life emerging in nature and reminds us to pay attention to the new energies stirring within us as well. There is a heavenly influx of grace and compassion this month enabling us to go forward in our lives.

Nissan is all about opening to newness and not being bound to the past. This month is about going forward in life. So do not waste time holding yourself hostage to the past. The past is over. Let go of trying to figure out the why's of your life with your mind. Trying to understand your life actually keeps you tied to the past. Live more in the present moment so as to receive Divine inspiration and blessing.

The month of Nissan is the headquarters for newness. Nissan is the time to let go of what keeps you limited, and create the space within you for newness. Nissan is the optimal time to receive the flow of new blessing to take you forward towards greater freedom and expanded love. A sign we are close to God is when everything feels new to us, full of wonder and possibilities.

What often keeps us feeling stuck in life is fear. We hold on to old habits, beliefs, behavior patterns and relationships that are uncomfortable and even toxic simply because they are familiar to us. What we know feels safe to us. What we do not know feels scary.

What if that is not true? What if letting go and taking steps forward into what is unknown is actually safer than holding on to familiar ego dysfunctional patterns that have previously blocked the flow of vitality in our lives. This is the month to have the courage to enter into what is unknown to us and open to new possibilities.

Listen this month to your soul's yearning to be more fully expressed and embodied in your life. Do not waste time resisting, denying, rationalizing, and numbing your heart because you are afraid. Seek protection in God. It is safe to be vulnerable. Being vulnerable before God is actually the safest place to be. It is safe to be in the not knowing. Give your life space to simply be without cluttering up your energy with activities that keep you busy but not fulfilled.

> Give your life space to simply be without cluttering up your energy with activities that keep you busy but not fulfilled.

Trust God and trust yourself and go deep inside to listen and open to the experience of being called or guided. Let go of the illusion that you are in control of your life, let go of your burdens and trust in God. The Gemara tells us: *Everything is in the hands of heaven except our awe of heaven.* According to the teachings in Ibn Paquda Jewish classic text,

> When we trust God we are blessed with the courage to move in new and expanded ways of being in our lives.

Duties of the Heart, trusting in God is the ticket to tranquility, blessing, and Divine protection. When we trust God we are blessed with the courage to move in new and expanded ways of being in our lives. Divine synchronicity so pronounced during this month helps us to remember that we are not alone. God is with us.

The epitome of the energy of the month is the holiday of Passover, the celebration of the miraculous departure of the Jewish people from Egypt. This Biblical story of the Jewish people's departure from Egypt by the hand of God is a message for the Jewish people and all the nations of the world for all times. The Passover story reminds Jews as well as all people that it is only God who has the power to move individuals and nations forward.

The Holy One could have redeemed the Jewish people through natural means, but the whole purpose of the exile and the redemption was for an everlasting and open display of Divine Revelation and miracles. With every plague, God revealed a different a different Divine emanation. Even God says in the Torah about the plagues: *Now you will fully realize that I am God*, in Exodus 10:2. The last plague was the most complete and intense revelation. It was not caused through an intermediary, as the previous plagues had been, but by God directly. *Around midnight, I will go out in the midst of Egypt and all the first born in the land of Egypt will die.* Exod. 11: 4-5. The revelation of God was said to be so intense that the souls of people left their physical bodies and died. The Angel of Death passed over the houses of the Jewish people who had poured blood on their doorposts as commanded. A significant percentage of the Jewish people actually perished during this plague because they did not prepare to protect their homes as instructed.

At the Passover Seder, we are reminded that this Exodus from Egypt was not just a one-time historical event. The Haggadah says: *In every generation, one should regard himself as though he personally had gone out of Egypt.* Ex.13:8. Metaphorically, we all feel a little bit still in Egypt, enslaved by the demands of the evil inclination—the *yetzer hara*. The Hebrew word for Egypt is *mitzraim* which means *narrow straits* to represent all the psychological, emotional, physical, and spiritual boundaries and constraints. Passover and throughout the month of Nissan is a propitious time to liberate oneself from one's internal and external constraints and make a personal exodus from our personal *mitzraim*.

Rabbi Yitzhok Luria, known as the Arizel, likened the descent of Jacob (the Jewish people) into Egypt to the soul entering a physical body. By residing in a physical body we each experience varying degrees of bondage. When we are not living and embodying our soul potential, we feel incomplete. There is emptiness and suffering within us when we are resisting the calls of our own soul and looking towards the physical world to nurture our holy soul. The soul will not be satisfied by our worldly accomplishments nor solely by anything in this physical world. Only when we strengthen the connection with our soul and our Creator, we are uplifted and we lift up the Divine sparks of all to whom we are attached. We then each will help restore harmony between the physical and spiritual world not just for ourselves but for everyone in the world.

Jews actually remember the Exodus many times each day. It is part of the liturgy of our daily, Shabbat and holiday prayer services. Its remembrance is contained within tefillin, those little black boxes on the forehead and arm to tie oneself to the Divine Presence. Remembering the Exodus is part of the Kiddush recited every Shabbat. The Baal Shem Tov suggested that we think of the Exodus at all times so we continually experience leaving places of constraint and moving to greater freedom.

The power of speech is the healing dimension for this month. It is through our own speech that we redeem or enslave ourselves. Rabbi Yitzchak Luria said that Pesach, the Hebrew word for Passover, is a conjugation of the words *peh*, the mouth, and *sach*, speaks, or, the mouth speaks. This is evidenced at the Seder where the main event is the telling of the story of the Exodus. The more questions we ask, either from the Haggadah or informally, the more the story will be told in greater depth. Kabbalah says that the highest form of speech is song. This level was reached on the seventh day of Passover, when the Jewish crossed the Red Sea and sang in unison the very same words. Song has the capacity to bring people together by unifying everyone's voices.

Words are also very important in Judaism. Words matter. The Torah states that the world was created through Divine speech. This is a metaphor because God is not a human being who speaks like we do. When the Torah tells us that God speaks, it is implying that everything in creation is Divine communication. Speech is used as a metaphor because speech is always dependent on the speaker to be heard. Made in the image of God, we create through speech as well.

It is interesting to note that Moses, our redeemer, had a speech impediment. He even initially refused his mission as redeemer of the Jewish people because he questioned how the Jewish people, much less Pharaoh, would hear and understand him. Some say that he stuttered because the world was not ready to hear his words.

The Torah records the conversation Moses had with God. Moses pleaded with God: *I beg you, I am not a man of words, not yesterday, not the day before, not from the very first time You spoke to me. I find it difficult to speak and find the right language.* God replies: *Who gave man a mouth? I will be your mouth and teach you what to say.* Exodus 4:10-12. Even though Aaron served as the mouthpiece for Moses, Moses was the mouthpiece for God. Through the words of Moses, reality changed.

This is the month we can overcome the ways we hold ourselves back from speaking our truth and carrying out our life mission. This is the month to allow our voices to be heard by others and even by ourselves. It is no accident that we are alive today so know that we each have something to contribute towards bringing peace into the world. Sometimes we do not know what we are going to say until we allow our souls to speak through us. This is often the best and preferable to thinking out beforehand what to say. It is important to give ourselves permission to speak when we feel called to do so. We each have the opportunity and privilege to serve as channels for God through our words, and our actions. And like Moses, our words can also change reality.

General Guidelines and Goals

The following guidelines and goals enable us to direct our energies in the ways that are optimal for our growth and transformation in accordance with the energy of this month. It is recommended that you read and meditate upon them often in the courage of the month. Reflect on their applicability to you and allow them to direct and inspire you often during this month.

1. CONNECT AND TRUST IN GOD.

There is a tremendous heavily influx of Divine compassion this month to lift us out of our ego-identified places of limitation and constraint. To go forward in our lives, we need to let go of the ways we have allowed fear, sadness and anger to limit our lives. When we trust God, we can accept that everything that has happened to us has served its purpose, even if we do not understand the whys of our lives. With this awareness, we can let go of the past, because our past does not define who we are now in the present nor who we will be in the future.

Trusting in God is said to be the ticket to inner peace, blessing, and protection according to teachings outlined in *Duties of the Heart*, a 12th century Jewish classic by Ibn Paquda. He tells us if we do not trust in God, we will put our trust elsewhere and God will withdraw providential care of us and leave us in the power in that which we trust. This sounds frightening to me. Furthermore, if we rely totally on our own wisdom, our own strength and industry, our labor will be in vain. Whatever we bring forth will not be sustainable. *Blessed is the person who trusts in the Lord and the Lord will be his trust.* Jeremiah 2:13. It is a blessing to trust in God. It is the key to all blessings.

Nissan is the month to move forward, even if nothing changes externally in your life, we can still move forward in our consciousness and in intensifying our Divine connection. Meditation, prayer, and doing mitzvot are the most powerful tools to move forward to greater inner freedom and well being.

As we grow and mature on our life journey, we naturally seek greater freedom from the limited and reactive ego states that have kept us enslaved to negative behaviors and limited concepts of who we thought we were or needed to be.

Within us is a passionate desire to be free to express who we really are and not feel obliged to live up to a false image of who we think other people imagine or need us to be. If there is something in your life that you no longer resonate with, know you do not have to stay in whatever you have felt that has limited you previously. Do not let fear stop you now. Fear disconnects you from your own soul, your own light and love. This is the month to live like you are not afraid to live. Trust in God and have the confidence to go forward in life.

People forfeit freedom in a variety of ways. Every addiction, obsession or compulsion limits a person's capacity for free choice and to move forward in one's life. Besides the obvious addictions in varying degrees to food, sex, and drugs, many people suffer some degree of compulsive or obsessive negative thinking that keeps them re-experiencing the pain of early childhood wounding. These people are frequently triggered and often blame other people or even themselves for their negative feelings and ineffective responses.

Just as the Jewish people cried out to God when the slavery in Egypt became too intense, so it is good this month to cry out when our personal existential pain becomes hard to bear. This cry humbles us to surrender, let go and go beyond the stories we tell ourselves. When we come to realize that the ego mind that is causing the stress and negativity cannot offer the solution or healing from our personal pain, we can let go of trying to figure out our life with our minds. Then we can surrender and truly begin our journey towards true freedom.

To become free, to be truly loving, we need to experience our attachment to that which is free, to that which is truly loving and that Being is God. Whether we acknowledge it or not, we are always connected to God because the soul that dwells within each of us is a part of God. Yet when we can distract ourselves, we lose access to our very own souls. Meditation, prayer, doing good deeds and spiritual practices are ways to experience greater alignment with our own souls and with God. We then become more aware of choices to be made between the higher knowing of the soul and the needs and desires of the ego mind. One way to discern the difference between the two is that the soul is peaceful and the ego mind is fraught with intense emotion. A sign of the contamination of a choice made by the ego is the tendency to compare oneself to others, to judge others and to want to be honored. Be patient and compassionate—the battle between the good inclination and evil inclination within each of us can be very challenging and profound.

Make inner peace a priority for you. Experiencing a state of inner peace assures us that we have made a connection to our souls. Always, make an effort to choose what your soul, or what you imagine God would want you to choose and not choose what your limited ego mind or the lust of the body wants. It would be helpful to frequently ask yourself and meditate on the question: What does God want of me?

Also this is a good month to take on a new *mitzvah*, a prescribed religious behavior to strengthen your God connection. Every mitzvah, every prayer, every meditation, if done with the right intention, can help liberate you from the demands and constraints of the ego mind. In so doing, it will be easier for you to make choices that will take you forward to greater and true freedom.

Be careful to resist the attempts of the ego mind to co-opt this behavior for its own purposes. There is such a thing as a spiritual ego, but it is still the ego masquerading as a more righteous or spiritual person. Sometimes, people may pretend to be who they are not, so people will think they are better, more righteous than who they really are. Such hypocrisy serves no purpose for nothing is hidden before God. For example, a person can pretend to be religiously observant but his religious practice is driven by the evil inclination, possibly a desire to be admired. My rebbe used to say the *yetzer hara* (evil inclination) wears a *strimmel*, the garb of the most religious.

The prophet Isaiah reminds us that there are no secrets before God: *With mouth and lips, they honor Me but their heart is far from Me.* God knows who you are and knows if you are sincere when you pray. You can never fool God nor fool your own soul. You on an ego level also know if your prayers are sincere and meaningful or not. Remember, God ultimately wants your heart, your love, and for you to be authentically the unique being God created you to be.

2. BE MINDFUL OF YOUR SPEECH.

King Solomon said in Proverbs 18:20-21, *A man's belly shall be filled with the fruit of his mouth. Death and life are in the power of the tongue.* We say in our daily prayer, *Guard your tongue from speaking evil and live long on the land.*

The Rambam (Maimonides) states that there are five categories of speech: 1. Virtuous speech that is a *mitzvah* like learning Torah, praying and so forth. 2. Forbidden speech such as *loshon hara,* criticizing oneself and others, gossip, lies, false testimony, and so forth. 3. Loathsome speech—idle conversations about current happenings, political intrigues, and so forth, 4. Desirable speech—such as discussion on how to improve oneself and others. 5. Permissible speech which is speech necessary for business and daily living.

Make a strong effort to increase virtuous and desirable speech, eliminate loathsome and forbidden speech, and limit permissible speech this month, Remember we each have the right to limit what we hear from others as well. We do not have to listen to *loshon hara* or any other form of loathsome speech. We can simply request to not have this kind of conversation and direct the conversation to a higher plane. Note how your energy increases when you engage in virtuous and desirable speech and decreases when you engage in forbidden or loathsome speech. It is however permissible to talk about other people if it is to protect them in a business dealing or in selecting a marriage partner.

The more mindful we are of our speech, the more powerful our words are when we do speak. That is why it is said that when a Tzaddik, a righteous person, speaks, God fulfills his decree. Guard your tongue. Don't waste words and your words will be more powerful. You can actually heal people with your words.

Widespread forbidden speech can destroy nations. We are taught that the Second Temple in Jerusalem was destroyed because we did not love each other. This baseless hatred was due to loathsome speech. It is very concerning today that there is so much animosity between people who hold different political affiliations, such as in Israel, America, and in many other places throughout the world.

Labeling people as extremists or as fascists for thinking differently creates divisiveness. Being unwilling or unable to talk with people who hold different political preferences is disconcerting. We must make great efforts to honor, love and appreciate all kinds of people, even if they hold different opinions than us. Most importantly, we must guard ourselves from speaking *loshon hara* for that contributes to baseless hatred. For example, it is appropriate to discuss or object to polices advocated by political parties without demonizing people for their differing opinions.

The *Chofetz Chaim (Hilchos Isurei Loshon hara)* says, *it seems obvious that the reason the holy Torah looks upon the transgression of loshon hara so strictly is because it incites the prosecuting angel against Klal Yisroel and through this many people are killed in many lands*. When Jews speak badly about others, we are creating prosecuting angels against ourselves and against all of Israel. So it behooves us to carefully watch our words. Make a strong effort to speak positive loving words and refrain from *loshon hara*.

3. AFFIRM THE PRESENCE, NOT THE ABSENCE OF GOD.

The world is filled with the glory of God. Rather than affirm our intrinsic Divine connection, we too often affirm the absence, the distance and our separation from God. We tell ourselves and others stories of how we have been victimized, how we have been abandoned, how God is punishing or how God is not there for us. Consequently we feel alone, often guilty, ashamed, depressed and angry in the face of life challenges. Holding on to these kinds of emotions blocks the flow of blessing and protection in your life. Let go of the past, feel and release these feelings that are rooted in the past, and lovingly open to simply being with yourself anew in the present.

Affirm that God is with you at all times. God is within you and within everything in creation. And, God also surrounds creation. This is what is meant by the Oneness of God—God is immanent and God is transcendent.

From our perspective there is outside and inside. From the Divine perspective, there is Oneness.

Trust that everything is happening for your highest good. Accept that what is happening in your life is Divine Will. Trust that God is supporting you through your life challenges. Always remember who your Creator is and how God is always with you, loving and supporting you to be the unique blessing that you are meant to be in this world.

This month make an effort to be more continually aware of the presence of God in daily life. This month a person can go forward in leaps and bounds, yet going forward always takes faith. Though there may be obstacles that seem to you insurmountable, like the Crossing of the Red Sea initially appeared to the Jews to be, but with faith, we each can go forward. This month is also an auspicious time to take some risks. When we live in the awareness of Divine Presence, we notice life is filled with small and large miracles every day. Just getting up each morning is a miracle. Life itself is a miracle, so always simply be grateful for the awesome privilege of being alive.

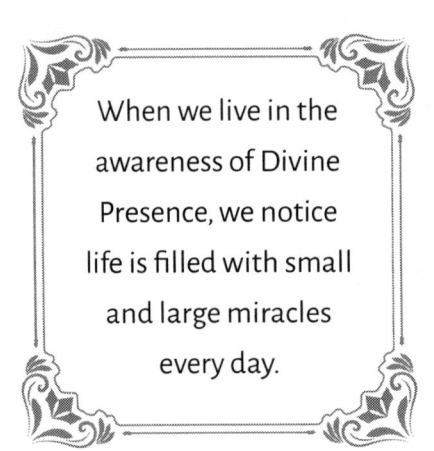

> When we live in the awareness of Divine Presence, we notice life is filled with small and large miracles every day.

4. BE WILLING TO EXPAND BEYOND YOUR COMFORT ZONE.

This is the month to be willing to live a more expanded version of your life. Your soul this month is nudging you to go forward in your life. So listen to your soul and not to your ego that may be resisting and frightened of life changes. Cultivate the courage to let go of what you know you have outgrown and go for what you previously thought was beyond or not possible for you.

Be open to new possibilities in your life that are unknown and not so familiar or habitual to you. Do things differently, meet new people, allow more of you to be seen and heard by others in new and different ways.

Appreciate your uniqueness. This month is the time to show the world who you really are.

5. FEED THE HUNGRY.

The Passover Seder begins with the following words: *Whoever is hungry, let him come and eat.* There are all kinds of hunger today. Probably the greatest hunger people face today is the hunger for family and community. Open your Passover Seder to friends and also to strangers.

One time I went to the store to pick up a few last things prior to the Seder and began talking to a Jewish woman there who did not have a Seder to go to so I invited her to mine. She added a lot to the awesome Seder we had. So from personal experience I can say that inviting strangers to your Seder will actually make your Seder more authentic and powerful.

It is traditional to give charity during this month to enable poor people throughout the world to celebrate the Passover holiday. Many organizations take on the mission to distribute Passover food to homebound elderly people and poor families throughout the world.

The Torah portions read this month tells us on numerous occasions to be kind to strangers for we were strangers in Egypt. Let's find a way to demonstrate kindness to widows, orphans, converts, poor and vulnerable people this month. In this way, we will become God's hands and feet and we will experience God's blessing more directly.

Astrological Sign: Aries

According to astrology, Aries is considered the first sign of the zodiac. It is a time of new beginnings. In its effort to evolve in a new way, the energy of Aries is willing to push past limitations and boundaries. The energy of Aries does not want to be defined by others, only by itself. Aries is a fire sign giving one energy and enthusiasm. Aries is a trail blazer and a leader.

The energy of Aries is about taking action in a very focused and direct way. Aries may often be focused on its own individuality that it may not consider the impact of how its actions affect others. Aries is considered the most impulsive sign. People born in Aries like to start new projects but often become impatient if these projects take too long to accomplish. They may take action without thinking things through so they can burn out or hurt others. We have to go forward this month but with mindfulness rather than recklessness.

Aries is ruled by the planet Mars. Mars was the Roman god of war. Aries comes from the Latin word for *ram* which is the symbol for Aries. The ram reminds us of the ram the Jewish people were commanded to slaughter in Nissan prior to the departure from Egypt. The ram had been an Egyptian god, a symbol of riches and power. Slaughtering something held in the greatest respect took a lot of courage and faith.

Aries is considered a masculine sign, aggressive, competitive and independent. The energy of Aries helps us to be self confident, decisive, assertive and courageous, empowering us to do new things this month. We can easily appreciate the resonance between Aries and Nissan.

Hebrew Letter: Hay

Sefer Yetzirah says that God crowned the letter *hay* for this month with the power over speech. The *Gemara* says there is no true speech except prayer from the mouth. The *hay* of this month is the final *hay* in the Divine Permutation YHVH. The final *hay* corresponds to the *sephira* of *malchut*, the kingship of God. The Divine Name for this sephira is Adonai.

The letter *hay* is such a holy letter that it appears twice in the Divine Name YHVH. Kabbalah says that God created this world with the letter *hay* and the world to come with the letter *yud*. The numerical value of the *hay* is five. It is no coincidence that there are five books of Moses, five fingers on each hand, five toes, and five levels of the soul. The Hebrew word for light, *ohr,* appears five times in the creation story.

Hebrew Tribe: Judah (Yehudah)

After giving birth to three sons, hoping that with each son her husband would love her, Leah gained an inner security and reached a higher state of consciousness. When she gives birth to Yehudah, her fourth son, she is no longer looking for her husband's love. She now stands strong, independent and connected to God on her own. She has secured her position as a mother of the Jewish people. The Torah reports that at Yehudah's birth, she says, *Now I will praise (odeh) the Lord. Therefore she called him Yehudah and left off bearing.* Gen 29:35. Yehudah is the only son of either Leah or Rachel who was not born out of pain, struggle, or competition.

The tribe of Yehudah is represented by the lion. The lion is the king of the animal world and the descendants of Yehudah became kings of the Jewish people. Jacob blesses him, saying: *Yehudah, your brothers shall praise you. The sons of your father shall bow down before you.* Gen.49:8. Everyone, even Joseph, recognized that Yehudah was like the king of the Jewish people in his time. As Yehudah was most prominent among the Twelve Tribes, so Nissan is the most prominent of months beginning the year according to the Torah.

The name Yehudah contains within it the Divine Name YHVH plus a *dalet*. The Hebrew word *dalet* means *door*. The name of this tribe is a doorway to God. That is why the kings and the Messiah come from Yehudah. Furthermore, the Jewish people are called Yehudim after Yehudah, indicating that all the tribes possess the attribute of thanksgiving that Yehudah embodied. All of this speaks to the majesty and importance of this month. More than other months, Nissan is a doorway to God.

The Torah records several incidents involving Yehudah to reveal the qualities and energies he represents. It was Yehudah along with Rueven who pleaded for the life of Joseph and finally convinced the brothers to sell Joseph rather than kill him. It was Yehudah who was strong enough to acknowledge publicly his sexual relations with a woman he thought was a prostitute but who turned out to be his own daughter in law. It was Yehudah who was willing to offer his own life in place of Benjamin. The energy of Yehudah is forthright and courageous. Like the impulsive energy described in the astrological sign of Aries, Yehudah is impulsive and makes mistakes but strong enough to admit them, repent and change. In this way, Yehudah demonstrates the kind of qualities needed for the leadership of the Jewish people.

Reb Shlomo of blessed memory used to say that Yehudah was symbolic of the *baal teshuva*, the person who does wrong but repents and Joseph represents the *tzaddik*, the righteous person who never does wrong. It is said that the *baal teshuva* is higher than the *tzaddik* because transforming negativity is more redemptive than never doing anything wrong. This is another reason why the Jewish people follow Yehudah, rather than Joseph, and are called Yehudim.

Divine Name Permutation: YHVH

God says to Moses: *I am Yud-Hay-Vav-Hay. I appeared to Abraham, Isaac, and Jacob as El Shaddai but I did not make myself known to them by My Name YHVH.* Exod.6:2-3.

YHVH is a wider and greater demonstration of Divine power. El Shaddai is a revelation of God experienced through nature. El Shaddai was the revelation of the Divine Name to righteous individuals, according to their capacity to receive. YHVH is the Divine Name of love and compassion independent of nature available to people regardless of their worthiness. It was this Divine Name that took the people out of Egypt and made them a holy nation. This is the Divine Name most commonly used in Jewish prayers.

The Divine permutation for this Name is in its proper and optimal placement for this month. This allows for the maximum flow of Divine blessings. The *yud* in the position of the world of Atzilut allows for a concentrated point of connection with Ain Sof. It expands in the letter *hay* in the world of Beriyah into the soul and is channeled through the *vav* in the world of Yetzirah into the heart and then expands to the *hay* in the world of Assiyah, the physical body.

Torah Portions

The Torah portions read during the month of Nissan speak in detail about sacrifices given in the Mishkon, the portable tabernacle for the Divine Presence, while the Jewish people were living in the desert. There were thanksgiving offerings and sin offerings for intentional and unintentional sins. Some offerings were obligatory and others were voluntary. Sacrifices were a way for the Jewish people to draw closer to God. When people sacrificed an animal, they were nullifying the animal part within themselves, letting go of the limiting parts of the self in order to be better able to receive the transmission of the holiness of God. We are told repeatedly throughout the Bible that the most important part of sacrifice is intention. To sacrifice something or to do religious acts in place of ancient sacrifices without the heart connection are empty and not meaningful to God. Yet done with proper intention, sacrifices and offerings forge a deeper connection to God within a person.

In the Torah portion of Shemini, Leviticus 9, on the eighth day, Aaron, the High Priest and brother of Moses, is told to slaughter a ram along with other animals and pour the blood on the sides of the altar. This command is reminiscent of the ram offering prior to the Passover holiday. The Passover holiday also lasts for eight days. Eight is symbolic of the supernatural, what is beyond the laws of nature. This is a month when the Divine Flow enables one to transcend the laws of nature.

The powerful story of Nadav and Avihu who died in the act of performing sacrifices is recorded in this Torah portion as well. From the simple reading of the text, it appears that their death was a punishment for offering sacrifices in an incorrect manner. Some say they were intoxicated with alcohol. Moses says to Aaron: *When God said, I will be sanctified before all the people, this event is what God was talking about.* Lev 10: 3.

Kabbalah generally sees their deaths as an act of grace. Their desire to be close to God was so great that their souls were liberated from the physicality of the body instantaneously. The Torah then devotes much time discussing animals that may and may not be eaten. If we eat animals that are not kosher, the Torah tells us there will be a blockage between the heart and the head, making it more difficult to access holiness.

The Torah portions give additional insight into the means of accessing freedom, what the energy of this month is all about. First sacrifice is important. Whether sacrifices are actual or symbolic, they must be performed with holy intention to both rectify sins and to also express gratitude if they are to open us to the Divine flow of blessing in the most powerful ways.

Second, this Torah portion tells us that what you take into your body is also important. If you are feeling blocked and unable to go forward in life, the Torah says it might be because you are eating not kosher animals. The Passover holiday is focused largely on food, on eating foods associated with the holiday and avoiding other foods. We are what we eat. So making food choices in alignment with our highest good is fundamental.

Holiday: Passover

HISTORY: The roots of the Passover are found in the Torah story that begins with the brothers of Joseph entering Egypt in search of food during a time of great famine. Joseph, who was ruling Egypt at that time, was distributing food to Egyptians and all foreign people seeking food. After being sold into slavery by his brothers, and cast into a prison for a crime he did not commit, Joseph, known as an interpreter of dreams in prison, had been called to interpret the dreams of Pharaoh and was now empowered to rule Egypt in behalf of the Pharaoh. Joseph recognizes his brothers but they do not recognize him. Rather than reveal his true identity immediately, Joseph tests his brothers to see if they regretted selling him into slavery. When the brothers express their regret for this act and the love for his brother Benjamin, Joseph reveals his true identity to his brothers and forgives them.

Joseph then invites his father, brothers, and their families to settle in the land of Goshen, the best land in Egypt during this challenging time. They were small in number initially but they prospered and became great in numbers and wealth while living in Goshen.

Over time, Joseph died and the memory of his reign faded. A new Pharaoh ruled in Egypt who, threatened by the power and proliferation of the Jewish people, instituted many measures to contain, limit, and oppress the Jewish people. During this time Moses, the redeemer was born and through Divine providence he was raised in Pharaoh's home by Pharaoh's own adopted daughter called by the Jewish people as Batya.

The oppression of the Jewish people increased until the Torah says: *We cried out to God, the God of our forefathers. God heard our cries, and saw our affliction, our misery, and our oppression. So God took us out of Egypt with a strong hand and an outstretched arm, with awesome power, with signs and wonders.* Deut.26: 7-8.

Prior to the miraculous departure from Egypt, the Jewish people had to perform three mitzvot: circumcision, the slaughter of the ram, and the sanctification of the moon. It was these mitzvot that gave them the strength to leave Egypt and all the impurity there. These mitzvot also teach us about the process of accessing freedom in our lives today.

Circumcision gave the Jewish people the strength to overcome the compulsion of physical desires because a free person is free of compulsion. By summoning up the courage and fearlessness to slaughter the ram, the symbol of an Egyptian god, they freed themselves from idolatry, the belief in powers other than God. When the blood was placed on the doorposts of their homes, God *passed over* those houses in the tenth plague that was the death of all firstborn which served as the basis for Passover.

The sanctification of the new moon made the Jews realize that everything changes like the moon. This gave them hope. The moon goes through cycles, and observing the moon, we learn that what is empty will be full and what is full will be empty. For the Jewish people, this was a reminder that times of oppression will be followed by times of emergence.

In sanctifying the new moon, in the month of Nissan, the Jewish people demonstrated through speech their power over time. The time of the new moon was called out and that established the timing for the holidays, for Jewish holidays are all based on the moon. With this mitzvah, the Jewish people gained the ability to call particular days holy.

Prior to the departure out of Egypt, the Egyptians and the Jewish people experienced the Ten Plagues in different ways as described in the Bible in Exodus 6-12, and in the *Haggadah,* read during the Passover Seder. After this, the Jewish people left Egypt quickly, and then a few days later experienced another miracle at the Crossing of the Red Sea. Exod. 14:21-15:20,

OBSERVANCE: The holiday of Passover lasts eight days. The first two days and the last two days have special restrictions outside the land of Israel. On those days, we light candles, have festive meals, go to synagogue for prayer services and refrain from work. On the days in-between, we can work but many people like to extend the holiday to be with family. Jews in Israel only celebrate the restrictions on the first and last day of the holiday.

The laws regarding the observance of Passover are more restrictive than those for any other holiday, which is somewhat paradoxical in that Passover is all about freedom. It is paradoxical that this holiday celebrating God's compassion and miraculous deliverance of the Jewish people requires the greatest preparation and effort. Many people begin preparing for Passover a month before, right after Purim.

It is also paradoxical that Passover, which may be thought of as the most particularly Jewish of the holidays because it celebrates the historical deliverance of the Jewish people from Egypt is the most universally observed Jewish holiday. Many Jews marginally connected to the Jewish people as well as non Jews make efforts to be at a Passover Seder or create a freedom Seder modeled after the traditional Seder. Though the text of the Hagaddah used at the Seder may be different, everyone at a Passover Seder will eat matzah, taste bitter herbs, sing, say prayers, and try to drink four cups of wine or grape juice.

Preparations for the holiday begin with the removal of *chometz* from one's possession. The Torah says: *During these seven days, no leaven should be found in your homes ... You must not eat anything leavened.* Exod.12:19-20. *Chometz* refers to grains such as wheat, rye, spelt, barley, and oats that are mixed with water and allowed to ferment. Though the Jewish law stipulates that one should not benefit from or even have possession of *chometz* during the holiday, the rabbis have devised a way for people to sell their *chometz* for the holiday to non Jews so they do not have to throw everything as was done in ancient times. Everything in the house is cleaned, *koshered*—made kosher—and prepared for Passover. Many people use this mitzvah as a time for intensive spring cleaning, and getting rid of what is no longer used or needed.

Ideally, as we search and clean our physical house, we also do a similar process in our *inner house* of our mind and heart. Spiritually, *chometz* is associated with pride, negativity, and whatever does not allow one to be in the moment, all parts of the ego mind and subconscious the keep one limited and bound to the past. Cleaning the house of *chometz* is a spiritual purification process for us on all levels of our being. As we remove and release our personal negativity symbolized by the *chometz*, we open to positive energy, creating greater possibilities for newness in our lives.

On the fourteenth of Nissan, a powerful ritual known as *bedika chometz,* the final search for *chometz,* takes place. Some pieces of *chometz* are placed throughout the house and the blessing is recited: *Blessed are you God King of the universe who has made us holy with His mitzvot and commanded us to remove chometz.* So this blessing will not be said in vain, one searches every room by the light of the candle and a feather to collect the *chometz* previously distributed. As one walks through one's home with a candle, without the benefit of electric light, it becomes a powerful way to look into one's heart and soul for *chometz*. This is one of those acts that one has to experience its transformative power firsthand.

Another powerful ritual is the burning of *chometz*. This is powerful, whether you do it yourself or bring your *chometz* to a synagogue and watch it burn along with the *chometz* of others. To me, watching the fire burning the *chometz* is the final release, the burning away of the limited ego states symbolized by the *chometz*. There is a wonderful feeling of freedom afterward. After that, a powerful prayer is said, through which people renounce all possession of *chometz*: *Any chometz in my possession which I did not see, remove or know about shall be nullified and become ownerless as the dust of the earth.*

Our words are important and complete this purification process. Though we may not have been successful in eliminating all possession of *chometz*, when we say these words, we wipe our hands of *chometz*. It no longer exists for us.

The main food for Passover is *matzah*. Matzah is symbolic of the unleavened bread that the Jewish people took with them to eat as they hurried to flee Egypt. The Torah tells us: *Eat matzah for seven days. By the first day you must have your homes cleared of all leaven.* Exod. 12:15. Made only of flour and water and baked within eighteen minutes so it does not rise or become leavened, *matzah* is called the bread of affliction and also the bread of freedom. Matzah is simple, humble, and in the moment.

My rabbi, Reb Shlomo, used to call *matzah* medicine. The Zohar calls it the food of healing. At your Passover Seder, experiment with eating the matzah silently to increase the full impact of this experience. If you can get handmade matzah, this experience will be stronger. As you eat the matzah, be aware that Jews all over the world are eating this same simple food, which Jews have eaten for thousands of years at this very time.

Affirmation for Seder

To be read prior to eating matzah at Seder or during the week.

I am the Lord who has taken you out of Egypt. Open your mouth wide and I will fill it. Tell me what you truly want. Your needs and your desires are important to Me. Pour your heart out to Me. (It will be more powerful if you actually open your mouth like a baby waiting to be fed and speak to the Creator about your needs)

> *Make a space for Me in your life. To give you what I want and what you really want, you need to let go of your old habits and limiting ideas of who you are and who I am. Change your vessels, open your heart, so you can receive something new from Me. I am your healer and your redeemer. I love you. I took you out of Egypt in the past and I will take you out from limitations and bondage in the future. I want you to be free and joyful. The holiday of Passover is a special time for Me to pour my light and love upon you if you are open to receive it.*
>
> *To best receive from Me, go on a Passover diet, eat simply, pray, sing, dance, be happy and have faith and trust in Me during this auspicious time. If you open your heart to Me and My Will, even just a little, I will liberate you from the fears and doubts that plague people who think that they can live life only by their own will. When you let go of the will of your personal ego, and attach yourself to My Will, I will bring you close to Me. You will be protected, and know a love and joy that is beyond this world. You can not experience the joy of true freedom without attaching yourself to Me. I love you more than you can fathom.*

To deepen the Seder experience, take time to understand the structure, content and context of the Seder as you read through it. Explore why certain things are included in the way they are. These questions and the answers you find through commentaries or within yourself enable a greater sharing among participants and a deeper revelation of Godliness at the table.

The Passover table is a time for discussion and singing. In addition to the four cups of wine and the four questions, Hallel, songs of praise, are sung during the Seder and thought the holiday. As I said previously, the Seder is filled with words and song and this reminds us of the healing of speech this month.

There are many wonderful *Haggadahs* available to guide your Passover Seder, so I will not review the Seder here. There are also many books, including cookbooks to guide you in preparing the special foods for the Seder and for the entire Passover holiday. It is great to have a variety of *Haggadahs* at your table so people can share the unique insights into the rituals composing the Seder.

Shir HaShirim (Song of Songs) is read on the second day of Passover. This mystical love poem expressing the passionate love between a man and woman written by King Solomon is a metaphor for the love between the Jewish people and God. The seventh and eighth days of Passover commemorate the miracle of crossing the Red Sea. On the eighth day of Passover, a final meal dedicated to the Messiah is eaten. At this time, we eat our last matzah and dream, talk, and sing about the final redemption. Passover offered a taste of redemption yet we trust that the final and complete redemption will come in the future. This will be a time when there will be no war and no illness, and everyone will be aware of the Oneness of God.

Meditation

The Divine permutation for this month is YHVH. The letters are in their proper placement. We are told that this powerful name of God was not given to Abraham, Isaac, or Jacob, but only to Moses. Some translate this name to mean: *I was, I am and I will be.* God is Being itself.

> Take a few minutes to center yourself with the breath Take slow deep breaths. Inhale from deep in the belly, to the rib cage, all the way to the chest, Hold the breath and then exhale from the mouth. Do this several times until you feel present and relaxed.
>
> Now as you inhale, visualize the letter Yud the middle of the head, Meditate on the *yud* and imagine that the letter radiates light and fills the head with light. Stay with this visualization for a few moments as long as you feel comfortable.

Then breathe in the letter *yud* again but on the exhalation, visualize the letter *hay* in the heart. Visualize that the letter *hay* offers shelter to the heart. The heart feels safe to open, allowing yourself to feel all the feelings that are in the heart. Stay with this visualization of the *hay*, allowing the heart to open as you love and accept yourself deeply on an emotional level. Do not judge or make yourself wrong for the feelings that are present for you. Sometimes negative feelings are a call from the inner child to love and accept oneself more deeply.

Breathe in the *yud* and exhale the *hay* with a few more breaths. Then visualize the *vav* connecting the heart to the genitals. Fill the torso with light. Stay with the straight line of letter *vav* and allow the light to penetrate all the organs in this part of the body that work so hard to sustain your physical embodiment. Allow this part of the body to relax and direct the light to any places where there may be tension.

Then place the final *hay* in the waist and legs. Be aware that you stand in this world. You can walk in this world metaphorically as well as literally. You have impact on the world.

Now coordinate the complete name of God with the breath. Breathe the *yud* into the head, exhale the *hay* in the heart, then breathe in the *vav* in the torso and exhale the final *hay* visualizing it in the waist and legs. Do this several times, optimally twenty-six times as this is the gematria for this Divine Name.

As you visualize the letters, you can say their names silently to yourself. What color are they? You may find that the colors of the letters actually change and this is a good sign. If they are black, see if you can visualize them as white. Allow each letter to permeate you deeply so you experience them in the core of your being.

MORE ADVANCED MEDITATION ON THE DIVINE NAME

Place yourself in a meditative state. Say the permutations of the letters of the Divine Name with the Hebrew vowel sounds SILENTLY to yourself. We have been instructed to **NOT SAY THESE PERMU-TATIONS OUT LOUD, even when alone.**

Breathe in light with the letter *yud* into the head to the count of ten and visualize the letter *yud* into your head and SILENTLY say YAH.

Exhale the letter *hay* and silently make the sound in your head HAH to the count of five as you see the letter *hay* in your heart and radiate the light through the heart with the letter *hay*.

Breathe in the letter VAV, seeing the VAV in your torso, to the count of six and SILENTLY say VAH. The VAV is the connector of the head, heart and body. So it is good to visualize the VAV and travel up and down it a few times before proceeding.

Then, on the exhalation visualize the final HAY in your waist and legs and SILENTLY say HAH to the count of five.

Do this at least TEN times. Remain focused and do not allow your mind to wander. It is important that the mind not wander.

If you have mastered the previous meditation, and your mind has not wandered much and you feel yourself ready and capable to hold the enhanced vibrations of this meditation, you can repeat the previous meditation but now using the other vowel sounds as demonstrated previously. YAH, YEH, YI, YU, AND YOH, with each letter in the Divine Name YHVH as described earlier.

Practical Recommendations

1. BE MINDFUL THIS MONTH TO FOCUS ON THE POSITIVE.

When we focus on the positive in our lives and are grateful, we open ourselves to receive the Divine Flow. When we focus on what is negative, and repeatedly telling ourselves stories how we are victims, we block the flow of blessing. Remember that the negative is usually tied to something in the past that no longer exists. When we feel sad or angry about what has happened in our lives, we may be denying the power of Divine Providence. Of course it may take time to heal from great losses or trauma, but during this month try not to allow the past to contaminate the gift and spiritual opportunity the present moment now offers you. There is always something new and beautiful to focus on in every moment.

When we pray, meditate, sing, dance, laugh, love, do acts of kindness, and feel grateful for everything, we change our energy. Give yourself time each day to do something positive for yourself or for others. Keeping a journal will help you make an effort to do something positive each day.

The great inventor Nicolas Tesla suggested: *If you want to find the secrets of the universe, think in terms of energy, frequency and vibration.* As we grow spiritually, we become more aware of ourselves as vibratory beings. We are embracing and raising our frequency, or resisting, blocking and lowering our vibration. Everything is recorded in our vibratory field of consciousness. As we change our energy with gratitude, prayer, meditation and doing good acts, we change our experience of life. It is that simple. When we volunteer to align with the Creator and be of Divine service, our energies are uplifted and we live on a higher frequency.

2. IDENTIFY WHO AND WHAT SUPPORTS YOU.

Imagine that in front of you lies a long straight path to the top of the hill. You begin at the bottom of the hill and you want to travel to the top. At the top of the hill is freedom, peace, and all that you want to open up to in your life right now.

As you travel on the path, imagine that you see people you know as well as people you do not know, even people from the Torah and Jewish history, cheering you onward and upward. Perhaps Moses, Avraham, Sarah, or Miriam are applauding you with each step you take. What do you imagine they would say to you? People are rooting for you to live a fulfilling meaningful life.

See yourself climbing upward and then visualize that you reach the top of the hill. Take a moment to receive all the wonderful feelings of accomplishment, and victory having reached the top of the hill. You have been Divinely supported to be victorious and capable of living your life. You have what it takes to go forward in your life. You have the confidence that you can grow through all of life challenges. Be thankful that Divine support enabled you to reach your goals.

When you volunteer to be of Divine service, to be used by God, know it is God working through you that enables you to accomplish what you do. So be grateful. Remember do not take personal credit for what God does for you and through you.

Joseph so beautifully modeled this humility when he was asked by Pharaoh to interpret Pharaoh's dreams. Joseph replied that he could not interpret dreams on his own but God would do it through him. Joseph spoke with so much authority and certainty that Pharaoh trusted him and elevated him to the second highest position in all of Egypt. It was because Joseph attributed his skill to God that he was respected and elevated. He was clearly seen as a channel for God's guidance and not just a human being.

A Tale to Live By

Many stories in all traditions remind us that whatever is happening in our lives is ultimately for the good. Here is one of the most known stories about this deeper truth in Judaism.

Rabbi Akiva was searching for lodging for the night but was refused by an inn keeper due to the rooster he was traveling with and the donkey he was riding. Rabbi Akiva was forced to camp outside. That night, his rooster and his donkey both die. And when each died, he said, *Gamzu l'Tova, this is also for the good.*

The next morning, he learns that robbers had murdered everyone who had been staying in the inn. If he donkey had brayed, or his rooster had crowed, he would have been heard and found and also killed. So their deaths saved Rabbi Akiva's life.

The rabbis are telling us how to meet misfortune and challenge in our lives. Though it may not appear so at the time, a person who trusts in God will be protected. All things are happening for people rather than against them. Sometimes when we may experience trials, we may feel ourselves descending away from God. Yet, when we trust in God, we experience ourselves ascending upwards higher than before we experienced our descent.

In this month of Nissan we receive glimpses of what the ultimate redemption will be when we trust in Divine Will. Everything happening to us and in the world is to take humanity forward to fulfill the Divine Purpose for Creation which is to create a conscious dwelling place for God in this physical world. For this higher consciousness to be embodied we have to let go of what is not true and cling only to what is true, and that is God.

8

Iyar

APRIL – MAY

ENERGY
Healing of the Body, Heart, and Soul

AREA OF HEALING
Thinking

ASTROLOGICAL SIGN
Taurus

HEBREW LETTER
Vav ו

HEBREW TRIBE
Issachar

DIVINE NAME PERMUTATION
YHHV

HOLIDAYS
Counting of the Omer
Lag B'Omer
Yom HaAtzmaut

A Personal Story

When I was in graduate school for a Master's Degree in Social Work in the mid 1970s, spirituality and meditation were certainly not part of the curriculum. Professionalism required a therapist to be value free, neutral and of course not advocate any belief in religion. Yet I knew from my own life that it was the opening to the experience of God that healed and strengthened me. As this was the most powerful vehicle for my own healing and personal transformation, I knew that this was what I wanted to share with my clients.

My primary goal as a therapist from the mid 1980s when I finally entered into private practice until even today is to help people to accept their thoughts, feelings and actions in a loving compassionate way so as to liberate themselves from the hold that judgment, anger, sadness, guilt, fear, and shame that have held them hostage. People usually come to therapy only because they are suffering. Though every person has a unique story, trials, and challenges, the ways I work with each person are similar. In addition to talking, my clients will be guided to experience meditation, psychotherapeutic and bio-energetic processes, Jewish teachings, inner-child work, and deep emotional release work to varying degrees as part of their therapeutic work with me. Most of my clients are also guided to develop or strengthen a spiritual or religious practice to support deepening connection with their own soul and God.

There have also been clients in my private practice suffering from tremendous physical pain in addition to emotional pain and I also have worked with a few clients who knew they would soon be actually dying. It is a holy privilege to be able to guide people in their last days and weeks by strengthening the intrinsic God connection that they are seeking at this auspicious time in their life journey. In one instance, I chanted the Shema for one client who was very close to death. Though she could not really talk at that time, and someone held the phone for her to be able to hear me, she was able to let me know that she heard me. Earlier when she was able to talk but still was in hospice, she asked me so sweetly and humbly how God would be willing to receive her when she only sought to come close to God when she really needed to experience her connection with God at this time of her dying. I assured her of God's love for her as well as my love for her. I sincerely felt that she really heard this message of love and was grateful and comforted as was I to share this message of love with her.

In addition to a fulfilling private practice in my home while living in Manhattan, I also worked as a therapist in a psychiatric clinic a few days each week for several years. I was actually hired by the head psychiatrist also executive director and owner of this clinic because he firsthand experienced my work in Jewish meditation. Because I was also a licensed social worker, he was able to charge insurance plans for the myriad of different services including meditation sessions that I offered at the clinic.

One of my primary responsibilities at the clinic was to offer meditation sessions to clients of all faiths and backgrounds to help them to move out of their heads and into their bodies, hearts and souls. When I helped these clients to activate their own faith, their transformation was quick and almost miraculous.

I particularly remember a female non-Jewish female client in her early 80s who came to the clinic because she was too anxious to eat. She was losing weight and becoming increasingly frail. I guided her to breathe into the belly in a way she did not really know how to do previously. I told her to accept that God is breathing and sustaining her right now with her every breath. Knowing that God was so close to her allowed her to relax and be able to enjoy food again. She believed in God but it was only intellectual and did not know how to integrate this belief in God into her life until she experienced this simple meditation. Once she did, she was cured of her eating disorder and able to eat again in only one session. Meditation helps us to move out of the head into a deeper more core awareness of ourselves and God.

God also was a very powerful healing force for a non-Jewish couple I worked with intensively for almost two years whose son had murdered his wife. I worked with each spouse individually and with them as a couple. Though the son did not feel guilty for this act, the parents did and they blamed themselves and each other. As they began therapy, they were in danger of getting a divorce, as well as losing their employment because they were not able to function effectively due to anxiety and depression. Their son was on death row.

With counseling this couple learned to listen and support each other's feelings. Their marriage actually strengthened. They were also guided to develop a meaningful prayer life that they never had previously. They prayed, meditated and recited psalms together daily. Additionally, they gave themselves time to talk and listen to each other daily without giving advice. As an aside, I instruct all my couples to talk, listen, and validate each other feelings without ever giving advice.

This couple also began to go on numerous Christian spiritual retreats and enlisted a whole network of people to pray for their son. The famous Sister Helen, known for ministering to people on death row, took up their cause. Many miracles occurred for this couple. Their lives were changed forever. They actually became better, more whole, more present, more loving and conscious people than they were before.

Being a therapist and spiritual guide is a great honor and awesome privilege for me. I have come to appreciate that in many ways, in our modern times, the therapy room is a place of revelation, one of the most holy and sacred places available to people today. It is here that people share their secrets, their deepest feelings, their fears, resistances, hopes, dreams and their fantasies. It is here that they discover and accept aspects of themselves that they did not or could not acknowledge even to themselves previously. Through the therapeutic process, people release the hold of the negative inclination, the judgmental inner critic, free up the *klippot*, the shells, of the wounded ego and awaken their awareness to the hidden sparks of their own holy soul, their true essence. In so doing it is like they give birth to a more conscious peaceful being, more in alignment with their most authentic selves.

When we open more to our most authentic selves, we become vessels to receive greater love and joy in our lives than we previously allowed. The month of Iyar is known as the most optimal time to do the inner healing work to prepare yourself to be an even larger vessel for something wonderful and new in the upcoming month of Sivan.

Energy: Healing of Body, Heart and Soul

Iyar is known as the month of healing. The Hebrew letters for the name Iyar spell out the initials of the verse, *Ani Yud-Yud Rofecha*, or, in English, I am God your Healer. Iyar is a time of detoxification, purification, and refinement of one's character traits. As spring begins to emerge more fully during the month of Iyar, we also begin to bring ourselves to a new order, a new alignment. Iyar is a time of letting go of what does not support our well being—what is toxic, what is false—a time for opening up to what does support our well being—what is true and what is real.

When many people hear that Iyar is the month for healing, most feel a combination of relief and gratitude for permission to bring forth their deeper issues. It takes a lot of energy to suppress feelings and so liberating to accept, feel and release them. The spiritual energy of the month of Iyar supports a deep level of release and healing in the easiest, most gentle and life-affirming way.

Iyar is the connection between the previous month Nissan, which hosts the holiday of Passover and the following month Sivan, which hosts the holiday of Shavuot. In Nissan, which marks the beginning of spring, there is a spiritual waking up to new possibilities, to new freedom within oneself. Passover marks the beginning of a new journey, a movement from internal or external constraint to greater freedom, expansiveness, and self expression that culminates in the receiving of the Torah and Divine Revelation in the month of Sivan, during the holiday of Shavuot.

The healing work of Iyar corresponds to the planting work done in Iyar. There is a spiritual practice of Counting the Omer that is discussed in this chapter in much detail later on that helps restore balance and harmony in our lives. When balance and harmony is restored, a person is better able to receive blessings.

Healing first begins with a careful discernment between ego states masquerading as the self and the soul, which is our true essence. Sometimes, it is not easy to discern the difference. As a general guide, we are most likely identified with an ego state if we find ourselves spending time justifying our position, analyzing, and judging the actions of ourselves and others or we feel frustrated and upset when life does not always happen according to our desires and what we feel we need. When any of these occurs, know that you are in an ego identified state and you need to relax to gain a greater and more expanded perspective.

To the extent we are identified with an ego state, we lack objectivity, we judge ourselves and others, we do not see the spiritual opportunity present in this life challenge and we lack trust and faith in God. When we do not trust God nor accept our life circumstances as an unfolding of Divine Will, we resist all the growth opportunities that are available to us. And we suffer. The more resistance we have, the more we make ourselves and others wrong, the greater the suffering we will endure. Resisting and refusing to accept life at it is takes so much energy and makes it hard to receive Divine blessings.

Asking questions like, *why me?* And, *why is this happening to me again?* These are often futile questions. Better questions are: *What is trying to emerge from within me from this challenge?* Or, *what is the good and blessing that I cannot see just yet but I trust is there?* If you need to ask questions, ask the kind of questions that empower you. And give yourself permission to listen and be with what is triggered within yourself when being with these questions.

In the Jewish classic, *Duties of the Heart*, the author Ibn Paquda tells us that no one can hurt us or benefit us without the permission of God, even if people exercise their free will and actually try to hurt us. He gives an example that a person could fire a gun at another person and miss hitting this person because it was not Divine Will that this person be hurt in this way at this time.

It is important that we see that it is always God who is talking to us through all of our life experiences. So stop blaming others or yourself for your painful experiences. When we do this, we are actually depriving ourselves of the consolation and fortitude needed for healing and spiritual growth. This is most unfortunate.

I am just reminded of a woman who came to one of my meditation classes at a local reform synagogue many years ago in Manhattan. After the class, she praised the breathing, the visualizations, the meditation was so very relaxing, but she was very annoyed and angry by my mention of the G word. She told me that she could not bear to hear of God even mentioned as a word. She explained her reason to me after class. She had prayed earnestly to God for the life of her beloved son. And her son died. Because God did not answer her prayer, she did not want to have anything to do with God ever again. How sad and even tragic that she deprived herself of the spiritual comfort and growth that connecting to God at this time of profound loss would offer her. I do not recall exactly what I said to her but I imagine I would have said something to her like I am so sorry for her loss and her pain and I am sorry that she is so angry that she cannot seek and receive comfort from the One Being who could truly comfort her. I doubt she would be so angry at God if she did not believe in God's power to save her son. In her mind, God could have saved her son's life but God simply chose not to do so. Therefore, she could not forgive God. I am sure I must have encouraged her to keep attending meditation classes for the relaxation they offered her. In time, I imagine that her anger would dissolve by the opening of the heart that meditation would offer her.

> One of the safest places to be is in the not-knowing, in our humility and vulnerability before God.

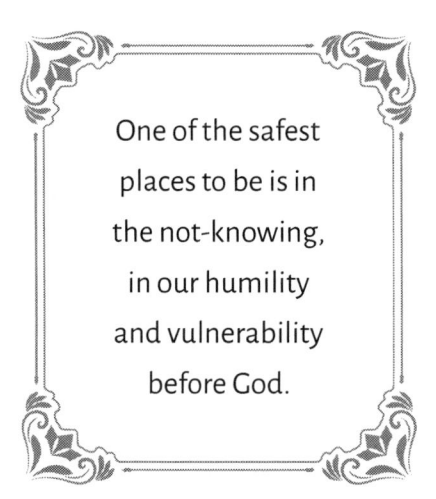

It is important to remember that life does not always make sense and we cannot always understand why certain things have happened as they have. Know that the best thing always is to call out to God and deepen our connection. One of the safest places to be is in the not-knowing, in our humility and vulnerability before God. When we can consciously be with what may have been previously unconscious such as our fears, our grief, our anger, and our doubts, we can liberate ourselves from the hold they have had in our life. Life is always revealing to us how conscious or unconscious we are.

Life is unfolding according to Divine Will whether we like what we are experiencing or not. If we know that everything is ultimately Divine

Will, we also know that there is always something good to extract from whatever happens to us. When we trust in God, we can stop focusing on the behavior of other people and our stories of victimhood and focus more on being open to receive blessings for healing, abundance, and love.

According to Kabbalah, all healing is administered through angels. Angels are conduits for the flow of Divine blessing into the physical world. The Talmud tells us that the grass would not grow were it not for an angel telling it to grow. Angels are messengers of God, and according to Judaism, we are surrounded by angels at all times.

The holy book, *The Way of God,* by Rabbi Moses Luzatto, reminds us a person can even overcome limitations imposed on him by physical law. *God's light is revealed to the highest angels and then transmitted to lower angels and then to people.* We do not pray to angels for angels only carry out the will and orders of God. I even read that it may not be safe to pray directly to angels. Pray to God to send the right angels to you. Some prayers are answered more quickly because they are offered with greater and purer intention. If our prayers are not answered it often means that we need to work on purification.

According to a section in *Gates of Holiness* by Rabbi Hayim Vital, the primary student of Rabbi Yitzchok Luria, *We create angels by everything that we do—good and bad angels, according to the actions of the person. If the intention is pure in doing a mitzvah like studying Torah or fulfilling another mitzvah, the angels we create are holy. If the mitzvah is not complete, the angel created is missing part of its light.*

There are differing opinions in Judaism about who and what angels really are. Maimonides, the Rambam, says that angels are spiritual forces. Nachmanides, the Ramban, says that angels are objective beings. Probably both are true. Angels are spiritual forces since we are told that we even create angels by our good deeds. But we are also told that angels are objective beings who can assume a physical form when necessary as did the three angels who visited Abraham in the Bible. I know many people who have sensed the presence of angels, heard them and several people who claim to have even seen them.

If a person is ill, he should see a doctor with a good reputation because he or she has greater angels working in conjunction with him or her, according to Kabbalah teachings. In Judaism, we generally do not believe that our healing comes from doctors but from God through the ministry of angels and then through doctors. All healing involves a level of surrender, a letting go and allowing oneself to receive Divine healing and angelic energies to flow to and through us. This may be new and challenging for many people who are used to being in control and feel that they have to do everything themselves or it does not happen. In these instances, an illness might be viewed as a spiritual initiation of letting go and opening to receive love and light from other people and ultimately from the Holy One.

General Guidelines and Goals

These guidelines and goals enable us to direct our energies in the ways that are optimal for our growth and transformation in accordance with the energy of this month. It is therefore recommended that you read and meditate upon them often in the course of the month. Reflect on their applicability to you and allow them to inspire you often during the month. Writing in a journal will be helpful to you.

1. DEVELOP A PLAN FOR HEALING THIS MONTH.

Purification and healing for this month is in the letting go of what does not support one's well being and the opening to what does. At the beginning of this month, take time to review your lifestyle, the quality of your life on the physical, emotional, intellectual, and spiritual levels. We live in a world that values superficiality over substance, fake virtue over true righteousness, and social media over loving intimate contact, so we are understandably out of alignment. Many of us are spiritually starved. In this month, we commit to a period of purification by choosing what is real and good over what is fake and only looks good.

Identify areas of your life that you would like to improve or expand upon. Identify behaviors and activities that do not support your well being.

Make a plan to begin new life affirming behaviors and activities that support you in that direction and reduce or eliminate destructive and negative behaviors.

For example, this month you may want to focus on your diet or exercise so you commit to eating more healthy food or have a plan of exercise for a few times every week. You also may want to focus on relationships so you choose to strengthen life affirming relationships and reduce or eliminate relationships that are draining or loathsome. State your goals and commit to a plan to carry them out for your own benefit.

2. MAKE INNER PEACE YOUR PRIORITY.

Most of us have largely been conditioned to look outside ourselves for love and tranquility when the love and peace that we naturally seek can only be found within. As a result of this tendency to look outside ourselves for love, approval and validation, we most likely will feel sad, angry, anxious, and think negative critical thoughts about ourselves and others when life does not happen according to our ego desires. Inner peace and trust in God becomes available to us when we let go of seeking validation and love from others.

Make a sincere conscious effort to choose peacefulness and trust in God over doubt and negativity. Do not allow your emotions, thoughts or bodily sensations to rob you of your inner natural peaceful state and Divine connection that is always available for you.

When we trust in God, we are peaceful, loving and even possibly joyful regardless of the circumstances we are experiencing. We trust that everything is taking place according to Divine Will and everything is ultimately for the good, even if we may not experience this in real time.

The awesome holy book, *Duties of the Heart*, reminds us that *when we trust in God, we are confident that whatever was destined for us will not be transferred to another. It will not come earlier nor later than at the time appointed.* Also in Duties of the Heart: *When a person trusts in the Creator, God will heal him of his sickness with or without any remedial measures.* Blessed be the person who trusts in God, and God will be his trust is in Jeremiah 17:7. This is a good mantra to repeat this month.

3. DEEPEN YOUR CONNECTION.

The month of Iyar is an optimal time to undertake or deepen a routine of Jewish spiritual practice that includes meditation, prayer, good deeds and more Torah observance as ways to open oneself to greater blessings and healing in one's life. Is there something that you can commit to that you are not currently doing? It is important to try to be consistent so as to receive the greatest benefit. Remember whatever you want to receive in your life, you cannot do it alone. The Jewish classic book, *Duties of the Heart*, warns: *A person relying on his own wisdom, on his own physical strength and industry will labor in vain and his plans for attaining his plans for attaining his aim will fall short of*, from: Fourth Treatise on chapter on Trust in God. Trusting in God is the key to tranquility and also to receiving blessings in whatever you do.

Learning Torah is considered by many to be a primary way to come close to God. For others it is prayer, meditation or doing mitzvot, acts prescribed by the Torah to deepen the connection with God. The traditional prayer book will offer tremendous insight into the Jewish wisdom about the nature of God and also inspire you to deepen your connection to God.

4. KABBALAH OF HEALING.

The body receives its spiritual nourishment from the soul through its good thoughts, feelings and acts. The body does not function if not for the life force energy of the soul. The soul infuses the body, heart, mind and spirit. When the body and soul enjoy the proper partnership, a person is healthy. Most of the practices in Judaism are directed to strengthening the connection of the body and soul.

According to Rabbi Hayim Vital, God made the body to clothe the soul according to the anatomy of the soul. Corresponding to the prescribed 613 commandments, the body has 248 spiritual limbs and 365 spiritual renews that are clothed within the physical limbs and function like pipes to bring blood and life force energy to the body. Vital wrote in Book Three of *Sharre Kedusha, Gates of Holiness*, that *every limb from the 248 limbs is given substance by a mitzvah that corresponds to that limb.*

Vital commented that what is even more nourishing and important are the *middot* (qualities) of a person. *Through our emotional qualities we connect our souls and God to our physical bodies. Or, we disconnect if we are overcome with anger and jealousy, and the soul begins to depart. By our negative thoughts, speech and actions, we set up blocks barriers between the flow of soul energy into the body.*

Disease begins in the spiritual dimension. If the disease is not attended to there, it will manifest on the physical level, forcing us to take note of the disharmony between the body and the soul. Illness is a weakening of the soul power to animate the body. The Tzemach Tzedek, the successor of the Alter Rebbe in the Lubavitch lineage, said that sickness comes from stagnation. The animal soul which desires pure physicality stops the Godly soul from cleaving to God.

The purpose of suffering is either to make people turn to God or to cleanse them of former sins so they will be able to absorb greater goodness into their lives in this lifetime or the next one. It is best not to dwell on reasons for becoming ill for that may lead to despair and self-pity. Rather we should focus on how to heal and become more God connected than previously.

It is vital that a sick person turn to God for all healing comes from God. The Tzemach Tzedek said that in turning to God we go beyond the world of cause and effect and are able to draw down the highest healing energy. God the Creator of the world is not limited to the laws of cause and effect. Similarly when we access our own soul, deepening our connection to God, we are also not limited to the laws of cause and effect. The soul has the ability to channel Divine healing energy to the body through prayer, meditation and mitzvot. When we do this, miracles are possible and even likely.

Faith in God is the greatest medicine for all healing comes from God. This is not to say that you should not take medicine unless you are on the level of embodying perfect faith in God or perfect faith in a Tzaddik. I know of many stories of people who listened to the guidance of the Lubavitcher Rebbe over that of doctors and were spared surgery, recovered from severe illnesses and gave birth to several children when they medically were told they could never give birth to even one child.

If we are sick, we need to consider the ways we may have blocked the flow of goodness into our lives. Sick people need to look out for internal anger and jealousy, accept these feelings and then release them. It is good to accept what is happening to you, rather than be angry about your circumstances. And then always trust in God that all is unfolding for your highest good. I have experienced personally several health challenges in my life but when I was healed, I had an unusual burst of creativity. My books were often written after a significant physical challenge of some sort. It was almost as if I had to go through the time of challenge to really make a commitment to be creative and not waste valuable time.

5. HEALING PAIN IN RELATIONSHIPS.

As a therapist, I see frequently that painful relationships are often why people enter into therapy because people tend to partner or marry people who afflict them in the very same ways they were afflicted as young children. These couples suffer after the "honeymoon" intoxication period is over. These kind of stressful marriages may offer people an opportunity to re-visit and heal childhood wounding. With therapeutic support, it is possible for a couple to become allies with each other so they can strengthen the bond between them and help each other to heal their personal childhood wounding together in a way that may be greater and more meaningful than working on themselves alone.

If however marriages or relationships are not loving or even become abusive after the courtship is over, and there is no willingness on the part of both people to work on the relationship, it may be better to leave sooner rather than later. For example, if a man does not demonstrate a capacity to bestow light and love, there is no reason for a woman to remain with him. No one should remain in a relationship where he or she feels less than or not good enough for their spouse.

When we love ourselves, we know that we do not have to prove ourselves lovable or good enough to be validated by another person to win their love. Most times if someone does not love him or herself they will not be able to love their spouse. We can leave unhappy partnerships or we can work on them. If we trust in God and we have done our best, if a relationship fails, we have to accept that the relationship was not meant to continue longer than it did.

It is helpful to know that every meaningful relationship we have with other people is either revealing the extent of our shadow, our own repressed dark emotions, or revealing our light, the love and vibrancy of our own soul. So take responsibility for your personal experience in relationships. It is a Divine appointment that we have the kind of relationships we have personally and also professionally. This is how we learn how to love, heal and liberate ourselves at the same time.

If you are experiencing pain in any relationship, become aware of the tendency to blame yourself, others, or God. Blaming others keeps you stuck, feeling like a victim. If you are in pain, feel your pain without blame. Love the child within you who is hurting. Be compassionate with yourself. Share your pain with others and especially with God. Call out for mercy and healing, Always ask yourself, *What am I learning and how can I grow from this challenging experience?* The answers will become clear to you.

6. BE WILLING TO DISCOVER AND ACCEPT THE TRUTH.

Healing comes from being connected to what is true and what is real. It is as simple as that. In situations where you feel pained or stressed, ask yourself if what you believe is absolutely true. Too often we become needlessly upset about something that is not relevant and not true. Too often, we regret the past, worry about the future and are overly concerned about what we imagine other people think. We waste so much precious time and energy through this kind of faulty imagination.

When you are upset, ask yourself: Am I being objective? If you are in a blaming or victim mode of thinking, know that you are not in touch with the whole truth. You are not being objective. If you cannot be objective, speak to someone who can help you be objective.

Healing requires a deep level of listening to oneself and being with oneself in the most honoring and respective way. When we have the courage to be with the truth of our being, we contact God and are then able to experience deep peace and healing regardless of what is happening externally.

Be particularly mindful this month to make optimal choices about where to direct your energy. As yourself often: Can I open and listen the voice of my own soul, the deep knowing inside myself that comes from inner stillness, or do I listen and react to the chatter and hysteria of the ego mind, which is loud and clamoring for my attention? Breathe deeply, meditate and give yourself time to find the inner stillness and listen to silence. Check out my meditation videos on You Tube to help you with holy listening.

7. COUNTING OF THE OMER.

The Counting of the Omer is a spiritual and religious practice linking Passover to Shavuot designed to bring special awareness to the spiritual opportunity available during these days. The practice of counting the Omer is cited in the Torah: *You shall count seven perfect Sabbaths from the day following the Passover holiday when you brought the omer as a wave offering until the day after the seventh Sabbath, when there will be fifty days. On the fiftieth day you may present new grain as a meal offering to God.* Lev. 23:15-16.

In ancient times when the Holy Temple stood in Jerusalem, the Omer was a daily ritual offering of barley. By offering barley, which represented simple animal food, one hoped to transform the simple unconscious instincts and behaviors into a higher more refined spiritual awareness. Offerings and sacrifices in the Holy Temple were ancient spiritual healing practices.

The Counting of the Omer helps people to do the inner work of refining the character traits of the ego on a daily systematic basis, so the pure energies of the *sefirot*, the Divine emanations, shine more powerfully through us. The Counting also helps a person to be aware of the preciousness of each day. People today count the Omer symbolically through prayer. Each week of the Counting of the Omer is devoted to reflection and meditation on a particular sephira in relation to other *sefirot*. For example, the first week is devoted to *hesed*, loving kindness. For that entire week we reflect upon the attribute of love and how we can better open to its many faces. The second week is devoted to *gevurah*, strength and we reflect on the ways we demonstrate strength, focus our energies and set boundaries. The month of Iyar begins with the sephira of *tiferet* compassion. Compassion is the most important trait to cultivate this month for our own healing. Each week is devoted to a different sephira in combination with the other *sefirot*.

There are many books to purchase and material online to support you in participating in this meaningful practice. I recommend the one by Rabbi Simon Jacobson.

8: BE FREE OF HABITUAL EMOTIONAL PATTERNS.

Too frequently, people define themselves by old patterns of emotions and behavior patterns that are so limiting. Every person has to open to the possibility that they can call forth new and varying emotional energies for different situations. For example, at times we have to be strong and set definitive boundaries. At other times, we have to be unconditionally loving, and have no boundaries. Not having the capacity to express what is appropriate in any given situation is detrimental to ourselves and others. We may have a propensity in one direction, for example, some of us are more kind than strong. We each need to cultivate and strengthen the whole spectrum of emotional capacities as presented in the Kabbalistic Tree of Life In this way, we become complete and balanced.

For example, the patriarch Abraham was known to embody the quality of *hesed*, loving kindness, but in his life he was constantly challenged to demonstrate *gevurah*, strength and setting boundaries. For example, it was not his nature nor desire to send his son Ishmael away, but he was challenged to do so. In this way, he gained the capacity to choose what is appropriate for every situation, rather than be limited by the feeling of *this is the way I am.*

Astrological Sign: Taurus

The astrological sign of this month is Taurus, ruled by the planet Venus. As an earth sign, Taurus informs us that the earthly plane is the arena for spiritual work now. The work of Iyar is to bring the spiritual illumination of the month of Nissan into the earthly plane. In Nissan—Aries, we move forward, and in Iyar—Taurus, we stabilize and integrate. When the sun is in Taurus, we feel connected to the earth and we sense that nature is pregnant with new life that will soon emerge in all its glory.

The planet Venus, which rules Taurus, imparts beauty and love to this month. As the mythological goddess of love and beauty, Venus is an agent of harmony, integrating parts and bringing them into the whole. There is an underlying energy of love to tap into this month that brings everything together, along with beauty that enables us to appreciate the relationship and balance between the parts. As always, but particularly this month, it is love, even Eros, that is a strong motivator for change. It is love that heals.

Taurus is symbolized by the bull. The prophet Isaiah says, *The bull knows his master*. Isa 1:3. The bull is said to have a level of discernment. Unlike the lamb in Nissan which does not work, we need to be like the bull this month and plod along. Iyar is a time of spiritual effort, step by step, day by day, like a bull. If we keep our goals in mind, our efforts will be meaningful and joyful.

Hebrew Letter: Vav

Like the month of Iyar, the letter *vav* is a connector; it connects time, space, and people to each other. In English, we would say *and* in place of the *vav*. As we learned earlier, Iyar connects the holiday of Passover celebrating the Exodus from Egypt to Shavuot, the holiday of receiving the Torah, which occurs in the beginning of the next month.

The *vav* has a numerical value of six. The Torah tells us that God created the world in six days. This corresponds to the six days of the week in which we do our work and to the six directions of the physical world. Iyar is the month of healing work in practical ways. Interestingly enough, the first *vav* that appears in the Torah is the sixth word in Hebrew: *In the beginning, God created heaven <u>and</u> earth*. The *vav* connects heaven and earth. Healing is also the connection between God and the body and heart and also between God and humanity.

In Kabbalah, the *vav*, the third letter in the tetragrammaton, YHVH is also a connector. The first two letters, *yud* (Y) and *hay* (H) refer to the spiritual light from above and the last *hay* is the vessel for this world. The *vav* connects heaven and earth. The *vav* represents the single line of light that connects the spiritual world to the physical world. Many Kabbalistic meditation exercises involve the letter *vav*.

According to Kabbalah, the *vav* is associated with *Zer Anpin*, which literally means *the small face* or *the son*. This refers to the six *sefirot*, the Divine attributes and channels by which we experience and connect with infinite Ain Sof. Those six attributes meditated upon in the Counting of the Omer are the following: *hesed*-loving kindness, *gevurah*-strength or restraint, *tiferet*-compassion and balance, *netzach*-victory and overcoming obstacles, *hod*-humility and splendor, *yesod*-foundation and bonding. The son also refers to *HaKodesh Borechu*, the Holy One Blessed be He. The *sefirot* each have unique Divine names associated with them and are used in many Kabbalistic meditative practices.

This month meditate on the letter *vav* in your body, bringing yourself into alignment on all levels of your being. In your meditation the *vav* can extend even beyond the physical body, for you are not limited to your physical body.

Hebrew Tribe: Issachar

The tribe associated with the month of Iyar is Issachar, Leah's fifth son. He was conceived on the night that Leah traded mandrakes, a fertility plant, with her sister, Rachel, for a night of conjugal rights with Jacob. At this time, Jacob was living exclusively with Rachel, so Leah had to actually buy a night with him. That night Leah tells Jacob: *I have hired (saker) you with my son's mandrakes.* Gen.30:16. When she bears the son she conceived that night, she names him Issachar. Because Leah so wanted to increase her participation in the development of the nation of Israel, she asserted herself in this way,

The men in the tribe of Issachar were the Torah scholars and were supported by the tribe of Zevulun. They represented the kind of thinking that is rooted in the Divine wisdom of the soul and the heart. The month of Iyar is devoted to the refinement and perfection of thought.

Divine Permutation YHHV

If we compare the permutation of the Divine Name for the month of Iyar to that of the previous month of Nissan, we find the third and fourth letters, the *vav* (V) and the *hay* (H) are reversed. This alerts us that there is a change in the flow of energy to the world of Yetzirah, which is the world of formation, the world of angels, the world of the heart, and in the world of Assiyah, the physical world, and the physical body. In particular the *hay* in the position of Yetzirah shows that there is expansiveness in the world of the heart and this is most important during this month.

The energy this month supports the opening of the heart. There is a greater flow of angelic blessings for healing this month. The letter *hay* in the position of Beriyah indicates that there is expansiveness in the mental dimension, the world of thought. The position of the *vav* in the world of Assiyah indicates an emphasis to bring light to the physical world, but the light is not fully manifested. As mentioned previously, this month is a planting time rather than a reaping time.

Torah Portions

Purification is a major theme reflected in the Torah portions for this month. The entire book of Leviticus, in which this month's Torah portions are found, is devoted to acquiring purity and holiness. The Torah portions throughout this month reiterate the words: *Be holy, for I Your God am holy*. And, *I am God*. Lev.19:2.

The Torah reminds us numerous times in the Torah portions of this month that the human being has the capacity to be holy like God. Because our soul is a part of God, we can be holy as God is holy. The Hebrew word for holy is *kedusha*, which means separate. Holiness is being separate from the world while also being fully embodied in this world. God is separate from the world, yet the world is filled with the glory of God. Our soul is holy because the soul is outside of the physical body, and extends even beyond this physical world, yet a part of the soul resides also within our physical bodies invigorating and sustaining the physical body for a limited amount of time that we are blessed to be embodied.

The Torah portions of this month teach us that it is the sanctification of the basic physical activities like food, sex, business, relationships, and in exchanging money that we may embody holiness in this physical world. We were created to be channels of the most sublime frequencies of Divine Love to this more physically dense world.

Being holy means to identify more with the immortality, wisdom, and peace of the soul rather than with the intensity of the ego identity that thrives to survive and be heard within the density of the physical body. We must always remember that we did not come here to accumulate physical possessions and achieve worldly accomplishments that we can not to take with us when we depart from our physical bodies. When we leave this physical world, we will only take with us the love we shared, the good deeds we performed for others, our awareness and consciousness of our Divine soul and our Divine connection for our journey to the next chapter for our soul.

In the Torah portion of Behar read this month are important teachings about the land of Israel and how to help impoverished people. Not only are we taught the laws providing rest every seven years for the physical land of Israel, we are also told to safeguard the holiness of impoverished people who were sold into "slavery" for a period of rehabilitation. *You should not subjugate him with hard labor—you shall fear God." Behar 25:43. 'For the Children of Israel are servants to Me, they are my servants, whom I have taken our of the land of Egypt, Behar 23:55.*

We are reminded in this month's Torah portion that the land of Israel belongs to God. We can not sell it permanently to others. We may think we are owners of the holy land but we must remember we are only temporary custodians of the land. The land of Israel belongs to God. This seems like an important reminder for people today. The Torah instructs us to return the land to the original owners at the end of fifty years, called the Jubilee. During the *Smittah* year, every seven years, the land was supposed to lay rest, no farming activity was to take place. Today there are rabbinic provisions to mindfully remember these Torah injunctions without actually fully carrying them out. Many people in Israel are particularly mindful of these injunctions and do their best to respect them as best as they can.

Holiday: Lag B' Omer

HISTORY: Lag B'Omer is the thirty -third day of the Counting of the Omer, or the eighteenth day of Iyar. Lag B'Omer commemorates the anniversary of the death, the *yahrzeit*, of the great Kabbalist Rabbi Simeon Bar Yochai, acclaimed author of one of the principal texts of Kabbalah, *The Zohar*.

Because of his spiritual radiance, Rabbi Simeon Bar Yochai was called the Holy Candle. Legend has it that during the time of the Roman occupation of Jerusalem in the second century, he lived in a cave with his son for twelve years surviving entirely off the fruit of a carob tree. It has been passed down through the centuries that there was a great awesome spiritual light at the time of his actual demise. As he was consciously leaving his body, he told people that he was happy because now he could be fully unified with God. For him dying was like going to the canopy of marriage.

Since ancient times, Jews have celebrated the *yahrzeit* (death anniversary) of Rabbi Simon Bar Yochai. This custom was strengthened by Kabbalah masters as Rabbi Yitchok Luria, the Arizel, and the Baal Shem Tov, the founder of the Chassidic movement. All the Chassidic groups even until today as well as religious and non-religious Jews celebrate Lab

B'Omer. No other rabbi receives such immense widely attended gatherings on their *yahrzeit*.

For those who honor this day and speak about the awesomeness of Rabbi Shimon Bar Yochai, this is a day of great spiritual light and joy. Because Rabbi Shimon Bar Yochai, nicknamed the Rashbi, revealed the secrets of Kabbalah, the mystical secrets of the Torah, Lag B'Omer is a day for receiving the secrets of the Torah.

Lag B'Omer also commemorates the end of the plague that killed twenty-four thousand students of Rabbi Akiva, who was also a great Kabbalist and commentator on the Talmud. Though Rabbi Akiva only began learning Torah at the age of forty, he was recognized as one of the leading scholars and rabbis in the world. Living during the second century in the period when Israel was occupied by Rome, it has been said that Rabbi Akiva encouraged his students to fight against the imperial power of Rome. Most of his students lost their lives in this battle or died in the plague. Though these students were considered the greatest Torah scholars in their day, the Oral Torah tells us that they died because they did not give sufficient honor to each other. They were knowledgeable in Torah but were jealous and competitive with each other. The impact of the five remaining holy students of Rabbi Akiva revived, sustained and enabled Judaism to flourish even after its defeat with Rome. The legacy of the revival of Judaism is also celebrated on Lag B' Omer.

OBSERVANCE: Today in Meron, a small city in the north of Israel where Rabbi Shimeon Bar Yochai is buried, thousands of people gather each year on Lag B'Omer to celebrate the *yahrziet* of this greatest saint with bonfires, music, drumming and hair cutting ceremonies of little boys of three years of age. In Chassidic and orthodox circles, many couples refrain from cutting their son's hair until the boys are three. One of the sources of this custom is the superstition that the lives of little boys are more vulnerable to Satan because as males they will perform more mitzvot than females.

Lag B' Omer in Meron is a glorious celebration. I encourage everyone to make an effort to attend at least once in their lifetime. I have attended a few times. There is nothing like it. It is a rare treat to be in such close proximity with Jews from so many Chassidic groups. The joy and love is very tangible. Being with the continual chanting and the drumming alters one's consciousness to the highest heights. I had one of my most powerful joyful ecstatic spiritual experiences on Lag B'Omer. In Meron. I was gifted with a glimpse of the awesomeness of the holy soul known as Rabbi Simeon Bar Yochai, and how he guides people and protects the nation of Israel to this very day.

Meditation

THREE AFFIRMATIONS TO CHANGE YOUR ENERGY

The Light of God illuminates darkness.
The Love of God erases fear.
The Power of God overcomes affliction, addiction and challenge.

Before you begin the practice of affirmations, take several deep breaths to center yourself. With each inhalation, allow yourself to expand and open. With each exhalation, allow yourself to let go of stress, regrets and worries of the future. As you continue to breathe, attend to the breath and allow the mind to quiet and become more aware of being simply being present. Sit in silence for a few moments and then prepare to repeat affirmations.

Repeat affirmations silently to yourself or out loud if you would like several times coordinated with the breath. If possible, meditate on one or each of these affirmations for five to ten minutes. Take time to be with the breath, recite and be with the affirmation. Meditate and pray with the affirmation and open to receive a shift in your energy and blessing.

Know that these affirmations are the truth. Know that God is the light, love and power of this universe. Breathe out your fears, your sadness, your anger, your sense of ego limitations because they are not truth. They are just what you became manipulated and habituated to believe as true, but they are not the real truth of who you are and who God is.

In meditation and prayer we come to experience that only God is the True Reality. Attach yourself to the True Reality and you will be brought into alignment with God. You will be liberated from the limitations of what you thought were true about yourself and you will open to the greater truth of your own soul, who you really are.

The light of God illuminates darkness.
(Repeat the affirmation out loud or silently with the breath for 5-15 slow conscious breaths.)

When I am attached to the Light of God, I radiate light. Darkness and negativity have no hold on me. I came here to radiate light. The Light of God disperses darkness which thrives on fear.

Be with this mantra for five to fifteen minutes. It will change your energy and it will change the energy of the people around you. You do not have to try to change them. The Light will change them for the better as well as you.

The love of God erases fear.
(Repeat the affirmation with the breath for 5-15 slow conscious breaths. If you like, sit with this affirmation for 5-10 minutes.)

Because God is loving us, there is no reason to fear. God is the power of love. The love of God erases fear. I do not have to fear someone will not love me or anything. God loves me. That is more than enough. I am safe and protected in God's love.

The power of God overcomes affliction, addiction or challenge.
(Repeat the affirmation with the breath for 5-15 slow conscious breaths. If you like, sit with this affirmation for 5 or 10 minutes.)

If you feel afflicted or are addicted in anyway and life feels beyond your control, repeat this mantra. Know this as the truth. God is the Creator and Power in this universe. There is no greater power in this world. Repeat and pray with the mantra, and let God heal, empower and protect you. Stay with this mantra as long as comfortable and take notice of what happens.

Repeat all of these three mantras and meditate upon throughout this month: *The light of God illuminates darkness. The love of God dissolves fears and resistance. The power of God is greater than any affliction, addiction or challenge. As you rep*eat these mantras, allow them to permeate you deeply. God is supporting, loving and protecting you in this moment and in every moment when you seek truth.

Listen to my YouTube channel for the guided meditations on the *Three Affirmations to Change Your Life.*

Practical Recommendations

1. BE PARTICULARLY CONSCIOUS OF YOUR DIET.

It was in the month of Iyar that manna came down for the Jewish people in the desert. During the time the Jews ate manna there was no illness or disease. At this time of year, the temperature begins to change in many places, so it is important to be sensitive to what the body needs and to adjust one's diet accordingly. Some may undertake a cleansing diet during this month to help the body to transition to another season. It is important to drink a lot of water. It was in Iyar that Miriam's well was established. The miraculous water supply for the Jewish people, attributed to the merit of Miriam, traveled with them as they wandered through the desert until Miriam's death. Though we need water for our continued survival, water is an important cleansing and purifying agent particularly this month. Make an effort to drink more water this month. If you can, take a glass of water right now.

2. CONSIDER BECOMING KOSHER OR VEGETARIAN.

Anyone who is spiritually sensitive and also eats meat, Jews and non-Jews alike, should consider eating only kosher meat. By buying kosher meat, you are assured that the animal was healthy when slaughtered and that it did not suffer in its demise. This is important to your physical and spiritual well being. It is said that animals slaughtered in a frightening non-kosher manner secrete a toxic chemical at the time of their slaughter, which we then consume. Unfortunately, however both kosher and non kosher animals are fed antibiotics and growth hormones that may pose health rises to consumers. Make an effort to find organic kosher meat that is not exposed to chemicals. We eat kosher food not only to be healthy but also as a way to align ourselves with Divine Will.

3. MAKE TIME TO PRAY AND MEDITATE EACH DAY.

Healing comes from moving from identifying with our physicality, ego needs and our emotions to that of attuning to the higher vibrations of our own soul. With prayer and meditation our consciousness ascends to the experience of the holiness of being in the present moment. When we open to the Divine Presence experienced in the present moment, we easily let go of negative thoughts and feelings that have kept us attached to a compromised and limited sense of self. The Jewish prayer book is also powerfully designed to facilitate this kind of ascension.

4. FIND A TEACHER OR SPIRITUAL GUIDE.

Being attached to a teacher or spiritual guide who can provide direction as well as objectivity for you is very helpful. For many of us it is essential. The ego mind is very clever and can easily deceive a person. An objective person who cares about your well-being and may be further along on the spiritual path has invaluable experience and guidance to offer you. If you cannot find such a mentor, find a friend with whom you can be spiritual buddies. A spiritual buddy is different than a friend for your focus together is solely directed to increasing your spiritual growth and letting go of the ways you have limited yourself. Spiritual buddies have soul conversations when they simply listen to each other without judgment, or advice giving, I call these truly holy conversations.

5. GIVE CHARITY WHEN ILL OR CHALLENGED.

According to Kabbalah, charity opens gates of healing and blessing for people. You should not feel that you are bribing God by giving charity. God cannot be bribed. Rather, you should consider how you expand and purify yourself by giving charity and how this enables you to receive a greater flow of Divine healing energy. We give charity for ourselves as well as to be of service or help to others.

A Tale to Live By

A person goes to the next world and has an opportunity to visit heaven and hell. He first goes to hell and sees that people there are looking very angry and unhappy, sitting around a table where there is lots of food. He looks more closely and sees that the people are not eating. Their elbows are locked in a straight position so they cannot bend their arms to put the food in their mouths. They are hungry and angry.

He goes to heaven and sees the very same scenario, Heaven looks just like hell. People are also there with straight arms, unable to bend their elbows, sitting around a table where there is lots of food. He looks again and sees that everyone there is smiling and happy.

Soon he perceives the reason for this. Unable to reach the food themselves, those in heaven take turns feeding each other.

The way to heal ourselves and transform challenging situations is to become a giver like God who is the ultimate giver. We always have opportunities to give to others and to give not at our own expense. By giving we resemble God and we are brought closer to God.

Become a giver not with an expectation of receiving, but simply for the joy of giving. The story reminds us that when we give, we also receive. Giving without expectation connects us to our Creator most directly and brings healing and blessing to ourselves and to the world.

9

Sivan

MAY – JUNE

ENERGY
The Art of Infinite Receiving

AREA OF HEALING
Subconscious Mind

ASTROLOGICAL SIGN
Gemini

HEBREW LETTER
Zayin ז

HEBREW TRIBE
Zevulun

DIVINE NAME PERMUTATION
YVHH

HOLIDAY
Shavuot

A Personal Story

It is never open on Shabbat, but perhaps it will open for you. My friend's eyes twinkled as she said those words to me. She then suggested that I journey alone, further from the women's synagogue buried in the caverns adjacent to the Kotel, by going left, down a flight of stairs, and through additional tunnels to pray by the Holy of Holies. In a state of awe and amazement I trembled and cried as I walked through the dimly lit winding paths and down the stairs to the most sacred site for the first time.

Soon, I found myself approaching a very simple place, resembling a cave. There were no special or elaborate ornaments marking the place, only three plastic chairs and two women dressed totally in white, sitting enraptured in prayer and meditation facing a blank wall. I claimed the remaining chair as mine and was transported to the realm of the Holy, where I felt totally loved and accepted as I was.

I can't recall all that transpired within me during the hours I stood and sat there in a state of awe. It felt like I was receiving a download of wisdom and deep spiritual insight on many subjects on the nature of reality and what will be in the future. And mostly, I felt myself in the presence of the most loving beautiful exquisite royal holy feminine energy.

Here is a part of what I received during my first meditation sitting at the cave that I want to share with you now. God's covenant with the Jewish people is real. There is no replacement for it. In the right time, all the prophecies will be fulfilled. The Shechinah, the Divine Feminine, has been waiting since the beginning of time, behind the veil of physicality to be redeemed from Her hiding to fill the world with love and blessing. When She is fully revealed in the world, our hearts will be opened, and there will be love and peace on all levels. Evil will have no jurisdiction.

She is eternally unified with *Ha Kodesh Baruch Hu*, the Divine Masculine, yet from time to time, when our hearts are truly open, it is She who gives us a glimpse of Her beauty and Her love. This is more than enough to sustain us until the great messianic day of Her total revelation.

Whenever I returned to the cave every time, there was always a group of women huddled there, reading psalms, meditating, and weeping gently. One time, when I was standing there in the third row from the wall, I was reflecting on the lack of a loving man in my life and I began to cry. Soon I found myself lovingly and gently moved to stand closer to the actual wall of the cave so I could rest myself directly upon the wall. I cried deeply from the core of my being, weeping alongside other women who were also weeping.

I can't imagine another place in the world where women of all ages and backgrounds are not ashamed or embarrassed to cry in front of strangers. There is such an unusual and special feeling of love and intimacy among the women there. I love the focus and devotion of the women. There is no frivolous speech, only silence and heartfelt soft words of prayer.

During one of my earlier visits to the holy cave, I became aware of horns and trumpets blasting. I listened closely and was guided to a stairwell, very close to the Holy of Holies cave. I learned then that there was a morning minyan that began at sunrise each day that had been going on for many years.

I was intrigued enough to make myself rise before 4:30 a.m. and walk very prayerfully alone in the dark through the Old City in order to attend this minyan. There are many reasons why I would not be comfortable attending this minyan. Besides being that it takes place so early, I am standing in a stairwell. I cannot even see the men for they are upstairs. I can't see the Torah. I am a bit of a feminist. I enjoy singing in prayer services, yet there is little or no singing here. I am not as observant as the women who frequent this minyan but none of this bothers me. I am actually grateful to the men for allowing me to be present in the stairwell. I even appreciate the total separation as it allows me and the women to go deeply into the prayer without the concern of being observed. It is a joy and honor to be with these holy women each morning.

This minyan is to me a rocket ship of prayer traveling through dimensions of time and space to Infinite Divine Holiness. I love the meditative quality of the service. The leader of the service will pause for a long time on a single word many times during the service. The male congregants are doing complex meditations at those times but I am happy to just be with that word as fully as I can be. Sometimes I feel no need to pray myself. I close my eyes and only have to open my heart to receive the sweet Divine nectar and vibrations from the prayers of these men. Here in this stairwell, I feel myself standing in the center of the universe.

One time, one of the male congregants of the upstairs minyan pointed out the man who had led the prayers that morning. I thanked the leader profusely, for I had received so much from the services he led. He immediately came over to me and put his hands over my head and blessed me. I was thrilled, for I felt as if I had been blessed by the High Priest. This gesture made me feel welcome and confirmed to me that I was in the right place.

Most of the times when the men exit through the stairs where the women were standing, I avert my eyes because I know that some of them might feel uncomfortable being seen. Other times they drape themselves with their prayer shawls so as to not look upon the women. Having shared this awesome experience of holiness, it almost feels too intimate to actually make eye contact. In years past I might have been offended by the lack of acknowledgment of my personhood. Now I am simply grateful to each of them, not only for what I have received spiritually for myself but for what these prayers offer to the Jewish people and the world at large. These men generally learn the depths of Kabbalah for a few hours prior to their morning prayers that begin around 4:00 or 4:30 a.m. I was blessed to attend this minyan for two months. Unfortunately, when I returned to Israel the following year, I was disheartened to discover that it was no longer possible for the women to stand in the stairwell or hear the prayers of this awesome minyan. What a blessing it was for me that I was able to do it for as long as I did.

Praying in the cave closest to the Holy of Holies with the women gave me a little taste of the holiness of the Holy Temple. When the Jewish people had the Holy Temple, the Divine Feminine was revealed to them. But due to selfishness and senseless hatred within the Jewish people, the Holy Temple was destroyed. Now we have only a wall of a cave and it is true that Her wall is moldy. She has been hidden for thousands of years, yet She is still present, so beautiful and loving. Every day, when I stand in the cave I am enveloped in Her presence, I feel Her and receive Her blessing. I am filled with visions of joy and ecstasy for the time when the Holy Temple will be restored. May She be revealed soon and may there be true peace in the world.

This month of Sivan is the headquarters for receiving. We receive many blessings in lives but receiving the revelation of the Shechinah, the Divine Feminine, is the greatest one of them all.

Energy: The Art of Receiving

The month of Sivan is known to be one of the most beautiful months of the year both physically and spiritually. Not only is nature blossoming this month, we also become more alive in Sivan. Sivan is a time of love, intimacy, unity, and creativity more than any other month. This is why more weddings take place during this month of May and June. Sivan is also considered an auspicious time for receiving clarity about one's life purpose along with the necessary guidance and blessing to live it.

Sivan is a time of expressed creativity, of bringing forth and communicating what is deep inside of us. As we open to the greater expansiveness possible this month, we become aware of the depths within us that we might not even conscious of previously. This brings greater freedom, love and joy.

Sivan arrives in the late spring. Having done the planting and healing work in the month of Iyar, in Sivan we enjoy the vibrancy of nature. Sivan is our time of fulfillment. We are now free to explore and to travel internally and externally. It is actually an auspicious time to travel. In Sivan, it becomes clearer to us where we are going and we can radiate and share ourselves with others in a more beautiful and direct way.

The whole month of Sivan is about increasing our capacity to receive from God. Many people know how to give and many more know how to take but fewer know how to truly receive. Sivan is a time of learning how to receive on all levels of being. To truly receive is to be open to be present without an agenda, accepting every moment gratefully as a Divine gift. The extent to which we are open determines what and how much we will receive. Life is so abundant and there is a flow of Divine blessings, particularly this month.

In the month of Sivan, it is easier to let go of thoughts, feelings, and actions which do not embody one's true essence. When we let go of ego-based feelings that are not rooted in truth, we naturally become vessels for something more expanded and authentic. It is good to spend time in nature this month to help us open and embrace the beauty of life itself. Being in nature also helps us become more loving and accepting of life as it is unfolding for us.

In the month of Sivan, we celebrate the holiday of Shavuot, which is the giving and receiving of the Torah. This phenomenal event could only take place during this beautiful month of Sivan. The Divine Revelation that took place on Shavuot offered a covenant, an everlasting partnership between the Jewish people and the Creator of the Universe. A deep Kabbalistic teaching informs us that the same spiritual energy manifested when a holiday occurred in Biblical times is available to us at the time of the month every year, making Shavuot a holiday for receiving an awesome tremendous Divine influx of blessing.

If we want to be capable of receiving Divine Revelation, we first have to be able to be in an open and loving heart. It is said that when the Jewish people received the Torah there were united in one heart, so unified that they were likened to one being. In the Torah passage describing Israel's encampment, the word encamped is written in the singular, rather than the plural form. It was unity that enabled the Israelites to receive the Torah.

The Torah was given in the desert because it is said that we each have to become like a desert in order to receive. We have to let go of our ego preferences and attachments, get out of the way, nullify ourselves and receive what God want to give us, which is much greater than anything we could imagine. It is we who limit ourselves, not God. If we experience ourselves as victims, if we blame other people for our problems, it is only because we have lost access to the wisdom and love of our own souls and are not open to receive what our souls and God wants to give to us.

This month we learn how to be proper vessels to receive Divine Revelation. We each receive according to our yearning and capacity to receive. This is the month to deeply yearn for Divine Revelation. The greater the yearning, the more sincere the yearning, the more we with receive. God will answer sincere prayers and respond to our true needs. Let us not be afraid to open ourselves to receive what is flowing through and within us. Let go of limiting concepts of who you think you are, and allow yourself to be guided to step more fully into the wonder of who you really are so as to fulfill your soul purpose in this world. We are each invited this month to go little deeper and consciously accept the Divine Flow of love and light that our souls have yearned for a long time to receive.

Sivan is also month for increased intimacy, love, and unity. This is also demonstrated by the giving and accepting of the Torah, which can only occur during this month. As a covenant likened to a marriage between the Jewish people and God, the Torah is an expression of love, commitment, dedication, and intimacy. It is interesting and no coincidence that May-June, in the month of Sivan, has always been a popular time for weddings.

Sivan is a wonderful time to deepen existing relationships and open to meeting new people who we will draw closely and easily to our heart. It is God who brings people together for we each have something to give and receive from each other.

There is an open-heartedness in this month of Sivan that makes it easy to bond with many different kinds of people. When we really know and internalize the deeper truth that we each were created by the one God, we can experience others as brothers and sisters, regardless of background, nationality and religion.

> The more we give from the Infinite well of blessing flowing through us, the more radiant we become and more blessings flow through us.

Every meeting with another person is best experienced as a Divine Appointment, a spiritual opportunity, to give love and blessings without the expectation of what you will receive in return. Here in lies the fulfillment of our soul purpose and also of our freedom. When we give without expectation, we experience ourselves as an Infinite well of blessing. If we give with expectation or conditionally we will suffer. As it has been said, love gives freely without demands. Otherwise it is business and not love. The more we give from the Infinite well of blessing flowing through us, the more radiant we become and more blessings flow through us.

General Guidelines and Goals

These guidelines and goals enable us to direct our energies in the ways that are optimal for our growth and transformation in accordance with the energy of this month. It is recommended that you and meditate upon them often in the course of the month. Reflect on their applicability to you and allow them to direct and inspire you this month.

1. NURTURE YOUR PERSONAL RELATIONSHIP WITH GOD.

If we want, we can feel that this world seems to run independently of God or we can feel that God is running and sustaining the world and the world is so beautiful. We can wonder where God is or we can experience everyone and everything permeated with Godliness. We have a choice. One choice leads to suffering and the other leads to love, peace, and joy regardless of what is happening outside of us. Deepen your choice to see God in everyone and everything this month.

Even though God may be hidden, God is the INFINITE TRUE REALITY who not only created every human being and everything in creation but Who remains ever-present to all. During this month and during other months, we raise our consciousness to a higher Divine frequency through prayer, meditation and doing good deeds. The Name Israel means *Yashar El*, and translated it means *straight to God*. As Jews we are entrusted to experience, embody, and share the direct revelation of the Divine in this physical world.

Take time this month to talk to God in your own words. Speak to God as if you were having a conversation with someone, like your best friend. Rabbi Nachman considered this kind of conversation as a powerful meditation practice. Even if you are not sure that you believe in God or in having a personal relationship with God, you can still talk to God about your confusion, ambivalence, and lack of belief. And most importantly, take time to pay attention and listen to any shifts and insights that occurs within you through this experience. God speaks to you through your higher self, your own soul in the moments of silence.

It is the practice of Staliner Chassidim to yell and scream to God in the loudest voice possible. You can hear them praying for blocks away. When people open their hearts and talk out loud to God in their own words for an extended period of time, they may even be prompted to yell, cry, and laugh as they release deep feelings. It used to happen frequently in my classes when I would guide the students to talk to God.

Reb Shlomo, my beloved teacher of blessed memory, however recommended that we speak to God softly. This is the most powerful and holy way. When a person whispers, it is like a holy wind rising from the depth of the soul. We tell our secrets in a low voice. Lovers whisper to each other. There is actually more fire in your words when you talk softly. So talk softly to the Creator. It is not that the Creator needs to know what is happening within you. There are no secrets before God. But the experience of talking with God in a soft voice will open you to receive in the most wonderful ways.

2. TREASURE YOUR OPPORTUNITIES TO GIVE.

You came into this world because it was Divine Will that you be physically embodied at this time. Always remember that you did not come to this world to receive from other human beings or to be defined or validated by them.

You came here to give what only you can give. By giving to others, you will discover and fulfill your life purpose and you will be blessed. Giving to others must be without expectation of what you will receive from them. That is business and not love.

When you answer the call to be of Divine service in this world, God will guide and bless you. God will work through you. You are simply the channel, and not the giver. So it is important to not take credit for what God does through you. A mantra to use in prayer and meditation might be *Use me. Guide me. May I be of Divine Service.* When you are in Divine service, and not that of your ego-identity, you will not burn out or be depleted but you will be renewed and energized.

If we do not feel appreciated as we would like to be for what we give and become resentful, the flow of Divine blessings through us will diminish or even cease. We must always remember that whatever service we are called to do, we are doing it for God, for our own soul and not to win praise from others.

3. INCREASE YOUR MEDITATION PRACTICE.

Meditation helps us to be more fully aware of the present moment. When we open to be in the present moment, we leave the boundaries of time and experience the awesomeness and holiness of eternity that is available in every moment. In this state, we access our own souls and we are able to receive what God wants to give us, which is more than anything we can imagine. This is a powerful month for meditation. Don't deprive yourself.

4. LEARN TORAH WITH A TEACHER OR FRIEND.

We first receive the Torah in this month. The study of Torah provides a powerful key to access the depths within you. Study by yourself and study with someone who can open the doors of Torah to you.

Though many question the relevance of the Five Books of Moses to modern times, it is because they do not have access to the holiness of Torah and only understand it very superficially. To them, Torah is merely literature and the stories of people long ago may not be relevant to people today. But, if the Torah were only stories, it would not have captivated the heart and soul of so many people for so long. It would not have served as a foundation for Christianity, Islam as well as Judaism. People do not kiss a book of literature, but they kiss the Torah. People have even risked their lives to save a scroll of Torah. Why? Make it your soul purpose this month to have glimpse of the answer to that question.

As a general rule, if your study of Torah does not fill you with greater love and devotion, you are not studying the true Torah. You must pray and if necessary cry and beg for the privilege of tasting the sweetness and holiness of Torah. I love the metaphor of Torah as a woman. She will not reveal her secrets until she is sure that she is truly loved. Pray for a teacher you can love and respect and who makes the Torah sweet and meaningful to you.

If you do not feel holier, more whole, more peaceful in a teacher's presence, he or she is not your teacher. You may gain some information from this person but find a teacher who revives your soul, who is loving, and who loves you.

My criterion for a spiritual teacher is that learning with this person opens my heart so I am more in touch with my own soul. I love such a person and intuitively I know this teacher also loves me even though I may not be privileged to even have a personal relationship with this person. I have loved rebbes from a distance because I feel the Divine Presence just by looking at them, listening to them, or seeing them dance from afar. A true spiritual teacher, a rebbe, is like an angel, a holy messenger.

I was blessed to learn closely with two Torah giants such as Rabbi Yitzchok Kirzner of blessed memory for several years and Rabbi Shlomo Carlebach of blessed memory for much longer. I describe Rabbi Kirzner as my floor for he gave me a place to stand in Torah, a foundation in Jewish classical texts, and Jewish spiritual practice. I describe Rabbi Shlomo Carlebach of blessed memory as my ceiling as he taught me how to reach into heaven and return with the highest blessings. It was also my destiny to have great awesome spiritual teachers outside of Judaism who indelibly impacted my soul in very unique and important ways as well.

5. DEEPEN YOUR RELATIONSHIP WITH LOVED ONES.

As we have learned, there is a great opportunity during this month of Sivan for love, unity, and intimacy. Add romance to your life. Buy flowers and gifts for loved ones. Extend yourself by doing favors and showing your appreciation to your loved ones, and open yourself to meeting new and different people. Fully receive and appreciate all that you are given by others. Most likely, you will meet people this month and you will feel immediately close to them as if you knew them for a long time. Soul connections are not bound by time and space.

6. TAP INTO YOUR CREATIVITY.

Spring is in full bloom during the month of Sivan and the Giving of the Torah represents the flowering of Divine Wisdom. This month is the month for creativity. Give yourself time to bring forth the creativity that is Divinely planted within you. Writing, music, dance and so forth may provide a medium of expression for you. Enjoy the creativity of others as well. Go to plays, concerts, and art shows this month.

In this month of such creativity, we can bring forth a new and more creative consciousness to even the most routine things in life. Cooking, making beds, and washing dishes can also offer creative moments. I once had a very powerful spiritual experience washing floors on my hands and knees because of my meditative consciousness done while performing this task.

Astrological Sign: Gemini

The astrological sign for this month is Gemini. An air sign, Gemini represents the energy that does not want to be contained. Air is ineffable. Mercury, the ruling planet of Gemini, was the Roman messenger of gods who flew from the heavens to the earth, constantly going back and forth between the worlds. Similarly, the Torah given this month is the messenger between heaven and earth.

People born under the sign of Gemini are free-spirited, always wanting their consciousness to ascend. Geminis want to leave the confines of the earth and fly to the heavens. Interested in ideas or any form of mental activity, Geminis are creative and skillful communicators. The planet of Mercury is associated with communication and intelligence.

Geminis are thought to be mercurial, quick to move from place to place, physically or mentally. Interestingly, this month the Torah documents the travel of the Jewish people in the desert. Sivan is a great month to travel internally as well as externally.

Gemini is the perfect month for the Giving of the Torah for many reasons. The freedom-seeking energy of Gemini is best expressed in the Torah which brings freedom and enables us to truly fly upward. Also appropriate to the theme of Torah is Gemini's symbol, the twins. Unlike most of the other months, which are represented by animals, Gemini has human twins as a symbol.

The significance of the twins has been explained by the great Kabbalist Rabbi Tzaddik HaCohen, who said the first three months of the year are associated with the three patriarchs. Nissan is the patriarch Abraham associated with the energy of *hesed*, loving-kindness. The month of Iyar is associated with the patriarch Isaac, who represents the energy of *gevurah*, judgment or strength. Gevurah is needed to do the healing work of Iyar. And, the month of Sivan is represented by Jacob. Jacob and Esau were twins. The energy of Jacob is *tiferet*, beauty and balance. *Tifere*t is the perfect synthesis of *hesed* and *gevurah*.

Hebrew Letter: Zayin

The Hebrew letter associated with Sivan is the *zayin*. The *zayin* looks like the *vav*, the letter for the previous month, to indicate that this month builds upon what went before. As the *vav* represents the straight and Divine light descending from the spiritual world to the physical world, the *zayin* represents the light that returns or ascends upward to a higher state of consciousness and revelation.

The *zayin* resembles a crown. In this month we receive the Torah, called the crown of creation, According to Rabbi Ginsburgh in his book *Aleph*

Beit, the *zayin* resembles the scepter of a king and conveys the royalty of this month. The king has the power to choose and is the ruler. In this month, God, the King, chooses to give the Torah to the Jewish people, making this month a time of tremendous blessing. The word *zayin* means weapon. The Torah is considered a weapon protecting us from the trials of life internally and externally.

The *zayin* is the seventh letter of the Hebrew alphabet and also has the numerical value of seven. Seven is a beloved letter in Judaism. Seven refers to Shabbat. Shabbat is also called the crown of creation. We work for six days of the week in order to receive the Shabbat, the seventh day which is God's gift to creation. Like the Torah, received this month, Shabbat is the container of the mysteries and secrets of creation. The Shabbat is a revelation of God expressed in the dimension of time.

Hebrew Tribe: Zevulun

According to the Arizel, Sivan is represented by the Tribe of Zevulun, the sixth son of Leah. The Hebrew word *zevul*, which means habitation, is the root of the name Zevulun. When Zevulun was born, Leah said, *Now my husband will dwell with me.* Gen.30:20. Leah was hoping that Jacob would live in her tent and love her the way she so much wanted.

Leah's statement is a metaphor for the indwelling of the Divine Presence. In Judaism, the husband is always a metaphor for God and the wife is either the Jewish people or the human soul. The passionate and animated energy of Zevulun reflects the abundance and the fulfillment of this month epitomized by the Divine Revelation of the Torah.

Zevulun was the tribe engaged in commerce. Its members, blessed with great wealth, provided for the material needs of the tribe of Issachar, who studied the oral transmission of the Torah and did not work. Being connected to the expansiveness and openness of the seas inspired a passion and joy of life in the tribe of Zebulon. They experience God in their involvement in the world.

This month we may easily tap into the energy of Zebulun to feel the passion and the vitality of life in this world. During this month, we are empowered to enjoy the abundance, beauty and Godliness of this world and share these blessings with others.

Divine Name Permutation: YVHH

In this month's permutation of YHVH, the *hay* (H) is in both the third and fourth positions, the world of Yetzirah and Assiyah, The *hay* in the world of Yetzirah indicates expansiveness of Divine light in the dimension of the heart via the activation of the high archangels, residing in this world. Its position in the world of Assiyah indicates expansiveness in our physical world. These positions inform us that there is a greater flow of blessing to the heart, more love energy this month and also a greater manifestation of Divine light and blessing in the physical world. This particular permutation of the Divine Name indicates abundance in the physical and emotional planes. This is what makes Sivan a month of love, intimacy and blossoming.

Torah Portions

Sivan usually introduces a new book of Torah, the book of Numbers, This book is known in Hebrew as B'Midbar, which is a word appearing in the first verse of the book that means, *In the desert*. The Torah was given in the desert, a place that cannot be claimed by anyone or anything, a no-man's land. According to Judaism and other traditions, the desert represents the nullification of the ego that is necessary to receive Divine inspiration. We have to release the clutter by which we limit and define ourselves and be more of an empty vessel to access who we are on the level of our soul.

This book of Torah provides an account of the wanderings of the Jewish people in the desert, all the challenges, rebellions, and mistakes the people made on the spiritual journey to the holy land during this time period. If we study these portions and allow them to enter us, we will see our own challenges reflected in their challenges. The Torah can be a mirror to gaze upon ourselves.

The first chapter of the book is called B'Midbar, and this portion is devoted to a detailed explanation of the counting of the Jewish people, the flags and banners of each tribe, and the place each tribe occupied. The Midrash, the Oral Torah, tells us that it was an honor and joy to be counted. Each person appeared in front of Moses and Aaron and gave his name. This chapter is always read before Shavuot. Though the chapter may appear irrelevant today, it conveys an important and timeless message about counting. Knowing that you and others count raises self-esteem which is a preparation for a relationship with God and receiving the Torah.

The next Torah portion, Nasso—Numbers 4:21-89—reveals the important formula for blessing people. *May HaShem bless and safeguard you. May HaShem illuminate His countenance for you and be gracious to you, May HaShem lift His countenance to you and establish peace for you.* Num.6:24-26. This is in alignment with the energy of blessing this month.

Toward the end of the month, however, the tone of the Torah portions begins to change in preparation for the next month of Tammuz. In Beha'asloscha, Numbers 11:10, it says *The people took to complaining.* Complaining is always an expression of resistance to Divine Will. These complaints reflected the dynamic tension between the physical and spiritual dimensions within people. Many Jews complained about the manna, the heavenly food they were given to sustain them in the desert. Though the Oral Torah tells us that the manna could taste like anything people wanted it to, even so, many of the people cried for meat. The manna did not provide the physical satisfaction of regular food. The cry for meat represented the cry for physicality and for fulfillment of physical desires. In the desert, all their physical needs were taken care of and there was nothing to do but be close to God. As wonderful as that was, it was also not easy for many to easily maintain the state of surrender necessary for this kind of Divine connection.

Many Jews in the desert simply did not want to live in such a supernatural realm, on the level of miracles, they wanted to return to a more ordinary reality where they experienced themselves as independent physical beings who do not receive what they need but participate in producing it.

The people asked, *Why did we leave Egypt?* Num 11;20. *A wind went forth and blew quail from the sea and spread them over the camp.* Num 11:31. The people were given meat. *You will eat it not for one day, not two days, not five days, not ten days, not twenty days, but for a whole month until it comes out of your nose and makes you sick ... For you have despised God, who is among you and you cried before Him.* The meat was in their mouths when God struck the people with a plague.

Also, in this Torah portion, Miriam and Aaron learn firsthand how their level of prophecy differed from that of Moses. For the sin of speaking words of criticism and judgment about the relationship Moses had with his wife, Miriam is stricken with a kind of severe leprosy. Miriam and Aaron had reasoned that because it was permissible for them to have a sexual relationship with their spouses, it might have been wrong for Moses to refrain from sexual relations with his wife Zipporah, especially when she wanted it so much. Miriam, in her conversation with Aaron, was advocating for Zipporah, who had cried to her about being separate from her husband. When Miriam's skin began to rot and be consumed by a plague, Moses cries out to God, Please *GOD heal her*. Those words are repeated by many today in praying for sick people. Miriam is healed, but God says that it was necessary for a quarantine to be imposed upon Miriam to teach Miriam and Aaron not to compare themselves to Moses. It may appear that HaShem even required that Moses be celibate. Miriam's quarantine actually renewed her. Afterward, she renewed her marriage with Caleb and was able to birth children that she was previously unable to have.

Complaining is the major theme for the preparation of the energy of the next month, Tammuz, a month of tests and judgment. As much as people want to receive, it is often hard for people to surrender and receive, particularly in this upcoming month. The ego identity asserts its own desires and its preferences. Resisting Divine Will as we will see is the primary source of all complaints and suffering.

Holiday: Shavuot

HISTORY: The holiday of Shavuot has four names that give us more information about it and the month of Sivan. First, the Torah calls Shavuot the Festival of Reaping. Exod. 23:16. This refers to the reaping of wheat. Shavuot is an agricultural holiday, marking the end of the spring harvest. Second, The Torah calls Shavuot the Day of the First Fruits (Bikurim). On this day, the first fruits were offered in the Holy Temple. Third, Shavuot is also called Festival of Weeks. The Hebrew word *shavu'a* means *week*. The Torah instructs us to count seven weeks—the Counting of the Omer—beginning on Passover. Shavuot is on the fiftieth day.

The *Zohar* tells us that the seven weeks in which the Omer is counted is likened to the seven days a woman counts after her monthly menses. Just as a woman would immerse herself in the *mikvah*, a ritual purification bath, and then be reunited with her beloved after the seventh day, so too is the community of Israel reunited with its beloved God on the fiftieth day, on Shavuot.

Finally, Shavuot is mostly called *Z'man Matan Toratainu*, which means, *The Giving of our Torah.* Interestingly, we are not told in the written Torah to commemorate the giving of the Torah on a specific date, like the instructions for Passover or Sukkot. The Torah says the Ten Commandments were given in the third month but it does not give the exact day.

The Torah says, *In the third month from the exodus of the Children of Israel from Egypt, on this day ...* Exod. 19:1. The rabbis concluded that it was the fiftieth day of the Counting of the Omer, the very same day as Shavuot. And, therefore, Shavuot was designated the holiday for the Giving of the Torah. The Torah reading selected for Shavuot is from the Torah portion of Yitro in Exodus that recounts the Giving of the Ten Commandments.

To better understand this holiday, take a little guided journey in your imagination, and feel free to use sets of the Hollywood movie, *The Ten Commandments*, if you like.

Take a few moments to imagine standing amidst the Jewish People. You have left Egypt in the most miraculous way on the fifteenth of Nissan, as recounted in the story of Exodus. After a battle with the Amalekites, an ancient tribe who went out of their way to attack the Jewish people, you arrive at the foot of the mountain on the first day of Sivan, the time of the new moon. On the first day you rest. On the second day, Moses, at God's instruction, begins to prepare everyone for the upcoming big event. Moses tells you and all those around you that everyone will be given the privilege of becoming a member of this holy nation, a kingdom of priests along with a set of mitzvot—commandments—to maintain their direct connection to the Divine Being who brought them out of Egypt. Your heart is filled with love for the privilege of being a part of this people. Allow your heart to open to love every Jew who is sharing this experience with you.

On the third day, Moses tells you not to ascend or touch the mountain lest you come too close and die. Moses instructs you to abstain from marital relations and cleanse your clothing, and says, *On the third day the Lord will descend before the eyes of all the people upon Mount Sinai.*

Moses is summoned to the top of Mount Sinai and you are with the people at the bottom of the mountain. It sounds from the Torah description that there was volcanic activity on Mount Sinai. The mountain was smoking and shuddering and there was lightning and thunder. Yet Moses ascends. Stand, and be ready to receive for as long as you are comfortable. What is your experience?

What did the people see or hear when standing at the foot of Mount Sinai? There is an ongoing debate about exactly what the people heard and what they experienced on that day. Some commentaries say people fainted upon hearing God's voice and had to be revived ten times, once after the recitation of each commandment. The act of fainting represents and demonstrates the realization that God is the true and only power, and that they as human beings did not have any real existence of their own, so they fainted. This commentary teaches us that people do not ever stand in truth on their own.

The *Gemara*, the primary commentary on the Torah, says that God actually placed the mountain upon the Jewish people forcing them to accept the Torah. Though many take this quite literally as an actual concrete occurrence, I think it is best understood as a metaphor. On one level we have a choice but on another level, the deeper things in life are beyond choice. They are expressions of who we are, and we would not be ourselves without them. Reb Shlomo expressed it in the following way: *Do I have choice whether I love my child?* The image of a mountain hanging above us was to impress upon us that life is possible with Torah and without Torah life is not possible. To reject Torah is to reject life. Because Torah is so integral to who we are, it is experienced as beyond choice.

Other commentaries such as from Ramban and Rashi, say that the Ten Commandments were given instantaneously, but the people could not comprehend them. After the first Two Commandments were repeated, they asked Moses to be an intermediary because they were not able to bear the intense holiness and power of the transmission. The people, upon seeing the flame and the smoke and hearing the thunder around the mountain, declared, *We will do and we will hear. Let God not speak to us lest we will die.* This became the trademark for the Jewish path emphasizing action over revelation. The Jewish people had faith in Moses to instruct them in what God wanted from them.

The Rambam concurs that the people heard the first Two Commandments, but they only heard the sound of the voice, they could not comprehend what was transmitted. Moses had to teach them. In the name of some Chassidic rebbes, my teacher Reb Shlomo said that the Jewish people did not hear anything. It was a revelation of pure silence, the silence of the aleph, the first letter in the Ten Commandments. I personally resonate with that explanation the most. Holy silence can be more powerful than words. Even this was too much for the people to bear.

Rabbi Moses Hayyim Ephraim of Sudylkow, of the 18th century, said that if the Jewish people had been willing to bear the Divine Revelation that they would not have been able to sin again. To have heard something directly from God is a very different than from Moses, a great prophet, but who is still a human being.

In the following Torah portion of Mishpatim, on the fifth day, *Moses, Aaron, Nadab, and Abihu, and seventy elders went up and they saw a vision of the God of Israel and beneath His feet was something like a sapphire brick like the essence of a clear blue sky.* Exod. 24; 9-10. This is the one mystical experience recorded in the Torah. Though we cannot make mystical experiences happen by our own will, they can happen to ordinary people. When they do happen, we receive a Divine gift that changes our lives forever. So sincerely keep your heart open to receive Divine gifts when you pray and meditate.

The *Gemara* tells us that the Torah was given to the Jewish people but the whole world was invited; the souls of many belonging to other nations were also present and also received the Torah at Sinai. Many of these people feel a strong attachment to the Jewish people and the principles of Judaism, and some of them choose to convert and become Jews.

Much of what is called Torah today is not simply the Ten Commandments or what is written in the Five Books of Moses. Much comes from the Oral Torah and was orally transmitted through generations until the time of the Holy Temple. But then it is also said that it never was written down in its entirety. Torah is still very much an oral transmission that a student receives from a teacher. For thousands of years, the body of wisdom known as Torah has been developed, intuited, and interpreted by the rabbis to respond to the needs of the time. The Ten Commandments serves as the foundation for Western civilization. History has shown us that societies weaken and collapse when they forsake these commandments, and they forsake God.

OBSERVANCE: The holiday of Shavuot is awarded the honor and holiness of the other major holidays with certain restrictions for its celebration to preserve and heighten its sanctity. Candles are lit. A festive meal is given in which Kiddish is received and Hallel, the special psalms of praise, are received as in the holiday of Passover and Sukkot.

Beautiful unique customs accompany Shavuot. Many synagogues decorate the prayer space with greens and flowers. At least on the first night and day, people traditionally eat dairy products with honey because the Torah is nourishing like milk and sweet like honey. Blintzes, cheesecake, and lasagna are popular foods during the holiday.

The book of Ruth is read, recounting the journey of childless Ruth as she accompanies her mother-in-law, Naomi, back to Israel after the death of her husband. By declaring her devotion and commitment to her mother-in-law, Ruth converts to Judaism. In a fantastic story, Ruth becomes not only a Jew, but a foremother of the House of David. Upon her arrival into Israel, Ruth is introduced to the king named Boaz, who is related to her mother-in law, Naomi. In a short time, Ruth conceives a son with Boaz, who is an old man who dies the next day. From this humble non-Jew comes the lineage of the Messiah. Ruth is envisioned as the perfect convert who is said to have demonstrated the same qualities of faith and selflessness that the Jewish people displayed when they received the Ten Commandments. The recitation of the book of Ruth inspires each Jew to be like Ruth to demonstrate selflessness and even though we may have been born Jewish we must also choose consciously to be a Jew to experience what that means.

The custom of staying up all night studying on the first night of Shavout is called *Tikkun Leil Shavuot*, which means: The Fixing of the Night of Shavuot. It is said that the Jews slept late the morning the Torah was given because they did not feel worthy to be present. It would appear that self-esteem was a problem even in those days. By staying up on the first night, we demonstrate our eagerness to learn and be connected to Torah. Though this custom is only four hundred or so years old, it is popular in many places that it seems like it is mandated but it is not. It was the custom of Reb Shlomo to stay up and learn the entire night.

Many people think that the Torah, the Five Books of Moses, or the commentaries, is only the study of the past. Torah also includes our current personal commentaries on what we study. Torah is best seen as a living, evolving and dynamic transmission. If it was not that, Judaism might not have survived and thrived as it has through time.

Meditation

Jews generally repeat the *Shema* prayer—Hear Israel, the Lord your God, the Lord is One—three to four times a day. The Shema is the Jewish ticket to the highest spiritual consciousness: that is, the consciousness that there ultimately is only God. Only God has True existence. Human beings are essentially a part of God and are not individuals with a separate existence from God.

Immersion in our God connection dissolves the limitations of the ego self. This experience of Divine consciousness gives us faith and trust that God is with us. When we experience firsthand that God believes in us, more than we believe in ourselves, we are then empowered to bring greater Godliness into our daily life.

> This meditation begins with focusing of the breath. Take five deep breaths from the lower abdomen to the rib cage to the chest, hold the breath and exhale through the mouth releasing stress. Let go of the thoughts of the day, the past, and the future, and focus on being present as fully as possible. Stay with the breath and enjoy being present.
>
> We begin by first focusing on the letters of the Shema, the *shin* and the *men,* and we substitute an *aleph* for the *ayin*; for *shin, men* and the *aleph* are the mother letters of the Hebrew alphabet.
>
> If you do not know the letters, you can meditate on the color and the sound of the letters.
>
> Visualize the *shin*. The *shin* represents the element of fire, the color is orange light, the sound is the Sh …
>
> Visualize the *shin* first in the head in orange light, make the sound of the *shin*, and imagine that the *shin* is holy fire, filling the head and purifying the mind of all thoughts that you would like to be purified from. Negative thoughts disappear in the presence of this holy fire.
>
> Repeat again the second time, and visualize that the entire torso is filled with holy fire. Access your willingness to enter into holy fire and to release what no longer serves your highest good, to release the fears, the doubts that keep you limited and fearful. Take a deep breath and make the sound of the *shin* as you visualize yourself filled with holy fire. Repeat this two more times.
>
> Now visualize the *mem* in blue light in the solar plexus, representing the element of water, and make the sound of the *mem*:

Mmm. Now visualize yourself by a natural body of water. Take a few moments to let go of the roles you play in your life, the clothes you wear, and see yourself totally naked before a body of water or a mikvah.

As you walk in, you access the desire to be cleansed and purified. And imagine yourself dunking in the water. Stay underwater to absorb the experience of being immersed in water. It is like returning to the womb. Repeat three or four times. And, when you are ready, walk out and return to the experience of sitting with your breath.

Now visualize the aleph, the silent aleph, representing the element of air on the top of your head. Hold the visualization of the letter for as long as comfortable, taking deep breaths.

Now we are ready to chant the words of the Shema. Take time to pause, listen, and be receptive in the spaces between the words. As we chant the Shema, we join the holy community of Jews who have been chanting the Shema many times, every day, for thousands of years.

We begin by chanting each word of the Shema. We first chant Shema, the call to listen, to quiet the mind, and be totally present. Stay with the breath for a few breaths and tune into holy listening. Then we move to the next word, Yisrael. We stay with the breath and feel ourselves connecting with the holy community of Israel who are currently chanting the Shema and have been chanting the Shema many times every day. The Hebrew word Yisrael is connected to the Hebrew words *yashar* (straight) and El (God). We claim ourselves as members of this holy community who go straight to the Creator. Take a moment to stay with the breaths and make this connection.

We then chant the Name of God, *Adonai*. If you like, visualize the letters the YHVH on your inner screen, and meditate on God that is greater than Creation. God is greater than creation. Stay with the breath. Then we chant out *Elohaynu*, our God, being in touch with the deeper truth that we each have a personal and collective relationship with God. Take a few breaths and absorb this experience. Then we chant out God's Name for the second time and if you like you can meditate on the letters of God's Name inside your body as the *yud* in the head, the *hay* in the heart, and *vav* in the heart to the genitals, and the *hay* in the waist and legs. We meditate on the immanence of God. God is within everyone and everything in this world. Pause for a few breaths if you like.

And then we chant out the final word Echod, meaning One. We meditate on the Oneness of God. From the Divine perspective there is no inside or outside, there is only Oneness. There is only God. You can chant Echod a few times to meditate more deeply on the Oneness of God. God is one. God is the True Realty and we are a part of this Oneness.

Take a few moments to meditate and incorporate this experience of Divine Oneness.

Chant the Shema daily and slowly with these *kavanot* (contemplations) as described above. With each exhalation, say another word.

Shema … Yisrael … Adonai … Eloheynu … Adonai … Echod …

Hear O Israel the Lord Your God, the Lord is One.

Listen … God is transcendent … God is immanent … God is One

In a whisper say the next line of the Shema: Baruch Shem, Kvod Malchuto L'olam Vaed. Blessed is the Name of His glorious Kingdom for all eternity.

When we say the Shema we meditate on each word to access the faith that God is a unity and is unified with all of creation and everything taking place in the world.

ADVANCED MEDITATION: THROUGH SPIRITUAL WORLDS

Take a few deep breaths to center yourself. Begin by becoming aware of the physical world and imagine that the whole world is enclosed in the letter *hay*. Now visualize the letter *hay* around your body. You are sitting in the shelter of the letter *hay*. This is the world of Assiyah. Breathe and enjoy the protection of the letter *hay*.

Now become aware that there is a vibrational angelic world beyond the density of this physical world of Assiyah. This is the world of Yetzirah. When we enter the consciousness of this world we become aware that we are surrounded by angels. Visualize the letter *vav* a few inches above the top of the head and imagine that there are angels traveling up and down the letter *vav*. The *vav* is a conductor of blessing of Divine Light. See the light of the *vav* entering into the letter *hay*, filling the letter *hay* with Divine Light.

The letter *vav* enters into the letter *hay* above it. This letter *hay*, the top letter *hay*, is filled with Divine Light. This letter *hay* is our ticket to entering the world of Beriyah, the consciousness of the Higher angels such as the Archangels, Michael, Gabriel, Uriel, and Raphael. And above the letter *hay* is the letter *yud*, a small point from which all the worlds emanate. The energy of all of creation is concentrated in this point. This is the world of Atzilut. This is the point of unity. Take time to meditate on each letter and reflect on the spiritual world it represents.

Now do this meditation in reverse order. Visualize the *yud* as a concentrated point of Divine light, twelve inches above the top of your head. Under the *yud*, visualize the *hay* and imagine that Divine light spreads through the *hay* and is contained within it. The *yud* and *hay* represent Abba and E'ma, the Divine Father and Divine Mother, the Divine Light coming from the highest worlds. Under the letter *hay* is the *vav*. The *vav* is the straight line that channels Divine light of the higher worlds to our physical world. Now see the light pour into the letter *hay* that surrounds your body. For the rest of the meditation, the focus is in sitting in the shelter of the letter *hay* (the Shechinah).

Visualize the light and love of God now surrounding and filling your body. This Divine Light is healing the organs within your body NOW. Breathe and accept the flow of this light throughout your body. Where you note some discomfort or need for healing in a part of the body, bring the breath and visualization of Light and love to that body part. Let the muscles in your body relax and open to the flow of blessing NOW.

Focus now on the eyes, allowing the eyes to be filled with Divine Light so you pray to see Divine Light in everything your eyes see in this world.

Now focus on your ears, the passageway of hearing, so you only hear the beauty and Godliness of this world.

Now focus on your mouth so you only speak words of kindness and Godliness. You will guard your words so they have more power when you do speak. You will not waste the awesome power of your speech on idle chatter.

Now focus on the nose, refining the power of smell. This refers to the power of our intuition, we can smell the fragrance of a person, experience Stay with the body until the entire body is saturated with Divine Light.

Focus now in the heart and open to the experience of being loved for who you really are. This may be a new experience for many people who somehow felt falsely that they were not good enough. Something was wrong with them. Let go and erase all these lies from your consciousness now. You are lovable and you are loved for who you are. You are more than good enough,

Now focus on the top of the head, the seat of your *neshama*, the soul, your inner knowing, and your higher consciousness. Direct your attention to the top of your head, your crown. Visualize that you are wearing a crown. NOW: Take time to absorb this visualization and feel the energy moving in the top of the head. You are wearing a crown. No one can take this away from you. It is who you are on a soul level. As you wear your crown in meditation and prayer, you receive guidance for your soul journey.

Now visualize the *yud* around twelve to twenty inches outside of your body. The immensity of your soul is outside of your body. Your soul, your energy field surrounds your body.

> Take time to experience and know your soul on this level so when the time comes to depart from your physical body it will be easier and possibly even pleasurable for you to do so.

Practical Recommendations

1. SET A SCHEDULE FOR TORAH STUDY.

Because the Torah was received in this month, it is a wonderful time to increase your Torah study. Because many of us live very busy lives it is easy to postpone Torah learning. If you are busy, it is fine to spend even a few minutes each day reading and studying spiritual books. All of this is part of Torah learning. It is fine to learn a little bit before you go to work, during a break in the course of the day, or before bed.

You will also receive the love and beauty of Torah even more if you learn with someone else. Learn with people who know more than you and people who know less.

According to *Duties of the Heart*, the Torah is the remedy for the spiritual maladies and moral diseases. *Thy word is a lamp to my feet and a light to my path.* Ps. 119;105. Learn Torah each day to enlighten your consciousness and heal yourself on every level of your being.

2. SPEND TIME IN NATURE.

Nature is particularly beautiful during this month so it is important to give yourself time to simply be in nature. Take off your shoes, stand and walk barefoot as long as you can. Hug trees, commune with flowers, look at the squirrels, frogs, ants, and whatever animals are roaming where you live. The Hebrew word for man is *Adam*, and the Hebrew word for nature is *adamah*, teaching us that we human beings are also a part of nature.

When we embrace ourselves as natural beings, we come into harmony with nature. We become grounded, peaceful and open to receive heavenly blessings.

3. THIS WORLD HAS A LOVING CREATOR.

There are people who say that the world came into existence by chance and without a Creator who caused, formed and sustains all of creation. Ibn Paquda, author of *Duties of Heart*, offers the following example to prove the falsehood of such a position.

If ink were to be poured accidentally on a blank sheet of paper would you expect that there would be poetry, lines, and words written as with a pen? If you brought a paper with words written as if by a pen, would you believe that what was on the paper was an accident? No, of course, you would affirm that it was impossible. If we look at the brilliance, awesomeness and the intricacy of creation we must attest that creation has a single Creator who has endowed all of creation with purpose, power, and wisdom of the Creator. Note this well, concludes Ibn Paquda.

This world has a Creator who imbued all of creation with Divine intelligence. This Creator sustains and guides creation according to Divine Will. Appreciate that everything in life has been made by this Infinite Intelligence Who is called and served by many different names in many paths and in many ways.

This awareness brings people together in love and harmony when they realize the there is only One God who created and guides each of us.

3. GIVE TO FAMILY AND FRIENDS THIS MONTH .

Tell them that you want to demonstrate love for them by giving something that they would like to receive. Mostly, people want to know that you love them and that they matter to you.

You came into this world to be a giver. To be a giver is to allow God to love and give through you. When you give in this way, you will be renewed rather than depleted. So give for the sake and joy of giving. Give without expectation. Do not expect that you will be appreciated for giving. If you have expectations, you will most likely be disappointed. Remember you came to this world to give. Giving is the answer to all your problems. Let God do magic through you and for you.

4. GIVE BLESSINGS TO PEOPLE YOU KNOW.

In one of the Torah portions this month, we receive the formula for blessing other people. Blessing is a powerful spiritual practice. A little known secret is that the best way to receive blessing is to bless others. In the course of the month, make an effort to bless at least five different people. The more people you bless, the better it is for you. You can even throw a blessing into casual conversation, such as, *God bless you*, or you can give a person a full blessing as described.

Take time to center yourself, quiet the mind as much as possible as you breathe and allow yourself to be open to Divine light and love. It is always present. Feel your yearning to be a channel for blessing with each breath. Reflect on the needs of the person in front of you and allow the words of blessing to flow through you. If you like, you may raise your hands above the top of the person's head. Our hands are powerful conduits of blessing.

You may begin the blessing with the following words, *May God bless you* or *May you be blessed*. Or if you like, you can say the traditional priestly blessing: *May HaShem (God)) bless you and safeguard you. May HaShem illuminate His countenance for you and be gracious to you. May HaShem turn His countenance to you and establish peace for you.*

5. BE HOSPITABLE.

Invite someone to your house for Shabbat or another meal. If you do not keep Shabbat, this will be a good way to start. If you do, you already know about this mitzvah. Sharing bread together is an important way to unite with Jews and with other people. Remember we do not have to agree with people to love them. We came here to love, not to have political opinions which may create separation from others who have different opinions than we do. Some of the disunity that we are experiencing as people today may be alleviated by simply sharing a Shabbat meal together.

6. INCREASE UNITY IN THE WORLD.

Wherever we are, we each have opportunities to bring more love and unity into the world. It could be something as simple as arranging a date between people or engaging in dialogue and really listening to people who hold different opinions than you do or whatever you feel called to do. It does not have to be a large effort. When we are dedicated to bringing light and love into the world we will be given opportunities to do so.

A friend of mine shared with me yesterday that he had spoken briefly with a woman ahead of him while waiting in line to purchase a coffee at Starbucks in Manhattan. He was surprised to discover that this woman paid for his coffee when he went to pay. She had already left before he could protest or thank her. This sweet and yet simple gesture surely increased love and unity in the world. I am even writing about it.

A Tale to Live By

This story was recorded in the wonderful online publication entitled Israel 365 on February 16, 2024. I loved this story so much that I included it even after the manuscript was completed. In 1946, shortly after the end of World War II, Rabbi Isaac Halevi Herzog, the Ashkenazi Chief Rabbi of Mandatory Palestine, traveled to Europe in the hopes of finding Jewish children who had survived the war. He visited a large monastery known to have sheltered Jewish children from death at the hands of the Nazis. How would he be able to identify Jewish children?

Rabbi Herzog asked the Reverend Mother of the monastery to gather all of the children in a large room. When they were all assembled, he cried out in Hebrew, "Hear, O Yisrael! The Lord is our God, the Lord is One." The sound of the Shema awakened memories within the children of these words being recited with their parents prior to bed. Known as the Shema, this fundamental Jewish prayer prompted an emotional reunion as dozens of children recognized the prayer and instantly ran toward him.

This newspaper article then cited stories where the recitation of the Shema also provided confirmation of Jewish identity more recently. On the very day of the start of the current October 7th conflict between Israel and Hamas, the Kalmanson brothers drove 100 kilometers on October 7th morning, from their home in Otniel to Kibbutz Be'eri, in order to help save the lives of other Jews. Thinking the Kalmansons were terrorists trying to fool them into coming out of hiding, the terrified members of the kibbutz refused to open the doors of their safe rooms. Their shouts of *we're reservists*, or, *we are Jews*, and even singing songs from the Jewish holidays were met with suspicion. It was only when they proclaimed the Shema that doors opened, revealing petrified kibbutz residents who had been hiding for over twelve hours. I imagined it was not just the words they proclaimed but the energy within the recited words that identified them as Jews.

One time in the 1980s when I was seeking to enter Israel at a particularly challenging time for Israel, I was questioned to prove my Jewish identity before I was allowed to enter. I chanted *Shema Israel ... HaShem Elohaynu HaShem Echod*. And then I began to chant my Bat Mitzvah Haftorah. "*Enough! Enough!*," they declared, after hearing only five words. Did they not like my singing? They were quick to allow me to enter Israel.

As a general rule, it is always good to chant the Shema at least twice a day, so as to strengthen our connection to God as Jews. The six words of the Shema remind us of Jewish unity, Jewish survival, and most importantly, that God is always with us. The Shema offers us a ticket to the experience of Divine Oneness—the highest spiritual awareness. And, most importantly, we feel ourselves as a part of the community of Israel which is always a blessing.

10

Tammuz

JUNE – JULY

ENERGY
Seeing Life as It is

AREA OF HEALING
Seeing

ASTROLOGICAL SIGN
Cancer

HEBREW LETTER
Chet ח

HEBREW TRIBE
Reuven

DIVINE NAME PERMUTATION
HVHY

HOLIDAY
The Seventeenth of Tammuz

My Little Holy Home in New York City

The double bed fits perfectly in the corner in my Manhattan studio apartment like a piece in a puzzle. Large decorative pillows around the outside rim of the bed allow the bed to also serve as a large couch for an overthrow of visitors.

The burgundy love seat frequently occupies the front of the non-working fireplace in the center of the apartment. The dining room table placed close to the large bay windows in the front of this first floor street level apartment almost seems like an outdoor cafe table. The cherry wood dining table expands with its additional leaves to sit twelve people for special occasions but usually is contracted to accommodate only myself on a daily basis.

The most beautiful possession in the apartment is a large woven wool rug, a tapestry of dark red, green, and golden colors. My mother bought it for me to cover up the ugly cracked wood floor. It is the most expensive and treasured gift I have ever received.

My New York City studio apartment also serves as my place of business. Several nights a week, for more than fifteen years, a circle of pillows and chairs, along with six large crystal bowls for toning are arranged for meditation classes for three to twenty or so people. Within the center of the circle, I burn four candles brightly illuminating the darkness of the room. With the exception of occasional street noises of conversations or cars riding by, a profound and holy silence pervades the room. Only words of the heart and soul are uttered here.

This old brownstone never renovated rent-stabilized studio apartment of mine on West 87th between West End Ave and Riverside Drive is very humble, even dingy by most standards. To the students and to me, this room is a portal to the higher worlds.

Healing takes place on all levels during meditation classes. Physical pain disappears and emotional stress vanishes. Deep mystical secrets are revealed. God is no longer hidden but found and experienced deep within ourselves. In this meditative circle, people share the most intimate secrets with each other.

One time a woman came to the meditation class on route to checking herself into a mental hospital. She feared she was going crazy and that she might even hurt herself. She had nothing to lose, so she thought she could stop into my humble abode and afterward, go check herself into the mental hospital. After a ninety minute class of guided meditation, she returned to her own home with the hope and faith to survive the crisis she was confronting without hospitalization or medication. God is a powerful healer. Due to the brief time of meditation, she saw that she needed not to collapse to survive and intuitively knew and envisioned that she could heal and be stronger than ever out of the hospital.

We learn this month that when we purify our seeing, we see that God is always with us, no matter what is happening externally or even emotionally within us. We learn this month that our homes can be holy temples. Our hearts can be transmitters for the Infinite Divine Presence for ourselves and others. And even our bodies can a temporary residence for God. God is in the world and within us. We just need to purify our eyes to see what is really present. What happens within us is much more important than what happens around us or seemingly to us.

(By the way, I no longer live in Manhattan and divide my time between Israel and Florida).

Energy: Seeing Life As It Is

Summer is fully upon us in the month of Tammuz. The sun is shining brightly, the days are their longest, and the heat of the summer is at its strongest. From a secular perspective, many think of the summer as a carefree time, a time to relax, travel and have fun, but according to Kabbalistic teachings, Tammuz is a heavy and challenging month. The heat one experiences this month is not just physical; it is also emotional and spiritual.

The physical and spiritual heat of this month often encourages us to make quick judgments about people and our own life situations that are based on externalities and not the truth or essence. If we are triggered emotionally and become reactive, this is a sign that we are not seeing the deeper truth of the situation. We frequently see things from our own vantage point. We rarely see the whole picture. Furthermore, we cannot see the impact from previous lifetimes as God can.

When we are triggered this month, always remember to take a few deep breaths to center yourself, question your assumptions, be discerning, and mindful. The most important lesson for this month is to recognize that what takes place in life this month is not what it first appears to be.

The healing opportunity of this month is seeing. The challenge this month is to see life as it is and not as we want or fear it to be. The question this month is, *Am I seeing things as they are or am I simply projecting my own needs, fears and desires onto a person or situation?*

When people project their own fears, anger, insecurities, and other unresolved feelings onto others, they are disempowered. It is hard to go forward in life if we are blaming others for our own weaknesses. The change in perception has to begin within ourselves. We are not responsible for the projections of others, only for our own. We must each come to see that there is no real benefit to experience ourselves as victims in any way.

No one has to be confined to an old narrative of low self-esteem and insecurity. We each have been Divinely given the freedom to choose life and all that is good in spite of what is taking place in the world or how we may have been programmed in our early years to not trust ourselves.

When we draw close to God and access our own souls, we know that we are not limited by the past unless we choose to be. We are also not affected by external forces or by other people unless we choose to disempower ourselves. Every moment offers us new possibilities. We can always choose to see our lives in a new and positive way that honors the highest expression of who we are. This is the deeper truth that liberates us from lies that so permeate the world today.

Everything in our lives is ultimately unfolding for our benefit, according to Divine Will and our soul destiny. Ibn Paquda in his classic book, *Duties of the Heart*, reminds us that whatever happens in the world is Divine Will. *No one can increase what God decreed shall be less. Nor decrease what God decreed shall be more. None can cause an event to happen earlier than God decreed that it shall happen later …"*

> This month is a time to realize and accept that God is in charge of everything in this world, even when what is happening does not feel good or right.

When we see and accept what is happening in our lives, we see the Divine Hand in our lives. Life is unfolding as it is because God is in charge of the world. When we resist what is happening in our lives, we suffer. This month is a time to realize and accept that God is in charge of everything in this world, even when what is happening does not feel good or right. When we open our eyes and our hearts and meditate, we can see clearly that God is Existence itself so God was always and is always present within all of Creation. As human beings we do not control reality. When we accept that God is in charge, we can be liberated from needless suffering and feelings of victimization. Furthermore, because God is always present, God is always available to support us when we call out sincerely from our hearts, wherever and whenever we do.

Tammuz is known as a time of judgment. During the month, we may be confronted with things from the past and find that we now have the opportunity to choose differently than we did previously. We can clear, heal, and let go of negative patterns in our relationships with others, with ourselves, and with God. Though challenges and tests take many forms and may occur on many different fronts in our lives, if we grow through them, we receive the Divine blessing inherent in them and come to see and appreciate what is really true. We then no longer are bothered by falsehoods or lies.

This may be hard, for what we held dear and true may be now seen as false and/or unnecessary. During this month, we are tested to see through appearances, and if it is necessary, internal and external structures will begin to break down to allow the true seeing to occur. This breakdown may not always occur by our conscious choice.

This is also the month of reversals, as the Divine Name permutation is reversed this month. What we held to be true may now be seen as false, and what is false may masquerade as the truth. We may think that one thing is happening, but in actuality it is the opposite. It is confusing, but all will become clear to us if we are open to see things as they are and not as want them to be. We live in a world where frequently what is good is viewed as evil and vice versa.

Kabbalah tells us that the months of the year are divided between Esau and Jacob. The months of Nissan, Iyar, and Sivan are given to Jacob. In these months, we find so many joyous Jewish holidays. The next three months, Tammuz, Av, and Elul are given to Esau. After many battles, Jacob reclaimed part of Av and all of Elul, but Tammuz is still totally in the domain of Esau. So the energy of this month is characteristic of the qualities attributed to Esau. Esau was said to be engaged in the physical world, involved in physical pleasures and warlike behavior. Esau was also known to be hypocritical, pretending to be righteous when he was not. Like the nature of Esau, Tammuz is a time when people engage in worldly and physical pleasures. It is a month to see easily the face of hypocrisy. Tammuz has been traditionally viewed as a time of challenge to the Jewish people. During this month, Israel has been more frequently forced to engage in defensive wars to stop the bombs directed at her from Gaza than during most other months.

The holiday of Tammuz is called, *The Seventeenth of Tammuz*. Unlike most Jewish holidays which commemorate happy redemptive events for the Jewish people, The Seventeenth of Tammuz is a day of fasting and repentance in keeping with the energy of this month. Many destructive events were reported to have occurred on this day. It is best known primarily for the breeching of the walls of Jerusalem that resulted in the destruction of the First and Second Holy Temples later in that year on the Ninth of Av.

We learn that the Temple was destroyed because people failed to see that the Temple was a reminder that God was in their midst and not only in the Temple itself. *They shall make me a sanctuary and I (God) will dwell in their midst*. Over time, people lost contact with the true significance of the Holy Temple. No longer serving the holy purpose for its creation, idols were placed in the Holy Temple, corruption was rampant, and the people consequently became divided. As the rabbis have told us, the destruction of the Holy Temple was due to the lack of love and unity between Jews.

Even after the breeching of the Wall surrounding Jerusalem took place, the people remained divided on how to cope as they awaited the inevitable destruction of the Holy Temple. The wealthy people of Jerusalem, with great financial and supply resources, offered to feed all the people in Jerusalem, yet the zealots who wanted war with Rome burnt what could have been the food supply for the people so as to motivate them to fight the Romans. It is obvious that people failed to see that God was present in their lives and that the Jewish people were created to love each other. When the Jewish people are united, they are Divinely protected. When the Jewish people are divided, they are very vulnerable to external enemies. What a painful and frightening this time must have been as the Jewish people awaited their defeat and the inevitable destruction of the Temple. During this war, many Jews perished, while many escaped and dispersed all over the world.

> The healing of seeing this month enables us to more easily see through appearance and deception.

Tammuz today is ultimately a wonderful month, but only if we know how to use its particular intense energy constructively. When we purify our seeing, open our hearts to see God in the world and within each of us, we grow in Tammuz in ways that may not be possible at any other time period of the year. The healing of seeing this month enables us to more easily see through appearance and deception. We may feel hurt or betrayed, but if we recognize that we have been given the gift of seeing life more clearly and honestly, we will be happy and uplifted. Through self-examination, we come to see that even what we have labeled as the negative experiences we have had in life have both deepened and humbled us and ultimately have had positive impact in our lives.

May we be blessed to find peace and love inside ourselves and in our relationship with God, even when what is happening externally may not be so peaceful. May we radiate blessings of calm, love and peace towards everyone we meet and thereby contribute to bringing forth the peace and love that we each are yearning for and what the world so needs.

General Guidelines and Goals

These guidelines and goals enable us to direct our energies in the ways that are optimal for our growth and transformation in accordance with the energy of this month.

1. OPEN TO SEE THINGS AS THEY ARE AND NOT AS YOU WANT THEM TO BE.

This is the month of healing through seeing. What we see reflects our thinking. We often do not see things as they really are and see only our projections. We may be comfortable or uncomfortable with what we see. Ask yourself often this month, *Am I seeing things as they are or am I simply projecting my own needs and desires onto this person or situation?*

This month is an auspicious time to see life more clearly. Do not be afraid to question your assumptions. Before taking an action, take note to consider whether you are looking for validation or permission from others or are you doing what you feel called to do on a soul level, no matter if anyone is aware of it or not.

This month is an optimal time to trust God, surrender to Divine Will, and experience inner peace regardless of what is happening externally. The Infinite Intelligence Who created all of life is in charge of your life. See Divine blessings in all of life experiences. There is always blessing.

2. DO NOT JUDGE OTHERS.

If you feel that you are going to judge someone or some situation in a harsh way, be sure to pray that your eyes and heart be opened so you can see more deeply what is true rather than pass judgment on seeing only superficially. *Master of the universe, please let my eyes be open to see the truth of what is rather than my own projections and false assumptions* is a good prayer for this month.

How we judge others is how we will be judged by the Heavenly Court. This point is illustrated in a saying in *Ethics of the Fathers*. Akiva ben Mahalalel says, *Consider three things and you will not come into the grip of sin. Know from where you came, to where you are going, and before whom you will give justification and reckoning*. The Hebrew words for justification and reckoning are *din ve chesbon*, which is translated as judgment and accounting. One would expect that it would say that first one makes an accounting and then one is judged. It is taught that when a person dies, he will be requested to make a judgment about someone else who has a similar situation to his own. It may be even his own, but he is not aware of that. How he judges that person will be how he is judged. For one's own self interest alone, it is always best to show compassion. God will judge us as we judge others.

3. BE FLEXIBLE.

Tammuz can be a month of reversals. We expect one thing to happen but something totally different happens. As much as may like to think we are in control, we need to accept our limitations, let go and invite God into our lives. We are not in control. God is. This is one of the deep teachings of this month.

Though it may be challenging, we must realize that whatever happens to us is an opportunity for growth and healing. We actually grow the most when confronting great challenges. As Tammuz is a month of judgment, we need to accept that nothing happens by chance and nothing is coincidental. Though we have free will, everything occurs by Divine Providence. This is the ultimate paradox. If and when we can accept what is happening in our lives with equanimity and trust in God, we will be happy even in hard times. Affirm to yourself that you are living the life you were meant to live, so do not invalidate yourself or your life. It is a privilege to be alive and to be you.

4. FEEL YOUR FEELINGS RATHER THAN BLAME OTHERS FOR THEM.

Too often people react to what they are feeling and are quick to blame others for not giving them what they want rather than communicate clearly and directly what they would like to receive. The expression of anger, moreover, makes it impossible for their underlying needs to be met by the person with whom they are angry.

No one is the cause for any of our feelings. So stop blaming others for your self-afflicted suffering, take responsibility and focus on loving yourself more. We cannot receive love from others unless we first love ourselves and love God. God created us in such a way to teach us that there are things that we must do for ourselves. No one can live our lives for us. No one can sleep for us. No one can eat for us. We each have to do these important life sustaining activities ourselves. So we need to be mindful that we first have to love ourselves. And we do not have to give ourselves up, to placate and validate others at our own expense to feel loved by others.

> We cannot receive love from others unless we first love ourselves and love God

Furthermore, we waste a lot of time and energy expecting other people to be different than they are. When we have expectations of others, we will often be disappointed and we will suffer. It is best to accept people for who they are and for who they are not. Accept yourself for who you are and who you are not. Complaining and being angry is considered one of the worst character traits, likened to idolatry. It does not help or change anything. It is simply a waste of time.

In this month, be mindful to feel your feelings without blaming others or even yourself. It is good to feel your feelings whatever they are and even weep with yearning for a more God connected life. If you allow yourself time to process and release your negative feelings rather than project or dump them onto others or even yourself, they will dissipate naturally. Your negative feelings are rooted in your ego identify and not within your soul. Your soul is a part of God and is always peaceful and wise. Feeling peaceful and wise is the best indicator that you have made a connection to your Divine soul. For the most part when we are angry or anxious, we must know that these feelings are ego driven so they can consciously be released.

5. BE INDIFFERENT TO PRAISE AND INSULT.

> Be in conversation with God more than with people.

What people say about others is usually more of a reflection of who they are than the person or people they are taking about for the most part. Do not allow yourself to feel devalued by others. Do not give up your passion to please or court favor from other people. Make yourself and your relationship with God your priority. Be in conversation with God more than with people.

5. WEEP FOR THE DIVINE PRESENCE.

If you feel separated from God and from the access to the peacefulness and joy of your own soul, it is often good to cry out for it. Do not numb or distract yourself but allow yourself to feel the depth of the impact of this loss of this Divine connection. It is actually a great blessing to feel grief over the pain of one's sins. Sins implied here means in the broadest definition as the ways we deprive ourselves of our innate capacity to receive the goodness the Creator has intended for us. Weeping in prayer is considered a blessing and not an expression of weakness.

When we make a connection that our sadness and grief is rooted in our inability to experience God in life, we may come to realize that we are actually crying for the Shechinah. Call to God from the depths of your heart and you will be Divinely comforted. Your tears are a portable mikvah, they will purify you and open your heart. As the Kotzker Rebbe said, *there is nothing more whole than a broken heart.*

Astrological Sign: Cancer

The astrological sign of Tammuz is Cancer, a term that in English has negative connotations, reminding us of the disease, and reflecting the serious challenges of this month. The Hebrew word for Cancer is *sartan* which means Satan, a name indicating the difficulty of the tests of this month.

The sign of Cancer is the crab, a not-kosher, unattractive, insect-like crustacean. Like the crab, the energy of this month and people born this month often have a hard outer shell and a soft center. The crab moves sideways, rarely forward to its goals. I have heard that for every step forward the crab takes, it takes two steps backwards.

The month of Tammuz is not a great time to go forward in one's life. It is not good to start new projects. The crab is tenacious, and tenacity is necessary this month. Tammuz is a good time to work on existing projects.

The ruling body of Cancer is the moon. The moon is always changing, making Tammuz an emotional roller coaster kind of time with many ups and downs in moods and feeling states. The moon affects the waters of the earth, and Cancer is a water sign. This month is a time of intense and varying feelings, accompanying by all kinds of desires which make this month one of emotional volatility more than other months.

The qualities associated with people born under the sign provide additional information about the energy of this month. People born under the sign of Cancer are known to be highly emotional and sensitive souls, albeit sometimes moody. They also are known to be intuitive, compassionate and nurturing. They are said to be strongly connected to the home for that offers them some stability and protection.

However, people born in this month have a tendency to be worriers. Like the crab, they may retreat into their shells, often hiding their sensitive feelings. Also like the crab, which has difficulty going forward in a direct way, people born in the month of Cancer are thought to make their desires known in subtle ways and may feel that they have to resort to deviousness when they are unable to approach or resolve a matter directly.

Hebrew Letter: Chet

Rabbi Yitchok Ginsburgh in his wonderful profound book, *Aleph Beit,* provides much information about each of the letters. The form of the *chet* is the combination of the two letters preceding it: The *vav* on the right which is the letter of Iyar, and the *zayin* on the left, which is the letter of Sivan, and a little line called a *chatoteret* that connects them. The *chatoteret,* which also begins with a *chet,* means *bridge.* From this we learn that what we accomplished in Iyar and Sivan prepares us for what we will do in Tammuz. When we put the *vav* and the *zayin* together, it forms the letter *chet,* which resembles a gateway.

Tammuz is a gateway into the summer. Tammuz represents another kind of gateway, a passageway that the soul must enter alone. Though the sun is shining brightly during this summer month, Tammuz can be a dark night of the soul that one must pass through before entering the light of the day.

The Hebrew word *chet,* which is the eighth letter of the Hebrew alphabet, means *transgression.* The word *chet* ends with the Hebrew letter aleph, the first letter of the Hebrew alphabet, is silent, *and* represents the one God. The Baal Shem Tov teaches that from this we learn that even when we sin, we transgress, God is with us. God may not be in the forefront but is always present in the background. The Talmud tells us that sight is the primary source of most transgressions. We see, we lust, we become heated in passion and we transgress. This month is the healing of seeing.

The letter *chet* is also the first letter of the world *chayim,* which means life, and also *chuppah,* which means canopy as in the covering used in weddings. Sin and transgression often can be a gateway to a better life, because they force people to confront themselves and what they have done so as to be empowered to grow, repair and become more whole than who they were previously.

Hebrew Tribe: Rueven

Reuven was the first born son of Leah and Jacob. As you may recall, Jacob wanted to marry Rachel but he was tricked into marrying her older sister first. On the wedding night, Jacob had sexual relations with Leah thinking she was Rachel. Out of this union, Reuven was conceived.

When Reuven was born, Leah said, *surely the Lord has looked upon my affliction and now my husband will love me.* Gen. 29:32. The name Reuven comes from the Hebrew word *re-eh* which means *to see.* Though Reuven *was* born out of deception, his name implies that a higher vision was present. Leah tricked Jacob, but still their marriage was supposed to be. The birth of Reuven was a sign validating the marriage. A general guideline for this month as expressed by the birth of Reuven is that what appears to be is not what is, but still it is supposed to be. Leah was not Rachel and never could be Rachel but her marriage to Jacob was still supposed to be. She is even buried for eternity near Jacob.

Leah and Rachel exemplify Tammuz's energy of reversals. Leah, the woman who tricked Jacob into marriage, bears him six sons and one daughter and is buried next to him for eternity. Rachel, the one he truly loved, is buried on the road apart from him. Be mindful of reversals the month. Remember, what appears to be happening may not be what is actually happening.

As the firstborn of Jacob, Reuven had a claim to leadership of the Jewish people but he saw that Joseph, the first born of Rachel and Jacob was more gifted and qualified for that position than he was. Though the brothers conspired to murder Joseph, Reuven defended Joseph to his brothers by suggesting that they place Joseph in a pit rather than murder him. Reuven even intended to return later to rescue Joseph. In this incident, Reuven modeled the capacity of love to let go of self-interest for the sake of truth.

Reuven was also a strong protector of his mother Leah. As we saw in Iyar, he gathered mandrakes to increase fertility and Leah ended up trading them with childless Rachel for a night with Jacob. Most children as young as Reuven may not want more siblings to share with their parents but Reuven knew that his mother so much wanted her husband's love and he did what he could to help her. As a result of the mandrakes he gathered, Issachar was born.

After Rachel's death, Jacob moved his bed into the tent of Bilhah, the handmaid of Rachel. As Leah's protector, Reuven was angry and offended by this move, so he moved his father's bed into his mother's tent. And to top it off, some midrashim say he even slept with Bilhah, and others say he did not. At any rate, he was criticized for overstepping his boundaries as Jacob's son.

On his deathbed, Jacob gave Reuven a blessing characteristic of the energy of this month. He says that Reuven expressed Jacob's power and his dignity but he is also *unstable like water*. Reuven acted upon his emotions: however, as well intended as they were, and this made him unfit for leadership of the Jewish people. Later on, the tribe of Reuven participated in the Korach rebellion against Moses, another reflection of the destructive energy of this month.

Before Moses died, he healed the blessing that Jacob had given to Reuven by saying, *Reuven shall live and not die and let his men be numbered*. Deut 33:6. Reuven had repented and it was accepted. Though he did not assume the leadership of the Jewish people as the first born, his tribe was blessed with strength, joy, and dignity. This blessing brings redemption to this month.

Divine Name Permutation: HVHY

The position of the letters in the permutation of the Divine Name for this month tell us much about the energy of this month. First, the letters are in the reverse order. Instead of YHVH which indicates the optimal flow of Divine energy. The order this month is HVHY. This reversed order tells us that this month is a time of judgment and that everything is reversed. Things will appear to be one way, but in actuality they are the opposite.

We note that the Yud (Y) occupies the world of Assiyah, our physical world, the world of action. The placement of the Yud in this world lets us know that not much is taking place on this plane of existence. Things are more hidden, asking us to see beyond appearances. This may not be a time to expend too much energy in doing and starting new projects. Tammuz is more an internal time. The Hay (H) in the world of Yetzirah informs us that the world of the heart, the world of emotions is very active, and very important. This is where one should focus.

It is very important this month to stop trying to figure out life with your mind but preferably focus on opening the heart to open to greater love. Expanding the heart with prayer and meditation and doing mitzvot to open the heart is the way to strengthen the connection between the heart and the higher spiritual worlds. The *vav* (V) in the world of Beriyah indicates that there is a flow from the world of Atzilut and Yetzirah. It is best this month to not process through the mind, but rather allow the mind be more of a vehicle to transmit the heavenly flow from above. This is not a time for critical analysis which only inhibits the flow of heavenly blessing. There is a great flow from above indicated by the Hay in the world of Atzilut, but one must know how to get one's mind out of the way and open the heart to receive the flow from above. Meditation is particularly helpful this month.

Torah Portions

The Torah portion for the beginning of the month of Tammuz often is the story of the spies sent out to survey the Land of Israel before the Jewish people entered it. Though God did not request this act, Moses responded to the need of the people to know what their next chapter on this journey would be. Most understood that their journey out of Egypt was not to remain in the desert forever, but was to go into the Promised Land that we call Israel today.

Upon seeing the inhabitants of the land, the spies, with the exception of two of them, reported that *we were like grasshoppers in our eyes and so we were grasshoppers in their eyes*. Num. 13:33. They murmured against Moses and Aaron saying, *If only we had died in the land of Egypt and if only we had died in the wilderness*. Num. 14:2.

They only saw their fear projected. They did not see things as they really were and most importantly they forgot that the land had been promised to them by God. They were afraid to enter the land and ultimately their fears and desires were fulfilled. I read recently that it is also possible that they feared they would lose the leadership roles they experienced while the Jewish people were in the desert, knowing that would all change once they actually entered the Land of Israel.

The incident of the spies is an important example of the mistake of *seeing* as it relates to the energy of this month. One has to be particularly mindful this month and consider whether what we see is true and whether it is simply our own fear projected.

The next Torah portion recounts the rebellion of Korach in Numbers 16. Two hundred and fifty men, leaders of the Jewish people, were followers of Korach and certain people from the tribe of Reuven. Reuvenites claimed that Moses had concentrated too much power in the hands of his family and tribe, the Levites, who served in the *Mishkon*, the Holy Tabernacle hosting the Divine Presence. Though they were jealous of Moses and Aaron and their tribes right to the priesthood, they did not express these feelings directly. They couched their argument in idealistic terms, claiming that *the entire assembly all of them are holy*. They implied and questioned, *Why should you elevate yourself above everyone else*. These arguments may sound good and even logical to the

> One has to be particularly mindful this month and consider whether what we see is true and whether it is simply our own fear projected.

rational mind, but they were not based in truth. They did not take into account the deeper truth of Divine Will. This is another example of discernment needed this month.

At the request of Moses, the ground opened and swallowed up those participating in this rebellion. Others carrying incense also perished in a flame. Many people were then angry and criticized Moses for the deaths of Korach and his supporters. Fourteen thousand of this group were punished and died in a plague. Though this was a small percentage of the Jewish people at this time, these deaths were still devastating, and reminiscent of the destructive quality of the energy of this month.

Also this month are reported the deaths of Miriam and Aaron, the sister and brother of Moses. Num. 20. In the merit of Miriam, the Jewish people had water. When she left her body, there was no longer any water. The Jewish people complained to Moses about the hardship of living in a desert without water. Even Moses becomes emotionally reactive in the Torah portions read this month as well and he strikes the rock to bring forth water rather than just speaking to it, as God had commanded. Moses was punished for this and could not enter the Land of Israel. Moses died alone in the desert. We have no idea where he is buried or even if he was buried.

The events of rebellion, punishment, death and loss portrayed in the Torah portions read during Tammuz reflect the intensity of the energy of this month. Tempers can run high at this time because people do not see the blessings that are present for them. Instead, there is constant complaining and lack of gratitude, and even Moses, our greatest prophet, overreacts.

Holiday: The Seventeenth of Tammuz

HISTORY: Unlike most Jewish holidays, which commemorate happy and redemptive events for the Jewish people, the Seventeenth of Tammuz is a day of fasting and repentance in keeping with the energy of this month.

The practice of fasting is a spiritual practice that redeems and transforms negative energy.

Many destructive events which have been said to take place on the Seventeenth of Tammuz are commemorated on this day. Moses broke the tablets when he descended from Mount Sinai on the Seventeenth of Tammuz upon seeing so many Jews worshiping the Golden Calf. The Golden Calf was built on that day and many Jews who had participated in the sin of the Golden Calf died on that day.

At the time of the First Temple, the daily offerings in the Temple ceased on this day due to a shortage of sheep. Some also say that an idol was placed in the Temple on that date. Furthermore it is said that on the Seventeenth of Tammuz Noah sent a dove out of the ark to see whether the water had receded sufficiently, but the dove could not find a dry place to rest and returned.

The Seventeenth of Tammuz is mostly significant for the following reason. The breeching of the walls of Jerusalem that resulted in the destruction of the First and Second Temples occurred on the Seventeenth of Tammuz. Jerusalem was under siege from the Seventeenth of Tammuz until Tisha B'Av, the ninth of Av, three weeks later. This was a time of waiting for the inevitable, a time of going inside oneself to find the spiritual resources to cope with what was unimaginable. This time from the Seventeenth of Tammuz to the Ninth of the month of Av is called The Three Weeks. Only this time known as The Three Weeks could contain this depth of brokenness. The Temple had served as the center of Jewish religious and communal life, so it was unclear what Jewish life would be like after that. Additionally, many people were murdered on this day as well.

OBSERVANCE: The Seventeenth of Tammuz is traditionally observed with a fast day that extends from the break of dawn until sunset. It is permissible to eat and drink the preceding night and even until dawn. This day of fasting does not have the same restrictions as the fasts of Yom Kippur and Tisha B'Av. Washing and wearing of leather shoes are permitted now but not during Yom Kippur or Tisha B'Av. People who do not fast well and who would be made ill from a fast are not required to fast on this day. However, people who do not fast are advised to eat simple foods and refrain from indulging in much food and drink. In addition to fasting, people are advised to engage in introspection, to review their actions, and repent of anything bad that they have done. During this time, many religious Jews refrain from listening to music, dancing, cutting their hair, and marriages until after Tisha B'Av, the ninth day of the next month.

During The Three Weeks, one is advised to be careful and avoid situations of danger more so than at other times of the year. Though travel is permitted, one is advised to exercise more care when traveling. Some people even choose not to fly in airplanes during this time, but that is a choice, it is not prohibited by Jewish law.

Meditation

In this month of spiritual darkness when the light of God is more hidden, we must learn to see the Divine Light in all of creation because on a deeper level this light is always present. The Bible tells us that light was the first creation. This light was created before anything else. The sun, the moon and the stars were created on later days. This first light, formed rather than created, on the first day, was spiritual light that did not originate from something physical. This light was a formation of the always present eternal Or Ain Sof, the Limitless Light, a Kabbalistic name for the Divine Existence prior to creation. Light is a metaphor for the Divine Influence. This spiritual light also has many names in Judaism such as the hidden light, holy light, inner light, and original light.

> The light we seek is a return to who we really are in our highest frequency vibration.

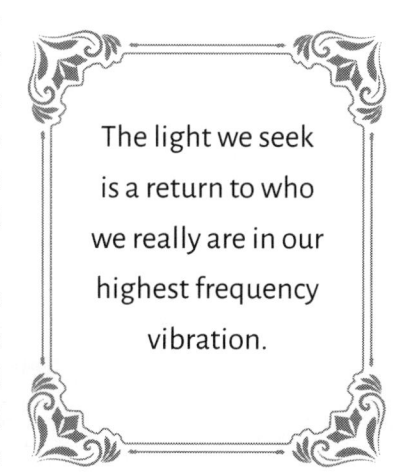

When we quiet the chatter of the mind and open the heart, we can begin to listen to the voice of our own soul and experience what the soul, our essential self, truly wants and needs. Most of us will hear the soul's yearning to return to limitless light of God. This is our spiritual home. We do not have to manufacture this desire, we just have to remove the obstacles we have placed to block the light. The light we seek is a return to who we really are in our highest frequency vibration. It does not matter what is happening externally to ourselves. This is why this is an important meditation to do during this month.

> ### LET THERE BE LIGHT MEDITATION
>
> Follow the instructions of this meditation at a pace that is comfortable for you. If possible, prepare a candle for this meditation. Find a comfortable seated position either on the floor with a pillow or on a chair. Allow the back to be straight, the shoulders to be relaxed. Imagine that there is a string connecting the top of the head to the ceiling.
>
> Begin by becoming aware of the breath. Take several long deep breaths to center yourself and bring your focus to the present moment. Breathe in through the nose and exhale through the mouth. With each exhalation, let go of the concerns of the day, let go of tension and stress. Breathe it out … As you inhale, focus on opening to greater energy and well being. Your awareness expands with each breath. With each deep inhalation and exhalation, allow yourself to pause in the space between the breaths. Allow the breath to become slower. As you inhale, get in touch with what you want to open to and receive within yourself from this meditation. What do you want to let go of within yourself?
>
> Your desire and intention will shape the quality of this meditation experience for you. Quiet the chatter of the mind and listen to the deep desires of the heart and soul within you. Are they what you would imagine that God, the Source and Sustainer of All life, would want for you?

Go deep inside to contact your personal desire for love, truth, holiness, for God's light, for the hidden light before creation. Open to the intensity of this yearning. If you like you can open your eyes and gaze at the candlelight before you. Alternate between closing your eyes and keeping them open.

If you like, listen to holy music or chant a niggun, a wordless melody of yearning expressing the yearning within you that is beyond words. Get in touch with your personal yearning through the chanting or singing. Then say a prayer that you be worthy of experiencing God's light and love directly: May I be worthy of experiencing the Divine Presence. Repeat this prayer silently to yourself several times. If you want, state it aloud or in a whisper.

Now repeat first silently to yourself the words *Ye He Ohr* (Let there be light). These are the first words reported to be said by God in the holy Torah ... *Ye He Ohr* ... Repeat these words as a mantra with the inhalation and exhalation silently. Then say to yourself: Let me experience Your light, Divine One (or however you address the Creator of the Universe). Let me experience Your Light, God. Let me experience the Light of the Divine Presence.

If you like, say these words now aloud. Repeat the words *Ye He Ohr* aloud. When you say *Ye he* allow the chin to rise to the ceiling. When you say *Ohr*, bring the chin down to the chest. Repeat as a chant *Ye he Ohr*, Let there be light. Feel free to say this loudly or softly, quickly or slowly. Repeat this chant for a few minutes and then come to rest in the silence. Absorb the frequency you generated by this repetition and heart opening.

Then visualize a luminous white light entering the body through the top of the head on the inhalation. And imagine that it enters deeply into the head and flows into the body with the exhalation. This Divine Light permeates the body and spreads particularly to all areas of the body in need of healing. This light caresses and heals you on all levels of your being, physically, emotionally, and spiritually.

To intensify your capacity to receive Divine light into your physical body, imagine a symbol like a Jewish star, a Hebrew letter, or any other symbol that has meaning for you. Visualize this symbol a few inches above the top of the head. In your imagination, endow this symbol with the power to radiate white light along with a sense of well being. This light removes tensions, negativity and toxicity. This light restores health and well being. Circulate this symbol through your physical body. Your consciousness is riding this symbol through the interior of your body. Make a conscious note of the areas where it is difficult to do this exercise and where it is easy. This will provide you with interesting and important information about what is happening within yourself

Begin by visualizing your symbol entering the body at the top of the head. Place this symbol in the middle of the head. That point is the midpoint between the front and back of the head and the ears. Allow your consciousness to rest upon the symbol. Experience the interior of the head from the vantage point of the symbol. Feel the vast universe inside your own head. Your symbol is radiating light in all directions within your head.

Ride the symbol as it traverses the interior of the head. The seven passageways to the soul are located in the head. Bring the symbol over to the eyes, visualizing that the symbol radiates its light into this passageway, purifying your power of vision. Pray that your vision is purified so that you see the good and see Godliness.

Now bring the symbol to the entrance of the nose and visualize that the symbol's light radiates through the nostrils, purifying your power of smell. Smelling refers to the power of intuition to sense the essence of the situation. Visualize the symbol going towards and into the mouth, purifying the power of speech. As you visualize the light purifying this passageway, pray that your speech be purified. The more purified your speech, more powerful words will be.

Now visualize the symbol traveling to the ears and purifying your hearing. Visualize the light of the symbol radiating through this passageway, and pray that your ears hear only good. The eyes, the ears, the nose, and the mouth are considered passageways for the soul. The soul empowers all these organs, giving us the power of seeing, hearing, smelling, and speaking.

Now visualize that your symbol travels to the neck, that long narrow passageway connecting the head with the rest of the body. Visualize your symbol traveling through this tunnel radiating light. Imagine that the symbol has the power to remove obstacles, to take away tensions so as to better permit the flow of soul energy of the head into the rest of the body. Ride your symbol with your consciousness and experience yourself traveling through the neck.

Now see your symbol going to the shoulders, releasing the tension and tightness of these muscles. It is said that we carry the burden of the world on our shoulders. We carry the should messages we have received on the shoulders. Continue to take deep breaths to release tensions throughout this exercise. Now float your symbol to the right arm to the right hand. Ride your symbol and experience your body from this vantage point. Visualize that your symbol radiates throughout your arm. As your symbol travels down the arms, feel that you open your capacity to give.

Now float your symbol up the right arm and then over to the left shoulder. Visualize your symbol traveling down the arm, radiating its light. Ride your symbol and experience your body from this vantage point. Note the difference between the right arm and hand and the left arm and hand. As you visualize the symbol traveling down the left arm, feel that you open your capacity to receive and contain energy. Now visualize your symbol floating up the left arm and going into the torso.

Ride your symbol in the torso, where so many vital organs of the body are located—the lungs, the heart, the intestine, the liver, the spleen. Visualize that your symbol radiates its light to all these organs. Your torso is being bathed in white light. Your symbol removes tensions and toxicities. You can say silently to yourself and if you want, even out loud: My heart is receiving Divine light. My heart is opening, My lungs are receiving light, My kidneys are receiving light, and My large intestine is receiving light. Call out and focus on all the organs in the torso. The entire torso is filling with white light, purifying and healing all the organs located in this center of your body. Experience gratitude for all your important and precious organs that work so hard to sustain your soul in a physical body.

Now bring your symbol to the pelvic and genital area of the body as well as the buttocks. This small condensed and concentrated area in the body, the seat of our sexuality, the seat of our reproduction, and the seat of elimination of impurities and toxicity of the body. Ride your symbol and experience yourself from this vantage point of your symbol.

Now bring your symbol to the right hip and leg and visualize that your symbol travels down the leg radiating light. Ride your symbol and experience yourself from this vantage point. The Divine emanation associated with the right leg is endurance, trust in victory. Then go up the right leg and repeat this exercise on the left leg. The Divine emanation associated with the left leg is humility, allowing what is essential to shine through. Note any difference between the right and left legs.

After you have completed this visualization, let go of the symbol, be aware of the breath, and focus on the body simply being open to receive.

Then imagine yourself in the Garden of Eden as a totally righteous person basking in the light of the Divine Presence. Breathe in the high vibrations. Accept these vibrations. Accept those vibrations and let them enter into your depths. Absorb this experience as fully as possible for as long as you like. This experience of who you are on a soul level is unaffected by what is happening in the world and in your personal life.

Practical Recommendations

1. MAKE INNER PEACE YOUR PRIORITY.

Make an effort to be mindful and calm this month and not act out from an emotionally wounded or heated place. This month is a time for feeling a range of deep, intense and varying feelings and desires. Be mindful to not make rash judgments this month. Make a sincere effort to not be reactive this month.

Be careful not to project your feelings onto others. It is a waste of time and energy to be upset expecting other people to be different than they are. Do not allow other people to define your value. Also remember that what people think of you is often their own projection. It is more about them than you.

Let go of the need to be validated by others. Give yourself time to be with your feelings without blaming others for what has been triggered within you. Maturity and self composure comes when we do not project our fears and wounding on to others and we are unaffected when others do so to us.

Choose always inner peace by seeking access and refuge in your own soul. Do not allow yourself to descend to the drama of the ego identity. Remember, you came to this world to radiate light, love, and peace, not to increase drama. As a general rule to be peaceful is to not expect from people for what only God can give to you. In this way, you will never be disappointed by others.

2. TAKE TIME TO BE QUIET AND MEDITATE.

This month is a time to be internal. There is a great heavenly flow this month but it is more hidden, so we need to be quiet and meditate to be able to receive. It is always good to spend time in nature. Hugging trees, listening to birds chirp, watching squirrels, and even industrious ants can be inspiring. There is a practice called grounding when you take off your shoes and stand directly on the physical ground. This helps you to unplug from all the noise and be grounded and more connected to nature.

3. SPEND TIME AT HOME.

This is not the month for extensive traveling around the world or even to be engaged in many external activities. During the month of Tammuz give yourself time to simply be at home with yourself and become closer to people you live with and love. Make your home more beautiful physically and spiritually. Your home is a miniature Holy Temple. Everything you are looking for can be found within yourself, right in your home.

A Tale to Live By

Here is another important story from my most favorite Jewish holy text, *Duties of the Heart,* reminding us to not entertain any fantasies and see clearly who we are and what this world is really is. I tell this story now from my memory so I may not include some embellishing details, but the essence of the story is clear.

There was a country in ancient times occupying an island in Pacific Ocean that had the custom of inviting a foreigner to rule over them for a limited period of time. At a certain time, unknown to the foreigner, he would have to depart from the kingdom and leave the possessions he had accumulated during his reign. Of course the residents of this country never told this secret to the foreigner selected to rule. Every appointed king worked very hard to build up and increase the wealth of the kingdom. How disappointed and upset they were to discover they would have to leave everything they worked hard to build in the kingdom.

There was a wise person who was selected to be king. But before he took his reign, he disguised himself and wandered among the citizens of this country to learn what the customs were in this kingdom. Eventually he was told this secret about the reign of the king. When he did take his reign, he devoted most of his time to taking wealth out of the kingdom as much as he could in the limited time granted to him to be king. When his time came to resign, he retired peacefully knowing that he had done his best to secure his standing after he departed from the throne.

This story reminds us to be mindful that we only have a limited amount of time to be physically embodied, so it is wise for us to devote our energies towards securing the kind of wealth from this world that we can take with us to the next world. Accumulating physical possessions, fame or ego accomplishments that we will not be able to take with us when we transition to the next world may not be the best use of our time and resources.

When I shared this story with my students, one of them responded that she did not like this story at all. Perhaps she did not appreciate the metaphor but she felt strongly that people should work hard in this world to make it a better place without any concern for how they would benefit from this labor. *What a most beautiful reflection* I told her. This was her first time attending my classes and unfortunately she did not come back after hearing this story. I seem to always have the sweetest and holiest people as students and even as visitors.

11

Av

JULY – AUGUST

ENERGY
The Wholeness of Brokenness

AREA OF HEALING
Hearing

ASTROLOGICAL SIGN
Leo

HEBREW LETTER
Tet ט

HEBREW TRIBE
Shimon

DIVINE PERMUTATION
HVYH

HOLIDAYS
Tisha B'AV
Tu B'AV

A Personal Story

Most of us have had many Tisha B'Av experiences in our lives. Those are the times when all that we wanted and all that we felt sustained us is taken away from us. When loved ones die, or worse, are murdered, marriages crumble, difficult heath challenges emerge, livelihoods lost, and homes and communities wiped out by hurricanes or violence, our hearts are broken. The pain is very great. We cry to God. And we cry for God, sometimes even more than we have cry for ourselves. God created this world to bestow love upon creation and not for suffering. Many of us have shed these kinds of holy tears at some time in our lives. And then when there are no more tears to cry, we become silent, we are humbled, and our lives then change for the better.

Here is just one of my many personal Tisha B'Av stories. After suffering the pain of being single and religiously observant for so many years, on Yud Tes Kislev in 1993, I am dragged to a Chabad celebratory event, and unexpectedly I meet a man whom I would soon marry.

The next day after our meeting, my future husband calls me. This man tracks down my phone number through a rabbi, who surprisingly gives him my phone number without even consulting me. I am sure the rabbi believed that I would never turn down this attractive man. My future husband calls to tell me that he is coming again to New York for business next week and he wants to take me out to dinner. Later I find out that I am the sole reason for this trip to NYC.

When he returns to New York the following week, we go to a candlelit kosher restaurant, a perfect place for a romantic entrapment. As the restaurant prepares to close its doors, we wake up from our intense conversation to notice that we are the only people in what had been earlier a busy night for the restaurant. I leave dinner with an ache in my heart and a pain in my solar plexus. I have been attacked by lust and longing. Is this what love that leads to marriage feels like? I do not know. I was never afflicted like this before.

An enormous, gorgeous, and expensive bouquet of flowers arrives at my home the very next day followed in a few days by a beautiful scarf and a train ticket to Boston for the following week. This man is serious! He already told me very clearly that he does not want to date me. He wants to marry me! I am being courted and wooed in a way that I never experienced before. Could it really be that my dream of being married to a handsome prince is really happening?

I am excited to be traveling to see him again and meet his spiritual family the following week. Even though my visit to Boston is only my second date with him, I am meeting all the significant people in this man's life, except for his biological family. I do not meet them until the actual wedding. Like Cinderella who has entered the ball and the glass slipper has just been placed on her foot, I am treated and cherished like a new bride by this group of married friends throughout the Sabbath celebration. At each meal, his friends raise their glasses in cheers to me and my future husband.

All the women I meet during this Shabbat like me. One of the women asks me to please move to Boston even if somehow I do not marry this man. I feel welcomed and loved by the women in this community in a way I never felt before. I know that if I were to marry this man, these women will be close friends and what a big blessing it would be for me to be connected to them.

I am eager to be married. So when he proposes to me, I say yes immediately, and we set our wedding date for as soon as possible.

The actual wedding takes place in about six weeks from our first date. The wedding is a four-hour drive from New York, but a rented bus transports my friends, family, and students from New York to celebrate, along with his friends. Even people we do not invite come to our wedding. Our wedding is a typical Chassidic wedding of people who have returned to Judaism. Like Woodstock, it is a happening. The band is great. The men and women are dancing separately but with great joy and zeal. During the wedding, my husband surprises me and plays the bass guitar, singing with the band a song he wrote just for me. I am thrilled. He is even a rock star.

After a few broken engagements, I am very happy to be married, feeling blessed to finally be entering the sanctity and joy of a Jewish marriage.

I actually love being married. I love shopping, cooking, cleaning, even doing laundry because it is for my beloved. No longer a feminist, I am instantly transformed into a traditional wife hoping and praying to be soon barefoot and pregnant. I love feeling part of a couple, seeing him daily, sleeping next to him even though he snores,

A month or so after the wedding, my husband must travel to Edmonton, Canada, for this new high-paying position he acquired a month or two prior to our wedding, almost immediately prior to meeting me. When we got engaged, I learn about this upcoming work commitment. I purchase long underwear for the weather to protect me from possibly thirty-degrees-below-zero weather. So soon after our wedding, we travel to the North West territories to live in a one bedroom rented apartment in a hotel near his place of employment. During our brief stay in Edmonton, we both experience intense food poisoning at separate times so severe we each need to go to the emergency room of a nearby hospital. I even have to go in an ambulance, as my blood pressure dropped significantly and I was unable to even drink water.

In less than two weeks after our return to Boston, my husband becomes very ill. The doctor tells us that he is testing my new husband of one and a half months for AIDS.

What a cruel joke God is playing on me. Have I been cursed rather than blessed? I feel like running, but I stay and marvel at the irony of this predicament. I make myself strong and go to all the doctor's appointments with him. I prepare special vegetable juices daily and nurse him back to health. I prayerfully await the results of all his laboratory tests. I do not tell anyone about this spiritual test, particularly my mother. How could I marry someone I did not really know? I know that I wanted to be married quickly, but I did not want to die because of it. I pray to God that I not be cursed.

Thankfully my husband heals and regains his strength, but soon, within a few days after his recovery, I take to the sick bed myself. I can't seem to hold food down. Walking a few blocks is a daunting task for me. In a short amount of time, I lose more than twenty pounds. I am very thin and frail. I do not know what is happening to me. In the beginning, my husband tries to take care of me. I often keep the bathroom door open just in case I need him to assist me. I feel so faint at times. I am worried I could collapse in the bathroom. I am so sick. I wonder how I can live with such discomfort. On many occasions, he rushes in to monitor my pulse and help me to the bed.

Through a variety of alternative medical care and spiritual healing from an Israeli healer along with conventional medical care, I slowly begin to improve. Just as I am beginning to feel somewhat better, my husband tells me he wants a divorce. *Please wait until I feel better*, I asked him. *We could try to have a good marriage, Let's give ourselves some time. If it does not work out after a few years, we could then divorce.* My arguments and even my tears do not persuade him. He has made his decision. He is impatient and wants to move forward in his life without a sick wife.

It is clear that my husband is really not interested in working on the marriage and has already arranged his work schedule so he is traveling extensively for the next few months. He is not available for counseling. I agree to be divorced. I do not want to be married to someone who does not want to be married to me. During our appearance before the Beit Din, I cry hysterically throughout the entire procedure, but the rabbis go through with it anyway. On the train back together, my then ex-husband tells me that he loves me and gives me a little gift. It was actually in the time period between Tisha B'Av and Tu B'Av that I receive my get (religious divorce).

After the divorce, I am emotionally devastated. I cry every day. I had so much wanted to be married, to even be blessed with a child and reside in that special and holy universe of Jewish *coupledom*. I soon enter therapy three times a week with a person who is training to be a therapist. I pay $10 a session. I do not have money to afford more at this time. I have not worked for more than a year. The truth is that I am not looking for great insight at the time, but am simply looking for someone to whom I can cry out my heart and mourn for the loss of the dream of marriage and children. I cry during the entirety of most sessions.

A few months after the divorce, I ultimately find comfort in writing. Books last. Relationships do not. In next four years, I write four books. Three of these books are published by mainstream publishers. How I, a person who had never written a book before, acquire book contracts that paid me royalties with no effort on my part is a miracle, a story in itself. I share this story in the Tishrei chapter.

Writing is the perfect antidote for my loneliness and heartbreak. When I am writing, I do not feel lonely nor sad. I am sharing the best part of myself and conversing with thousands of people energetically. I love the act of writing. Writing also allows me to access my own soul and deepen my knowledge of Judaism. With each book, I feel I am initiated into a deeper wisdom.

My books over time bring invitations for me to teach all over America as well as expand my practice as a therapist. For over a decade I've traveled extensively to teach over the US, to Israel, and even to England for a Limmud Conference. All of a sudden, I am also sought after as a therapist by people facing divorce, relationship problems, or serious health challenges. It is clear to me that I am better able to help my clients because I have gone through challenges similar to what they are confronting. I am very busy professionally. I am teaching meditation in New York several nights a week in my home or local synagogues. God is my comfort. I find myself again and feel good being me. I have been resurrected and renewed.

Energy: The Wholeness of Brokenness

Av is considered the most emotionally intense volatile month of the year, a roller coaster of feelings. Much of the impact of the negative challenges of this month can be diminished if we are mindful and really listen to ourselves and others.

Misunderstanding what is heard and jumping to conclusions are the source of many problems in this month. In the Land of Israel and in many places in the world, Av is physically the hottest month. This heat is reflected on the emotional and spiritual planes of our lives as well.

Av means father in Hebrew. The father is a symbol of love and giving in Judaism. By this name we know that whatever happens in this month, even bad things, will ultimately be for good. The analogy of a child learning to walk illustrates this underlying principle and the process of growth for this month. At first, the child is supported by the parent. At a certain point, the parent lets go so the child will learn to walk on his or her own. Sometimes the child falls, which may be painful, but the parent is still nearby. Eventually, through various attempts and trials, the child learns to walk. The falls taken are all part of the learning process.

As a general rule and especially this month, we must give up trying to understand why things have happened in our lives as they have. We do not have access to the full picture of what is needed for our growth. We do not know the karma we accrued in former life incarnations. Only God knows what we need to go forward in our lives so trusting God allows us to accept life events, even challenging events, with grace. From that place of acceptance, we can then open ourselves for blessing.

The goodness of this month is further indicated by the fact that the letter associated with this month, *tet,* is the first letter of the word tov, which means good. The Talmud tells us that in the future, even the sorrowful days of Av will be transformed into days of joy. Even though challenging life events take place this month or at other times of the year, it is important to trust that good will emerge out of life challenges.

The *Gemara* however states that the luck of Jews is bad in the month of Av. Jews should avoid going to court even if they have a good case and are favored to win. This month is not an optimal time to negotiate new business contracts either, especially during the period of time known as *The Nine Days.*

Av hosts the saddest day of the year, Tisha B'Av, which commemorates the destruction of the First and Second Temples in Jerusalem thousands of years ago. As sad and tragic as this time was, we must accept that it was Divine Will that the Temples were destroyed and Jews were dispersed throughout the world.

When God initially asks the Jewish people to build a Mishkon, a holy Tabernacle in the desert to serve as the prototype for the Holy Temple in Jerusalem, it was to unify the people so God could be experienced within them. God had instructed the Jewish people in the Torah, *Make me a sanctuary and I will dwell within you or in your midst.* Exod. 25:8. The verse does not say *in it,* but within, or among you. The Hebrew is clear, telling us that the purpose of the external Temple is to experience the internal presence of God. It was not that the physical structure was so important, it was the vehicle for the interior experience. In the building of the Mishkon, everyone was asked to donate one half a shekel, no one could give more for this was an opportunity for everyone to participate equally. This was a fundamental demonstration of the equality of all Jews. We each have a direct and equal access to the Holy One.

In ancient times the Jewish people believed that the Holy Temple in Jerusalem was the meeting place between the Jewish people and God. The Jewish people were divided into the Kohanim, the priests, the Levites, serving the Kohanim in priestly duties, and Israelite, the common people. This is a collective hierarchy accepted by the Jewish people since then until today to serve the holy mission of the Jewish people with particular roles assigned to each group. Most Jews today know whether they are Kohanim or from the Levite tribe or Israelites.

Several times a year, the Jewish people would journey to the Holy Temple in Jerusalem to offer sacrifices and receive blessings and atonement for their sins. Jewish prophets informed us that through the service of the Jewish people in the Holy Temple, all nations of the world would be blessed. Its destruction is a loss to the world, not just to the Jewish people. For many religious people, the Temple was a microcosm of the universe. When the Temple stood, the spiritual and physical worlds were said to be connected. The destruction of the Temple meant that the Shechinah, the Feminine Divine Presence, no longer had a special home.

After the destruction of the Holy Temple, the rabbis instituted rituals in Jewish law so the Jewish people could have the experience of the Temple within their own homes and even within themselves. In many ways, the destruction of the Holy Temple democratized Judaism. Now with rabbinic law in place, everyone could serve God in their home like the priests did in the Holy Temple. Shabbat and holiday tables are likened to the altar of offerings in the Holy Temple. The candles we light for Shabbat and holidays remind us of eternal Divine light burning in the Holy Temple. The bread and salt at the Shabbat and holiday meals reminds us of the sacrificial wheat offerings. Every marriage was even said to offer a taste of the Holy of Holies from the Holy Temple.

When people become trapped in externalities, the form and structure, they may easily forget that the real purpose of everything is to facilitate the internal experience of the Divine Presence. This is what we each must remember this month. Sometimes we learn this best through loss.

If there is loss in your life, particularly this month, it is safe and good to feel the pain of your loss but also to accept it as a growth opportunity. Through loss, we learn what it essential. As we go deeper inside ourselves, we experience that we can never lose what is essential and intrinsic to who we are on a soul level. That which is real and true can never be taken away from us.

Toward the middle of this month of Av, there is greater clarity and openness. The first Sabbath after Tisha B'Av is called Shabbos Nachamu, the Sabbath of Consolation. The energy of the month then shifts dramatically. Having entered into the depths of our souls earlier in the month and possibly lost our fantasies for fulfillment through externalities, we now have access to our own souls and that of others in a new and deeper way. Hope and love are now rekindled. It is now a good time to travel and connect with others and open to the joy of love in life again.

This shift in the energy of this month takes place on the full moon of the month Av. This time is what the Talmud describes as the most joyous day of the year known as Tu B'Av, the fifteenth of the month of Av. Tu B'Av was celebrated historically as the time when there was such love and joy in the air that women would dance before the men and marriages took place on the basis of just one glance.

Tu B'Av is ultimately the celebration of the Divine Feminine, the immanence of God. God is not just in heaven but experienced in our midst. In Judaism, God is not only masculine. There are two faces of the Divine that are closest to us: the Divine Masculine, aka *Hakodesh Borechu,* the Holy One Blessed by He, and the Divine Feminine known as the *Shechinah,* the Divine Presence. On Tu B'Av, there is an arousal from below associated with a shift in the energy towards the revelation of the Divine Feminine.

It is no coincidence that these two polar events take place during the same month because in fact they are interconnected. These holidays reveal the dual character of the energy of the month and model for us a very important spiritual principle. Out of destruction comes rebirth and newness. Though these historical events occurred thousands of years ago, both occurred in this month and reflect the kind of emotional intensity still present during this month even today.

General Guidelines and Goals

These guidelines and goals enable us to direct our energies in the ways that are optimal for our growth and transformation in accordance with the energy of this month. It is recommended that you read and meditate upon them often during the course of this month. Reflect on their applicability to you, and allow them to direct and inspire you often during this month.

1. LISTEN TO WHAT IS SAID AND WHAT IS NOT SAID.

This month is dedicated for the healing of hearing. It is important to truly listen to others this month. We do not always correctly listen to what is said in words, nor do we always hear what is not said and implied in silence. Be mindful this month particularly to ask for clarification of what has been said, so you do not make any false assumptions. Be careful not to emotionally react without fully thinking about what you have heard this month.

> It is important to truly listen to others this month.

Make an effort to listen to people respectfully who are different than you without judgment. Today, people often have difficulty listening and respecting people who may hold different political opinions than they do.

Not only do people not have the capacity to dialogue with people with different opinions, some people may even resort to name-calling. I have been even called an idiot by people who hold different opinions than I do when I have tried to engage respectfully in dialogue. The inability to engage in dialogue seems to becoming increasingly difficult these days in America.

Israel was equally divided before October 7th. I heard the following in synagogue what someone said in Israel. *Before October 7th, many Israelis hated each other and were ready to kill each other. Now, after October 7th, we are willing to die for each other.* Jews are not thinking left or right. They are united. May Jews stay united.

2. CREATE OPPORTUNITIES FOR DEEP LISTENING.

Now is the time to share your pain with others and be open to hearing their pain as well. Sharing our vulnerability with others allows us to bond more deeply. In the sharing of our humanness and pain, we become close to each other and to God. Allow yourself to be humbled. When we have been truly humbled we are not afraid to acknowledge our vulnerability to ourselves and others. This humility brings rectification and healing.

3. GUARD AGAINST JUDGING YOURSELF AND OTHERS.

One of the reasons given for the destruction of the Holy Temple was because people did not love each others. This is called *sinas chinam*, causeless hatred. We each have to guard against our tendencies for spreading causeless hatred.

One of the causes of *sinas chinam* is egotism. Watch for the tendency to judge others, or even to see ourselves better or worse than others. We must let these tendencies go if they come up during the course of the month. Let us not be so petty or superficial.

Judging oneself or others creates feelings of separation from others. Watch out particularly for the tendency to be jealous of other's accomplishments and let that go of jealousy as quickly as you can. Remember that no one can have what is not intended for them. And we each can have only what we have the vessels to receive at this time. If we were supposed to have more, we would have more.

4. BE CAREFUL OF YOUR SPEECH.

Refrain from gossip or speaking negatively about others or even oneself. Judaism recognizes the power of words and has many laws about what should and should not be said. When we speak badly about a person, it backfires on us and hurts us energetically. If we need to say something to another that may in any way be perceived as criticism, we should do it directly and respectfully, and only if we feel that person will be able to hear what we have said. Otherwise, we need to be silent. So much unnecessary pain, particularly in this month, is caused by speaking without considering the impact our words will have on others.

5. BECOME MORE GIVING AND LOVE UNCONDITIONALLY.

The antidote to *sinus chinam* is love, unconditional love. All true love is unconditional. If love is conditional it is more like business than love. Unfortunately the business mentality has entered into the realm of our personal relationships. People too often give to others with the specific expectation of receiving something in return. If they don't get what they want or expect, they often withdraw their love. They may call it love, but it is really business. In spite of all their *giving*, they continue to feel isolated and lonely.

> Giving for the simple joy of giving without intention of receiving is pure and healing.

Giving for the simple joy of giving without intention of receiving is pure and healing. When we give in this way, our spiritual frequency is raised and we are brought into greater alignment with God, because God is the ultimate giver. This pure kind of giving builds true loving relations. Every day there are opportunities to give, small and large, without considering what you will receive in return. Make an effort this month to simply give for the joy of giving.

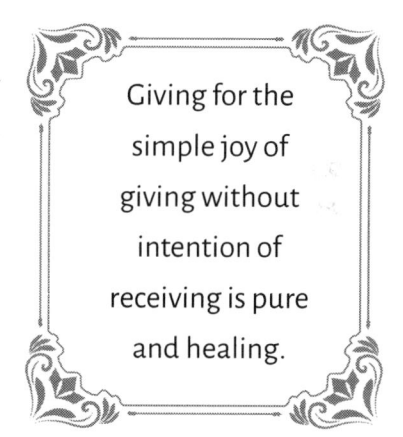

Reb Dessler, in his book, *Strive for Truth,* reveals an important insight about the nature of love. We don't first love people and then give to them. Rather, we first give to people and then we come to love them. According to Reb Dessler, if you want to have a lot of friends, give to many people.

6. OPEN TO THE DIVINE FEMININE IN YOUR DAILY LIFE.

Though the Holy Temple was destroyed during this month, God is still present in our lives. The Divine Feminine refers to the Divine immanence that is always present in our lives and in the world. It is the blessing of the Divine Feminine that maintains our physical existence in this physical plane. When we acknowledge that every human being came out of the womb of a woman, our appreciation of the Feminine, both human and Divine, is heightened.

It is the denial of the Divine Feminine that causes pain, alienation, and suffering in the world. When God is only experienced as *Ha Kodesh Borechu*, the Holy One Blessed be He, as the Divine Masculine that is transcendent, we are always looking towards heaven to connect with God. God is experienced as separate from ourselves. As a result, we may not experience our inherent oneness with people, with life itself, and with God. We are disconnected from the Divine Feminine when we do not experience or accept Divine Providence as operational in our daily lives, in our relationships with others, and in our homes. The revelation of the Divine Feminine reveals to us that God is present in every event in the world and even in our personal lives. The awareness and acceptance of this Divine Revelation brings tremendous feelings of love, peace, and connection.

As we grow spiritually, we experience God more as the Ultimate True Reality. In the deepest experience of the True Reality, we know that nothing truly exists other than God. Ultimately, we as human beings do not have real and everlasting existence of our own. Only God does. Through the nullification of our personal selves, it is our attachment and our absorption in God that we experience true aliveness. As it is said, *Only those who cling to YHVH are alive.*

This month take time to open and expand your awareness of the Divine Feminine. Studying Torah, praying, doing mitzvot, meditation, and even being in nature may help us to have a direct experience of the Shechinah, the Divine Feminine. It is through the agency of the Divine Mother and the Shechinah that we receive comfort and consolation during this month and throughout the year. Even when we are not engaged in a prescribed spiritual activity, we can be aware and connect with the ever present Divine Feminine. We know we have made this connection when our hearts are bursting with love, every moment feels new and beautiful, we trust in Divine Will and in the words of our holy prophets.

Astrological Sign: Leo

This month of Leo is ruled by the sun. The sun is a metaphor for spiritual energy. Kabbalah teaches us, however, the greater the positive energy, the greater potential for negative energy, a range especially demonstrated during this month.

The sun is a fire sign and Leo exhibits the two qualities of the first sign, its ability to impassion or enliven and its ability to destroy. In Tisha B'Av and Tu B'Av, the two holidays in this month, we see both aspects of fire revealed. Fire is purifying, illuminating, and transformational if it is properly channeled and contained. God is compared to fire. A fire that burns and does not consume. God is often described as holy fire.

Without fire, there is no passion. Without passion, nothing happens in the world. But fire can be also destructive and dangerous if it is uncontrolled. What can take a long time to build, fire can quickly destroy.

The energy of Leo in the month of Av is fire, while the previous month of Tammuz is represented by the crab, which is introverted. Av is represented by the lion, which is extroverted. When necessary, the lion roars to let everyone know that he is the king and that he will do everything he can to protect his territory. He wants and demands to be the center of attention. As we see, the lion struts around the jungle in his dignified and majestic way.

People born under the sign of Leo are known to resemble the lion. They like to be the center of attention. They are known to be generous, somewhat flamboyant and courageous. They can also be vain and ostentatious. Many world leaders are born under the sun sign of Leo. Interestingly, the Messiah, according to Judaism, will come from the tribe of Judah, which is associated with the lion. And the Talmud tells us that the Messiah is to be born on Tisha B'Av, a holiday occurring this month.

Like the lion, we all may feel a passionate desire to be heard, noticed, and make a difference, particularly this month. If this desire is channeled appropriately, this month will be a time of great creativity and generosity. If not, there may be pretentiousness and egotism that leads to needless strife. If we can be sensitive to this energy and give each other needed acknowledgement and validation, much conflict may be avoided.

Hebrew Letter: Tet

Tet is the first letter in the word *tov* which means *good*. The letter *tet* indicates that Av is ultimately a good month. The Gemara says the if one sees a *tet* in a dream, it is a sign that something good will happen.

If we examine the form of the letter *tet*, it looks like vessel with an inverted rim. It does not pour out, but contains within it. Moreover it is likened to a womb. As such the *tet* represents what is hidden, the potential contained within creation and within each person.

This idea is further supported by the numerical value of *tet,* which is nine. The number nine reminds one of the nine months of pregnancy. *Tet* connotes the power of pregnancy, the power to conceal and contain within oneself all that is good. Recall that the *chet*, the letter of the previous month, resembled a wedding canopy. This month is the impregnation. The birthing process begins in the next month known as Elul.

As an aside, the number nine is the numerical value of the word *emet* which means *truth*. The numerical value of aleph, the first letter, is one, *mem*, is forty but it is counted as four and the value of *tet* is four hundred but this is also counted as four, totaling nine. It is truth that is liberating, even if it sometimes forces us to relinquish comfortable illusions, which can be difficult for some to do. Some of the loss we experience this month may be more about the discovery and impact of truth in our lives. As hard as this process is, truth is necessary and good. It is so important and ultimately strengthening.

After each phrase in the six day creation story of the world, God pronounced it as *good*. By saying *good*, God is telling us that creation is a vessel to contain within it the goodness of God. Interestingly, the word *tov* is the thirty-third word in the Torah, reminding us of Lag B'Omer in the month of Iyar, the thirty-third day of the counting of the Omer. Though the word *tov* appears many times in the creation story presented in Genesis, it only appears one more time in the entire Torah. The other time used the word *Tov* is used is to describe Moses at the time of his birth, because of the light that shone within him.

Meditating on the letter *tet* this month will open you to the experience of what is intrinsically good, even though it may be concealed. In your meditation, visualize the letter *tet*. Trace it on your inner screen. Be with the letter *tet*. Merge with the letter *tet*. And if you like, project yourself and your life inside the letter *tet*.

Hebrew Tribe: Shimon

The tribe of Shimon, the second son of Leah, represents the energy of Av. The name Shimon is derived from the Hebrew word *shimo'a* which means *to hear*. The whole month of Av is devoted to the healing of hearing. Looking at incidents recorded in the Torah about Shimon—his mistakes, passion, and emotional intensity—provides us clues about the energy of this month and directs us to be mindful of our own human passions.

When Leah named her son Shimon she said *Because the Lord has heard that I was hated he has therefore given me this son also Gen.29:33*. Because these are such strong words for a mother to use at the time of a child's birth, it is easy to see how this child might have been emotionally scarred from birth. Like his older brother Rueven, he carried the legacy of being a child of a woman who felt less than appreciated and even hated, because Jacob favored her sister, Rachel. Leah's sentiments in naming Shimon may have predisposed him to be somewhat volatile with a chip on his shoulder, so to speak. Much of Shimon's actions might be seen as an effort of a son to defend and rectify the perceived lower status of his mother.

Shimon was most known as the passionate defender of his sister Dinah. Dinah had wandered independently into town and was kidnapped and sexually violated by the prince of the region, Shechem. Though rape was commonplace there, he however fell in love with Dinah. His father, the ruler of region, went to ask Jacob for her hand in marriage to his son. Jacob's sons were infuriated and devised a plan requiring the men of the region including the price to be circumcised as a condition for marriage to Jewish women. The ruler and prince believed them and all the men in the region circumcised themselves. On the third day after the circumcision, when they were most weak, Shimon organized an attack that resulted in their deaths. The Torah tell us, *"And it came to pass when they were in pain that two of the sons of Jacob, Shimon and Levi, Dinah's brothers took each man his sword and came upon the city and slew all the males."* Gen. 34:25. Fearing the consequences of such violence, Jacob confronted them about what they did, saying *"You have brought trouble on me, making me odious among the inhabitants of the land."* (v 30) but Simon and Levi responded without remorse, *"Should he be allowed to treat our sister as a prostitute."* (v 31)

The events of this story are as troubling to many readers today as they were to Jacob and later rabbinic sages. Was it right that all the men of the city be killed because of the actions of the prince? Torah commentaries attempt to justify it saying that the men in Shechem were lewd, immoral and rape was commonplace, an accepted every day occurrence there.

Shimon's zealotry and passionate emotions also made him a leader in the plan to kill his brother Joseph, the first son of the beloved wife Rachel, Instead of being killed, due to the persuasion of Reuven, his older brother, Joseph was sold into slavery. As terrible as all this was, it is considered part of the Divine plan to bring Joseph and then the Jewish people to Egypt, as had been prophesied to Abraham years before.

At the time of his death, Jacob assembled all his sons to bless them. But instead of blessing Shimon, Jacob tells him that he disapproves of the evil actions he did, and that his soul would not shield him from responsibility. He lets Shimon know that his tribe will lose its separate identity and be dispersed within Israel. The tribe of Shimon was absorbed into the tribe of Judah and became teachers, for this profession enabled them to do the learning they needed to do.

One more incident concerning the tribe of Shimon is recorded in the Torah (Num, 25:6-15) Zimri, an elder and a prince in the tribe of Shimon, fell in love with Cosbi, a princess in Miriam, a non-Jew. The Torah tell us that they were having sexual relations in front of Moses tent, as a challenge to the authority of Moses, and they were slain by Pinchas, known as a young zealot. Did Pinchas act correctly in killing the couple? Kabbalah deepens the question by telling us that Zimri and Cosby were soul mates and a reincarnation of Dinah and Shechem. They may have thought they acted with pure intentions to bring in a new order. The Jewish people were initially very upset by their deaths, but God approves of Pinchas's actions. Pinchas is rewarded the covenant of peace, which is God's way of saying however that he now needed to learn the ways of peace.

Shimon is the perfect representative of the energy of Av because he is the passionate zealot. We see that, throughout history, it was passionate zealotry that led to the divisiveness and destructiveness characteristic of this month. But in the time of the Messiah, the passionate energy of this month will be transformed.

Divine Name Permutation: HVYH

In examining the permutation for this month, we see a reversal of the letters, the hay (H) and vav (V) are usually in them order of Vav and Hay and they now are reversed and occupy first and second rather than the optimal third and fourth positions. This reversal indicates judgment and this judgment applies to the first two weeks of the month. The yud (Y) and the hay (H) are in the proper order and though they are now in the third and fourth positions it indicates a time of mercy and compassion that we find in the last two weeks of the month.

The permutation for this month is like the one for Tammuz except the last two letters are reversed. The yud is now in the world of Yetzerah and the hay is in the world of Assiyah. This month the emphasis is not in the heart but in the world of Assiyah, the physical world. The Godly Light enters into the world of Assiyah, our physical world, more easily and directly and we experience this during the last weeks of this month. The heart must be quieted, become small like the yud, so the Divine Light can flow into this world.

Torah Portions

With this month we enter into a new book of Torah, entitled *Devarim*, or Deuteronomy. Devarim literally means "words" and this book is the words of Moses as he recounts the high points of Israel's journey from Mount Sinai and tries to prepare the Jewish people for the challenges they will face in this next phase of their journey. It is distinguished from the earlier books in which Moses functions as a scribe for God's words; here, Moses talks to the people as a human being. He even shares his very human feelings, his deep grief and disappointment about not being able to go into the land of Israel with the rest of the Jewish people.

In addition to recounting events, this book includes basic teachings and spiritual practices of Judaism. The Shema, the basic declaration of faith used in the Jewish prayer book, is taken from this book, as is the practice of saying blessings after eating. The Ten Commandments are repeated, in the Torah portion of Va'eschanan, read on Shabbat Nachamu, the Sabbath of Consolation, the Sabbath after Tisha B'Av. The reading of the Ten Commandments is once again a sign of forgiveness. It hints at the forgiveness of Yom Kippur when Moses obtained forgiveness for the sin of the Golden Calf and returned with a second set of tablets.

But mostly this book is an instruction manual for the future. It even includes predictions of all the catastrophes that the Jewish people will experience in the years to come. And if we look at history, we see that these predictions were fulfilled. Moses tells the Jewish people that they will enter the land but not follow God's ways, so they will be scattered. He tells them they will yearn for God, however and eventually be brought back to the land. God will not abandon the Jewish people—an important message for this month of Av.

Moses speaks here in both theoretical and practical ways. He tells the people that God is not beyond them, but available to them. He reviews the laws of *kashrut*, tithing, the observance of the holidays and many other practices designed to preserve the holiness of the people.

In Deuteronomy, Moses prepares the people for the tests and challenges they will have to face in entering the land of Israel. Some of these teachings seem particularly relevant today. Several times he reminds the people that Israel is God's gift to them, not because they are better than other people but only because of God's compassion and covenant with them. It is in the land of Israel that the Jewish people will be better used by God to fulfill the Divine intention for creation.

Beginning on the Shabbat after Tisha B'Av, we read each week for seven weeks a Haftorah; that is, a special section from the prophets to offer consolation to the people. This represents the healing and compassion energy of the latter part of the month, which extends into the next month of Elul.

Holiday: Tisha B'av

HISTORY: Tisha B'Av, the Ninth of Av, has historically been a painful day for the Jewish people. Though it primarily commemorates the destruction of the First and Second Temples in Jerusalem, throughout history, many other terrible persecutions and destruction events are recorded to have occurred on Tisha B'Av.

The first recorded event was on Tisha B'Av itself when the Jewish people heard and believed the reports of the spies who scouted the land of Israel and advised them to not enter the land. The whole purpose of the departure out of Egypt was to enter the land God promised to the Jewish people. For this, the Jewish people were condemned to wander in the desert for forty years until the whole first generation of Jews who fled Egypt during the Exodus had died. Legend has it that the Jews did not die of natural causes during the time they were in the desert. What was said to happen was that a certain percentage of them, approximately fifteen thousand people, would die each Tisha B'Av. According to the legend, people would build graves for themselves. On Tisha B'Av they would lie in these graves, go to sleep and some would not awaken in the morning.

Throughout history, Jews endured discrimination and persecution in almost every country they resided, and Tisha B'Av was often the time when the worst incidents occurred. The Jews were expelled from England in 1290, from France in 1306, from Spain in 1492, all on Tisha B'Av. The Talmud was burned in Paris in 1244 on Tisha B'Av. The deportation from the Warsaw ghetto to Treblinka in 1942 began on Tisha B'Av. In modern times, the terrorist bombings from Gaza into the Land of Israel frequently began on Tisha B'Av. It sometimes feels like the enemies of the Jewish people know about our calendars and when we are most vulnerable to attacks.

Tisha B'Av is most known as the day commemorating the destruction of the First and Second Temples in Jerusalem. Although the First Temple remained standing for hundreds of years, prophets had predicted its downfall because of the widespread idolatry in the Temple itself and throughout the country. One of the prophets, Zechariah, was even beheaded by Jews who did not want to listen to his prophecies. With such internal divisiveness, the Jewish people were vulnerable. The Babylonians destroyed the First Temple on Tisha B'Av in 586 BCE.

When the Babylonians were conquered by the Persians, the Jewish people were allowed to return to Israel and rebuild the Temple. Soon Persia was conquered by Greece. Israel, under the domain of Greece, was greatly influenced by Hellenism, and that also threatened the purity of the Temple and Torah. After the Maccabees miraculously defeated the Syrian-Greek Empire, Israel was later conquered by Rome, the emerging dominant world power. The Jewish people were quick to form an alliance with Rome to protect Jerusalem and the Holy Temple.

With considerable juggling to appease the Roman Empire, Israel was relatively stable for a long time. Though the Second Temple was destroyed by Rome, the real problem cited by the rabbis for its destruction was the internal divisiveness within the Jewish people and not Rome.

The few stories in the Talmud used to explain the destruction of the Holy Temple point to the causeless hatred between the Jews. We do not know if the stories are actually true but their message is what is important and particularly relevant even today when there is frequently considerable Jewish divisiveness. It is the lack of Jewish unity then and today that makes Israel vulnerable to the aspirations of other nations who seek her harm and destruction.

> It is the lack of Jewish unity then and today that makes Israel vulnerable to the aspirations of other nations who seek her harm and destruction.

The most famous incident of senseless hatred given in the Talmud is between Bar Kamtza and Kamtza. Though no reason was given, they were enemies, but inadvertently, Bar Kamtza was invited to a party of Kamtza. When he arrived at the party, he was asked to leave by the host. Bar Kamtza wanted to stay and offered to compensate his host financially for what he would eat and drink during the party. His offer was refused. He even offered to pay for half and then for all the expenses of the party if he was allowed to stay. His offer was rejected, and he was physically ejected from the banquet in a most embarrassing and public way.

Bar Kamtza then said to himself, *Since the rabbis at the banquet did not rebuke the host for the way he treated me, it is evident that what he did was acceptable to them. I will go and spread slander against the rabbis in the royal palace.* And he did just that. He went to Caesar and told him, *The Jews have rebelled against you.*

To verify this claim, he suggested, *Send them an animal sacrifice and see whether they offer it in their Temple.* Caesar sent a fine calf with Bar Kamtza. On his return trip to Jerusalem, Bar Kamtza caused a blemish in the calf's upper lip that he knew would make the animal unacceptable for offering according to strict orthodox standards. The rabbis considered offering it anyway because they did not want to ruin their relations with Rome. But they were overruled by a group of zealots who did not want to compromise the standards regarding animal sacrifices and allow people to think they could offer blemished animals in the future. The rabbis even considered killing Bar Kamtza so he would not inform Caesar that his offering had been refused, but ultimately they did not do that either. So eventually this simple incident is used to explain that it was Jew against Jew that was the origin of the Roman war against the Jewish people.

Another painful incident occurs later on after the war had already started. There were those who wanted to negotiate with the Romans, knowing that any military effort would be devastating and unsuccessful, and those who wanted war, believing that God would make them victorious. The wealthy people of Jerusalem offered to sustain the Jewish people with food and wood that was estimated to last for twenty one years. The *baryoni,* the zealots who advocated the overthrow of Roman rule through war alone, burned the storehouses of wheat and barley and wood, so the Jewish people would have no option but to fight. Along with the Roman soldiers, they did not allow anyone to leave the besieged city.

The Second Temple was destroyed also on Tisha B'Av in 70 CE. Over one million Jews died fighting for independence. Many others died of starvation and by crucifixion. Many ancient Biblical curses predicting what would happen if the Jews did not fulfill Divine Will while living in the Land of Israel were fulfilled during this time period. In addition to the death and degrading behaviors of war, there was a religious crisis.

Could Judaism continue to exist if there were no Temple? Many people questioned whether Judaism could or should survive without the Holy Temple. Rabbi Yohanan Ben Zakkai escaped from Jerusalem and negotiated with the Roman authorities for the Jewish people to control the nearby city of Yavneh. There he rebuilt a Judaism that is most known today. In so doing, he made Judaism more accessible and democratic than it had been before. The rabbis, rather than the priests or prophets, became the principal keepers of the faith. By following rabbinic law, every Jew could be like the high priest, every home and synagogue could be like the Holy Temple.

Nevertheless, the rebuilding of the Holy Temple in the Land of Israel has never been forgotten and is still envisioned as an essential base of operation needed for the Jewish people to fulfill their spiritual mission of uplifting the world. Because the holiness and potency of this mission, the ownership of Israel has been brutally contested throughout history by those who seek to dominate the world for their own nefarious purposes. The enemies of the Jewish people are tremendously threatened by the possibility of the rebuilding of the Holy Temple.

From the beginning of the inception of the Jewish people, it was the Divine plan to settle them in the center of the world like Israel, rather in the Himalayas or in island in the Pacific Ocean where they would be separated from much of the world. It is in the Land of Israel, surrounded by enemies more numerous, that the Jewish people can be better used by God to uplift the world.

Twice the Jewish Holy Temple in Jerusalem was destroyed and the majority of Jews were murdered or expelled from the Land of Israel. To escape persecution and death, some of these Jews converted to Islam or Christianity depending on the dominant religion of the country that now hosted them. Now many of these converts are returning to Judaism and even immigrating to Israel.

The Land of Israel was largely uninhabited for two thousand years, ever since the Second Holy Temple was destroyed. God tells us in the Bible, *I will make your cities a waste. I will bring the Land into desolation. Then I will remember My servant Jacob and I will remember the Land.* Lev. 26:32. There was a drought in the Land of Israel for more than one thousand and eight hundred years. When the State of Israel was established, the rain miraculously resumed.

Then, many prophecies spoke of the rise and rebuilding of Israel, such as: *The cities in the Land of Israel will be inhabited, the ruins will be rebuilt. I will make it better than it ever was.* Ezek. 36:10-11. Israel is now a very vibrant country. We clearly see the fulfillment of these prophecies. Due to Divine blessings, the Jewish people have transformed the desert into gardens and farms. They have even exported their innovative agricultural techniques and so much more to help many other countries to thrive.

Though very small in size and in population, with few natural resources, tiny Israel appears to be a great threat to much larger nations with greater populations, and endowed with more natural resources. The world even seems to be obsessed with Israel and compromising its security. For example, most of the business of the United Nations is about condemning Israel for crimes Israel did not commit while ignoring censoring countries who commit heinous crimes against their own people and against Israel. This obsession with Israel and the jealousy of the nations of the world against Israel was highlighted long ago in Biblical prophecies.

Nations condemning Israel fail to see the gifts that Israel offers to the world. Rather, the rulers of these countries who hate Israel are most likely fearful that the goodness, freedom, and democracy that Israel embodies is a threat to the oppressive hold that these rulers have on their own people. Quite simply, many of these rulers fear that the existence of Israel jeopardizes their personal power, status, and wealth. Their jealousy reminds us of the need to fix our hearing this month. It is just a matter of time until the inhabitants of the world are willing to hear the truth about Israel and dismiss all the lies promulgated against her.

As an aside, at the time of the Second Temple, Christianity was one sect among many within Judaism. Christian Jews prayed in synagogues and kept all the Jewish holidays. After the destruction of the Temple, they eventually separated from Judaism. Though Jews following Christianity were initially persecuted by the Romans, they sought to differentiate themselves from the Jews and appease the Romans. Once Rome accepted Christianity and established the Church to promulgate a new form of Christianity to attract membership beyond that of Jews, this new form was different than what the early Jews practicing Christianity followed. In recent times, interestingly enough, more Christians are seeking to accept more Jewish practices as a way to connect with Jesus. Christian organizations such as Christians United for Israel (CUFI) have been Israel's best friends. Christians from many countries throughout the world travel to Israel in great numbers.

OBSERVANCE: Tisha B'Av is a day of abstinence. Next to Yom Kippur, it is the most widely observed fast day. The fast begins on sundown and ends on sundown of the next day. During this time, no food or drink is taken and sexual relations are also prohibited. The synagogues are dimly lit just with candles and in many places people sit on the floor or on low benches as they would if they were morning the loss of a loved one. People wear sneakers rather than leather shoes. There is little social greeting or socializing. The smiles, warm greetings and embraces so prevalent during other holidays are absent now. If you knew nothing about the holiday beforehand, you might think that people were either unfriendly or depressed. The atmosphere is very subdued and everyone is encouraged to be inwardly focused and self-reflective.

In my orthodox synagogue, that of Reb Shlomo Carlebach, the *mechitza*, the divider separating the men and women during prayer services, is removed and women participate in the service along with the men. This dramatizes the important message that we are all together in loss and grief. The book of Lamentations, known as *Eicha*, written by the prophet Jeremiah, is chanted.

On Tisha B'Av morning, the traditional *tallis*, the prayer shawl, and *tefillin*, the phylacteries, are not worn. There is none of the usual singing during prayer services. The Torah reading from Deuteronomy is read when Moses forecasts the exile and destruction of the Jewish people for not keeping Divine Will so as to encourage them to return to God when this occurs.

The *Book of Kinot* is also chanted. The *kinot* are the assembled poems recounting terrible occurrences of destruction and pain experienced by the Jewish people throughout history. In New York and many other places there are movies, often about the Holocaust as well as lectures about suffering of the Jewish people throughout time.

Every year, I find it awesome to witness the solemn observance of Tisha B'Av. Reflecting that this practice has continued for thousands of years is quite humbling. Grieving for the loss of the Holy Temple for so long on the holiday of Tisha B'Av is a powerful testimony for the claim of the Jewish people to Jerusalem and to the Temple Mount.

When Napoleon witnessed Jewish people fasting and weeping on Tisha B'Av, he inquired as to the reason. Amazed to learn that they were weeping over an event that happened thousands of years before, Napoleon remarked that this people would be victorious in the end. In 1967, the Jewish people captured all of Jerusalem and even the Temple Mount. At the time, the Israeli government was not willing to stand up the pressure exerted by the United States, Europe, and Arab nations, and relinquished control of the Temple Mount to Jordan though Israel remains still involved in its security.

In recent years, there has been increased desire in many sections within the Jewish people to enter into this most holy space to the Jewish people known as the Temple Mount. More Jews entered the Temple Mount in 2023 alone than ever since 1967. However, there are still strict regulations, such as not allowing Jews to pray, taking any holy books there, and visiting only within restricted parameters. My girlfriend was actually arrested many years ago because she simply closed her eyes and meditated to soak up the holy vibrations of being there. I went twice to the Temple Mount. My very first time, I went with Rabbi Yehudah Glick, a Temple Mount activist, and a few other people, We were escorted by both Arab and Israeli military with big guns to make sure we would not pray when we were there. Another time, I took a non-Jewish friend with me to visit the Temple Mount. They welcomed her warmly. I was greeted coldly. They searched my pocketbook extensively, not hers, to make sure I did not have any Jewish literature there, and they gave me a stern warning to not pray while visiting the Temple Mount. They seem to be very afraid of the power of prayer of any Jew.

Rebuilding the Holy Temple continues to be a passionate desire among many Jews. Many people may not be aware that since the destruction of the Holy Temple in Jerusalem, hundreds of thousands of Jews from all over the world have prayed three times a day for thousands of years to return to Jerusalem, their ancestral homeland, and rebuild the Holy Temple to be a source of light and blessing for the entire world. Many may also not be aware that hundreds and thousands of Jews will not even eat a piece of bread without uttering such prayers. At every Jewish wedding for two thousand years, a glass is broken to remind us that our joy as Jews is diminished because we have not yet built the Holy Temple on the Temple Mount.

There are even holy Jews who awaken each night and literally cry about the destruction of the Holy Temple thousands of years ago. I have actually witnessed this intense sobbing on a few occasions when I was unable to sleep at night when living in the Old City in Jerusalem and went to the Kotel for inspiration and comfort in the middle of the night. These tears were not just for the physical embodiment of the Holy Temple, but Jews also yearn and weep for the realization of the promise that the Third Holy Temple be established as a place for all people, a platform to bring peace and love into the world for all people. I have seen and met such holy Jewish people living in Israel even today. These people are not famous nor widely known. If only the world would realize this holy mission of the Jewish people, they would support them in claiming and rebuilding of the Temple Mount so the nations could all be so blessed.

Holiday: Tu B' Av

HISTORY: Tu B'Av is the fifteenth day of Av. The moon is full and shining as bright as it will at the time in this month. On the sixteenth day of the month, the moon already begins to diminish. The days begin to get shorter on Tu B'Av. The weather begins to shift, and the scent of fall is now in the air, even though there may be many more hot days ahead.

The Oral Tradition records this day as the day when the death of the Jewish people in the desert stopped. As mentioned previously, a certain percentage of the Jewish people died every Tisha B'Av in the years prior to entering the Land of Israel. It was told that Jews would enter their graves as in past years and but on Tu B'Av were surprised to find that no one died. They thought they had possibly miscalculated the day, but when the full moon appeared they knew that the curse was lifted and they would live to enter the holy land. So Tu B'Av was regarded as a sign that the sin of the spies was forgiven. It was established as a day of general forgiveness and purification.

Tu B'Av is regarded as the most joyous day in the Jewish calendar. On this day, at the time when the Holy Temple was standing, young maidens would all dress in white dresses and dance before the men. This was most unusual, for generally men and women were separated in public gatherings. On Tu B' Av, the women would flirt, and with their eyes, say. *Look at me.* And in one look, marriages were made. It was on this day that the people from various tribes would meet for the purpose of marriage. Every marriage brought joy not just to the couple, but also to the tribal community and to God. Because the women danced before the men, Tu B'Av was considered a day celebrating the rise and revelation of the Divine Feminine. Tu B'Av remains a day for increased love and joy.

The full moon in each month is often revered as a high point of the energy for that month. The major holidays such as Sukkot and Passover occur at the time of the full moon. The fifteenth of Av is even a more special full moon because it immediately follows the introspective periods of time known as The Three Weeks, The Nine Days, and Tisha B'Av. Because the spiritual descent into darkest and saddest time is greatest during the Nine Days and Tisha B'Av, the ascent into the light and healing is also the greatest at the time of the full moon this month. The full moon is a powerful testimony that light will emerge from the darkest of times.

The Jewish calendar turns on an axis of Tu'B Shevat and Tu B'Av. Tu B'Shevat is at the time of the full moon in the month of Shevat and signals the flow of blessing from above, a time of expansiveness and Divine blessings as evidenced in the holidays of Passover and Shavuot.

Tu B'Av signals a time for the awakening of blessing from below, a time of the Feminine, a time of turning inward as demonstrated with holidays like Rosh Hashanah, Yom Kippur, and Sukkot. Tu B'Av is forty days before the twenty-fifth of Elul, which marks the beginning of creation. Forty days is a mystical number in Judaism. Human beings were created on the first day of Tishrei, six days later.

OBSERVANCE: This Jewish Sadie Hawkins day known as Tu B'Av has been resurrected in several communities, but not quite as it was in ancient times. On Tu B'Av today, at least in Manhattan when I lived there, there were numerous singles events. Often times, at these events, the women would also dress in white and even dance in front of the men in the hope that sparks will be ignited that could possibly lead to marriages. Through my own organization at the time, we did special and unique kind of meditative single events every Tu B'Av in Manhattan.

For married couples, Tu B'Av is a time to rekindle their love. Gazing at the beloved and receiving the gaze of the beloved is always a wonderful spiritual practice, but particularly on Tu B'Av. This gazing is best done outside at the time of the full moon.

Meditation

Many people have experienced trauma in life and are often afraid to feel painful feelings. Sometimes people are overwhelmed by these feelings so they shut down and numb themselves. Sometimes they engage addictive behaviors like drugs, food, or watching television so as to not feel their feelings. This is so unfortunate because these behaviors block their heart and limit their capacity to receive the goodness of life's blessings.

There is no reason to avoid or be afraid to feel one's painful feelings. These feelings do not define who we really are. Meditation may help us to release deep wounded feelings because we learn to not identify with them as the essence of who we really are. We may experience them but they do not limit or define who we are.

> Take deep breaths to center yourself. Take note of the physical body and any sensations, tensions, or any particular awareness in any part of the body. Use the breath to further relax the body. Take time to extend awareness and breath around the entire body to continue to relax the body as best as you can.
>
> When the physical body is relaxed, become aware of the emotional

> body without judgment. Where in your body do you hold certain feelings? Some people hold feelings in their shoulders, or in their stomach, in their chest, or in their face. Where do you hold your feelings?
>
> Allow yourself to be with any feelings that may arise within you. Experience your feelings without judgment, no need to understand, explain, or rationalize these feelings. Just be with your feelings. It is beautiful to be vulnerable and feel one's feelings. As you open to your feelings, you may hear that voice inside you that says, This is too painful, too overwhelming. Simply, take a few deep breaths to relax. Feelings are just feelings that are rooted in past experiences. Allow yourself to open, be compassionate and gentle with yourself as you feel the feelings you have resisted or avoided previously.
>
> If you are in touch with a loss during this time of meditation, give yourself time to feel your loss. If this loss involves another, you may want to visualize the person and talk to him or her about this loss. You may note other feelings present for you such as guilt, betrayal, hurt, and anger mixed in the sadness. Give yourself permission to feel those feelings without judgment. For example, you may notice first the feeling of anger. Be with that as fully as possible. We can be angry at a person who is no longer in our lives. Then as we go deeper inside, we may find under the anger there is a feeling of sadness or hurt. After being with those feelings, one may find the desire of love, the longing to be loved. And as we stay with this feeling, we may experience the great love inside of ourselves. At a certain point there will be silence and a deep peace. When we have fully released the feelings that are connected to our ego identity, we access the feelings of our own soul. When we experience peace and joy, we know that we have touched our very soul.

As I write this now, I am reminded of the experience of the most unusual funeral of my most beloved teacher, Rabbi Yitzchak Kirzner, that may illustrate these teachings. The rabbis who spoke at the funeral went from publicly expressing anger towards him for dying—*How could you leave us?*—First in anger, even yelling, and then openly crying without restraint. Rabbis then shared how they had prayed for him and even tried to bribe God for his life. Finally they concluded with sharing how inspired and empowered they were for having known him. As the rabbis cried, so did most people at the funeral. This was a very unique experience. There were several thousand people at his funeral. Most everyone was crying. So many tears were shed that day. I never knew until then how tremendously loved Rabbi Kirzner was by the Torah community in Boro Park New York.

I came home from this funeral and went to bed exhausted, never having been at a funeral so real and profound. Rabbi Kirzner was always the most real and authentic teacher. All the time he was teaching, he knew he was dying, so he only wanted to be honest. He did not hide behind any platitudes or typical things Jewish teachers often say. For Rabbi Kirzner, there was simply no time for any pretense of any kind.

His funeral was his last and most awesome teaching for me about the importance of being real and authentic. These holy rabbis, some of them well known and highly respected in their communities, were not ashamed to cry openly in public. I never had witnessed such a display of raw emotion by so many people before. I saw firsthand how such tears were holy. These tears did not display weakness but rather the courage to cry and share the depth of one's heart to God before other people. I also came to understand that when I weep deeply, like I did for my teacher that day, and as I would on the future occasions when I wept over personal losses, that my tears were also holy. I came to also see that my tears were not even personal. My tears were and are always for the Shechinah who also weeps within me.

Practical Recommendations

1. DELAY INTERACTIONS THAT MAY BE DIFFICULT.

As we have learned earlier in this chapter, tempers can be easily ignited during The Nine Days. I mentioned this to a few friends who said that they wished they had known this earlier and had delayed challenging interactions until after the Nine Days. Unfortunately, they had unnecessary skirmishes with people that were quite stressful in the beginning of the month.

Be extra sensitive and empathic this month. If we take time before we react to a negative situation, we will most likely respond in a way that is much calmer and constructive than if we reacted immediately.

2. REVIEW RELATIONSHIPS WITH PEOPLE YOU DO NOT LIKE.

Many of us have people in our lives we may not like. We avoid them and try to have as little to do with them as possible. These people may be people who are close to us, either members of our family, or people at work, or in synagogue so we can't totally ignore them. Most likely they have hurt us numerous times. We have not yet forgiven them and we continue to carry resentment and anger towards them. We expect them to be different than they are. During this month, simply make a list of people and consider working on letting go of your anger, so you can move on.

3. DO NOT SPEAK NOR LISTEN TO *LOSHON HARA*.

Loshon hara means evil speech—malicious gossip, saying bad things about other people, even if they are true, putting people down, etc. Since the area of healing this month is hearing, pay careful attention to both what you speak and what you hear. The Jewish laws regarding speech are very detailed and profound. Set barriers around what you will allow yourself to hear. For example, according to Jewish law, it is only permissible to hear derogatory words about another if you are planning to do business or marry this person.

For example, if you knew two people who are planning to enter a business together or a marriage, it would be permissible for you to warn one about the other if you knew that one of them would not be an honorable or responsible partner. Otherwise, it is not necessary to talk badly about other people. It only weakens the flow of blessing in your life. Take note how you feel when you curtail speaking and listening to *loshon hara*.

4. GIVE TO PEOPLE YOU KNOW AND DO NOT KNOW.

Because historically this was a time shaped by petty conflict between people, this time requires proactive steps to heal conflict. Stretch yourself with giving of your time, attention, love, and resources to heal conflict. Be careful to not give to the point that you begin to feel resentful, but give only out of a generous and loving spirit within you. Paradoxically, the greatest benefits from giving are to the giver. It is quite liberating to give without thinking of your personal gain. If you are feeling sad or broken-hearted this month, make an effort to give to someone or some worthy cause or organization. Giving brings joy to the giver.

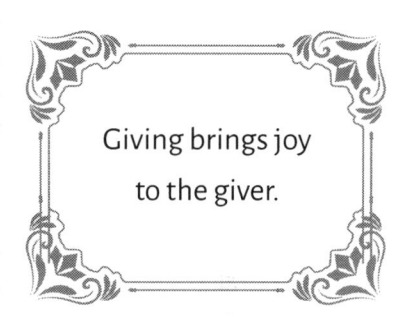

> Giving brings joy to the giver.

A Tale to Live By

The following is a story of the Jewish people's expulsion out of their Land and returning to rebuild the Land. It may also be a parable for the story of the human being finding blessing and peace within oneself.

There was once a beautiful garden situated around a magnificent castle where the most benevolent wise king resided. In this garden grew the most beautiful flowers in the whole world, unlike any other ever known to man. The people of the kingdom worked hard clearing and fertilizing the Garden of Life because they loved life and the king who was so good to them.

Over time, the people began to take credit for the beauty of the gardens and started to forget that the beauty of the garden was only due to the love of the Good King and not because of their personal efforts. Once they started to take credit for the beautiful gardens, they also stopped appreciating the other blessings the Good King had given to them. They began to think that some people deserved more than others as some people seemed to be closer to the king than others. They forgot that it was their devotion to the king that made them united and successful. They no longer saw the Good King in their midst and saw each other as separate from each other.

Simultaneously, around the same time, people from all over the world began to visit this magnificent garden and view the beautiful flowers. They returned to their own land and reported to their own kings what they witnessed. Their kings were not as loving to their subjects as the Good King was. They even abused and exploited their subjects for their own benefit. They surely did not inspire their people to clear, fertilize, and irrigate their king's land like the Good King had done. Consequently, the weeds in their gardens grew and choked the flowers so everything perished in these kingdoms. Their kingdoms resembled the Gardens of Death where no life flourished.

The nations of the world became jealous and wanted to destroy the beauty of the garden of the Good King. They sent hordes of people to invade and destroy the Garden of Life, banishing and murdering the children of this land. They built palaces on top of the ruins of the previous beautiful gardens of life. Soon the land they occupied was desolate just like the lands they had came from. The beautiful lakes, streams, and rivers that once provided water to the beautiful Garden of Life became swamps. There was no rain because these people did not love the Good King who was the source of water for the land.

The exiled people of the Garden of Life never forgot their land, and they prayed and dreamed of returning to their former homeland. They suffered greatly at the hand of other nations. They repented for their arrogance and pledged to be humble before the Good King if only they could return to the land of the Garden of Life. However, the kings of the world would not allow them to return because they did not want to see the restoration of the beautiful Garden of Life.

After many more years of strife and tumult between the various worldly kings, the people of the Garden of Life were able to return on the condition that they share the land with the people of the Garden of Death who also occupied their homeland. Once there, the people of the Garden of Life dedicated their lives to rebuilding their ancient beautiful gardens to the Good King. Though the people of the Garden of Death kept trying to undermine the people of the Garden of Life, the Good King promised them in the end of times that they would never be exiled again. They believed the Good King and took comfort in the prophets who offered visions to inspire them. In time, they prayed that everyone would wake up to know what a blessing the Garden of Life is to the world. And they continue to pray that to this very day.

Prophecies from Amos and others prophets provide hope that in the right time the Jewish people would return to Land of Israel and never to be exiled again. *Behold, the days are coming says the Almighty ... I will bring back the captives of My people Israel. They will rebuild desolate cities and settle them. They will plant vineyards and drink their wine, they will cultivate gardens and eat their fruits. I will plant them on the Land and they will never be uprooted from their Land that I have given them.* Amos 9:14-15.

We have seen the fulfillment of these prophecies for the establishment of the State of Israel in our time. Even though the nations of the world still seek to undermine the Jewish people living in the land of Israel, so many Biblical prophecies assure us that they will not be successful. The Torah reminds us that: *Those who bless you (Israel and the Jewish people) will be blessed. Those who curse you will be cursed.* Gen. 27-29. For their own sake, the nations of the world must wake up and support Israel rather than pay a terrible price for undermining Israel's claim to the Land given to them by the Creator.

*inspired by a parable by Asher Najer.

12

Elul

AUGUST – SEPTEMBER

ENERGY
Forgiving and Returning to Inner Stillness

AREA OF HEALING
Action

ASTROLOGICAL SIGN
Virgo

HEBREW LETTER
Yud י

HEBREW TRIBE
Gad

DIVINE PERMUTATION
HHVY

HOLIDAY
Selichot

A Personal Story

During this month of Elul, as the last month of the Jewish calendar, we naturally reflect on the ways we may have done things during this past year or in our lives as a whole, things that we regret. Sometimes even with the passing of time we are unable to release the guilt and shame we still may feel about some of these actions. During this month, we also become aware of many good actions we could have taken but did not. It is during this month of Elul, we begin to make amends for both of these errors as well as make a commitment to turn our lives in a more positive direction. Here is one example of my seeking forgiveness and turning in a new direction.

After college, I attended my first yoga class. I loved it, and continued to go to yoga classes a few times a week. The hypocrisy of smoking after engaging in consciously breathing as guided in the yoga classes I attended soon became unbearable to me. I finally had to acknowledge that I was addicted to smoking. I had given away my free will and belief in the power of God to a simple cigarette. I tried many times to quit smoking but I was unsuccessful in overcoming my addiction to smoking on my own. It eventually occurred to me to create a ritual that would support me to quit smoking. And that actually worked.

In my prayers, I mentally offered my addiction to cigarettes along with actual cigarettes on a makeshift altar for some of the previous actions that I continued to feel guilty about and felt there was nothing I could do in the present time to amend, repair, or reverse what I had done previously. I cried to God, I asked God for forgiveness for what I had done, and I prayed to God to support me to live a better more Divinely connected life.

Interestingly enough at the time, I did not throw away all my cigarettes. That act was initially too frightening for me due to my limited faith in

God's power. I still carried a pack of cigarettes with me everywhere, just in case I really needed to have a cigarette. To take a cigarette would however have to be a conscious choice on my part. Though I gave myself the safety net of choosing a cigarette in a dire situation, I never took another cigarette again. One day, about a month later, as I was riding on a bus, a poor person directly begged me for a few cigarettes. How did he know that I was carrying a pack of cigarettes? With a little initial hesitation on my part, I ultimately had the courage and strength to let go of a pack of cigarettes, the very pack of cigarettes I carried at all times, just in case I needed one. This request was actually a gift to me because it helped me to realize that I could let go of my need for smoking.

Stopping smoking was very hard for me but with Divine help through this ritual, I was successful. Because it was not easy for me, some of the guilt I had carried inside myself was mitigated. It was a sacrifice of some sort for me. Eventually, I came to understand that I had to forgive myself, let go and dedicate my life in a new and more positive direction. There was no point continuing to feel guilty for something I did and could not repair. I did not realize it at the time, but I was following many of the steps in popular Twelve Step programs that ask people to turn their addiction, whatever it is, over to God and open to receive Divine support. I had never heard of the Twelve Step programs at that time in my life.

I was recently comforted by reading the following sentences in this life changing awesome book for me I bought and studied in my mid twenties, *Duties of the Heart*, by Ibn Paquda. In this book, the author reminds the reader that, *the sacrifices to God are a broken spirit, a broken and contrite heart, O God, Thou will not despise.* Psalms 51:19. *When a person has a broken heart, he attains a kind of humility that is the road to nearness to God. The worthiness to stand before God is then not far off.* Ibn Paquda goes on to tell us that this person will be accepted by God and be pleasing to God no matter what he or she has done. The gates of repentance are fortunately and always open to us but particularly during this month. When we sincerely engage in repentance, we often experience an immediate reward of greater inner peace and self love. I hope this teaching is meaningful to a few people who are reading this personal account.

Energy: Returning to the Inner Stillness within Change

Elul is known in Judaism as the headquarters for *Teshuvah*, which literally means *to return*. Teshuvah has many facets to it. In its most common usage, it often connotes a return to or an acceptance of a greater level of Jewish observance. It also refers to the acknowledgment of an error, the resultant feeling of regret, and the commitment to correct a situation and behave differently in the future. On the deepest and most mystical level, Teshuvah is the return to inner wholeness, beauty, and potential, a return to the soul and its innate connection with the Divine. Teshuvah is the healing and letting go of what we believe keeps us separate from others and God, and from being who we really are. Teshuvah asks us to take real steps to strengthen our connection with God.

Rav Kook summed it up in the following way: *When one forgets the essence of one's own soul, when one distracts their mind from attending to the substantive content of their own inner life, everything becomes confused and uncertain. The primary role of Teshuvah … is for the person to return to their true selves, to the root of their soul.* Orot HaTshuva 15:10.

The month of Elul begins somewhere toward the middle to end of August and continues to the middle or end of September. Even though the heat may still be strong in Elul, there is a subtle change in the quality of light upon the arrival of Elul. We begin to sense that fall will soon be upon us. In many places in the world, the days will become shorter, the air begins to cool, and the leaves will once again turn into beautiful colors before they fall to the ground. We will see before our very eyes the cyclical dance of nature. Some of us will greet these changes with joy and some with regret. Nevertheless, the natural changes will occur. Nature will turn inward once again, and so will we.

As we both witness and experience the inevitable cycles of life, we are drawn inward to the consciousness within us that does not change.

Through the spiritual grace of this month, it is easy to get in touch with what is pure and constant within us. It is interesting to note that the astrological sign for this month is Virgo, which is symbolized by a virgin. This is the only astrological sign that is feminine.

According to Kabbalistic teachings, the feminine refers to our capacity to receive. Kabbalah tells us that this is hinted to in Proverbs 18:22: *Who finds a (virgin) wife finds great good.* Elul sweetens the judgment energy of the two previous months, Tammuz and Av, and brings a hidden goodness. As our consciousness turns inward this month, we access a certain detachment enabling us to become more aware of the ways we have strayed from embodying our highest potential during this past year. We can more objectively see the good and the not-so-good within us.

As the last month in the Jewish calendar, we naturally find ourselves reviewing, assessing, and evaluating our accomplishments, challenges, and shortcomings of the entire year. What soul qualities were we encouraged to develop and express during the year? What lessons did we need to learn? What were the dominant themes of this past year? It may be meaningful for you to take time to write responses to these questions.

When we have undergone challenging experiences during this last year or in our lifetime, we must not think of ourselves as victims, but rather appreciate that all our experiences actually offered us opportunities to grow and to also be of greater service in the world. Who is to know if that is why God chose for us these challenging experiences?

For example, some of us may have experienced a challenging experience like a rape or a scary health diagnosis and have learned something about how to deepen our connection to God as a result of these experiences. This spiritual growth allows us to be of greater service to others. Not only is it more likely that we will have more compassion to people who have had similar experiences, we know how to be with them in their places of pain. We understand in a way that others who have not had the experience do. We often have something meaningful to share with others who are going through the experiences similar to what we have gone through. They are usually more open to listen to what we have to share with them because we have been there ourselves.

As we review the past year, many of us will be brought to new levels of appreciation for the personal relationships that have nourished us in this last year. Others of us will be more aware of unfinished business and the work needed to heal relationships so we can truly open to newness in the coming year. During the month of Elul, we get in touch with what the essence of what is important in life.

The entire month of Elul is a time for spiritual accounting. For those who've had a relatively easy year, it may be easier to come to terms with the year. Those who have had a difficult year may become discouraged, feel burdened by sins or mistakes made, and question one's capacity for real change. Know that despair is natural at this time and temporary but it can be a powerful launching pad for the teshuvah experience. We are not really stuck even though we may tell ourselves that we are.

When we call out to God from this place of humility, we will find that there is a unique heavenly grace that we can draw upon during this month. It becomes clear to us that we really want something pure and deep and we cannot do this on our own. The gates of heaven are open during this month.

This is the month to open our channels to receive the blessings we want in our lives and in the world. During this month, it is natural to allow ourselves to be vulnerable, to be humble, as we deepen our acceptance that there is a God who created the world and everything.

> During this month, it is natural to allow ourselves to be vulnerable, to be humble, as we deepen our acceptance that there is a God who created the world and everything.

The first letters of the Hebrew verse, *Ani Ledodi vidodi li*—I AM MY BELOVED'S AND MY BELOVED IS MINE in Song of Songs 6:3, spell out Elul. There is a unique, intimate, and loving closeness between God and people during this last month of the Jewish calendar. It is said that in Elul God wanders in the fields close to people, while on Rosh Hashanah God sits on His throne like a King. The metaphor of God sitting on His throne as King expresses the awe inspired by our awareness of God as the Creator and ruler of everything.

The perceived distance between us and God is reduced in Elul. God is very close to us this month, and the experience of God's unconditional love is very accessible now. Nevertheless, we must want it, and we must work for it.

Kabbalah talks about two kinds of awakenings: from above to below, and from below to above. In Nissan, which hosts Passover, there is an awakening from above, a flow of heavenly grace from the spiritual world to this physical world. In Elul, there is also a flow from above but we have to initiate it with our actions and spiritual yearning. The inner work we do and our yearning enables us to receive and integrate grace and blessings into our lives in a way we would not do if they were just given to us.

The month of Elul is the month of spiritual preparation for the High Holidays. The inner work of spiritual accountability and returning to one's true essence done during this month of Elul affects our capacity to stand before God and draw down blessings for the coming year.

Historically, Elul is the time period during which Moses returned to Mount Sinai to plead for forgiveness for the sin of the Golden Calf. As we forgive ourselves and others, we open to a greater Divine Revelation. Much has been written about the benefits and importance of forgiveness. As difficult as it might be, forgiveness is often the best thing that we can do for ourselves. When we forgive, we let go of limiting thoughts and behaviors, we accept what has happened in our lives, and we are more open for Divine blessing in our lives. Though forgiveness is a spiritual practice for the entire year, it is a major theme for this month of Elul.

The quality of teshuvah is in the air, whether people are consciously undertaking the process of repentance and self evaluation or not. During this month, you may find that you are brought into contact with people you have not seen for a while and are now given an opportunity to heal the relationship in a way that was not possible before. You may have unexpected telephone calls *out of the blue* as well. You may even find that you are revisiting places and situations that on a conscious level you would not have chosen to do: nevertheless, these offer you opportunities to release residual negativity so you can truly go forward in your lives.

On the other hand, if you feel a desire to connect with someone you haven't had contact with for a while, listen to your inner voice and follow your heart. It is generally a good time to reach out to people you want to be close to and wish them a happy and healthy new year. Many of us will be brought to new levels of appreciation for the personal relationships that have nourished us in this last year as well as the accomplishments we were able to achieve. Others of us will be more aware of our unfinished business needed to heal relationships. This is all good.

The shofar is traditionally blown every day in Elul, except Shabbat, in synagogues to wake us up and highlight the inner turning of this month and the powerful awakening possible to our own soul. The shofar reminds us that our lives can become deeper and more expressive of our soul purpose. During the moments of shofar blowing, it is easy to let go of resentments and judgments that have previously limited us. This upcoming year can be a truly new and amazing year for us, even if the external circumstances surrounding our lives remain the same.

General Guidelines and Goals

These guidelines and goals enable us to direct our energies in the ways that are optimal for our growth and transformation in accordance with the energy of this month. It is recommended that you read and meditate upon them often in the course of the month. Reflect on their applicability to you and allow them to direct and inspire you often this month.

1. COMPLETE UNFINISHED BUSINESS AND MAKE PLANS.

Personal transformation and growth can begin only from where we are. Take time to review where you are now. Be as honest and objective as you can be in the following reflections. Write a brief description and evaluation of your correct status for each one in this book or in your journal.

Reflect on your physical well-being, your health, diet, and living situation. Are you satisfied or would you prefer some improvement?

Reflect on your emotional well being, your relationships with family, friends, colleague, and community. Are you satisfied or are you open to expansion? How would you define your general disposition?

Reflect on your spiritual well being: your inner prayer life, your connection to God and to Judaism or the religious path you follow. When you pray or meditate, is your heart into it? When you learn Torah are you excited? How much time do you actually devote to your spiritual growth? Are you satisfied or open to enhancement?

Accepting ourselves and acknowledging the areas in our lives that need rectification, improvement, and expansion is the foundation for growth. In preparing for the new year, reflect on what you would like to let go of, what you would like to maintain, and what you want to bring more fully into the upcoming new year. If you find yourself in painful abusive situations at home or in the work place, ask yourself if you want or need to continue this in the next year.

Remember, if nothing changes, nothing changes. If we do what we have done in the past, most likely we will get what we always got. Most of us want more than what we have, yet do not know how to really change. Begin to formulate a plan to rectify the areas in your life that are not in accordance with what you really want.

2. DO THE WORK OF TESHUVAH.

When we do teshuvah, we acknowledge the mistakes we have made and the actions we have taken that are not in accordance with how we really want to live in the world. This is not an easy process but it is necessary if we are to grow and become the people we truly want to be. The teshuvah process asks us to assume responsibility for our actions, to feel regret for the mistakes we have made, and to commit to do differently in the future. Finally, we make penance for any suffering we have caused. Here are some guidelines to assist you in this reevaluation process.

Identify particular actions, behavior patterns, and personality tendencies that you would like to change. Without making a vow, because Jews do not generally make vows, state how you plan to change your behavior in one or two ways. What compensation are you willing to offer for the pain and suffering you caused yourself, others, and God?

3. FORGIVE GOD, YOURSELF, AND EVERYONE.

Forgiveness may be an ongoing process. It is not always easy because the ego likes to be right, in control, especially when we feel we have been wronged. Though forgiveness is a great gift we can give to another, it is primarily an act of compassion towards ourselves. Anger and resentment keep us bound to limiting ideas of who we are, that we feel like victims, that we are emotionally stuck, and so on. Forgiveness and compassion purify, heal and liberate us so we can feel free to grow.

Forgiveness does not mean we condone negative behavior, nor do we deny our angry or hurt feelings. However, forgiveness asks us to see beyond the limits of our personality or that of the person who hurt us and open our heart to love. Though forgiveness may be experienced as an act of grace, forgiveness is often a process and may take some time. It is easier to forgive others and even ourselves when we are willing to take responsibility for the negativity we have experienced. In most cases, we may simply have allowed ourselves to enter into or remain in situations that were hurtful to us.

In the act of forgiveness we substitute compassion for blame, and we trust ourselves and God that we have grown and will continue to grow from the pain and challenge we have experienced. Forgiveness is complete when we gain insight into how the challenges and difficulties we have faced in this last year support our growth.

During the month, reflect on relationships in which you may still harbor resentment or anger. Reflect on relationships with people whom you may have hurt and who may harbor anger towards you. Reflect on the ways you have been judgmental or unforgiving with yourself. Work on forgiveness this month, so you will be open to new blessings in the coming year.

It may be important to tell the person who has hurt you and who you continue to have anger or resentment towards about what they have done to you. This gives them an opportunity to apologize and make amends. It is much easier to let go of your anger and resentment and forgive someone who wants to be forgiven. And similarly, if you have possibly hurt someone it is important for you to ask for forgiveness from anyone you knowingly hurt or might have been hurt by you. Because we may have hurt someone unknowingly, ask people whether you have hurt them, so you can ask them for forgiveness. I have heard stories of people whose lives suffered because they did not receive forgiveness for pain they caused others. Once forgiven, life blessings opened up for them. If forgiveness has not occurred, take time to do this special meditation about forgiveness.

> **MEDITATION FOR FORGIVENESS**
>
> Call to mind a person or people who hurt you, and to whom you continue to hold feelings of anger and resentment. Silently say in your heart. **I forgive you, I forgive you for whatever pain you have caused me intentionally and unintentionally.** Speak to the person about how they have hurt you and how you want to forgive them, and how and also what you may not want and want to continue in a relationship that feels abusive or hurtful to you.
>
> Ask God to help you have love and compassion for this person and also for yourself. Reflect on the pain this person must have felt inside to mistreat you. Realize that the abuse and disrespect you experienced was ultimately not about you, but usually people who are abusive are often projecting. Make a decision to not personalize any abuse.
>
> By affirming yourself, you can forgive this person and you can forgive yourself for staying in abusive relationships for as long as you have. Embrace and love yourself and be willing to leave abusive and disrespectful relationships.

4. REPLACE THE INNER CRITIC WITH THE INNER CARETAKER.

Many people may have received messages about themselves as children, messages that have become a part of how they experience themselves as adults. Though people know intellectually these ideas have no basis in truth, they do not know it emotionally. As a result, they continue to feel deep inside that they are not good enough, not smart enough, not entitled to have the feelings that they do—all the things they were told as children—even though they may be externally very successful in their lives as adults. They continue to judge themselves harshly as adults and feel shame about things that have happened in their lives.

Take note of the inner critic, that negative voice within you that judges and criticizes you and others. Do not get into an extended battle with that part of yourself. Simply make an effort to substitute a loving, caring, nurturing voice in its place. Tell yourself how beautiful, wonderful and lovable you really are. Accentuate the loving voice within you until it becomes integrated and prominent. Look to see the light rather than the darkness. Remember that the glass is half full rather than half empty.

5. MEDITATE AND IDENTIFY WITH YOUR INNER WITNESS.

Completing one year and preparing for the next year is a time of major transformation. In times of change, it is helpful to anchor our awareness to the part of us that is constant and does not change. As we meditate, we access the witness part of ourselves. This witness consciousness is greater than our minds and bodies. From this place of awareness within us, we have objectivity and detachment. Identify with this listening awareness rather than the content of your life experiences. Experience yourself as more than your body, emotions, and thoughts. Our true identity is the pure Divine soul that is a part of God.

All meditation techniques help us access this listening awareness of ourselves that does not change and is always present. Meditation can be brief, even five to fifteen minutes is enough. If you prefer, it can be longer. However long the practice is, a daily meditative or prayer practice will deepen your experience and its impact on your life.

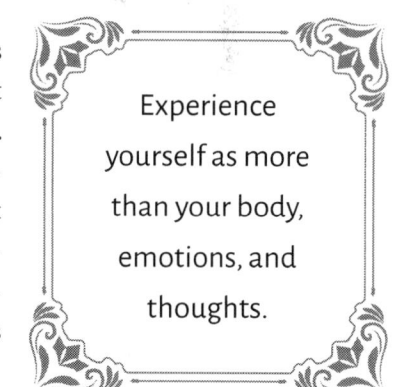

> Experience yourself as more than your body, emotions, and thoughts.

6. DEEPEN YOUR RELATIONSHIP WITH GOD.

Elul is the optimal time to develop intimacy with the Divine. In addition to formalized prayer and meditation, this is the month to take time to talk directly to God in your own words. Share your hopes, dreams, fears, challenges, and pain. Ask for God's help, strength, and guidance to help you to change in the ways you want.

If it is hard for you to talk to God in this way, you can ask for help. Plead and beg if necessary for this relationship. A relationship with God is the most important relationship in your life. If you are not sure whether you believe in a personal God who hears the needs of individuals or even if such a being as God exists, pretend that you do enough so you can speak to God about your resistance and doubt. When you take time to speak, also take time to listen to any changes that occur within you as you speak.

Astrological Sign: Virgo

The qualities of Virgo reveal much of the energy of this month of Elul. First, the sign is represented by the virgin. The virgin symbolizes purity and modesty. The virgin represents that part of us that has remained pure, untainted, and unchanged by the vicissitudes of life. It is this deep part within us, the pure holy soul, which calls for our attention this month.

The virgin symbolizes the feminine energy that is dominant his month. Feminine energy, according to Kabbalah, is grounded, detail oriented, and more practical than masculine energy. Virgo is an earth sign which further suggests that the focus this month is practical. Indeed, this is the month for the healing of action.

Like Gemini (Sivan), Virgo is ruled by the planet Mercury. Mercury, the mythological messenger of the gods, represents communication as well as the reasoning and analytical powers of the mind. People born under this sign are known for these qualities as is the energy of this month.

Quite different from the exuberance and emotional intensity of Av's Leo of the previous month, the energy of Virgo is introspective and disciplined. While people born in the previous month might be flamboyant and passionate with a desire to be the center of attention, people born in Virgo tend to be conservative by nature, analytical, more emotionally restrained, and detail-oriented.

With a gift for systematic organization, Virgos tend to be observers rather than leaders. They often prefer to work behind the scenes. They are great problem solvers. They tend to stand back in life, observing and analyzing in order to better understand the underlying dynamics so they can act more purposefully when they finally act.

According to astrology, the best Virgo energy supports introspection, analysis and objectivity, and at its worst, judgment and aloofness.

Hebrew Letter: Yud

The Hebrew letter for the month of Elul is the *yud*. The smallest letter in the Hebrew alphabet, the *yud* is simply a point. The *yud* is a part of all letters and represents the essential life force energy in all the letters.

According to Kabbalah, creation began with a *yud*, representing the original point of entry of the Infinite light into the finite. As the smallest letter in the alphabet, the *yud* represents the self-nullification of the ego necessary for coming close to God. The *yud* is the essential point. The *yud* represents the soul, in its most pristine state and the level of its union with the Divine. The *yud* is the first letter in the name Yisrael (Israel) and is also the first letter in the word Yehudi (Jew). It is the first letter in the names of many of the Biblical prophets, such as Yehousha (Joshua), Yirmiyahu (Jeremiah), and Yoel (Joel). Many holy words, names, and things begin with the letter *yud*.

The numerical value of the *yud* is ten. Ten is accepted as the basis for the universal number system. Ten represents plurality but it contains within itself the initial and essential unity. It is no coincidence that we have ten fingers, ten toes, Ten Sefirot, Ten Commandments, and ten people as a requirement for a prayer minyan (a quorum).

Meditating on the *yud* this month supports the inner turning to the most essential inner point within us. Place the *yud* on your inner screen, meditate upon it and merge with it, and let it teach you the secrets of the power of becoming small.

Hebrew Tribe: Gad

When Leah saw that her sister, Rachel, had given her maid servant to Jacob to bear a child and she conceived a child, Leah gave her maidservant Zilpah to Jacob. Leah names the first child of this union Gad. Gad means *good fortune*. Gen. 30:11. This name is a sign of the good energy of this month.

When the Jewish people were entering the Land of Israel, the tribe of Gad requested the land not in Israel but east of the Jordan. They expressed their willingness to join in the fight with the other tribes for the Land of Israel and only afterward would they then return to the land they preferred. Moses complied with their request and blessed them with extraordinary strength and good fortune. During the conquest of the Land of Israel, the tribe of Dan even marched in front of other tribes. Because of their generosity and courage, their territory was larger than the territory of any of the other tribes. Living on the border, they remained continually protective of Israel.

Commentators on the Torah like Rashi have also said that Gad chose the land on the east side of the Jordan because they wanted to remain close to Moses who would not enter the Land of Israel as well. They guarded the burial site of Moses, and they guarded the Land of Israel.

Gad is the perfect tribe to represent the energy of this month of Elul. Gad, the tribe that served and protected the borders of the Land, represents the month that is on the border of one year and the next. We need to tap into the strength of Gad to review the last year and prepare for the coming year. Gad is the energy that defines boundaries. Boundaries are important. Many problems in life occur because people have diffused boundaries. They do not distinguish the past from the present or future. During the month of Elul, we are better able to make these needed distinctions.

When boundaries are clear, we can assume responsibility for ourselves and make choices about extending ourselves to others. As Gad did with the other tribes of Israel, Gad is the energy that both defines boundaries and is willing to extend beyond them when necessary. This Gad kind of knowing, so essential this month, enables us to know our own boundaries between ourselves and others, as well as make distinction between the past and future.

The Prophet Elijah came from the tribe of Gad. Interestingly, the Oral Torah says that Pinchas, who slew the elder Zimri, the Prince of the Tribe of Shimon, along with Cosby, his young concubine, is said to reincarnate as the prophet Elijah. Pinchas was rewarded for this courageous act of murder. The plague also stopped after this murder. It is predicted that Elijah will blow the shofar and bring the people back to the Land of Israel. It is this returning to the Land, and to the essence of oneself, to our very souls, that the shofar awakens us.

Divine Permutation: HHVY

The permutation of the Divine Name for this month is HHVY. From the placement of the *hays* in the first and second positions, we can appreciate the expansiveness of the higher worlds of Atzilut and Beriyah. The letters in these spiritual worlds channel and shape the flow of light above creation. The *hay* is a feminine letter, so we once again see the prominence of the feminine in this month. The two *hays* in the first and second position indicate that we need to turn inside and upward first before taking any action.

The position of the last letter in this permutation which corresponds to our physical world, known as Assiyah, is occupied by the letter *yud* (Y). As we learned previously, the *yud* is the smallest letter in the Hebrew alphabet, just a dot. Even to sound the letter *yud*, the mouth has to close almost immediately so only a minuscule amount of air is released. The *yud* in this position indicates that at this time spiritual light is dim and hidden in the physical world. We have to nullify ourselves, reach deep inside ourselves and beyond ourselves to experience the tremendous light available in the higher worlds or dimensions. The *vav* (V) in the position of the world of Yetzirah is the only letter that is in its optimal and usual placement. This placement corresponding to the heart informs us that the heart is the direct channel through which we draw down light.

This permutation demonstrates that the energy of this month is reflective rather than active. Taking time to go inside so as to contact the higher levels of our being will be most productive during this month.

Torah Portions

The first Torah portion of this month is usually Deuteronomy 18:1-20:20, beginning with Shoftim, which means Judges. Moses is instructing people to appoint judges who will judge righteously and objectively. So this begins the process of judging oneself for the month of Elul. To judge oneself, we need to access the part of ourselves which can be objective and can review and reflect.

The next Torah portion, Ki Setzei in Deuteronomy 21-26, begins with: *When you will go out to war against your enemies, God will deliver them into your hand. You see among the captives a woman who is beautiful in form and you desire her, you may take her for a wife.* Deut. 21:10-11. Though these are instructions for war, they are interpreted by Jewish mysticism as instruction for the inner battle that occurs during this month. The enemies are internal but with Divine help during this month we can access the soul; that is, the beautiful woman. This is the battle that we each must wage at this time. The Torah gives us guidance in how to be victorious. We are told that we can take this woman, but *shave her head, remove the garment of captivity from her.* Deut. 21:12-13. Basically, strip yourself of all the external garments of self so you experience yourself as the true intrinsic goodness of the Divine Soul, which is your true soul essence.

The next Torah portion, Ki Tavo, begins: *When you enter the Land, you shall take the first fruits ... and go to a place where God will choose to make*

His name dwell. Deut.26: 1-2. The declaration mandated in the verses was to purify the soul and connect with the Land. The willingness to offer one's first fruits strengthens one's devotion and connection to God. The chapter lists the blessings we received for aligning with Divine Will and the curses for not doing so.

The Rambam reminds us to do mitzvot from a place of love rather than fear. We should do God's Will because it connects us to truth and to God rather than due to fear of suffering negative consequences for having done acts that were not in accordance with Divine Will.

Holiday: Selichot

HISTORY: Selichot literally means *forgiveness* and refers to special prayers said during Elul. The daily recitation of these prayers along with the sounding of the shofar during this month is rooted in the Torah. Moses returned to Mount Sinai to ask for forgiveness for the Jewish people for the sin of the Golden Calf on the new moon of Elul. He returned with new tablets on Yom Kippur. This forty day period between the new moon of Elul and Yom Kippur has been historically designated for repentance and forgiveness.

During ancient times, the shofar was sounded each day to remind the people that Moses was pleading for God's forgiveness for their sins as well as to facilitate the process of teshuvah within the people themselves.

OBSERVANCE: Today, in synagogues around the world, special prayers of repentance and forgiveness along with the sounding of the shofar occur daily to commemorate this Biblical forty day period. The shofar blowing is the wake-up call for the soul. If you go to synagogue morning services during the week, you will hear the shofar blasts.

There are four different sounds made by shofar blasts. Some sounds are long and steady and pierce the depth of the heart and soul. Other sounds are short and broken and open us up to the experience of brokenness of our hearts. Hearing the shofar blasts turns us inward to open our hearts and be with our selves in a deeper way. The shofar blasts help us to experience the teshuvah process of purification.

On the Saturday night approximately a week before Rosh Hashanah, is a special midnight service known as Selichot when prayers of penitence along with the Thirteen Attributes of Divine Compassion are recited. The translation of the Thirteen Attributes is the following:

Adonai, Adonai, God is merciful, and gracious, long suffering, abundant in loving kindness and truth, guarding loving-kindness to the thousandth generation, forgiving transgression, iniquity and misdeeds, and cleansing and not holding guilt. Exod. 34-6. This verse is repeated many times on the holiday of Yom Kippur.

Many of these prayers were composed before the seventh century. Although historically these prayers were said during the days between Rosh Hashanah and Yom Kippur known as the Ten Days of Teshuvah in the eleventh century, this practice was extended to the entire month of Elul.

According to Kabbalah teachings, the gates of compassion open at midnight. That is why the service for Selichot usually takes place at midnight. The Thirteen Attributes were said to have been received by Moses as the way to solicit Divine forgiveness and will be recited until the messianic time.

Meditation

The meditation mantra for this month is *Ani Le Dodi vi Dodi li*. The first letters of the Hebrew verse, Ani Ledodi vidodi li, meaning *I am my beloved and my beloved is mine* from Song of Songs 6:3, spell out Elul. It is good to make it a habit to repeat this mantra with the breath throughout the month to deepen your Divine connection. This month we affirm Divine love as the foundation of who we are as human beings. The Infinite Power and Intelligence that we call God created this world and all that is within it to bestow love and goodness upon all. Even though there is still suffering in the world and we may personally experience suffering at this time, this mantra reminds us that within the midst of the suffering there is always love and a growth opportunity. Whatever is happening, we can let go of what is limiting and open to what is deeper, more fulfilling and empowering within ourselves. Recognizing the miraculous gift of simply being alive regardless of what is happening in life elevates us to deepen our connection with the Creator so we can receive greater blessing.

> As you begin this meditation, focus on the breath as we always do. Take breaths from deep in the abdomen to the rib cage to the chest, hold the breath to your comfort level, and then let go of the breath through the mouth. I like to inhale through the mouth or nostrils and exhale through the mouth as if I were blowing out the light of a candle. Take deep breaths until you feel yourself moving more fully into the present moment. When stress is released, inhale and exhale through the nostrils.
>
> Then, be aware that God is breathing you and sustaining. You do not breathe by your own will but by Divine Will. You live now only because it is Divine Will that you do so. When it is no longer Divine Will that you continue to be embodied, God will no longer breathe you and your soul will leave your body. The soul will generally depart when the soul has fulfilled what it can of its soul purpose in this incarnation.
>
> Repeat the mantra Ani Ledodi vi Dodi li. Feel yourself as the beloved by God and God is also your beloved. As you repeat this mantra, soak in the experience of being loved by God and access your love for God. Stay with this mantra for as long as you are comfortable doing so. Allow yourself to relax with this mantra, to feel bathed in love and compassion with this mantra. End the meditation by returning your focus to the breath and take a moment to be aware of what you internalized during your time of meditation.

WRITING MEDITATION

In the month of Elul, we review the events of the past year. Take a few moments to identify highlights from this past year. If you may want to even construct a calendar to better identify and write down the significant events in the months in which they occurred during this past calendar year in your journal.

Consider that these events whether they were challenges or joyful accomplishments that they were orchestrated by God to help you fulfill your soul purpose for your life, the reason for the embodiment for your soul. What lessons were most prominent for you? What were the themes for this past month?

After review and reflection, take a piece of paper and begin to write as if God is talking to you about this last year and the upcoming new year that will soon be upon you.

This is what I want to say to you ... And continue to write stream of consciousness. Do not think too much and see what comes through you. Perhaps you will gain insight into the lessons and growth opportunities these experiences afforded you.

OR write stream of consciousness with the following cue: *This past year was a time in my life when I ...*

Regardless of which writing exercise you choose, or you can choose to do both, turn inward and write what you feel most intuitively expresses what the year was for you. This writing is for you. It is not necessary for you to share it with anyone. You can do so if you choose to do so but that is your choice alone. If you write in a journal, it will be available for you to refer to at a future time.

Practical Recommendations

1. DO A SPIRITUAL ACCOUNTING FOR THE YEAR.

As if you were watching a movie of your life, allow yourself to review, reflect, and re-experience the themes of the past year. Outline the major events, accomplishments, and challenges of the past year on a piece of paper. Or in your journal under the headlines: Fall (Tishri, Cheshvan, Kislev), Winter (Tevet, Shevat, Adar), Spring (Nissan, Iyar, Sivan), and Summer (Tammuz, Av, Elul). Record the feeling tone and themes of each portion of the year. Consider what remains unfinished in your relationships and projects. Reflect upon the way you shared in the joys and sorrows of members of your family and community. What relationships were strengthened in this last year? What relationships were diminished or challenged?

2. MAKE FORGIVENESS PART OF YOUR DAILY PRACTICE.

In the course of the year, there are many opportunities to focus on the spiritual practice of forgiveness because it is so important. Forgiving others is so important that there is a prayer in the prayer book to be said every night before sleep. You might find it helpful to recite this prayer every night during this month: *Master of the Universe, I hereby forgive anyone who angered or antagonized me or who sinned against me, whether he did so accidentally, willfully, carelessly or purposefully, whether through speech, deed, thought, or notion, whether in this transmigration or another transmigration, I forgive. May no man be punished because of me. May it be Your Will my God, God of my forefathers, that I sin no more."

The prayer of forgiveness helps us to forgive everyone who has harmed us or our property, in this lifetime or previous lifetimes.

3. SEND NEW YEAR CARDS WITH A PERSONAL NOTE AND BLESSING.

This simple gesture becomes an opportunity to heal and strengthen relationships with others. Take time to call people you are connected to or want to connect to more in the coming year. Express your appreciation for what they have meant to you in your life.

4. BLESS PEOPLE WITH A HAPPY AND HEALTHY NEW YEAR.

It is customary to bless everyone we encounter with a happy and healthy new year. Blessing others allows us to be a channel of Divine blessing. As we bless, so are we blessed. The more people we bless, the more we will feel blessed.

Bless people you love and people you do not yet love. You can do this alone or you can do this in person with the person you want to bless. You can also easily give a quick blessing in almost any conversation or you can do an extended blessing meditation.

> **MEDITATION FOR BLESSING OTHERS**
>
> Visualize someone on your inner screen or take an opportunity to stand in front of a person you want to bless. Consider what this person wants and needs and open to bless him or her in ways beyond what this individual would even request. Utter a blessing first in your mind, and then speak the words of the blessing out loud.
>
> You may want to begin with: May you be blessed … Or, May God bless you … Or, You are blessed with … And allow the outpouring of your heart be expressed in words and in emotion. If the person you are blessing is not in front of you, visualize that he or she accepts the blessing and says Amen to the blessing you have just given. If the person is in front of you, remind him to say Amen if he has not done so. Amen seals the blessing.

5. SAY PSALMS.

The recitation of psalms, *tehillim*, is said to have the power to cleanse and purify a person. There are several different kinds of books of psalms but the psalms are universally numbered in every book. For thousands of years, Jews, Christians and Moslems have turned to the psalms for comfort and strength. It is a particularly beneficial practice during the month of Elul.

As you say a psalm, seek to find yourself in the psalm and feel its relevance and application to your life. If possible, say the psalm in Hebrew, even if your Hebrew is not good. It is also fine to say the psalms in English or the language you are most comfortable with. If you are feeling sad, it is recommended to say psalms 3, 6, 13, 22, 31, and 51. Psalm 23 is a basic and most popular one that is always relevant and said every Shabbat.

It is a traditional Jewish practice to repeat Psalm 27 daily during this month. Repeat and meditate on the verses of this psalm as a mantra and see how your consciousness is lifted upward.

> God is my light and salvation: Whom shall I fear, God is the strength of my life, whom shall I be afraid.
> One thing I ask of God, one thing I seek, that I may dwell in the house of God all the days of my life.
> God, hear my voice when I call, be gracious to me.

A Tale to Live By

This is a beautiful and important story attributed to the Maharal of Prague.

There was once a great king who called into his presence his most loyal and trusted subject. He entrusted to his care a very precious vessel for a given amount of time. The subject, however, became negligent in the care of the vessel, and one day the vessel accidentally broke. The subject was seized with great anxiety. He had to find a way to restore it to its original form so he would be able to face the king when he had to return the vessel lent to him.

He sought the counsel of the wisest people. What was he to do? They told him that he would have to confess to the king. There is no other recourse. He then went to the people who were closest to the king for their guidance. They too offered no help. Desperate, it occurred to him to go to the person who had manufactured the vessel. He pleaded with him to put it back together but was told that it was impossible. This vessel given to him was unique, and it could not be duplicated or fixed. The king would know the difference. He was very clear and could not be persuaded.

Everyone told him that the king would be enraged but that he still had to confess to the king. There was no other choice. The loyal subject finally accepted that he had no alternative but to throw himself at the king's mercy. He meekly presented himself with the broken vessel and confessed what happened. The king responded: *It is all right. I use broken vessels. I know that you sought the counsel of others and they advised you according to their own perspective, but it is only I who can say I use broken vessels.*

This story is such a beautiful metaphor for our lives. We were each entrusted with a beautiful holy soul to guard and elevate during our time on Earth. While in the physical world, we are often out of touch with our own soul and her mission for entering into a physical world.

We are all challenged in this world to remember and fulfill the purpose we came into this world. In the course of life, most of us have been distracted. We make mistakes and do things which are not in accordance with our soul purpose. We fail too frequently to honor or nourish sufficiently our access to our beautiful souls.

If we are honest with ourselves, we discover that we are all broken. Like the person in the story, we run everywhere trying to heal and fix our lives. Too often we do not feel better despite all our efforts to feel better. All our attempts to feel whole fail because we do not address the root cause for our failure to live a purposeful life.

This story reminds us to accept our brokenness, to be honest and humble, and realize that we cannot be whole without God. We have no recourse but to go directly to God. Only our connection with God, our Creator, can truly mend us. Only God knows how to use our broken vessels and transform our pain, mistakes, fears, doubts, anger, and questions. Our willingness to be honest, vulnerable, and humble before our Creator is what opens the gates for us to receive what we truly want and need in our lives. Whenever we surrender and connect with God, we are immensely grateful for the gift of our human existence, no matter what is happening in our lives.

Eventually all of us will find our own personal way to make our direct connection to our souls and to God. Some of us will do it sooner or more easily than others, but eventually we will all do, even, if it is right before the time of our death or immediately after our death.

ANOTHER TALE TO LIVE BY FOR THE MONTH OF ELUL

I love this wonderful story about the power of Teshuvah so I decided to include a second inspirational story for this month.

One Friday afternoon, the wife of the great Seer of Lublin went out into the street hoping someone would pass by so she could ask for money to purchase Shabbat candles. Just at that moment, a rich married man who was on route to visit a prostitute saw her distress and stopped to ask if he could be of assistance to her. She told him that she did not have money to buy Shabbat candles. So he gave her the money and she blessed him with the light of Shabbat.

As this was happening, the Rebbe, the Seer of Lublin, was immersed in prayer much longer than typical for him. His students asked him what was taking so long when he finally returned to waking consciousness. He told them his soul ascended to heaven and he was confronted by angels who questioned his wife's authority to bless this married man who frequented prostitutes. How could she do such a thing!

The Seer responded to the angels: *This man is wicked only because he never tasted the light of Shabbat.* On his way home from synagogue, the Seer actually met this rich man who asked him: *May I please spend a Shabbat with you. I am yearning to experience this light of Shabbat.*

The Seer responded: *Yes, of course. Please join us for Shabbat.* This rich man became a most devoted student of the Seer of Lublin. He supported him and his followers and even became one of his successors.

Conclusion

In closing, I thank each of you for reading, studying, internalizing, applying and sharing this book with others. I have written this book from my heart. I hope you have experienced love and blessings throughout the book. Though I have not yet been privileged to meet most of you, I feel energetically and spiritually connected to everyone who reads and studies this book. This is why I chose to share more intimate personal stories in this edition than I did in any of my previous books.

Many Jews especially after October 7th refer to this new chapter in time as "End of Days" or "Birth Pangs of the Messianic Era." There are leaders in other faith traditions who also speak of these times similarly as an auspicious time for global transformation. For many, life as we have known has already changed dramatically or now feels suddenly more fragile and volatile.

For some of us the state of the world appears to be getting rapidly worse. In addition to fighting Hamas, it looks like at the time of this writing that Israel will have to fight on multiple fronts against neighboring terrorist groups also seeking her destruction. Anti-Semitism is rising noticeably all over the world along with an increase in crime, inflation, homelessness, and violence as well. Friends of Israel seem to be dwindling in their support while support for Islamic terrorist entities is increasing all over the world. Chants to Free Palestine, Death to Israel, Death to America and even death to Jews are expanding in frequency and intensity. It appears to be increasingly difficult for many to seemingly discern lies from truth, good from evil.

The challenges of these times may humble many of us but that is good. In the midst of adversity, more and more people will eventually find that we have no other choice but to surrender to that which is greater than ourselves. In our own unique ways, we will each come to see and accept that the Creator is the One in charge of all of creation, so ultimately there will be good for all those who love what is good. It is not that these times ask us to be passive and merely accept life as it is unfolding. No, we are asked to be morally clear, discerning, responsive and empowered to align, embody and advocate actively for what is good and true. It is my prayer that this book supports your empowerment and faith. We each have the opportunity to love and bring greater harmony into this world.

The ultimate purpose of this book is to help you, my dear reader, live more consistently in the Divine Flow for it is only there we find love that is not dependent on anything external. It is only there that we feel protected and peaceful regardless of what is happening in our lives and in the world. And most importantly, it is only there that we experience ourselves as a part of God and not as isolated, fragile, frightened, and limited human beings, struggling to survive rather than thrive.

It is my prayer that Jews and good people of other traditions wake up to the love that the One God, our Creator, wants us to feel towards ourselves and each other. May we cast aside ridiculous feelings of pettiness and jealousy and love ourselves and each other. When the Jewish people are unified, or any people with a similar spiritual foundation for their peoplehood are unified, they are invincible because it is Divine Will that we love each other.

May our light and love be increasingly stronger and wipe out the negative forces that seek to divide us and make us afraid. The enemies of God, of all that is good and true, will do their best to make us afraid so our deepened connection to God is so vital today. GOD IS REAL. GOD IS THE TRUE REALITY. We need not be afraid of external forces. When it is the right time for the anticipated prophesied second Divine Revelation to happen, it will take place. Until then, we simply need to be patient, do our part and use the gift of our time wisely and respectfully.

As an aside, I personally take comfort in Biblical prophecies. I trust that there will be joy and blessing for those who align with the Jewish people, even during these times of challenge. There is a reason why enemies of freedom and all that is good and true in the world particularly hate the Jewish people and seek to destroy the one and only Jewish state of Israel on the planet by any means possible to them. To support Israel and the Jewish people now is to support light over darkness, good over evil. Take comfort and know that what is happening today is all part of the Divine Plan, so it will ultimately be good.

Now is a time of a great spiritual opportunity. Remember you are not defined or limited by what is happening externally in this world. Rather you are God's hands and feet endowed with a holy mission to bring and reveal greater love and faith into this world. It is for this reason that you incarnated into the density of this physical world. Thank you for all that you are and all that you do and will do in the near future to be ambassadors of love and light. I love you.

Love, Triple M. Melinda, Mindy, Miriam Shulamit

P.S. If you would like to buy over 15 copies at a very special discount to spread the holy teachings in this book, please let me know at Ribner@msn.com. There are so many people who need to be spiritually fortified by the love, spiritual opportunity and blessings that are directly available within them. Please help me reach them. The teachings in this book will help protect and empower readers so as to go through these intense times more peacefully and joyfully. I am happy to make free copies available to people continuing to experience trauma from October 7th. Please help me reach them.

Please sign up for newsletter or to attend free meditation sessions at www.melindaribner.com.

Subscribe to the Melinda Ribner YouTube channel to view guided short and extended meditations, interviews, and teachings.

You are also welcome to sign up for free special zoom Rosh Chodesh gatherings based on this book.

Melinda Ribner can also be reached at Mindyribner@gmail.com

About the Author

Melinda Ribner has taught Jewish meditation since 1978 at synagogues of all affiliations throughout America, at respected New Age centers, and in many places in Israel. She received *semicha* (ordination) from Rabbi Shlomo Carlebach of blessed memory, and Rabbi Zalman Schacter Shalomi of blessed memory to teach Jewish meditation and provide spiritual counsel to individuals and couples. Melinda (Mindy) began teaching on Zoom towards the beginning of COVID and continues to offer free classes ever since. She has made available short and extended meditation sessions available at Melinda Ribner You Tube channel, also available for free.

Melinda is a formerly licensed and certified social worker in private practice since 1982 and uses personalized meditation with clients as part of treatment on zoom and in person. She is the author of *Everyday Kabbalah: A Practical Guide for Jewish Meditation, New Age Judaism: Ancient Wisdom for the Modern World, Kabbalah Month by Month: A Year of Spiritual Practice* and *Personal Transformation, The Secret Legacy of Biblical Women: Revealing the Divine Feminine* and *Biblical Women Who Changed the World: Ancient Wisdom and Prophecy for Today.* And now, *Living in the Divine Flow: Monthly Spiritual Gifts and Blessings.*

To contact her directly mindyribner@gmail.com for speaking engagements, meditation workshops and counseling. Sign up for her free newsletter at Melindaribner.com.

Acknowledgments

To my most wonderful brother, Stephen Ribner, who has been the biggest consistent personal support throughout my life. I am very grateful to have been blessed with such an extraordinary and loving brother. May my dear brother be blessed with good health, much joy and a very long beautiful life.

To all my awesome spiritual teachers, alive or departed, who guided, encouraged, and inspired me to be the person I wanted to be and do the work I felt called to do. You changed my life for the better forever. I am eternally grateful.

To all my friends in Israel and America who loved and inspired me over so many years. Thank you for all the love and kindness you showed me. I will always be grateful to you.

To my beautiful students and therapy clients who offered me opportunities to grow and express who I am on a soul level. I grew and became a better person and teacher because of your support and love. I am grateful to you.

To my beautiful departed sweet loving parents, uncle, and aunt, I miss you, even after all these years. I continue to be grateful for all the love and guidance you generously gave me throughout my life. May your souls continue to ascend to ever higher places of love in the next world.

Made in the USA
Columbia, SC
18 September 2024

e66fbbe7-2b56-4900-8df3-60d8be997a91R01